Python Feature Engineering Cookbook

A complete guide to crafting powerful features for your machine learning models

Soledad Galli

Python Feature Engineering Cookbook

Associate Group Product Manager: Niranjan Naikwadi
Publishing Product Manager: Nitin Nainani
Book Project Manager: Hemangi Lotlikar
Senior Editor: Tiksha Abhimanyu Lad
Technical Editor: Sweety Pagaria
Copy Editor: Safis Editing
Proofreader: Tiksha Abhimanyu Lad
Indexer: Manju Arasan
Production Designer: Joshua Misquitta and Alishon Mendonca
Senior DevRel Marketing Executive: Vinishka Kalra

First published: January 2020
Second edition: October 2022
Third edition: August 2024

Production reference: 1260724

Published by Packt Publishing Ltd.
Grosvenor House
11 St Paul's Square
Birmingham
B3 1RB, UK.

ISBN 978-1-83588-358-7

www.packtpub.com

This book would not have been possible without the dedicated efforts of those who contribute to the Python open source ecosystem for data science and machine learning. We often overlook the fact that these contributors are real people with families, jobs, and hobbies, who generously allocate their time to develop these essential tools. I am deeply grateful to the developers of scikit-learn and pandas, pivotal libraries for data analysis and processing, as well as the maintainers of tsfresh and category encoders. A special acknowledgment goes to Nathan Parsons, current maintainer of Featuretools, for his invaluable support in crafting Chapter 8 of this book.

I am grateful to my editor, Tiksha Abhimanyu Lad, and her team for their invaluable support in bringing this book to fruition. Special thanks to our technical reviewer, Hector Patiño, for meticulously reviewing the code and recipes, ensuring smooth execution, and providing valuable resources to our readers.

A heartfelt thank you to my friend Chris Samiullah for his invaluable support in my growth as a software developer.

Finally, I am grateful to the users and contributors of Feature-engine for their unwavering support, feedback, and engagement, which have been instrumental in shaping the functionality of the library. Lastly, I owe a debt of gratitude to my students, whose feedback and encouragement have helped me become a better instructor and writer.

Thank you all for your invaluable contributions to this endeavor.

– Soledad Galli

Foreword

From convolutional neural networks to XGBoost, when it comes to machine learning, it's easy to focus too much on the algorithms. But as the saying goes, *"Garbage in, garbage out."* The quality of the features can be more important than the machine learning algorithm itself. Despite advances in feature learning, such as embedding in neural networks, feature engineering remains as important as ever. Particularly when dealing with categorical, numerical, and time-series features, feature engineering is a critical skill. With the right features, you can greatly improve model performance and ensure that models are more interpretable and robust.

Sole is a remarkable data science and machine learning educator. She has taught tens of thousands of students through her online courses on topics ranging from machine learning interpretability to hyperparameter optimization. It's fantastic that she has taken on this timeless topic of feature engineering. Her approach is direct, pragmatic, and practical. As the author of the popular Feature-engine, a Python library for feature engineering, and a respected machine learning educator, Sole is uniquely qualified to cover this topic.

The third edition of this book, which you have in your hands now, provides updated guidelines for selecting methods based on the data and the model. It also covers the integration of scikit-learn with pandas through the recently released `set_output` API. Finally, it covers automating feature creation using decision trees.

Whether you are a beginner or an experienced practitioner, this book will provide you with practical insights, lots of code examples, and various techniques to improve your machine learning models through effective feature engineering.

Christoph Molnar

Author of Interpretable Machine Learning and Modeling Mindsets

Contributors

About the author

Soledad Galli is a bestselling data science instructor, book author, and open source Python developer. As the leading instructor at Train in Data, Sole teaches intermediate and advanced courses in machine learning that have enrolled 64k+ students worldwide and continue to receive positive reviews. Sole is also the developer and maintainer of the Python open source library Feature-engine, which offers an extensive array of methods for feature engineering and selection.

Sole worked as a data scientist in finance and insurance companies, where she developed and put into production machine learning models to assess insurance claims and credit risk and prevent fraud.

Sole has been selected multiple times as a LinkedIn voice in data science. She is passionate about sharing her knowledge and experience, and that is why you'll often hear her talking at meetups, podcasts, or authoring articles online.

Sole is constantly looking for people like you, who can support her in enhancing the functionality of Feature-engine or delivering more and better courses, so if you are interested, contact her over social media or at her Train in Data website.

About the reviewer

Hector Patiño Rivera has been involved with machine learning for geosciences since 2015, especially for subjects related to satellite imagery. He has a strong knowledge of Python and SQL and is a proficient developer of PostgresQLS, ArcGIS, QGIS, and more GIS-related software. He is an experienced Django developer. When Hector is not programming, he loves playing tennis and hanging out with his friends.

Table of Contents

2

Encoding Categorical Variables   43

3

Transforming Numerical Variables   83

4

Performing Variable Discretization   113

5

Working with Outliers   153

6

Extracting Features from Date and Time Variables   177

7

Performing Feature Scaling   203

8

Creating New Features   229

9

Extracting Features from Relational Data with Featuretools   269

10

Creating Features from a Time Series with tsfresh   307

11

Extracting Features from Text Variables   339

Preface

Python Feature Engineering Cookbook, covers almost every aspect of feature engineering for tabular data, including missing data imputation, categorical encoding, variable transformation, discretization, scaling, and the handling of outliers. It also discusses how to extract features from date and time, text, time series, and relational datasets.

This book will take the pain out of feature engineering by showing you how to use open source Python libraries to accelerate the feature engineering process, via multiple practical, hands-on recipes. Throughout the book, you will transform and create new variables utilizing `pandas` and `scikit-learn`. Additionally, you'll learn to leverage the power of four major open source feature engineering libraries – Feature-engine, Category Encoders, Featuretools, and tsfresh.

You'll also discover additional recipes that weren't in the second edition. These cover imputing missing data in time series, creating new features with decision trees, and highlighting outliers using the median absolute deviation. More importantly, we provide guidelines to help you decide which transformations to use, based on your model and data features. You'll know exactly what, why, and how to implement each feature transformation.

Who this book is for

This book is for machine learning and data science students and professionals, as well as software engineers involved in deploying machine learning models, who seek to enhance their skills in data transformation and feature creation for improved model training. It is designed for anyone interested in or currently engaged in feature engineering, providing clear guidance on what to do, how to do it, and why it matters. This resource goes beyond basic knowledge, offering practical insights and detailed explanations to help you master feature engineering effectively.

What this book covers

Chapter 1, *Imputing Missing Data*, explores techniques to replace missing values with suitable estimates for numerical, categorical, and time series data. It covers both single and multiple imputation methods and demonstrates how to streamline the imputation process using scikit-learn and Feature-engine.

Chapter 2, *Encoding Categorical Variables*, covers methods to transform categorical variables into numerical features. It begins with common techniques such as one-hot and ordinal encoding and then explores adaptations for high cardinality and linear models. The chapter also discusses domain-specific methods, such as weight of evidence, and demonstrates how to encode highly cardinal variables using methods such as target encoding, ensuring that you understand how to regularize the process to avoid overfitting.

Chapter 3, *Transforming Numerical Variables*, discusses when and why you need to transform variables for use in machine learning models. Then, it shows you different variable transformation functions and highlights which types of variables each function is best suited for. By the end of this chapter, you'll understand when you need to transform your variables and why you apply the logarithm or the square root, among other functions.

Chapter 4, *Performing Variable Discretization*, introduces the concept of discretization, highlighting its uses in machine learning. The chapter then explores various discretization methods, detailing their advantages and limitations. It covers the basic equal-with and equal-frequency discretization procedures, as well as discretization using decision trees and k-means. Finally, it pairs discretization with encoding to return variables that are monotonic with the target.

Chapter 5, *Working with Outliers*, presents methods to identify outliers and understand their characteristics. It then discusses techniques to remove outliers or adjust their values to fit within accepted boundaries, utilizing pandas and Feature-engine.

Chapter 6, *Extracting Features from Date and Time Variables*, describes how to create features from dates and time variables. It covers how to extract date and time components from features, as well as how to combine datetime variables and how to work with different time zones.

Chapter 7, *Performing Feature Scaling*, covers methods to put the variables on a similar scale. It discusses standardization, how to scale to maximum and minimum values, and how to perform more robust forms of variable scaling. You'll also find guidelines about which method to use, based on your model and variables.

Chapter 8, *Creating New Features*, describes various methods to combine existing variables to generate new features. It shows the use of mathematical operations to combine features based on domain knowledge. Then, it discusses how to transform features through the sine, cosine, and the use of splines. Finally, it shows you the value of creating features from one or more variables through decision trees.

Chapter 9, *Extracting Features from Relational Data with Featuretools*, introduces relational datasets and then moves on to explain how we can create features at different data aggregation levels, utilizing Featuretools. You will learn how to automatically create dozens of features from numerical and categorical variables, datetime, and text.

Chapter 10, *Creating Features from a Time Series with tsfresh*, discusses how to automatically create hundreds of features from time series data for use in supervised classification or regression. You'll leverage the power of tsfresh to automatically create and select relevant features from your time series.

Chapter 11, Extracting Features from Text Variables, explores effective methods to clean and extract features from short text segments for use in supervised learning models. The chapter covers techniques to count words, sentences, and characters and measure lexical diversity. Additionally, it guides you through text cleaning processes and demonstrates how to build feature matrices by counting words.

To get the most out of this book

This book provides practical tools and techniques to streamline your feature engineering pipelines, allowing you to enhance code quality and simplify processes. The book explores methods to transform and create features to effectively train machine learning models with Python. Therefore, familiarity with machine learning and Python programming will benefit your understanding and application of the concepts presented.

The recipes have been tested in the following library versions:

- `category-encoders == 2.6.3`
- `Feature-engine == 1.8.0`
- `featuretools == 1.31.0`
- `matplotlib==3.8.3`
- `nltk=3.8.1`
- `numpy==1.26.4`
- `pandas==2.2.1`
- `scikit-learn==1.5.0`
- `scipy==1.12.0`
- `seaborn==0.13.2`
- `tsfresh==0.20.0`

Software/hardware covered in the book	OS requirements
Python 3.9 or greater	Windows, macOS, or Linux

Note that earlier or newer versions of the Python libraries may prevent code from running. If you are using newer versions, make sure to check their documentation for any recent updates, parameter name changes, or deprecation.

If you are using the digital version of this book, we advise you to type the code yourself or access the code via the GitHub repository (the link is available in the next section). Doing so will help you avoid any potential errors related to the copying and pasting of code.

Download the example code files

You can download the example code files for this book from GitHub at `https://github.com/PacktPublishing/Python-Feature-Engineering-Cookbook-Third-Edition`. If there's an update to the code, it will be updated on the existing GitHub repository.

We also have other code bundles from our rich catalog of books and videos available at `https://github.com/PacktPublishing/`. Check them out!

Conventions used

There are a number of text conventions used throughout this book.

`Code in text`: Indicates code words in text, database table names, folder names, filenames, file extensions, pathnames, dummy URLs, user input, and Twitter handles. Here is an example: "We used `year`, `month`, and `quarter` to capture the year, month, and quarter, respectively, in new columns of the DataFrame."

A block of code is set as follows:

```
date = "2024-05-17"
rng_hr = pd.date_range(date, periods=20, freq="h")
rng_month = pd.date_range(date, periods=20, freq="ME")
df = pd.DataFrame({"date1": rng_hr, "date2": rng_month})
```

Any command-line input or output is written as follows:

```
pip install yellowbrick
```

> **Tips or important notes**
> Appear like this.

Sections

In this book, you will find several headings that appear frequently (*Getting ready*, *How to do it...*, *How it works...*, *There's more...*, and *See also*).

To give clear instructions on how to complete a recipe, use these sections as follows:

Getting ready

This section tells you what to expect in the recipe and describes how to set up any software or any preliminary settings required for the recipe.

How to do it...

This section contains the steps required to follow the recipe.

How it works...

This section usually consists of a detailed explanation of what happened in the previous section.

There's more...

This section consists of additional information about the recipe to make you more knowledgeable about it.

See also

This section provides helpful links to other useful information for the recipe.

Get in touch

Feedback from our readers is always welcome.

General feedback: If you have questions about any aspect of this book, mention the book title in the subject of your message and email us at `customercare@packtpub.com`.

Errata: Although we have taken every care to ensure the accuracy of our content, mistakes do happen. If you have found a mistake in this book, we would be grateful if you would report this to us. Please visit `www.packtpub.com/support/errata`, select your book, click on the **Errata Submission Form** link, and enter the details.

Piracy: If you come across any illegal copies of our works in any form on the internet, we would be grateful if you would provide us with the location address or website name. Please contact us at `copyright@packt.com` with a link to the material.

If you are interested in becoming an author: If there is a topic that you have expertise in and you are interested in either writing or contributing to a book, please visit `authors.packtpub.com`.

Share Your Thoughts

Once you've read *Python Feature Engineering Cookbook*, we'd love to hear your thoughts! Scan the QR code below to go straight to the Amazon review page for this book and share your feedback.

https://packt.link/r/1835883591

Your review is important to us and the tech community and will help us make sure we're delivering excellent quality content.

Download a free PDF copy of this book

Thanks for purchasing this book!

Do you like to read on the go but are unable to carry your print books everywhere?

Is your eBook purchase not compatible with the device of your choice?

Don't worry, now with every Packt book you get a DRM-free PDF version of that book at no cost.

Read anywhere, any place, on any device. Search, copy, and paste code from your favorite technical books directly into your application.

The perks don't stop there, you can get exclusive access to discounts, newsletters, and great free content in your inbox daily

Follow these simple steps to get the benefits:

1. Scan the QR code or visit the link below

https://packt.link/free-ebook/978-1-83588-358-7

2. Submit your proof of purchase
3. That's it! We'll send your free PDF and other benefits to your email directly

1
Imputing Missing Data

Missing data—meaning the absence of values for certain observations—is an unavoidable problem in most data sources. Some machine learning model implementations can handle missing data out of the box. To train other models, we must remove observations with missing data or transform them into permitted values.

The act of replacing missing data with their statistical estimates is called **imputation**. The goal of any imputation technique is to produce a complete dataset. There are multiple imputation methods. We select which one to use, depending on whether the data is missing at random, the proportion of missing values, and the machine learning model we intend to use. In this chapter, we will discuss several imputation methods.

This chapter will cover the following recipes:

- Removing observations with missing data
- Performing mean or median imputation
- Imputing categorical variables
- Replacing missing values with an arbitrary number
- Finding extreme values for imputation
- Marking imputed values
- Implementing forward and backward fill
- Carrying out interpolation
- Performing multivariate imputation by chained equations
- Estimating missing data with nearest neighbors

Technical requirements

In this chapter, we will use the Python libraries Matplotlib, pandas, NumPy, scikit-learn, and Feature-engine. If you need to install Python, the free Anaconda Python distribution (`https://www.anaconda.com/`) includes most numerical computing libraries.

`feature-engine` can be installed with `pip` as follows:

```
pip install feature-engine
```

If you use Anaconda, you can install `feature-engine` with `conda`:

```
conda install -c conda-forge feature_engine
```

> **Note**
>
> The recipes from this chapter were created using the latest versions of the Python libraries at the time of publishing. You can check the versions in the `requirements.txt` file in the accompanying GitHub repository, at `https://github.com/PacktPublishing/Python-Feature-engineering-Cookbook-Third-Edition/blob/main/requirements.txt`.

We will use the **Credit Approval** dataset from the *UCI Machine Learning Repository* (`https://archive.ics.uci.edu/`), licensed under the CC BY 4.0 creative commons attribution: `https://creativecommons.org/licenses/by/4.0/legalcode`. You'll find the dataset at this link: `http://archive.ics.uci.edu/dataset/27/credit+approval`.

I downloaded and modified the data as shown in this notebook: `https://github.com/PacktPublishing/Python-Feature-engineering-Cookbook-Third-Edition/blob/main/ch01-missing-data-imputation/credit-approval-dataset.ipynb`

We will also use the **air passenger** dataset located in Facebook's Prophet GitHub repository (`https://github.com/facebook/prophet/blob/main/examples/example_air_passengers.csv`), licensed under the MIT license: `https://github.com/facebook/prophet/blob/main/LICENSE`

I modified the data as shown in this notebook: `https://github.com/PacktPublishing/Python-Feature-engineering-Cookbook-Third-Edition/blob/main/ch01-missing-data-imputation/air-passengers-dataset.ipynb`

You'll find a copy of the modified data sets in the accompanying GitHub repository: `https://github.com/PacktPublishing/Python-Feature-engineering-Cookbook-Third-Edition/blob/main/ch01-missing-data-imputation/`

Removing observations with missing data

Complete Case Analysis (CCA), also called list-wise deletion of cases, consists of discarding observations with missing data. CCA can be applied to both categorical and numerical variables. With CCA, we preserve the distribution of the variables after the imputation, provided the data is missing at random and only in a small proportion of observations. However, if data is missing across many variables, CCA may lead to the removal of a large portion of the dataset.

> **Note**
>
> Use CCA only when a small number of observations are missing and you have good reasons to believe that they are not important to your model.

How to do it...

Let's begin by making some imports and loading the dataset:

1. Let's import `pandas`, `matplotlib`, and the train/test split function from scikit-learn:

```
import matplotlib.pyplot as plt
import pandas as pd
from sklearn.model_selection import train_test_split
```

2. Let's load and display the dataset described in the *Technical requirements* section:

```
data = pd.read_csv("credit_approval_uci.csv")
data.head()
```

In the following image, we see the first 5 rows of data:

	A1	A2	A3	A4	A5	A6	A7	A8	A9	A10	A11	A12	A13	A14	A15	target
0	b	30.83	0.000	u	g	w	v	1.25	t	t	1	f	g	202.0	0	1
1	a	58.67	4.460	u	g	q	h	3.04	t	t	6	f	g	43.0	560	1
2	a	24.50	NaN	u	g	q	h	1.50	t	f	0	f	g	280.0	824	1
3	b	27.83	1.540	u	g	w	v	3.75	NaN	NaN	5	t	g	100.0	3	1
4	b	20.17	5.625	u	g	w	v	1.71	t	f	0	f	s	120.0	0	1

Figure 1.1 – First 5 rows of the dataset

3. Let's proceed as we normally would if we were preparing the data to train machine learning models; by splitting the data into a training and a test set:

```
X_train, X_test, y_train, y_test = train_test_split(
    data.drop("target", axis=1),
    data["target"],
```

```
        test_size=0.30,
        random_state=42,
)
```

4. Let's now make a bar plot with the proportion of missing data per variable in the training and test sets:

```
fig, axes = plt.subplots(
    2, 1, figsize=(15, 10), squeeze=False)

X_train.isnull().mean().plot(
    kind='bar', color='grey', ax=axes[0, 0], title="train")
X_test.isnull().mean().plot(
    kind='bar', color='black', ax=axes[1, 0], title="test")

axes[0, 0].set_ylabel('Fraction of NAN')
axes[1, 0].set_ylabel('Fraction of NAN')

plt.show()
```

The previous code block returns the following bar plots with the fraction of missing data per variable in the training (top) and test sets (bottom):

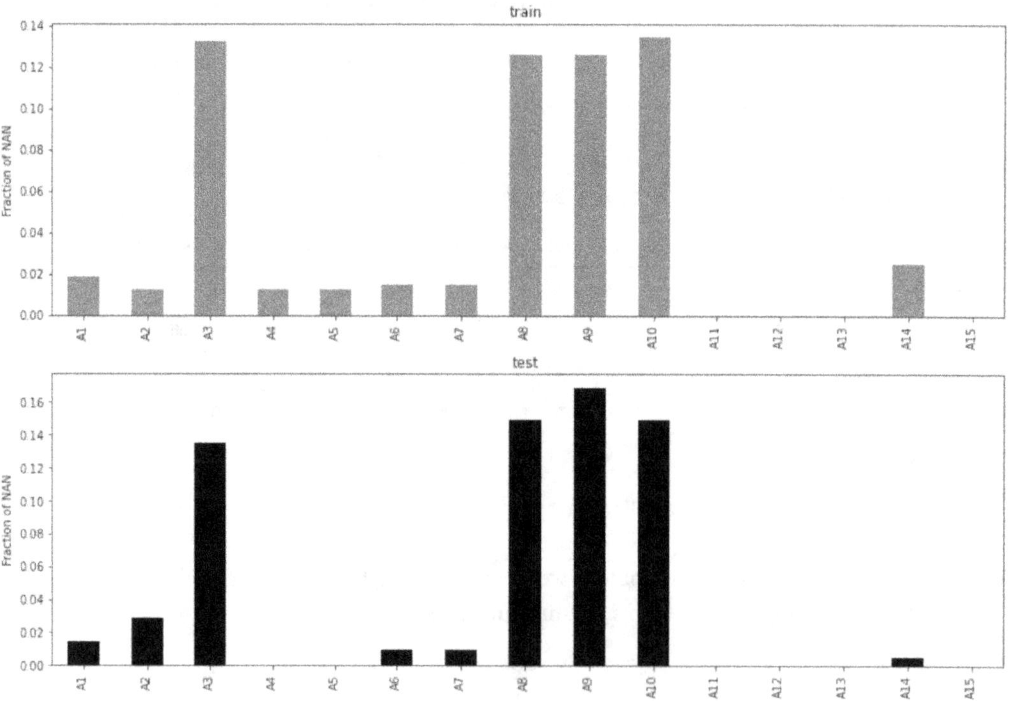

Figure 1.2 – Proportion of missing data per variable

5. Now, we'll remove observations if they have missing values in any variable:

```python
train_cca = X_train.dropna()
test_cca = X_test.dropna()
```

> **Note**
>
> pandas' `dropna()` drops observations with any missing value by default. We can remove observations with missing data in a subset of variables like this: `data.dropna(subset=["A3", "A4"])`.

6. Let's print and compare the size of the original and complete case datasets:

```python
print(f"Total observations: {len(X_train)}")
print(f"Observations without NAN: {len(train_cca)}")
```

We removed more than 200 observations with missing data from the training set, as shown in the following output:

```
Total observations: 483
Observations without NAN: 264
```

7. After removing observations from the training and test sets, we need to align the target variables:

```python
y_train_cca = y_train.loc[train_cca.index]
y_test_cca = y_test.loc[test_cca.index]
```

Now, the datasets and target variables contain the rows without missing data.

8. To drop observations with missing data utilizing `feature-engine`, let's import the required transformer:

```python
from feature_engine.imputation import DropMissingData
```

9. Let's set up the imputer to automatically find the variables with missing data:

```python
cca = DropMissingData(variables=None, missing_only=True)
```

10. Let's fit the transformer so that it finds the variables with missing data:

```python
cca.fit(X_train)
```

11. Let's inspect the variables with NAN that the transformer found:

```python
cca.variables_
```

The previous command returns the names of the variables with missing data:

```
['A1', 'A2', 'A3', 'A4', 'A5', 'A6', 'A7', 'A8', 'A9', 'A10',
 'A14']
```

12. Let's remove the rows with missing data in the training and test sets:

```
train_cca = cca.transform(X_train)
test_cca = cca.transform(X_test)
```

Use `train_cca.isnull().sum()` to corroborate the absence of missing data in the complete case dataset.

13. `DropMissingData` can automatically adjust the target after removing missing data from the training set:

```
train_c, y_train_c = cca.transform_x_y( X_train, y_train)
test_c, y_test_c = cca.transform_x_y(X_test, y_test)
```

The previous code removed rows with nan from the training and test sets and then re-aligned the target variables.

> **Note**
>
> To remove observations with missing data in a subset of variables, use `DropMissingData(variables=['A3', 'A4'])`. To remove rows with nan in at least 5% of the variables, use `DropMissingData(threshold=0.95)`.

How it works...

In this recipe, we plotted the proportion of missing data in each variable and then removed all observations with missing values.

We used pandas `isnull()` and `mean()` methods to determine the proportion of missing observations in each variable. The `isnull()` method created a Boolean vector per variable with `True` and `False` values indicating whether a value was missing. The `mean()` method took the average of these values and returned the proportion of missing data.

We used pandas `plot.bar()` to create a bar plot of the fraction of missing data per variable. In *Figure 1.2*, we saw the fraction of nan per variable in the training and test sets.

To remove observations with missing values in *any* variable, we used pandas' `dropna()`, thereby obtaining a complete case dataset.

Finally, we removed missing data using Feature-engine's `DropMissingData()`. This imputer automatically identified and stored the variables with missing data from the train set when we called the `fit()` method. With the `transform()` method, the imputer removed observations with nan in those variables. With `transform_x_y()`, the imputer removed rows with nan from the data sets and then realigned the target variable.

See also

If you want to use `DropMissingData()` within a pipeline together with other Feature-engine or scikit-learn transformers, check out Feature-engine's `Pipeline`: `https://Feature-engine.trainindata.com/en/latest/user_guide/pipeline/Pipeline.html`. This pipeline can align the target with the training and test sets after removing rows.

Performing mean or median imputation

Mean or median imputation consists of replacing missing data with the variable's mean or median value. To avoid data leakage, we determine the mean or median using the train set, and then use these values to impute the train and test sets, and all future data.

Scikit-learn and Feature-engine learn the mean or median from the train set and store these parameters for future use out of the box.

In this recipe, we will perform mean and median imputation using `pandas`, `scikit-learn`, and `feature-engine`.

> **Note**
>
> Use mean imputation if variables are normally distributed and median imputation otherwise. Mean and median imputation may distort the variable distribution if there is a high percentage of missing data.

How to do it...

Let's begin this recipe:

1. First, we'll import `pandas` and the required functions and classes from `scikit-learn` and `feature-engine`:

    ```python
    import pandas as pd
    from sklearn.model_selection import train_test_split
    from sklearn.impute import SimpleImputer
    from sklearn.compose import ColumnTransformer
    from feature_engine.imputation import MeanMedianImputer
    ```

2. Let's load the dataset that we prepared in the *Technical requirements* section:

    ```python
    data = pd.read_csv("credit_approval_uci.csv")
    ```

3.   Let's split the data into train and test sets with their respective targets:

```python
X_train, X_test, y_train, y_test = train_test_split(
    data.drop("target", axis=1),
    data["target"],
    test_size=0.3,
    random_state=0,
)
```

4.   Let's make a list with the numerical variables by excluding variables of type object:

```python
numeric_vars = X_train.select_dtypes(
    exclude="O").columns.to_list()
```

If you execute `numeric_vars`, you will see the names of the numerical variables: `['A2',
'A3', 'A8', 'A11', 'A14', 'A15']`.

5.   Let's capture the variables' median values in a dictionary:

```python
median_values = X_train[
    numeric_vars].median().to_dict()
```

> **Tip**
>
> Note how we calculate the median using the train set. We will use these values to replace missing
> data in the train and test sets. To calculate the mean, use pandas `mean()` instead of `median()`.

If you execute `median_values`, you will see a dictionary with the median value per variable:
`{'A2': 28.835, 'A3': 2.75, 'A8': 1.0, 'A11': 0.0, 'A14': 160.0,
'A15': 6.0}`.

6.   Let's replace missing data with the median:

```python
X_train_t = X_train.fillna(value=median_values)
X_test_t = X_test.fillna(value=median_values)
```

If you execute `X_train_t[numeric_vars].isnull().sum()` after the imputation,
the number of missing values in the numerical variables should be 0.

> **Note**
>
> pandas `fillna()` returns a new dataset with imputed values by default. To replace
> missing data in the original DataFrame, set the `inplace` parameter to `True`: `X_train.
> fillna(value=median_values, inplace=True)`.

Now, let's impute missing values with the median using `scikit-learn`.

7. Let's set up the imputer to replace missing data with the median:

```python
imputer = SimpleImputer(strategy="median")
```

> **Note**
>
> To perform mean imputation, set `SimpleImputer()` as follows: `imputer = SimpleImputer(strategy = "mean")`.

8. We restrict the imputation to the numerical variables by using `ColumnTransformer()`:

```python
ct = ColumnTransformer(
    [("imputer", imputer, numeric_vars)],
    remainder="passthrough",
    force_int_remainder_cols=False,
).set_output(transform="pandas")
```

> **Note**
>
> Scikit-learn can return numpy arrays, pandas DataFrames, or `polar` frames, depending on how we set out the transform output. By default, it returns numpy arrays.

9. Let's fit the imputer to the train set so that it learns the median values:

```python
ct.fit(X_train)
```

10. Let's check out the learned median values:

```python
ct.named_transformers_.imputer.statistics_
```

The previous command returns the median values per variable:

```python
array([ 28.835,    2.75,    1.,    0., 160.,    6.])
```

11. Let's replace missing values with the median:

```python
X_train_t = ct.transform(X_train)
X_test_t = ct.transform(X_test)
```

12. Let's display the resulting training set:

```python
print(X_train_t.head())
```

We see the resulting DataFrame in the following image:

```
     imputer__A2  imputer__A3  imputer__A8  imputer__A11  imputer__A14  \
596        46.08        3.000        2.375           8.0         396.0
303        15.92        2.875        0.085           0.0         120.0
204        36.33        2.125        0.085           1.0          50.0
351        22.17        0.585        0.000           0.0         100.0
118        57.83        7.040       14.000           6.0         360.0

     imputer__A15 remainder__A1 remainder__A4 remainder__A5 remainder__A6  \
596        4159.0             a             u             g             c
303           0.0             a             u             g             q
204        1187.0             b             y             p             w
351           0.0             b             y             p            ff
118        1332.0             b             u             g             m

    remainder__A7 remainder__A9 remainder__A10 remainder__A12 remainder__A13
596             v           NaN              t              t              g
303             v           NaN              f              f              g
204             v             t              t              f              g
351            ff             f              f              f              g
118             v             t              t              t              g
```

Figure 1.3 – Training set after the imputation. The imputed variables are marked by
the imputer prefix; the untransformed variables show the prefix remainder

Finally, let's perform median imputation using `feature-engine`.

13. Let's set up the imputer to replace missing data in numerical variables with the median:

```python
imputer = MeanMedianImputer(
    imputation_method="median",
    variables=numeric_vars,
)
```

> **Note**
>
> To perform mean imputation, change `imputation_method` to `"mean"`. By default
> `MeanMedianImputer()` will impute all numerical variables in the DataFrame, ignoring
> categorical variables. Use the `variables` argument to restrict the imputation to a subset of
> numerical variables.

14. Fit the imputer so that it learns the median values:

```python
imputer.fit(X_train)
```

15. Inspect the learned medians:

```python
imputer.imputer_dict_
```

The previous command returns the median values in a dictionary:

```
{'A2': 28.835, 'A3': 2.75, 'A8': 1.0, 'A11': 0.0, 'A14': 160.0,
'A15': 6.0}
```

16. Finally, let's replace the missing values with the median:

```
X_train = imputer.transform(X_train)
X_test = imputer.transform(X_test)
```

Feature-engine's `MeanMedianImputer()` returns a `DataFrame`. You can check that the imputed variables do not contain missing values using `X_train[numeric_vars].isnull().mean()`.

How it works...

In this recipe, we replaced missing data with the variable's median values using `pandas`, `scikit-learn`, and `feature-engine`.

We divided the dataset into train and test sets using scikit-learn's `train_test_split()` function. The function takes the predictor variables, the target, the fraction of observations to retain in the test set, and a `random_state` value for reproducibility, as arguments. It returned a train set with 70% of the original observations and a test set with 30% of the original observations. The 70:30 split was done at random.

To impute missing data with pandas, in *step 5*, we created a dictionary with the numerical variable names as keys and their medians as values. The median values were learned from the training set to avoid data leakage. To replace missing data, we applied `pandas'` `fillna()` to train and test sets, passing the dictionary with the median values per variable as a parameter.

To replace the missing values with the median using `scikit-learn`, we used `SimpleImputer()` with the `strategy` set to `"median"`. To restrict the imputation to numerical variables, we used `ColumnTransformer()`. With the `remainder` argument set to `passthrough`, we made `ColumnTransformer()` return *all the variables* seen in the training set in the transformed output; the imputed ones followed by those that were not transformed.

> **Note**
>
> `ColumnTransformer()` changes the names of the variables in the output. The transformed variables show the prefix `imputer` and the unchanged variables show the prefix `remainder`.

In *step 8*, we set the output of the column transformer to `pandas` to obtain a DataFrame as a result. By default, `ColumnTransformer()` returns `numpy` arrays.

> **Note**
>
> From version 1.4.0, `scikit-learn` transformers can return numpy arrays, pandas DataFrames, or `polar` frames as a result of the `transform()` method.

With `fit()`, `SimpleImputer()` learned the median of each numerical variable in the train set and stored them in its `statistics_` attribute. With `transform()`, it replaced the missing values with the medians.

To replace missing values with the median using Feature-engine, we used the `MeanMedianImputer()` with the `imputation_method` set to `median`. To restrict the imputation to a subset of variables, we passed the variable names in a list to the `variables` parameter. With `fit()`, the transformer learned and stored the median values per variable in a dictionary in its `imputer_dict_` attribute. With `transform()`, it replaced the missing values, returning a pandas DataFrame.

Imputing categorical variables

We typically impute categorical variables with the most frequent category, or with a specific string. To avoid data leakage, we find the frequent categories from the train set. Then, we use these values to impute the train, test, and future datasets. `scikit-learn` and `feature-engine` find and store the frequent categories for the imputation, out of the box.

In this recipe, we will replace missing data in categorical variables with the most frequent category, or with an arbitrary string.

How to do it...

To begin, let's make a few imports and prepare the data:

1. Let's import `pandas` and the required functions and classes from `scikit-learn` and `feature-engine`:

    ```python
    import pandas as pd
    from sklearn.model_selection import train_test_split
    from sklearn.impute import SimpleImputer
    from sklearn.compose import ColumnTransformer
    from feature_engine.imputation import CategoricalImputer
    ```

2. Let's load the dataset that we prepared in the *Technical requirements* section:

    ```python
    data = pd.read_csv("credit_approval_uci.csv")
    ```

3. Let's split the data into train and test sets and their respective targets:

    ```python
    X_train, X_test, y_train, y_test = train_test_split(
        data.drop("target", axis=1),
        data["target"],
    ```

```
        test_size=0.3,
        random_state=0,
    )
```

4. Let's capture the categorical variables in a list:

```
categorical_vars = X_train.select_dtypes(
    include="O").columns.to_list()
```

5. Let's store the variables' most frequent categories in a dictionary:

```
frequent_values = X_train[
    categorical_vars].mode().iloc[0].to_dict()
```

6. Let's replace missing values with the frequent categories:

```
X_train_t = X_train.fillna(value=frequent_values)
X_test_t = X_test.fillna(value=frequent_values)
```

> **Note**
>
> `fillna()` returns a new DataFrame with the imputed values by default. We can replace missing data in the original DataFrame by executing `X_train.fillna(value=frequent_values, inplace=True)`.

7. To replace missing data with a specific string, let's create an imputation dictionary with the categorical variable names as the keys and an arbitrary string as the values:

```
imputation_dict = {var:
    "no_data" for var in categorical_vars}
```

Now, we can use this dictionary and the code in *step 6* to replace missing data.

> **Note**
>
> With pandas `value_counts()` we can see the string added by the imputation. Try executing, for example, `X_train["A1"].value_counts()`.

Now, let's impute missing values with the most frequent category using `scikit-learn`.

8. Let's set up the imputer to find the most frequent category per variable:

```
imputer = SimpleImputer(strategy='most_frequent')
```

> **Note**
>
> `SimpleImputer()` will learn the mode for numerical and categorical variables alike. But in practice, mode imputation is done for categorical variables only.

9. Let's restrict the imputation to the categorical variables:

```
ct = ColumnTransformer(
        [("imputer",imputer, categorical_vars)],
        remainder="passthrough"
        ).set_output(transform="pandas")
```

> **Note**
>
> To impute missing data with a string instead of the most frequent category, set `SimpleImputer()` as follows: `imputer = SimpleImputer(strategy="constant", fill_value="missing")`.

10. Fit the imputer to the train set so that it learns the most frequent values:

```
ct.fit(X_train)
```

11. Let's take a look at the most frequent values learned by the imputer:

```
ct.named_transformers_.imputer.statistics_
```

The previous command returns the most frequent values per variable:

```
array(['b', 'u', 'g', 'c', 'v', 't', 'f', 'f', 'g'],
dtype=object)
```

12. Finally, let's replace missing values with the frequent categories:

```
X_train_t = ct.transform(X_train)
X_test_t = ct.transform(X_test)
```

Make sure to inspect the resulting DataFrames by executing `X_train_t.head()`.

> **Note**
>
> The `ColumnTransformer()` changes the names of the variables. The imputed variables show the prefix `imputer` and the untransformed variables the prefix `remainder`.

Finally, let's impute missing values using `feature-engine`.

13. Let's set up the imputer to replace the missing data in categorical variables with their most frequent value:

```
imputer = CategoricalImputer(
    imputation_method="frequent",
    variables=categorical_vars,
)
```

> **Note**
>
> With the `variables` parameter set to None, `CategoricalImputer()` will automatically impute all categorical variables found in the train set. Use this parameter to restrict the imputation to a subset of categorical variables, as shown in *step 13*.

14. Fit the imputer to the train set so that it learns the most frequent categories:

```
imputer.fit(X_train)
```

> **Note**
>
> To impute categorical variables with a specific string, set `imputation_method` to `missing` and `fill_value` to the desired string.

15. Let's check out the learned categories:

```
imputer.imputer_dict_
```

We can see the dictionary with the most frequent values in the following output:

```
{'A1': 'b',
 'A4': 'u',
 'A5': 'g',
 'A6': 'c',
 'A7': 'v',
 'A9': 't',
 'A10': 'f',
 'A12': 'f',
 'A13': 'g'}
```

16. Finally, let's replace the missing values with frequent categories:

```
X_train_t = imputer.transform(X_train)
X_test_t = imputer.transform(X_test)
```

If you want to impute numerical variables with a string or the most frequent value using `CategoricalImputer()`, set the `ignore_format` parameter to True.

`CategoricalImputer()` returns a pandas DataFrame as a result.

How it works...

In this recipe, we replaced missing values in categorical variables with the most frequent categories or an arbitrary string. We used `pandas`, `scikit-learn`, and `feature-engine`.

In *step 5*, we created a dictionary with the variable names as keys and the frequent categories as values. To capture the frequent categories, we used pandas `mode()`, and to return a dictionary, we used pandas `to_dict()`. To replace the missing data, we used pandas `fillna()`, passing the dictionary with the variables and their frequent categories as parameters. There can be more than one mode in a variable, that's why we made sure to capture only one of those values by using `.iloc[0]`.

To replace the missing values using `scikit-learn`, we used `SimpleImputer()` with the `strategy` set to `most_frequent`. To restrict the imputation to categorical variables, we used `ColumnTransformer()`. With `remainder` set to `passthrough`, we made `ColumnTransformer()` return all the variables present in the training set as a result of the `transform()` method.

> **Note**
>
> `ColumnTransformer()` changes the names of the variables in the output. The transformed variables show the prefix `imputer` and the unchanged variables show the prefix `remainder`.

With `fit()`, `SimpleImputer()` learned the variables' most frequent categories and stored them in its `statistics_` attribute. With `transform()`, it replaced the missing data with the learned parameters.

`SimpleImputer()` and `ColumnTransformer()` return NumPy arrays by default. We can change this behavior with the `set_output()` parameter.

To replace missing values with `feature-engine`, we used the `CategoricalImputer()` with `imputation_method` set to `frequent`. With `fit()`, the transformer learned and stored the most frequent categories in a dictionary in its `imputer_dict_` attribute. With `transform()`, it replaced the missing values with the learned parameters.

Unlike `SimpleImputer()`, `CategoricalImputer()` will only impute categorical variables, unless specifically told not to do so by setting the `ignore_format` parameter to `True`. In addition, with `feature-engine` transformers we can restrict the transformations to a subset of variables through the transformer itself. For `scikit-learn` transformers, we need the additional `ColumnTransformer()` class to apply the transformation to a subset of the variables.

Replacing missing values with an arbitrary number

We can replace missing data with an arbitrary value. Commonly used values are `999`, `9999`, or `-1` for positive distributions. This method is used for numerical variables. For categorical variables, the equivalent method is to replace missing data with an arbitrary string, as described in the *Imputing categorical variables* recipe.

When replacing missing values with arbitrary numbers, we need to be careful not to select a value close to the mean, the median, or any other common value of the distribution.

> **Note**
>
> We'd use arbitrary number imputation when data is not missing at random, use non-linear models, or when the percentage of missing data is high. This imputation technique distorts the original variable distribution.

In this recipe, we will impute missing data with arbitrary numbers using `pandas`, `scikit-learn`, and `feature-engine`.

How to do it...

Let's begin by importing the necessary tools and loading the data:

1. Import `pandas` and the required functions and classes:

    ```python
    import pandas as pd
    from sklearn.model_selection import train_test_split
    from sklearn.impute import SimpleImputer
    from feature_engine.imputation import ArbitraryNumberImputer
    ```

2. Let's load the dataset described in the *Technical requirements* section:

    ```python
    data = pd.read_csv("credit_approval_uci.csv")
    ```

3. Let's separate the data into train and test sets:

    ```python
    X_train, X_test, y_train, y_test = train_test_split(
        data.drop("target", axis=1),
        data["target"],
        test_size=0.3,
        random_state=0,
    )
    ```

    We will select arbitrary values greater than the maximum value of the distribution.

4. Let's find the maximum value of four numerical variables:

    ```python
    X_train[['A2','A3', 'A8', 'A11']].max()
    ```

    The previous command returns the following output:

    ```
    A2        76.750
    A3        26.335
    A8        28.500
    A11       67.000
    dtype: float64
    ```

    We'll use 99 for the imputation because it is bigger than the maximum values of the numerical variables in *step 4*.

5. Let's make a copy of the original DataFrames:

```
X_train_t = X_train.copy()
X_test_t = X_test.copy()
```

6. Now, we replace the missing values with 99:

```
X_train_t[["A2", "A3", "A8", "A11"]] = X_train_t[[
    "A2", "A3", "A8", "A11"]].fillna(99)
X_test_t[["A2", "A3", "A8", "A11"]] = X_test_t[[
    "A2", "A3", "A8", "A11"]].fillna(99)
```

> **Note**
>
> To impute different variables with different values using pandas `fillna()`, use a dictionary like this: `imputation_dict = {"A2": -1, "A3": -1, "A8": 999, "A11": 9999}`.

Now, we'll impute missing values with an arbitrary number using `scikit-learn`.

1. Let's set up `imputer` to replace missing values with 99:

```
imputer = SimpleImputer(strategy='constant', fill_value=99)
```

> **Note**
>
> If your dataset contains categorical variables, `SimpleImputer()` will add 99 to those variables as well if any values are missing.

2. Let's fit `imputer` to a slice of the train set containing the variables to impute:

```
vars = ["A2", "A3", "A8", "A11"]
imputer.fit(X_train[vars])
```

3. Replace the missing values with 99 in the desired variables:

```
X_train_t[vars] = imputer.transform(X_train[vars])
X_test_t[vars] = imputer.transform(X_test[vars])
```

Go ahead and check the lack of missing values by executing `X_test_t[["A2", "A3", "A8", "A11"]].isnull().sum()`.

To finish, let's impute missing values using `feature-engine`.

4. Let's set up the `imputer` to replace missing values with 99 in 4 specific variables:

```
imputer = ArbitraryNumberImputer(
    arbitrary_number=99,
```

```
            variables=["A2", "A3", "A8", "A11"],
    )
```

> **Note**
>
> `ArbitraryNumberImputer()` will automatically select all numerical variables in the train set for imputation if we set the `variables` parameter to None.

5. Finally, let's replace the missing values with 99:

```
X_train = imputer.fit_transform(X_train)
X_test = imputer.transform(X_test)
```

> **Note**
>
> To impute different variables with different numbers, set up `ArbitraryNumberImputer()` as follows: `ArbitraryNumberImputer(imputater_dict = {"A2": -1, "A3": -1, "A8": 999, "A11": 9999})`.

We have now replaced missing data with arbitrary numbers using three different open-source libraries.

How it works...

In this recipe, we replaced missing values in numerical variables with an arbitrary number using `pandas`, `scikit-learn`, and `feature-engine`.

To determine which arbitrary value to use, we inspected the maximum values of four numerical variables using pandas' `max()`. We chose 99 because it was greater than the maximum values of the selected variables. In *step 5*, we used pandas `fillna()` to replace the missing data.

To replace missing values using `scikit-learn`, we utilized `SimpleImputer()`, with the `strategy` set to `constant`, and specified 99 in the `fill_value` argument. Next, we fitted the imputer to a slice of the train set with the numerical variables to impute. Finally, we replaced missing values using `transform()`.

To replace missing values with `feature-engine` we used `ArbitraryValueImputer()`, specifying the value 99 and the variables to impute as parameters. Next, we applied the `fit_transform()` method to replace missing data in the train set and the `transform()` method to replace missing data in the test set.

Finding extreme values for imputation

Replacing missing values with a value at the end of the variable distribution (extreme values) is like replacing them with an arbitrary value, but instead of setting the arbitrary values manually, the values are automatically selected from the end of the variable distribution.

We can replace missing data with a value that is greater or smaller than most values in the variable. To select a value that is greater, we can use the mean plus a factor of the standard deviation. Alternatively, we can set it to the 75th quantile + IQR × 1.5. **IQR** stands for **inter-quartile range** and is the difference between the 75th and 25th quantile. To replace missing data with values that are smaller than the remaining values, we can use the mean minus a factor of the standard deviation, or the 25th quantile – IQR × 1.5.

> **Note**
>
> End-of-tail imputation may distort the distribution of the original variables, so it may not be suitable for linear models.

In this recipe, we will implement end-of-tail or extreme value imputation using `pandas` and `feature-engine`.

How to do it...

To begin this recipe, let's import the necessary tools and load the data:

1. Let's import `pandas` and the required function and class:

```
import pandas as pd
from sklearn.model_selection import train_test_split
from feature_engine.imputation import EndTailImputer
```

2. Let's load the dataset we described in the *Technical requirements* section:

```
data = pd.read_csv("credit_approval_uci.csv")
```

3. Let's capture the numerical variables in a list, excluding the target:

```
numeric_vars = [
    var for var in data.select_dtypes(
        exclude="O").columns.to_list()
    if var !="target"
]
```

4. Let's split the data into train and test sets, keeping only the numerical variables:

```
X_train, X_test, y_train, y_test = train_test_split(
    data[numeric_vars],
    data["target"],
    test_size=0.3,
    random_state=0,
)
```

5. We'll now determine the IQR:

```
IQR = X_train.quantile(0.75) - X_train.quantile(0.25)
```

We can visualize the IQR values by executing `IQR` or `print(IQR)`:

```
A2        16.4200
A3         6.5825
A8         2.8350
A11        3.0000
A14      212.0000
A15      450.0000
dtype: float64
```

6. Let's create a dictionary with the variable names and the imputation values:

```
imputation_dict = (
     X_train.quantile(0.75) + 1.5 * IQR).to_dict()
```

> **Note**
>
> If we use the inter-quartile range proximity rule, we determine the imputation values by adding 1.5 times the IQR to the 75th quantile. If variables are normally distributed, we can calculate the imputation values as the mean plus a factor of the standard deviation, `imputation_dict = (X_train.mean() + 3 * X_train.std()).to_dict()`.

7. Finally, let's replace the missing data:

```
X_train_t = X_train.fillna(value=imputation_dict)
X_test_t = X_test.fillna(value=imputation_dict)
```

> **Note**
>
> We can also replace missing data with values at the left tail of the distribution using `value = X_train[var].quantile(0.25) - 1.5 * IQR` or `value = X_train[var].mean() - 3 * X_train[var].std()`.

To finish, let's impute missing values using `feature-engine`.

1. Let's set up `imputer` to estimate a value at the right of the distribution using the IQR proximity rule:

```
imputer = EndTailImputer(
     imputation_method="iqr",
     tail="right",
     fold=3,
```

```
        variables=None,
    )
```

> **Note**
>
> To use the mean and standard deviation to calculate the replacement values, set `imputation_method="Gaussian"`. Use `left` or `right` in the `tail` argument to specify the side of the distribution to consider when finding values for the imputation.

2. Let's fit `EndTailImputer()` to the train set so that it learns the values for the imputation:

    ```
    imputer.fit(X_train)
    ```

3. Let's inspect the learned values:

    ```
    imputer.imputer_dict_
    ```

    The previous command returns a dictionary with the values to use to impute each variable:

    ```
    {'A2': 88.18,
     'A3': 27.31,
     'A8': 11.504999999999999,
     'A11': 12.0,
     'A14': 908.0,
     'A15': 1800.0}
    ```

4. Finally, let's replace the missing values:

    ```
    X_train = imputer.transform(X_train)
    X_test = imputer.transform(X_test)
    ```

Remember that you can corroborate that the missing values were replaced by using `X_train[['A2','A3', 'A8', 'A11', 'A14', 'A15']].isnull().mean()`.

How it works...

In this recipe, we replaced missing values in numerical variables with a number at the end of the distribution using `pandas` and `feature-engine`.

We determined the imputation values according to the formulas described in the introduction to this recipe. We used pandas `quantile()` to find specific quantile values, or pandas `mean()` and `std()` for the mean and standard deviation. With pandas `fillna()` we replaced the missing values.

To replace missing values with `EndTailImputer()` from `feature-engine`, we set `distribution` to `iqr` to calculate the values based on the IQR proximity rule. With `tail` set to `right` the transformer found the imputation values from the right of the distribution. With `fit()`, the imputer learned and stored the values for the imputation in a dictionary in the `imputer_dict_` attribute. With `transform()`, we replaced the missing values, returning DataFrames.

Marking imputed values

In the previous recipes, we focused on replacing missing data with estimates of their values. In addition, we can add missing indicators to *mark* observations where values were missing.

A missing indicator is a binary variable that takes the value 1 or `True` to indicate whether a value was missing, and 0 or `False` otherwise. It is common practice to replace missing observations with the mean, median, or most frequent category while simultaneously marking those missing observations with missing indicators. In this recipe, we will learn how to add missing indicators using `pandas`, `scikit-learn`, and `feature-engine`.

How to do it...

Let's begin by making some imports and loading the data:

1. Let's import the required libraries, functions, and classes:

```
import pandas as pd
import numpy as np
from sklearn.model_selection import train_test_split
from sklearn.impute import SimpleImputer
from sklearn.compose import ColumnTransformer
from sklearn.pipeline import Pipeline
from feature_engine.imputation import(
    AddMissingIndicator,
    CategoricalImputer,
    MeanMedianImputer
)
```

2. Let's load and split the dataset described in the *Technical requirements* section:

```
data = pd.read_csv("credit_approval_uci.csv")
X_train, X_test, y_train, y_test = train_test_split(
    data.drop("target", axis=1),
    data["target"],
    test_size=0.3,
    random_state=0,
)
```

3. Let's capture the variable names in a list:

```
varnames = ["A1", "A3", "A4", "A5", "A6", "A7", "A8"]
```

4. Let's create names for the missing indicators and store them in a list:

```
indicators = [f"{var}_na" for var in varnames]
```

If we execute `indicators`, we will see the names we will use for the new variables: `['A1_na', 'A3_na', 'A4_na', 'A5_na', 'A6_na', 'A7_na', 'A8_na']`.

5. Let's make a copy of the original DataFrames:

```
X_train_t = X_train.copy()
X_test_t = X_test.copy()
```

6. Let's add the missing indicators:

```
X_train_t[indicators] =X_train[
        varnames].isna().astype(int)
X_test_t[indicators] = X_test[
        varnames].isna().astype(int)
```

> **Note**
>
> If you want the indicators to have `True` and `False` as values instead of `0` and `1`, remove `astype(int)` in *step 6*.

7. Let's inspect the resulting DataFrame:

```
X_train_t.head()
```

We can see the newly added variables at the right of the DataFrame in the following image:

	A1	A2	A3	A4	A5	A6	A7	A8	A9	A10	...	A13	A14	A15	A1_na	A3_na	A4_na	A5_na	A6_na	A7_na	A8_na
596	a	46.08	3.000	u	g	c	v	2.375	NaN	t	...	g	396.0	4159	0	0	0	0	0	0	0
303	a	15.92	2.875	u	g	q	v	0.085	NaN	f	...	g	120.0	0	0	0	0	0	0	0	0
204	b	36.33	2.125	y	p	w	v	0.085	t	t	...	g	50.0	1187	0	0	0	0	0	0	0
351	b	22.17	0.585	y	p	ff	ff	0.000	f	f	...	g	100.0	0	0	0	0	0	0	0	0
118	b	57.83	7.040	u	g	m	v	14.000	t	t	...	g	360.0	1332	0	0	0	0	0	0	0

Figure 1.4 – DataFrame with the missing indicators

Now, let's add missing indicators using Feature-engine instead.

8. Set up the imputer to add binary indicators to every variable with missing data:

```
imputer = AddMissingIndicator(
    variables=None, missing_only=True
    )
```

9. Fit the imputer to the train set so that it finds the variables with missing data:

```
imputer.fit(X_train)
```

> **Note**
>
> If we execute `imputer.variables_`, we will find the variables for which missing indicators will be added.

10. Finally, let's add the missing indicators:

```python
X_train_t = imputer.transform(X_train)
X_test_t = imputer.transform(X_test)
```

So far, we just added missing indicators. But we still have the missing data in our variables. We need to replace them with numbers. In the rest of this recipe, we will combine the use of missing indicators with mean and mode imputation.

11. Let's create a pipeline to add missing indicators to categorical and numerical variables, then impute categorical variables with the most frequent category, and numerical variables with the mean:

```python
pipe = Pipeline([
    ("indicators",
        AddMissingIndicator(missing_only=True)),
    ("categorical", CategoricalImputer(
        imputation_method="frequent")),
    ("numerical", MeanMedianImputer()),
])
```

> **Note**
>
> `feature-engine` imputers automatically identify numerical or categorical variables. So there is no need to slice the data or pass the variable names as arguments to the transformers in this case.

12. Let's add the indicators and impute missing values:

```python
X_train_t = pipe.fit_transform(X_train)
X_test_t = pipe.transform(X_test)
```

> **Note**
>
> Use `X_train_t.isnull().sum()` to corroborate that there is no data missing. Execute `X_train_t.head()` to get a view of the resulting datafame.

Finally, let's add missing indicators and simultaneously impute numerical and categorical variables with the mean and most frequent categories respectively, utilizing scikit-learn.

13. Let's make a list with the names of the numerical and categorical variables:

```python
numvars = X_train.select_dtypes(
    exclude="O").columns.to_list()
catvars = X_train.select_dtypes(
    include="O").columns.to_list()
```

14. Let's set up a pipeline to perform mean and frequent category imputation while marking the missing data:

```python
pipe = ColumnTransformer([
    ("num_imputer", SimpleImputer(
        strategy="mean",
        add_indicator=True),
    numvars),
    ("cat_imputer", SimpleImputer(
        strategy="most_frequent",
        add_indicator=True),
    catvars),
]).set_output(transform="pandas")
```

15. Now, let's carry out the imputation:

```python
X_train_t = pipe.fit_transform(X_train)
X_test_t = pipe.transform(X_test)
```

Make sure to explore `X_train_t.head()` to get familiar with the pipeline's output.

How it works...

To add missing indicators using pandas, we used `isna()`, which created a new vector assigning the value of `True` if there was a missing value or `False` otherwise. We used `astype(int)` to convert the Boolean vectors into binary vectors with values 1 and 0.

To add a missing indicator with `feature-engine`, we used `AddMissingIndicator()`. With `fit()` the transformer found the variables with missing data. With `transform()` it appended the missing indicators to the right of the train and test sets.

To sequentially add missing indicators and then replace the nan values with the most frequent category or the mean, we lined up Feature-engine's `AddMissingIndicator()`, `CategoricalImputer()`, and `MeanMedianImputer()` within a `pipeline`. The `fit()` method from the `pipeline` made the transformers find the variables with nan and calculate the mean of the numerical variables and the mode of the categorical variables. The `transform()` method from the `pipeline` made the transformers add the missing indicators and then replace the missing values with their estimates.

> **Note**
>
> Feature-engine transformations return DataFrames respecting the original names and order of the variables. Scikit-learn's `ColumnTransformer()`, on the other hand, changes the variable's names and order in the resulting data.

Finally, we added missing indicators and replaced missing data with the mean and most frequent category using `scikit-learn`. We lined up two instances of `SimpleImputer()`, the first to impute data with the mean and the second to impute data with the most frequent category. In both cases, we set the `add_indicator` parameter to `True` to add the missing indicators. We wrapped `SimpleImputer()` with `ColumnTransformer()` to specifically modify numerical or categorical variables. Then we used the `fit()` and `transform()` methods from the `pipeline` to train the transformers and then add the indicators and replace the missing data.

When returning DataFrames, `ColumnTransformer()` changes the names of the variables and their order. Take a look at the result from *step 15* by executing `X_train_t.head()`. You'll see that the name given to each step of the pipeline is added as a prefix to the variables to flag which variable was modified with each transformer. Then, `num_imputer__A2` was returned by the first step of the pipeline, while `cat_imputer__A12` was returned by the second step of the pipeline.

There's more...

Scikit-learn has the `MissingIndicator()` transformer that just adds missing indicators. Check it out in the documentation: `https://scikit-learn.org/stable/modules/generated/sklearn.impute.MissingIndicator.html` and find an example in the accompanying GitHub repository at `https://github.com/PacktPublishing/Python-Feature-engineering-Cookbook-Third-Edition/blob/main/ch01-missing-data-imputation/Recipe-06-Marking-imputed-values.ipynb`.

Implementing forward and backward fill

Time series data also show missing values. To impute missing data in time series, we use specific methods. Forward fill imputation involves filling missing values in a dataset with the most recent non-missing value that precedes it in the data sequence. In other words, we carry forward the last seen value to the next valid value. Backward fill imputation involves filling missing values with the next non-missing value that follows it in the data sequence. In other words, we carry the last valid value backward to its preceding valid value.

In this recipe, we will replace missing data in a time series with forward and backward fills.

How to do it...

Let's begin by importing the required libraries and time series dataset:

1. Let's import `pandas` and `matplotlib`:

    ```python
    import matplotlib.pyplot as plt
    import pandas as pd
    ```

2. Let's load the air passengers dataset that we described in the *Technical requirements* section and display the first five rows of the time series:

    ```python
    df = pd.read_csv(
        "air_passengers.csv",
        parse_dates=["ds"],
        index_col=["ds"],
    )
    print(df.head())
    ```

    We see the time series in the following output:

    ```
                    y
    ds
    1949-01-01    112.0
    1949-02-01    118.0
    1949-03-01    132.0
    1949-04-01    129.0
    1949-05-01    121.0
    ```

> **Note**
>
> You can determine the percentage of missing data by executing `df.isnull().mean()`.

3. Let's plot the time series to spot any obvious data gaps:

    ```python
    ax = df.plot(marker=".", figsize=[10, 5], legend=None)
    ax.set_title("Air passengers")
    ax.set_ylabel("Number of passengers")
    ax.set_xlabel("Time")
    ```

The previous code returns the following plot, where we see intervals of time where data is missing:

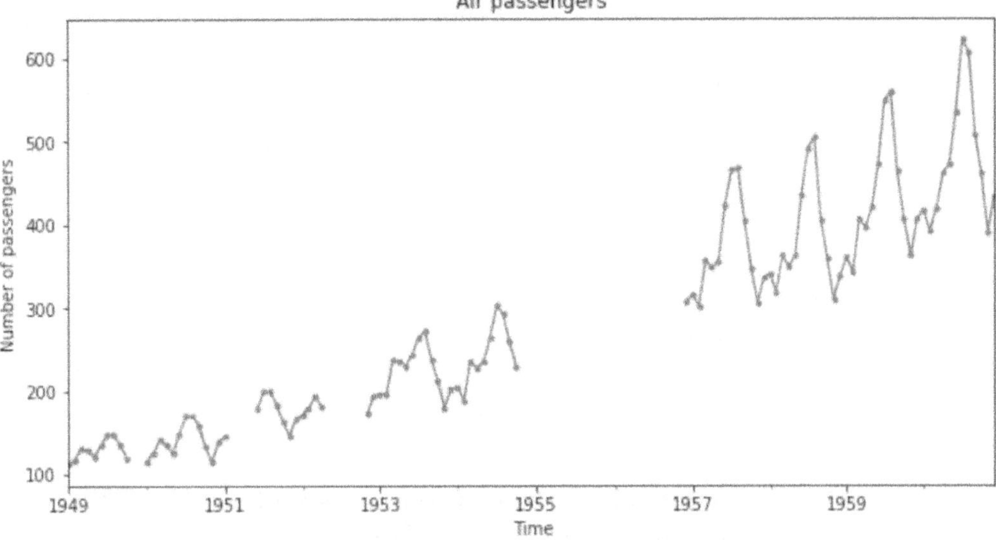

Figure 1.5 – Time series data showing missing values

4. Let's impute missing data by carrying the last observed value in any interval to the next valid value:

```
df_imputed = df.ffill()
```

You can verify the absence of missing data by executing `df_imputed.isnull().sum()`.

5. Let's now plot the complete dataset and overlay as a dotted line the values used for the imputation:

```
ax = df_imputed.plot(
    linestyle="-", marker=".", figsize=[10, 5])
df_imputed[df.isnull()].plot(
    ax=ax, legend=None, marker=".", color="r")
ax.set_title("Air passengers")
ax.set_ylabel("Number of passengers")
ax.set_xlabel("Time")
```

The previous code returns the following plot, where we see the values used to replace nan as dotted lines overlaid in between the continuous time series lines:

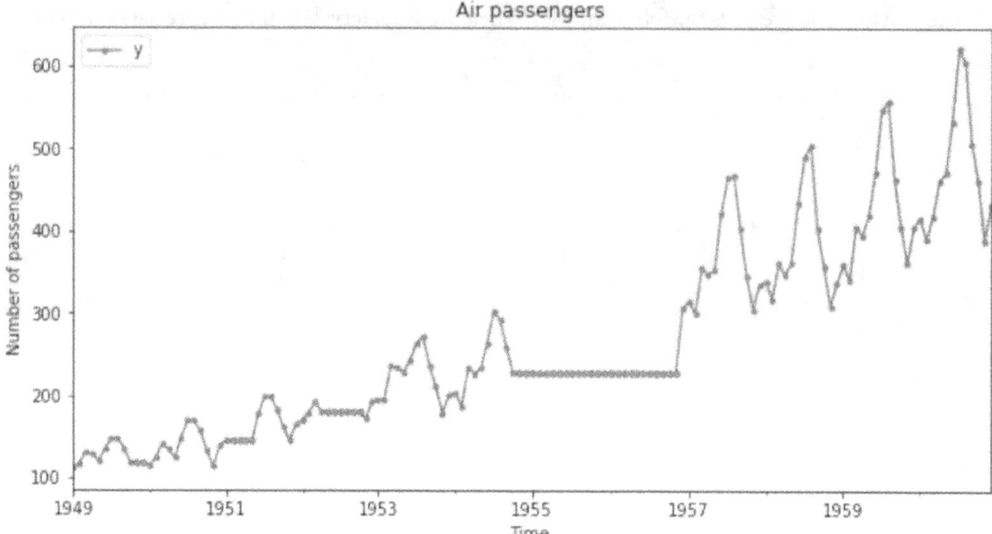

Figure 1.6 – Time series data where missing values were replaced
by the last seen observations (dotted line)

6. Alternatively, we can impute missing data using backward fill:

```
df_imputed = df.bfill()
```

If we plot the imputed dataset and overlay the imputation values as we did in *step 5*, we'll see the following plot:

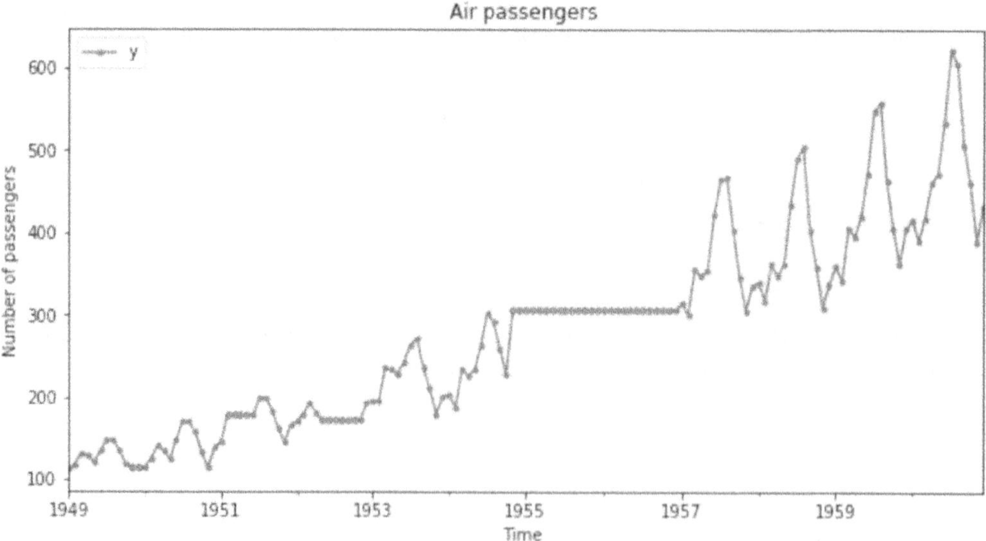

Figure 1.7 – Time series data where missing values were replaced by backward fill (dotted line)

> **Note**
>
> The heights of the values used in the imputation are different in *Figures 1.6 and 1.7*. In *Figure 1.6*, we carry the last value forward, hence the height is lower. In *Figure 1.7*, we carry the next value backward, hence the height is higher.

We've now obtained complete datasets that we can use for time series analysis and modeling.

How it works...

pandas `ffill()` takes the last seen value in any temporal gap in a time series and propagates it forward to the next observed value. Hence, in *Figure 1.6* we see the dotted overlay corresponding to the imputation values at the height of the last seen observation.

pandas `bfill()` takes the next valid value in any temporal gap in a time series and propagates it backward to the previously observed value. Hence, in *Figure 1.7* we see the dotted overlay corresponding to the imputation values at the height of the next observation in the gap.

By default, `ffill()` and `bfill()` will impute all values between valid observations. We can restrict the imputation to a maximum number of data points in any interval by setting a limit, using the `limit` parameter in both methods. For example, `ffill(limit=10)` will only replace the first 10 data points in any gap.

Carrying out interpolation

We can impute missing data in time series by using interpolation between two non-missing data points. Interpolation is the estimation of one or more values in a range by means of a function. In linear interpolation, we fit a linear function between the last observed value and the next valid point. In spline interpolation, we fit a low-degree polynomial between the last and next observed values. The idea of using interpolation is to obtain better estimates of the missing data.

In this recipe, we'll carry out linear and spline interpolation in a time series.

How to do it...

Let's begin by importing the required libraries and time series dataset.

1. Let's import `pandas` and `matplotlib`:

    ```
    import matplotlib.pyplot as plt
    import pandas as pd
    ```

2. Let's load the time series data described in the *Technical requirements* section:

```python
df = pd.read_csv(
    "air_passengers.csv",
    parse_dates=["ds"],
    index_col=["ds"],
)
```

> **Note**
>
> You can plot the time series to find data gaps as we did in *step 3* of the *Implementing forward and backward fill* recipe.

3. Let's impute the missing data by linear interpolation:

```python
df_imputed = df.interpolate(method="linear")
```

> **Note**
>
> If the time intervals between rows are not uniform then the `method` should be set to `time` to achieve a linear fit.

You can verify the absence of missing data by executing `df_imputed.isnull().sum()`.

4. Let's now plot the complete dataset and overlay as a dotted line the values used for the imputation:

```python
ax = df_imputed.plot(
    linestyle="-", marker=".", figsize=[10, 5])
df_imputed[df.isnull()].plot(
    ax=ax, legend=None, marker=".", color="r")
ax.set_title("Air passengers")
ax.set_ylabel("Number of passengers")
ax.set_xlabel("Time")
```

The previous code returns the following plot, where we see the values used to replace nan as dotted lines in between the continuous line of the time series:

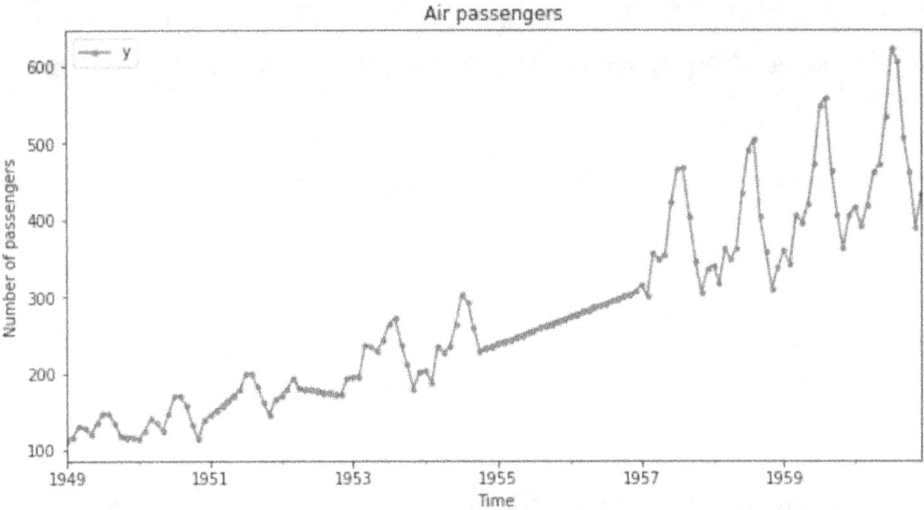

Figure 1.8 – Time series data where missing values were replaced by linear
interpolation between the last and next valid data points (dotted line)

5.   Alternatively, we can impute missing data by doing spline interpolation. We'll use a polynomial
of the second degree:

```
df_imputed = df.interpolate(method="spline", order=2)
```

If we plot the imputed dataset and overlay the imputation values as we did in *step 4*, we'll see
the following plot:

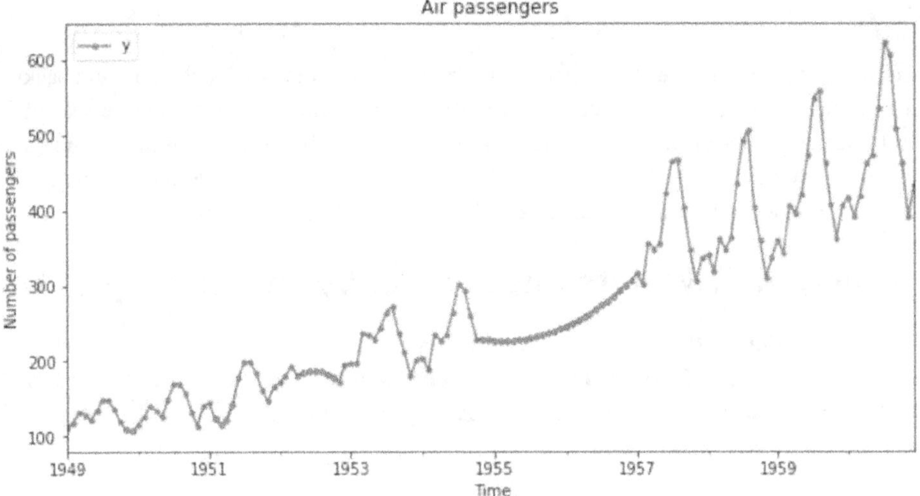

Figure 1.9 – Time series data where missing values were replaced by fitting a second-
degree polynomial between the last and next valid data points (dotted line)

> **Note**
>
> Change the degree of the polynomial used in the interpolation to see how the replacement values vary.

We've now obtained complete datasets that we can use for analysis and modeling.

How it works...

pandas `interpolate()` fills missing values in a range by using an interpolation method. When we set the `method` to `linear`, `interpolate()` treats all data points as equidistant and fits a line between the last and next valid points in an interval with missing data.

> **Note**
>
> If you want to perform linear interpolation, but your data points are not equally distanced, set `method` to `time`.

We then performed spline interpolation with a second-degree polynomial by setting `method` to `spline` and `order` to 2.

pandas `interpolate()` uses `scipy.interpolate.interp1d` and `scipy.interpolate.UnivariateSpline` under the hood, and can therefore implement other interpolation methods. Check out pandas documentation for more details at `https://pandas.pydata.org/pandas-docs/stable/reference/api/pandas.DataFrame.interpolate.html`.

See also

While interpolation aims to get better estimates of the missing data compared to forward and backward fill, these estimates may still not be accurate if the times series show strong trend and seasonality. To obtain better estimates of the missing data in these types of time series, check out time series decomposition followed by interpolation in the *Feature Engineering for Time Series Course* at `https://www.trainindata.com/p/feature-engineering-for-forecasting`.

Performing multivariate imputation by chained equations

Multivariate imputation methods, as opposed to univariate imputation, use multiple variables to estimate the missing values. **Multivariate Imputation by Chained Equations** (MICE) models each variable with missing values as a function of the remaining variables in the dataset. The output of that function is used to replace missing data.

MICE involves the following steps:

1.   First, it performs a simple univariate imputation to every variable with missing data. For example, median imputation.

2.   Next, it selects one specific variable, say, `var_1`, and sets the missing values back to missing.

3.   It trains a model to predict `var_1` using the other variables as input features.

4.   Finally, it replaces the missing values of `var_1` with the output of the model.

MICE repeats *steps 2 to 4* for each of the remaining variables.

An imputation cycle concludes once all the variables have been modeled. MICE carries out multiple imputation cycles, typically 10. That is, we repeat *steps 2* to *4* for each variable 10 times. The idea is that by the end of the cycles, we should have found the best possible estimates of the missing data for each variable.

> **Note**
>
> Multivariate imputation can be a useful alternative to univariate imputation in situations where we don't want to distort the variable distributions. Multivariate imputation is also useful when we are interested in having good estimates of the missing data.

In this recipe, we will implement MICE using scikit-learn.

How to do it...

To begin the recipe, let's import the required libraries and load the data:

1.   Let's import the required Python libraries, classes, and functions:

```python
import pandas as pd
import matplotlib.pyplot as plt
from sklearn.model_selection import train_test_split
from sklearn.linear_model import BayesianRidge
from sklearn.experimental import (
    enable_iterative_imputer
)
from sklearn.impute import (
    IterativeImputer,
    SimpleImputer
)
```

2. Let's load some numerical variables from the dataset described in the *Technical requirements* section:

```python
variables = [
    "A2", "A3", "A8", "A11", "A14", "A15", "target"]
data = pd.read_csv(
    "credit_approval_uci.csv",
    usecols=variables)
```

3. Let's divide the data into train and test sets:

```python
X_train, X_test, y_train, y_test = train_test_split(
    data.drop("target", axis=1),
    data["target"],
    test_size=0.3,
    random_state=0,
)
```

4. Let's create a MICE imputer using Bayes regression, specifying the number of iteration cycles and setting `random_state` for reproducibility:

```python
imputer = IterativeImputer(
    estimator= BayesianRidge(),
    max_iter=10,
    random_state=0,
).set_output(transform="pandas")
```

> **Note**
>
> `IterativeImputer()` contains other useful arguments. For example, we can specify the first imputation strategy using the `initial_strategy` parameter. We can choose from the mean, median, mode, or arbitrary imputation. We can also specify how we want to cycle over the variables, either randomly or from the one with the fewest missing values to the one with the most.

5. Let's fit `IterativeImputer()` so that it trains the estimators to predict the missing values in each variable:

```python
imputer.fit(X_train)
```

> **Note**
>
> We can use any regression model to estimate the missing data with `IterativeImputer()`.

6. Finally, let's fill in the missing values in both the train and test sets:

```python
X_train_t = imputer.transform(X_train)
X_test_t = imputer.transform(X_test)
```

> **Note**
>
> To corroborate the lack of missing data, we can execute `X_train_t.isnull().sum()`.

To wrap up the recipe, let's impute the variables with a simple univariate imputation method and compare the effect on the variables' distribution.

7. Let's set up scikit-learn's `SimpleImputer()` to perform mean imputation, and then transform the datasets:

```python
imputer_simple = SimpleImputer(
    strategy="mean").set_output(transform="pandas")
X_train_s = imputer_simple.fit_transform(X_train)
X_test_s = imputer_simple.transform(X_test)
```

8. Let's now make a histogram of the A3 variable after MICE imputation, followed by a histogram of the same variable after mean imputation:

```python
fig, axes = plt.subplots(
    2, 1, figsize=(10, 10), squeeze=False)
X_test_t["A3"].hist(
    bins=50, ax=axes[0, 0], color="blue")
X_test_s["A3"].hist(
    bins=50, ax=axes[1, 0], color="green")

axes[0, 0].set_ylabel('Number of observations')
axes[1, 0].set_ylabel('Number of observations')

axes[0, 0].set_xlabel('A3')
axes[1, 0].set_xlabel('A3')

axes[0, 0].set_title('MICE')
axes[1, 0].set_title('Mean imputation')

plt.show()
```

In the following plot, we see that mean imputation distorts the variable distribution, with more observations toward the mean value:

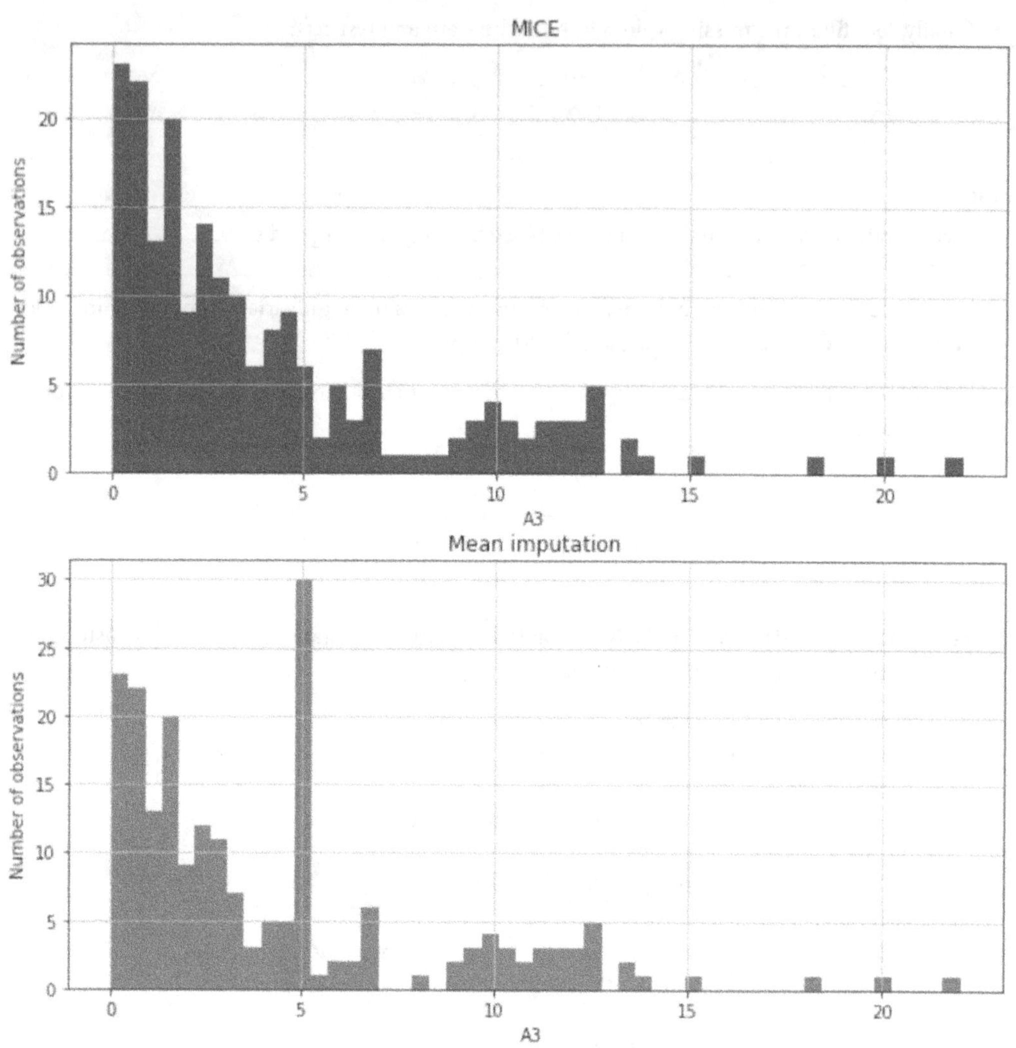

Figure 1.10 – Histogram of variable A3 after mice imputation (top) or mean imputation (bottom), showing the distortion in the variable distribution caused by the latter

How it works...

In this recipe, we performed multivariate imputation using `IterativeImputer()` from `scikit-learn`. When we fit the model, `IterativeImputer()` carried out the steps that we described in the introduction of the recipe. That is, it imputed all variables with the mean. Then it selected one variable and set its missing values back to missing. And finally, it fitted a Bayes regressor to estimate that variable based on the others. It repeated this procedure for each variable. That was one cycle of imputation.

We set it to repeat this process 10 times. By the end of this procedure, `IterativeImputer()` had one Bayes regressor trained to predict the values of each variable based on the other variables in the dataset. With `transform()`, it uses the predictions of these Bayes models to impute the missing data.

`IterativeImputer()` can only impute missing data in numerical variables based on numerical variables. If you want to use categorical variables as input, you need to encode them first. However, keep in mind that it will only carry out regression. Hence it is not suitable to estimate missing data in discrete or categorical variables.

See also

To learn more about MICE, take a look at the following resources:

- A multivariate technique for multiplying imputing missing values using a sequence of regression models: `https://www.researchgate.net/publication/244959137`

- *Multiple Imputation by Chained Equations: What is it and how does it work?*: `https://www.jstatsoft.org/article/download/v045i03/550`

Estimating missing data with nearest neighbors

Imputation with **K-Nearest Neighbors** (**KNN**) involves estimating missing values in a dataset by considering the values of their nearest neighbors, where similarity between data points is determined based on a distance metric, such as the Euclidean distance. It assigns the missing value the average of the nearest neighbors' values, weighted by their distance.

Consider the following data set containing 4 variables (columns) and 11 observations (rows). We want to impute the dark value in the fifth row of the second variable. First, we find the row's k-nearest neighbors, where $k=3$ in our example, and they are highlighted by the rectangular boxes (middle panel). Next, we take the average value shown by the closest neighbors for variable 2.

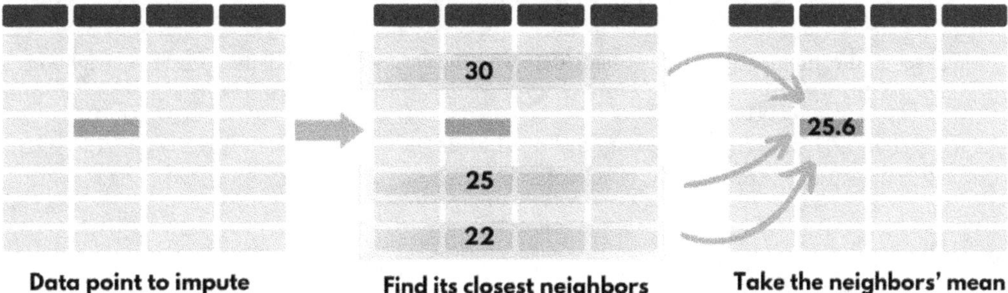

Figure 1.11 – Diagram showing a value to impute (dark box), the three closest rows to the value to impute (square boxes), and the values considered to take the average for the imputation

The value for the imputation is given by (value1 × w1 + value2 × w2 + value3 × w3) / 3, where w1, w2, and w3 are proportional to the distance of the neighbor to the data to impute.

In this recipe, we will perform KNN imputation using scikit-learn.

How to do it...

To proceed with the recipe, let's import the required libraries and prepare the data:

1. Let's import the required libraries, classes, and functions:

    ```
    import matplotlib.pyplot as plt
    import pandas as pd
    from sklearn.model_selection import train_test_split
    from sklearn.impute import KNNImputer
    ```

2. Let's load the dataset described in the *Technical requirements* section (only some numerical variables):

    ```
    variables = [
        "A2", "A3", "A8", "A11", "A14", "A15", "target"]
    data = pd.read_csv(
        "credit_approval_uci.csv",
        usecols=variables,
    )
    ```

3. Let's divide the data into train and test sets:

    ```
    X_train, X_test, y_train, y_test = train_test_split(
        data.drop("target", axis=1),
        data["target"],
        test_size=0.3,
        random_state=0,
    )
    ```

4. Let's set up the imputer to replace missing data with the weighted mean of its closest five neighbors:

    ```
    imputer = KNNImputer(
        n_neighbors=5, weights="distance",
    ).set_output(transform="pandas")
    ```

> **Note**
>
> The replacement values can be calculated as the uniform mean of the k-nearest neighbors, by setting `weights` to `uniform` or as the weighted average, as we do in the recipe. The weight is based on the distance of the neighbor to the observation to impute. The nearest neighbors carry more weight.

5. Find the nearest neighbors:

```
imputer.fit(X_train)
```

6. Replace the missing values with the weighted mean of the values shown by the neighbors:

```
X_train_t = imputer.transform(X_train)
X_test_t = imputer.transform(X_test)
```

The result is a pandas DataFrame with the missing data replaced.

How it works...

In this recipe, we replaced missing data with the average value shown by each observation's k-nearest neighbors. We set up `KNNImputer()` to find each observation's five closest neighbors based on the Euclidean distance. The replacement values were estimated as the weighted average of the values shown by the five closest neighbors for the variable to impute. With `transform()`, the imputer calculated the replacement value and replaced the missing data.

2

Encoding Categorical Variables

Categorical variables are those whose values are selected from a group of categories or labels. For example, the `Home owner` variable with the values of `owner` and `non-owner` is categorical, and so is the `Marital status` variable with the values of `never married`, `married`, `divorced`, and `widowed`. In some categorical variables, the labels have an intrinsic order; for example, in the `Student's grade` variable, the values of `A`, `B`, `C`, and `Fail` are ordered, with `A` being the highest grade and `Fail` being the lowest. These are called **ordinal categorical variables**. Variables in which the categories do not have an intrinsic order are called **nominal categorical variables**, such as the `City` variable, with the values of `London`, `Manchester`, `Bristol`, and so on.

The values of categorical variables are often encoded as strings. To train most machine learning models, we need to transform those strings into numbers. The act of replacing strings with numbers is called **categorical encoding**. In this chapter, we will discuss multiple categorical encoding methods.

This chapter will cover the following recipes:

- Creating binary variables through one-hot encoding
- Performing one-hot encoding of frequent categories
- Replacing categories with counts or the frequency of observations
- Replacing categories with ordinal numbers
- Performing ordinal encoding based on the target value
- Implementing target mean encoding
- Encoding with the Weight of Evidence
- Grouping rare or infrequent categories
- Performing binary encoding

Technical requirements

In this chapter, we will use the `Matplotlib`, `pandas`, `NumPy`, `scikit-learn`, `feature-engine`, and Category Encoders Python libraries. If you need to install Python, the free Anaconda Python distribution (`https://www.anaconda.com/`) includes most numerical computing libraries.

`feature-engine` can be installed with `pip`:

```
pip install feature-engine
```

If you use Anaconda, you can install `feature-engine` with `conda`:

```
conda install -c conda-forge feature_engine
```

To install Category Encoders, use `pip` as follows:

```
pip install category_encoders
```

We will use the **Credit Approval** dataset from the *UCI Machine Learning Repository* (`https://archive.ics.uci.edu/`), licensed under the CC BY 4.0 creative commons attribution: `https://creativecommons.org/licenses/by/4.0/legalcode`. You'll find the dataset at this link: `http://archive.ics.uci.edu/dataset/27/credit+approval`.

I downloaded and modified the data as shown in this notebook: `https://github.com/PacktPublishing/Python-Feature-engineering-Cookbook-Third-Edition/blob/main/ch02-categorical-encoding/credit-approval-dataset.ipynb`.

You'll find a copy of the modified data set in the accompanying GitHub repository: `https://github.com/PacktPublishing/Python-Feature-engineering-Cookbook-Third-Edition/blob/main/ch02-categorical-encoding/`.

> **Note**
>
> Before encoding categorical variables, you might want to impute their missing data. Check out the imputation methods for categorical variables in *Chapter 1, Imputing Missing Data*.

Creating binary variables through one-hot encoding

One-hot encoding is a method used to represent categorical data, where each category is represented by a binary variable. The binary variable takes a value of 1 if the category is present, or 0 otherwise.

The following table shows the one-hot encoded representation of the `Smoker` variable with the categories of `Smoker` and `Non-Smoker`:

Variable	Smoker	Non-Smoker
Smoker	1	0
Non-Smoker	0	1
Non-Smoker	0	1
Smoker	1	0
Non-Smoker	0	1

Figure 2.1 – One-hot encoded representation of the Smoker variable

As shown in *Figure 2.1*, from the Smoker variable, we can derive a binary variable for Smoker, which shows the value of 1 for smokers, or the binary variable for Non-Smoker, which takes the value of 1 for those who do not smoke.

For the Color categorical variable with the values of red, blue, and green, we can create three variables called red, blue, and green. These variables will be assigned a value of 1 if the observation corresponds to the respective color, and 0 if it does not.

A categorical variable with k unique categories can be encoded using $k-1$ binary variables. For Smoker, k is 2 as it contains two labels (Smoker and Non-Smoker), so we only need one binary variable ($k - 1 = 1$) to capture all the information. For the Color variable, which has 3 categories ($k = 3$; red, blue, and green), we need 2 ($k - 1 = 2$) binary variables to capture all the information so that the following occurs:

- If the observation is red, it will be captured by the red variable (red = 1, blue = 0)

- If the observation is blue, it will be captured by the blue variable (red = 0, blue = 1)

- If the observation is green, it will be captured by the combination of red and blue (red = 0, blue = 0)

Encoding into $k-1$ binary variables is well suited for linear models. There are a few occasions in which we may prefer to encode the categorical variables with k binary variables:

- When training decision trees, since they do not evaluate the entire feature space at the same time

- When selecting features recursively

- When determining the importance of each category within a variable

In this recipe, we will compare the one-hot encoding implementations of pandas, scikit-learn, and feature-engine.

How to do it...

First, let's make a few imports and get the data ready:

1. Import pandas and the train_test_split function from scikit-learn:

    ```python
    import pandas as pd
    from sklearn.model_selection import train_test_split
    ```

2. Let's load the Credit Approval dataset:

    ```python
    data = pd.read_csv("credit_approval_uci.csv")
    ```

3. Let's separate the data into train and test sets:

    ```python
    X_train, X_test, y_train, y_test = train_test_split(
        data.drop(labels=["target"], axis=1),
        data["target"],
        test_size=0.3,
        random_state=0,
    )
    ```

4. Let's inspect the unique categories of the A4 variable:

    ```python
    X_train["A4"].unique()
    ```

    We can see the unique values of A4 in the following output:

    ```
    array(['u', 'y', 'Missing', 'l'], dtype=object)
    ```

5. Let's encode A4 into *k-1* binary variables using pandas and then inspect the first five rows of the resulting DataFrame:

    ```python
    dummies = pd.get_dummies(
        X_train["A4"], drop_first=True)
    dummies.head()
    ```

> **Note**
>
> With pandas' get_dummies(), we can either ignore or encode missing data through the dummy_na parameter. By setting dummy_na=True, missing data will be encoded in a new binary variable. To encode the variable into *k* dummies, use drop_first=False instead.

Here, we can see the output of *Step 5*, where each label is now a binary variable:

```
        Missing            l        u          y
   596    False    False    True    False
   303    False    False    True    False
   204    False    False   False     True
   351    False    False   False     True
   118    False    False    True    False
```

6.   Now, let's encode all the categorical variables into *k-1* binaries:

```
X_train_enc = pd.get_dummies(X_train, drop_first=True)
X_test_enc = pd.get_dummies(X_test, drop_first=True)
```

> **Note**
>
> pandas' get_dummies() will encode all variables of the object, string, or category type by default. To encode a subset of the variables, pass the variable names in a list to the columns parameter.

7.   Let's inspect the first five rows of the resulting DataFrame:

```
X_train_enc.head()
```

> **Note**
>
> When encoding more than one variable, get_dummies() captures the variable name – say, A1 – and places an underscore followed by the category name to identify the resulting binary variables.

We can see the binary variables in the following output:

	A2	A3	A8	A11	A14	A15	A1_a	A1_b	A4_l	A4_u	...	A7_j	A7_n	A7_o	A7_v	A7_z	A9_t	A10_t	A12_t	A13_p	A13_s
596	46.08	3.000	2.375	8	396.0	4159	True	False	False	True	...	False	False	False	True	False	True	True	True	False	False
303	15.92	2.875	0.085	0	120.0	0	True	False	False	True	...	False	False	False	True	False	False	False	False	False	False
204	36.33	2.125	0.085	1	50.0	1187	False	True	False	False	...	False	False	False	True	False	True	True	False	False	False
351	22.17	0.585	0.000	0	100.0	0	False	True	False	False	...	False	False	False	False	False	False	False	False	False	False
118	57.83	7.040	14.000	6	360.0	1332	False	True	False	True	...	False	False	False	True	False	True	True	True	False	False

Figure 2.2 – A transformed DataFrame showing the numerical variables followed by the one-hot encoded representation of the categorical variables

> **Note**
>
> pandas' get_dummies() will create one binary variable per category seen in a DataFrame. Hence, if there are more categories in the train set than in the test set, get_dummies() will return more columns in the transformed train set than in the transformed test set, and vice versa. To avoid this, it is better to carry out one-hot encoding with scikit-learn or feature-engine.

Let's do one-hot encoding using `scikit-learn` instead.

8. Let's import the encoder and `ColumnTransformer` from `scikit-learn`:

```python
from sklearn.preprocessing import OneHotEncoder
from sklearn.compose import ColumnTransformer
```

9. Let's create a list with the names of the categorical variables:

```python
cat_vars = X_train.select_dtypes(
    include="O").columns.to_list()
```

10. Let's set up the encoder to create *k-1* binary variables:

```python
encoder = OneHotEncoder(drop="first",
    sparse_output=False)
```

> **Note**
>
> To encode variables into *k* dummies, set the `drop` parameter to None. To encode only binary variables into *k-1*, set the `drop` parameter to `if_binary`. The latter is useful because encoding binary variables into *k* dummies is redundant.

11. Let's restrict the encoding to the categorical variables:

```python
ct = ColumnTransformer(
    [("encoder", encoder, cat_vars)],
    remainder="passthrough",
    force_int_remainder_cols=False,
).set_output(transform="pandas")
```

12. Let's fit the encoder so that it identifies the categories to encode:

```python
ct.fit(X_train)
```

13. Let's inspect the categories that will be represented with binary variables:

```python
ct.named_transformers_["encoder"].categories_
```

The transformer will add binary variables for the following categories:

```
[array(['Missing', 'a', 'b'], dtype=object),
 array(['Missing', 'l', 'u', 'y'], dtype=object),
 array(['Missing', 'g', 'gg', 'p'], dtype=object),
 array(['Missing', 'aa', 'c', 'cc', 'd', 'e', 'ff', 'i', 'j', 'k', 'm',
        'q', 'r', 'w', 'x'], dtype=object),
 array(['Missing', 'bb', 'dd', 'ff', 'h', 'j', 'n', 'o', 'v', 'z'],
       dtype=object),
 array(['f', 't'], dtype=object),
 array(['f', 't'], dtype=object),
 array(['f', 't'], dtype=object),
 array(['g', 'p', 's'], dtype=object)]
```

Figure 2.3 – Arrays with the categories that will be encoded into binary variables (one array per variable)

> **Note**
>
> scikit-learn's OneHotEncoder() will only encode the categories learned from the train set. If there are new categories in the test set, we can instruct the encoder to ignore them, return an error, or replace them with an infrequent category, by setting the handle_unknown parameter to ignore, error, or infrequent_if_exists.

14. Let's encode the categorical variables:

```
X_train_enc = ct.transform(X_train)
X_test_enc = ct.transform(X_test)
```

    Make sure to inspect the result by executing X_test_enc.head().

15. To get familiar with the output, let's print the variable names of the resulting DataFrame:

```
ct.get_feature_names_out()
```

    In the following image, we see the names of the variables in the transformed DataFrame:

```
array(['encoder__A1_a', 'encoder__A1_b', 'encoder__A4_l', 'encoder__A4_u',
       'encoder__A4_y', 'encoder__A5_g', 'encoder__A5_gg',
       'encoder__A5_p', 'encoder__A6_aa', 'encoder__A6_c',
       'encoder__A6_cc', 'encoder__A6_d', 'encoder__A6_e',
       'encoder__A6_ff', 'encoder__A6_i', 'encoder__A6_j',
       'encoder__A6_k', 'encoder__A6_m', 'encoder__A6_q', 'encoder__A6_r',
       'encoder__A6_w', 'encoder__A6_x', 'encoder__A7_bb',
       'encoder__A7_dd', 'encoder__A7_ff', 'encoder__A7_h',
       'encoder__A7_j', 'encoder__A7_n', 'encoder__A7_o', 'encoder__A7_v',
       'encoder__A7_z', 'encoder__A9_t', 'encoder__A10_t',
       'encoder__A12_t', 'encoder__A13_p', 'encoder__A13_s',
       'remainder__A2', 'remainder__A3', 'remainder__A8',
       'remainder__A11', 'remainder__A14', 'remainder__A15'], dtype=object)
```

Figure 2.4 – Arrays with the names of the variables in the resulting DataFrame

> **Note**
>
> `ColumnTransformer()` changes the name and order of the variables during the transformation. If the variable was encoded, it will append the `encoder` prefix and if the variable was not modified, it will append the `remainder` prefix.

To wrap up the recipe, let's perform one-hot encoding with `feature-engine`.

16. Let's import the encoder from `feature-engine`:

```
from feature_engine.encoding import OneHotEncoder
```

17. Let's set up the encoder so that it returns *k-1* binary variables:

```
ohe_enc = OneHotEncoder(drop_last=True)
```

> **Note**
>
> `feature-engine`'s `OneHotEncoder()` encodes all categorical variables by default. To encode a subset of the variables, pass the variable names in a list: `OneHotEncoder(variables=["A1", "A4"])`. To encode numerical variables, set the `ignore_format` parameter to `True` or cast the variables as objects.

18. Let's fit the encoder to the train set so that it learns the categories and variables to encode:

```
ohe_enc.fit(X_train)
```

> **Note**
>
> To encode binary variables into *k-1*, and other categorical variables into *k* dummies, set the `drop_last_binary` parameter to `True`.

19. Let's explore the variables that will be encoded:

```
ohe_enc.variables_
```

The transformer found and stored the variables of the object or categorical type, as shown in the following output:

```
['A1', 'A4', 'A5', 'A6', 'A7', 'A9', 'A10', 'A12', 'A13']
```

20. Let's explore the categories for which dummy variables will be created:

```
ohe_enc.encoder_dict_
```

The following dictionary contains the categories that will be encoded in each variable:

```
{'A1': ['a', 'b'],
 'A4': ['u', 'y', 'Missing'],
```

```
    'A5': ['g', 'p', 'Missing'],
    'A6': ['c', 'q', 'w', 'ff', 'm', 'i', 'e', 'cc', 'x', 'd', 'k',
'j', 'Missing', 'aa'],
    'A7': ['v', 'ff', 'h', 'dd', 'z', 'bb', 'j', 'Missing', 'n'],
    'A9': ['t'],
    'A10': ['t'],
    'A12': ['t'],
    'A13': ['g', 's']}
```

21. Let's encode the categorical variables in train and test sets:

```
X_train_enc = ohe_enc.transform(X_train)
X_test_enc = ohe_enc.transform(X_test)
```

If we execute `X_train_enc.head()`, we will see the following DataFrame:

	A2	A3	A8	A11	A14	A15	A1_a	A1_b	A4_u	A4_y	...	A7_z	A7_bb	A7_j	A7_Missing	A7_n	A9_t	A10_t	A12_t	A13_g	A13_s
596	46.08	3.000	2.375	8	396.0	4159	1	0	1	0	...	0	0	0	0	0	1	1	1	1	0
303	15.92	2.875	0.085	0	120.0	0	1	0	1	0	...	0	0	0	0	0	0	0	0	1	0
204	36.33	2.125	0.085	1	50.0	1187	0	1	0	1	...	0	0	0	0	0	1	1	0	1	0
351	22.17	0.585	0.000	0	100.0	0	0	1	0	1	...	0	0	0	0	0	0	0	0	1	0
118	57.83	7.040	14.000	6	360.0	1332	0	1	1	0	...	0	0	0	0	0	1	1	1	1	0

Figure 2.5 – Transformed DataFrame with numerical variables followed by
the one-hot encoded representation of the categorical variables

Note how the A4 categorical variable was replaced with A4_u, A4_y, and so on.

> **Note**
>
> We can get the names of all the variables in the transformed dataset by executing `ohe_enc.get_feature_names_out()`.

How it works...

In this recipe, we performed a one-hot encoding of categorical variables using `pandas`, `scikit-learn`, and `feature-engine`.

`pandas`' `get_dummies()` replaced the categorical variables with a set of binary variables representing each of the categories. When used on the entire dataset, it returned the numerical variables, followed by the one-hot encoded representation of each seen category in every variable of type object, string, or categorical.

> **Note**
>
> `pandas` will return binary variables for every category seen in a dataset. In practice, to avoid data leakage and anticipate deployment eventualities, we want to return dummy variables for categories seen in a training set only. So, it is safer to use `scikit-learn` and `feature-engine`.

`OneHotEncoder()` from `scikit-learn` or `feature-engine` learned the categories that should be represented by binary variables from the train set when we applied `fit()`. With `transform()`, `scikit-learn` returned just the binary variables, whereas `feature-engine` returned the numerical variables followed by the one-hot encoded representation of the categorical ones.

`scikit-learn`'s `OneHotEncoder()` encodes all variables by default. To restrict the encoding to categorical variables, we used `ColumnTransformer()`. We set the output of `transform()` to `pandas` to obtain the resulting data as a DataFrame.

> **Note**
>
> One-hot encoding is suitable for linear models. It also expands the feature space. If your dataset contains many categorical variables or highly cardinal variables, you can restrict the number of binary variables by encoding the most frequent categories only. You can do this automatically with both `scikit-learn` and `feature-engine` as we describe in the *Performing one-hot encoding of frequent categories* recipe.

There's more...

We can also perform one-hot encoding using the Category Encoders Python library: `https://contrib.scikit-learn.org/category_encoders/onehot.html`.

To limit the number of binary variables, we can choose which categories to encode and which to ignore; check out a Python demo in the following article: `https://www.blog.trainindata.com/one-hot-encoding-categorical-variables/`.

Performing one-hot encoding of frequent categories

One-hot encoding represents each variable's category with a binary variable. Hence, one-hot encoding of highly cardinal variables or datasets with multiple categorical features can expand the feature space dramatically. This, in turn, may increase the computational cost of using machine learning models or deteriorate their performance. To reduce the number of binary variables, we can perform one-hot encoding of the most frequent categories. One-hot encoding the top categories is equivalent to treating the remaining, less frequent categories as a single, unique category.

In this recipe, we will implement one-hot encoding of the most popular categories using `pandas`, `Scikit-learn`, and `feature-engine`.

How to do it...

First, let's import the necessary Python libraries and get the dataset ready:

1. Import the required Python libraries, functions, and classes:

    ```python
    import pandas as pd
    import numpy as np
    from sklearn.model_selection import train_test_split
    ```

2. Let's load the Credit Approval dataset and divide it into train and test sets:

```python
data = pd.read_csv("credit_approval_uci.csv")
X_train, X_test, y_train, y_test = train_test_split(
    data.drop(labels=["target"], axis=1),
    data["target"],
    test_size=0.3,
    random_state=0,
)
```

> **Note**
>
> The most frequent categories need to be determined in the train set. This is to avoid data leakage.

3. Let's inspect the unique categories of the A6 variable:

```python
X_train["A6"].unique()
```

The unique values of A6 are displayed in the following output:

```
array(['c', 'q', 'w', 'ff', 'm', 'i', 'e', 'cc', 'x', 'd', 'k',
'j', 'Missing, 'aa', 'r'], dtype=object)
```

4. Let's count the number of observations per category of A6, sort them in decreasing order, and then display the five most frequent categories:

```python
X_train["A6"].value_counts().sort_values(
    ascending=False).head(5)
```

We can see the five most frequent categories and the number of observations per category in the following output:

```
A6
c     93
q     56
w     48
i     41
ff    38
Name: count, dtype: int64
```

5. Now, let's capture the most frequent categories of A6 in a list by using the code in *Step 4* inside a list comprehension:

```python
top_5 = [x for x in X_train[
        " A6"].value_counts().sort_values(
            ascending=False).head(5).index
]
```

6. Let's add a binary variable per top category to a copy of the train and test sets:

```python
X_train_enc = X_train.copy()
X_test_enc = X_test.copy()
for label in top_5:
    X_train_enc[f"A6_{label}"] = np.where(
        X_train["A6"] == label, 1, 0)
    X_test_enc[f"A6_{label}"] = np.where(
        X_test["A6"] == label, 1, 0)
```

7. Let's display the top 10 rows of the original and encoded variable, A6, in the train set:

```python
X_train_enc[["A6"] + [f"A6_{
    label}" for label in top_5]].head(10)
```

In the output of *Step 7*, we can see the A6 variable, followed by the binary variables:

	A6	A6_c	A6_q	A6_w	A6_i	A6_ff
596	c	1	0	0	0	0
303	q	0	1	0	0	0
204	w	0	0	1	0	0
351	ff	0	0	0	0	1
118	m	0	0	0	0	0
247	q	0	1	0	0	0
652	i	0	0	0	1	0
513	e	0	0	0	0	0
230	cc	0	0	0	0	0
250	e	0	0	0	0	0

Let's now automate one-hot encoding of frequent categories with `scikit-learn`.

8. Let's import the encoder:

```python
from sklearn.preprocessing import OneHotEncoder
```

9. Let's set up the encoder to encode categories shown in at least 39 observations and limit the number of categories to encode to 5:

```python
encoder = OneHotEncoder(
    min_frequency=39,
    max_categories=5,
    sparse_output=False,
).set_output(transform="pandas")
```

10. Finally, let's fit the transformer to the two high cardinal variables and then transform the data:

```python
X_train_enc = encoder.fit_transform(X_train[
    ['A6', 'A7']])
X_test_enc = encoder.transform(X_test[['A6', 'A7']])
```

If you execute `X_train_enc.head()` you'll see the resulting DataFrame:

	A6_c	A6_i	A6_q	A6_w	A6_infrequent_sklearn	A7_bb	A7_ff	A7_h	A7_v	A7_infrequent_sklearn
14	0.0	0.0	1.0	0.0	0.0	0.0	0.0	0.0	1.0	0.0
586	0.0	0.0	0.0	0.0	1.0	0.0	0.0	1.0	0.0	0.0
140	0.0	0.0	0.0	0.0	1.0	0.0	0.0	1.0	0.0	0.0
492	0.0	0.0	0.0	0.0	1.0	0.0	0.0	0.0	1.0	0.0
350	0.0	0.0	0.0	0.0	1.0	0.0	0.0	0.0	0.0	1.0

Figure 2.6 – Transformed DataFrame containing binary variables for those categories with at least 39 observations and an additional binary representing all remaining categories

To wrap up the recipe, let's encode the most frequent categories with `feature-engine`.

11. Let's set up the one-hot encoder to encode the five most frequent categories of the A6 and A7 variables:

```
From feature_engine.encoding import OneHotEncoder
ohe_enc = OneHotEncoder(
    top_categories=5,
    variables=["A6", "A7"]
)
```

> **Note**
>
> The number of frequent categories to encode is arbitrarily determined by the user.

12. Let's fit the encoder to the train set so that it learns and stores the most frequent categories of A6 and A7:

```
ohe_enc.fit(X_train)
```

13. Finally, let's encode A6 and A7 in the train and test sets:

```
X_train_enc = ohe_enc.transform(X_train)
X_test_enc = ohe_enc.transform(X_test)
```

You can view the new binary variables in the transformed DataFrame by executing `X_train_enc.head()`. You can also find the top five categories learned by the encoder by executing `ohe_enc.encoder_dict_`.

How it works...

In the first part of this recipe, we worked with the `A6` categorical variable. We inspected its unique categories with `pandas' unique()`. Next, we counted the number of observations per category using `pandas' value_counts()`, which returned a `pandas` series with the categories as the index and the number of observations as values. Next, we sorted the categories from the one with the most to the one with the least observations using `pandas' sort_values()`. We then reduced the series to the five most popular categories by using `pandas' head()`. We used this series in a list comprehension to capture the names of the most frequent categories. After that, we looped over each category, and with NumPy's `where()`, we created binary variables by placing a value of `1` if the observation showed the category, or `0` otherwise.

We discussed how to use `OneHotEncoder()` from `scikit-learn` and `feature-engine` in the *Creating binary variables through one-hot encoding* recipe. Here, I will only highlight the parameters needed to encode the most frequent categories.

To encode frequent categories with `scikit-learn`, we set the `min_frequency` parameter to `39`. Hence, categories shown in less than `39` observations were grouped into an additional binary variable called `infrequent_sklearn`.

To encode frequent categories with `feature-engine`, we set the `top_categories` parameter to `5`. Hence, the transformer created binary variables for the `5` most frequent categories only. Less frequent categories will show a `0` in all the binary variables.

There's more...

This recipe is based on the winning solution of the **Knowledge Discovery and Data** (**KDD**) 2009 mining cup, *Winning the KDD Cup Orange Challenge with Ensemble Selection* (`http://proceedings.mlr.press/v7/niculescu09/niculescu09.pdf`), where the author's limited one-hot encoding to the 10 most frequent categories of each variable.

Replacing categories with counts or the frequency of observations

In count with counts or frequency of observations" or frequency encoding, we replace the categories with the count or the fraction of observations showing that category. That is, if 10 out of 100 observations show the `blue` category for the `Color` variable, we would replace `blue` with `10` when doing count encoding, or with `0.1` if performing frequency encoding. These encoding methods are useful when there is a relationship between the category frequency and the target. For example, in sales, the frequency of a product may indicate its popularity.

> **Note**
>
> If two different categories are present in the same number of observations, they will be replaced by the same value, which may lead to information loss.

In this recipe, we will perform count and frequency encoding using pandas and feature-engine.

How to do it...

We'll start by encoding one variable with pandas and then we'll automate the process with feature-engine:

1. Let's start with the imports:

```
import pandas as pd
from sklearn.model_selection import train_test_split
from feature_engine.encoding import CountFrequencyEncoder
```

2. Let's load the Credit Approval dataset and divide it into train and test sets:

```
data = pd.read_csv("credit_approval_uci.csv")
X_train, X_test, y_train, y_test = train_test_split(
    data.drop(labels=["target"], axis=1),
    data["target"],
    test_size=0.3,
    random_state=0,
)
```

3. Let's with counts or frequency of observations" capture the number of observations per category of the A7 variable in a dictionary:

```
counts = X_train["A7"].value_counts().to_dict()
```

> **Note**
>
> To find the frequency instead, execute `X_train["A7"].value_counts(normalize=True).to_dict()`.

If we execute `print(counts)`, we'll see the count of observations per category of A7:

```
{'v': 277, 'h': 101, 'ff': 41, 'bb': 39, 'z': 7, 'dd': 5, 'j':
5, 'Missing': 4, 'n': 3, 'o': 1}
```

4. Let's replace the categories in A7 with the counts in a copy of the data sets:

```
X_train_enc = X_train.copy()
X_test_enc = X_test.copy()
X_train_enc["A7"] = X_train_enc["A7"].map(counts)
X_test_enc["A7"] = X_test_enc["A7"].map(counts)
```

Go ahead and inspect the data by executing `X_train_enc.head()` to corroborate that the categories have been replaced by the counts.

To apply this procedure to multiple variables, we can use `feature-engine`.

5. Let's set up the encoder so that it encodes all categorical variables with the count of observations:

```
count_enc = CountFrequencyEncoder(
    encoding_method="count", variables=None,
)
```

> **Note**
>
> `CountFrequencyEncoder()` will automatically find and encode all categorical variables in the train set. To encode only a subset of the variables, pass the variable names in a list to the `variables` argument. To encode with the frequency instead, use `encoding_method="frequency"`.

6. Let's fit the encoder to the train set so that it stores the number of observations per category per variable:

```
count_enc.fit(X_train)
```

7. The encoder found the categorical variables automatically. Let's check them out:

```
count_enc.variables_
```

The previous command returns the names of the categorical variables in the train set:

```
['A1', 'A4', 'A5', 'A6', 'A7', 'A9', 'A10', 'A12', 'A13']
```

8. Let's print the count of observations per category per variable:

```
count_enc.encoder_dict_
```

The previous attribute stores the mappings that will be used to replace the categories:

```
{'A1': {'b': 335, 'a': 144, 'Missing': 4},
 'A4': {'u': 363, 'y': 115, 'Missing': 4, 'l': 1},
 'A5': {'g': 363, 'p': 115, 'Missing': 4, 'gg': 1},
 'A6': {'c': 93,
  'q': 56,
  'w': 48,
  'i': 41,
  'ff': 38,
  'k': 38,
  'aa': 34,
  'cc': 30,
  'm': 26,
  'x': 24,
  'e': 21,
  'd': 21,
  'j': 8,
  'Missing': 4,
  'r': 1},
 'A7': {'v': 277,
  'h': 101,
  'ff': 41,
  'bb': 39,
  'z': 7,
  'dd': 5,
  'j': 5,
  'Missing': 4,
  'n': 3,
  'o': 1},
 'A9': {'t': 256, 'f': 227},
 'A10': {'f': 271, 't': 212},
 'A12': {'f': 263, 't': 220},
 'A13': {'g': 441, 's': 38, 'p': 4}}
```

Figure 2.7 – Dictionary containing the number of observations per category, for each variable; these values will be used to encode the categorical variables

9. Finally, let's with counts or frequency of observations" replace the categories with counts in the train and test sets:

```
X_train_enc = count_enc.transform(X_train)
X_test_enc = count_enc.transform(X_test)
```

Check out the result by executing `X_train_enc.head()`. The encoder returns pandas DataFrames with the strings of the categorical variables replaced with the counts of observations, leaving the variables ready to use in machine learning models.

How it works...

In this recipe, we replaced categories with the count of observations using `pandas` and `feature-engine`.

Using `pandas'` `value_counts()`, we determined the number of observations per category of the A7 variable, and with `pandas'` `to_dict()`, we captured these values in a with counts or frequency of observations" dictionary, where each key was a unique category, and each value the number of observations for that category. With `pandas'` `map()` and using this dictionary, we replaced the categories with the observation counts in both the train and test sets.

> **Note**
>
> The count of observations for the encoding should be obtained from the train set to avoid data leakage. Note that new categories in the test set will not have a corresponding mapping and hence will be replaced by nan. To avoid this, use `feature-engine`. Alternatively, you can replace the nan with 0.

To perform count encoding with `feature-engine`, we used `CountFrequencyEncoder()` and set `encoding_method` to `'count'`. We left the `variables` argument set to `None` so that the encoder automatically finds all the categorical variables in the dataset. With `fit()`, the transformer found the categorical variables and stored the observation counts per category in the `encoder_dict_` attribute. With `transform()`, the transformer replaced the categories with the counts, returning a `pandas` DataFrame.

> **Note**
>
> If there are categories in the test set that were not present in the train set, the encoder will raise an error by default. You can make it ignore them, in which case they will appear as nan, or encode them as 0.

See also

You can also carry out count and frequency encoding with the Python library Category Encoders: `https://contrib.scikit-learn.org/category_encoders/count.html`.

For some useful applications of count encoding, check out this article: `https://letsdatascience.com/frequency-encoding/`.

Replacing categories with ordinal numbers

Ordinal encoding consists of replacing the categories with digits from *1* to *k* (or *0* to *k-1*, depending on the implementation), where *k* is the number of distinct categories of the variable. The numbers are assigned arbitrarily. Ordinal encoding is better suited for non-linear machine learning models, which can navigate through arbitrarily assigned numbers to find patterns that relate to the target.

In this recipe, we will perform ordinal encoding using `pandas`, `scikit-learn`, and `feature-engine`.

How to do it...

First, let's make the import and prepare the dataset:

1. Import `pandas` and the data split function:

    ```python
    import pandas as pd
    from sklearn.model_selection import train_test_split
    ```

2. Let's load the Credit Approval dataset and divide it into train and test sets:

    ```python
    data = pd.read_csv("credit_approval_uci.csv")
    X_train, X_test, y_train, y_test = train_test_split(
        data.drop(labels=["target"], axis=1),
        data["target"],
        test_size=0.3,
        random_state=0,
    )
    ```

3. To encode the A7 variable, let's make a dictionary of category-to-integer pairs:

    ```python
    ordinal_mapping = {k: i for i, k in enumerate(
        X_train["A7"].unique(), 0)
    }
    ```

    If we execute `print(ordinal_mapping)`, we will see the digits that will replace each category:

    ```
    {'v': 0, 'ff': 1, 'h': 2, 'dd': 3, 'z': 4, 'bb': 5, 'j': 6,
    'Missing': 7, 'n': 8, 'o': 9}
    ```

4. Now, let's replace the categories in a copy of the DataFrames:

    ```python
    X_train_enc = X_train.copy()
    X_test_enc = X_test.copy()
    X_train_enc["A7"] = X_train_enc["A7"].map(ordinal_mapping)
    X_test_enc["A7"] = X_test_enc["A7"].map(ordinal_mapping)
    ```

    Go ahead and execute `print(X_train["A7"].head())` to see the result of the previous operation.

    Next, we'll carry out ordinal encoding using `scikit-learn`.

5. Let's import the required classes:

    ```python
    from sklearn.preprocessing import OrdinalEncoder
    from sklearn.compose import ColumnTransformer
    ```

> **Note**
>
> Do not confuse `OrdinalEncoder()` with `LabelEncoder()` from `scikit-learn`. The former is intended to encode predictive features, whereas the latter is intended to modify the target variable.

6. Let's set up the encoder:

```
enc = OrdinalEncoder()
```

7. Let's make a list containing the categorical variables to encode:

```
cat_vars = X_train.select_dtypes(include="O").columns.to_list()
```

8. Let's restrict the encoding to the categorical variables:

```
ct = ColumnTransformer(
    [("encoder", enc, cat_vars)],
    remainder="passthrough",
    force_int_remainder_cols=False,
).set_output(transform="pandas")
```

> **Note**
>
> Remember to set `remainder` to `"passthrough"` to make the `ColumnTransformer()` return the un-transformed variables as well.

9. Let's fit the encoder to the train set so that it creates and stores representations of categories to digits:

```
ct.fit(X_train)
```

> **Note**
>
> By executing `ct.named_transformers_["encoder"].categories_`, you can visualize the unique categories per variable.

10. Now, let's encode the categorical variables in the train and test sets:

```
X_train_enc = ct.transform(X_train)
X_test_enc = ct.transform(X_test)
```

Go ahead and execute `X_train_enc.head()` to check out the resulting DataFrame.

> **Note**
>
> `ColumnTransformer()` will mark the encoded variables by appending `encoder` to the variable name. The variables that were not modified show the `remainder` prefix.

Now, let's do ordinal encoding with `feature-engine`.

11. Let's import the encoder:

```
from feature_engine.encoding import OrdinalEncoder
```

12. Let's set up the encoder so that it replaces categories with arbitrary integers in the categorical variables specified in *Step 7*:

```
enc = OrdinalEncoder(
    encoding_method="arbitrary",
    variables=cat_vars,
)
```

> **Note**
>
> `feature-engine`'s `OrdinalEncoder()` automatically finds and encodes all categorical variables if the `variables` parameter is None. Alternatively, it will encode the variables indicated in the list. In addition, it can assign the integers according to the target mean value (see the *Performing ordinal encoding based on the target value* recipe).

13. Let's fit the encoder to the train set so that it learns and stores the category-to-integer mappings:

```
enc.fit(X_train)
```

> **Note**
>
> The category to integer mappings are stored in the `encoder_dict_` attribute and can be accessed by executing `enc.encoder_dict_`.

14. Finally, let's encode the categorical variables in the train and test sets:

```
X_train_enc = enc.transform(X_train)
X_test_enc = enc.transform(X_test)
```

`feature-engine` returns `pandas` DataFrames where the values of the original variables are replaced with numbers, leaving the DataFrame ready to use in machine learning models.

How it works...

In this recipe, we replaced categories with integers assigned arbitrarily.

We used pandas' `unique()` to find the unique categories of the A7 variable. Next, we created a dictionary of category-to-integer and passed it to pandas' `map()` to replace the strings in A7 with the integers.

Next, we carried out ordinal encoding using `scikit-learn`'s `OrdinalEncoder()` and used `ColumnTransformer()` to restrict the encoding to categorical variables. With `fit()`, the transformer created the category-to-integer mappings based on the categories in the train set. With `transform()`, the categories were replaced with integers. By setting the `remainder` parameter to `passthrough`, we made `ColumnTransformer()` concatenate the variables that are not encoded at the back of the encoded features.

To perform ordinal encoding with `feature-engine`, we used `OrdinalEncoder()`, indicating that the integers should be assigned arbitrarily through `encoding_method`, and passed a list with the variables to encode in the `variables` argument. With `fit()`, the encoder assigned integers to each variable's categories, which were stored in the `encoder_dict_` attribute. These mappings were then used by the `transform()` method to replace the categories in the train and test sets, returning DataFrames.

> **Note**
>
> When a category in the test set is not present in the training set, it will not have a mapping to a digit. `OrdinalEncoder()` from `scikit-learn` and `feature-engine` will raise an error by default. However, they have the option to replace unseen categories with a user-defined value or `-1`, respectively.

`scikit-learn`'s `OrdinalEncoder()` can restrict the encoding to those categories with a minimum frequency. `feature-engine`'s `OrdinalEncoder()` can assign the numbers based on the target mean value, as we will see in the following recipe.

There's more...

You can also carry out ordinal encoding with `OrdinalEncoder()` from Category Encoders. Check it out at `http://contrib.scikit-learn.org/category_encoders/ordinal.html`.

Performing ordinal encoding based on the target value

In the previous recipe, we replaced categories with integers, which were assigned arbitrarily. We can also assign integers to the categories given the target values. To do this, first, we calculate the mean value of the target per category. Next, we order the categories from the one with the lowest to the one with the highest target mean value. Finally, we assign digits to the ordered categories, starting with *0* to the first category up to *k-1* to the last category, where *k* is the number of distinct categories.

This encoding method creates a monotonic relationship between the categorical variable and the response and therefore makes the variables more adequate for use in linear models.

In this recipe, we will encode categories while following the target value using pandas and feature-engine.

How to do it...

First, let's import the necessary Python libraries and get the dataset ready:

1. Import the required Python libraries, functions, and classes:

```
import pandas as pd
import matplotlib.pyplot as plt
from sklearn.model_selection import train_test_split
```

2. Let's load the Credit Approval dataset and divide it into train and test sets:

```
data = pd.read_csv("credit_approval_uci.csv")
X_train, X_test, y_train, y_test = train_test_split(
    data.drop(labels=["target"], axis=1),
    data["target"],
    test_size=0.3,
    random_state=0,
)
```

3. Let's determine the mean target value per category in A7, then sort the categories from that with the lowest to that with the highest target value:

```
y_train.groupby(X_train["A7"]).mean().sort_values()
```

The following is the output of the preceding command:

```
A7
o          0.000000
ff         0.146341
j          0.200000
dd         0.400000
v          0.418773
bb         0.512821
h          0.603960
n          0.666667
z          0.714286
Missing    1.000000
Name: target, dtype: float64
```

4. Now, let's repeat the computation in *Step 3*, but this time, let's retain the ordered category names:

```
ordered_labels = y_train.groupby(
    X_train["A7"]).mean().sort_values().index
```

To display the output of the preceding command, we can execute `print(ordered_labels)`:
`Index(['o', 'ff', 'j', 'dd', 'v', 'bb', 'h', 'n', 'z', 'Missing'],`
`dtype='object', name='A7')`.

5. Let's create a dictionary of category-to-integer pairs, using the ordered list we created in *Step 4*:

```
ordinal_mapping = {
    k: i for i, k in enumerate(ordered_labels, 0)
}
```

We can visualize the result of the preceding code by executing `print(ordinal_mapping)`:
`{'o': 0, 'ff': 1, 'j': 2, 'dd': 3, 'v': 4, 'bb': 5, 'h': 6, 'n':`
`7, 'z': 8, 'Missing': 9}`

6. Let's use the dictionary we created in *Step 5* to replace the categories in A7 in a copy of the datasets:

```
X_train_enc = X_train.copy()
X_test_enc = X_test.copy()
X_train_enc["A7"] = X_train_enc["A7"].map(
    ordinal_mapping)
X_test_enc["A7"] = X_test_enc["A7"].map(
    ordinal_mapping)
```

> **Note**
>
> If the test set contains a category that is not present in the train set, the preceding code will introduce np.nan.

To visualize the effect of this encoding, let's plot the relationship of the categories of the A7 variable with the target before and after the encoding.

7. Let's plot the mean target response per category of the A7 variable:

```
y_train.groupby(X_train["A7"]).mean().plot()
plt.title("Relationship between A7 and the target")
plt.ylabel("Mean of target")
plt.show()
```

We can see the non-monotonic relationship between categories of A7 and the target in the following plot:

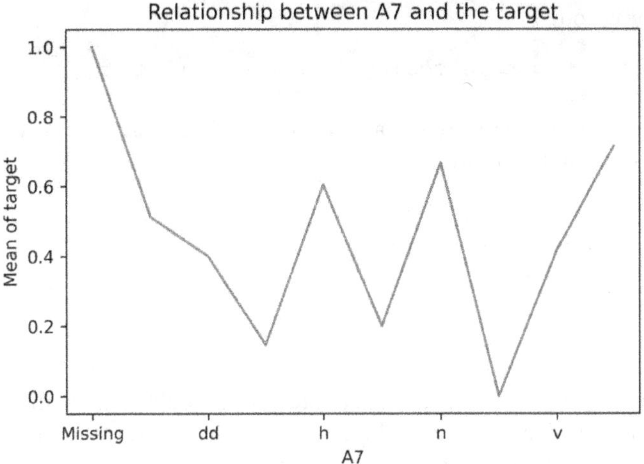

Figure 2.8 – Mean target value per category of A7 before the encoding

8. Let's plot the mean target value per category in the encoded variable:

```
y_train.groupby(X_train_enc["A7"]).mean().plot()
plt.title("Relationship between A7 and the target")
plt.ylabel("Mean of target")
plt.show()
```

The encoded variable shows a monotonic relationship with the target – the higher the mean target value, the higher the digit assigned to the category:

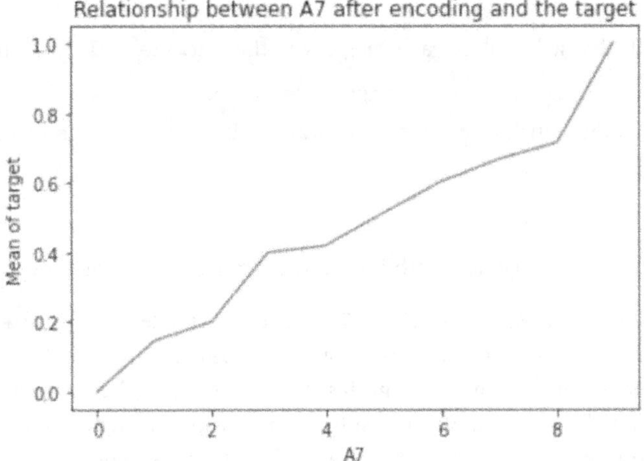

Figure 2.9 – Mean target value per category of A7 after the encoding.

Now, let's perform ordered ordinal encoding using `feature-engine`.

9. Let's import the encoder:

```
from feature_engine.encoding import OrdinalEncoder
```

10. Next, let's set up the encoder so that it assigns integers based on the target mean value to all categorical variables in the dataset:

```
ordinal_enc = OrdinalEncoder(
    encoding_method="ordered",
    variables=None)
```

> **Note**
>
> `OrdinalEncoder()` will find and encode all categorical variables automatically. To restrict the encoding to a subset of variables, pass their names in a list to the `variables` argument. To encode numerical variables, set `ignore_format=True`.

11. Let's fit the encoder to the train set so that it finds the categorical variables, and then stores the category and integer mappings:

```
ordinal_enc.fit(X_train, y_train)
```

12. Finally, let's replace the categories with numbers in the train and test sets:

```
X_train_enc = ordinal_enc.transform(X_train)
X_test_enc = ordinal_enc.transform(X_test)
```

> **Note**
>
> You'll find the digits that will replace each category in the `encoder_dict_` attribute.

Check out the output of the transformation by executing `X_train_enc.head()`.

How it works...

In this recipe, we replaced the categories with integers according to the target mean.

In the first part of this recipe, we worked with the A7 categorical variable. With pandas' `groupby()`, we grouped the data based on the categories of A7, and with pandas' `mean()`, we determined the mean value of the target for each of those categories. Next, we ordered the categories with pandas' `sort_values()` from the ones with the lowest to the ones with the highest target mean response. The output of this operation was a pandas series, with the categories as indices and the target mean as values. With pandas' `index`, we captured the ordered categories in an array; then, with Python dictionary comprehension, we created a dictionary of category-to-integer pairs. Finally, we used this dictionary to replace the category with integers using pandas' `map()`.

> **Note**
>
> To avoid data leakage, we determine the category-to-integer mappings from the train set.

To perform the encoding with `feature-engine`, we used `OrdinalEncoder()`, setting the `encoding_method` to `ordered`. We left the argument variables set to `None` so that the encoder automatically detects all categorical variables in the dataset. With `fit()`, the encoder found the categorical variables and assigned digits to their categories according to the target mean value. The categorical variables' names and dictionaries with category-to-digit pairs were stored in the `variables_` and `encoder_dict_` attributes, respectively. Finally, using `transform()`, we replaced the categories with digits in the train and test sets, returning `pandas` DataFrames.

See also

For an implementation of this recipe with Category Encoders, visit this book's GitHub repository: `https://github.com/PacktPublishing/Python-Feature-engineering-Cookbook-Third-Edition/blob/main/ch02-categorical-encoding/Recipe-05-Ordered-ordinal-encoding.ipynb`.

Implementing target mean encoding

Mean encoding or **target encoding** maps each category to the probability estimate of the target attribute. If the target is binary, the numerical mapping is the posterior probability of the target conditioned to the value of the category. If the target is continuous, the numerical representation is given by the expected value of the target given the value of the category.

In its simplest form, the numerical representation for each category is given by the mean value of the target variable for a particular category group. For example, if we have a `City` variable, with the categories of `London`, `Manchester`, and `Bristol`, and we want to predict the default rate (the target takes values of 0 and 1); if the default rate for `London` is 30%, we replace `London` with `0.3`; if the default rate for `Manchester` is 20%, we replace `Manchester` with `0.2`; and so on. If the target is continuous – say we want to predict income – then we would replace `London`, `Manchester`, and `Bristol` with the mean income earned in each city.

In mathematical terms, if the target is binary, the replacement value, S, is determined like so:

$$S_i = n_{i(y=1)}/n_i$$

Here, the numerator is the number of observations with a target value of *1* for category *i* and the denominator is the number of observations with a category value of *i*.

If the target is continuous, S, this is determined by the following formula:

$$S_i = \frac{\Sigma y_i}{n_i}$$

Here, the numerator is the sum of the target across observations in category i and n_i is the total number of observations in category i.

These formulas provide a good approximation of the target estimate if there is a sufficiently large number of observations with each category value – in other words, if n_i is large. However, in many datasets, there will be categories present in a few observations. In these cases, target estimates derived from the precedent formulas can be unreliable.

To mitigate poor estimates returned for rare categories, the target estimates can be determined as a mixture of two probabilities: those returned by the preceding formulas and the prior probability of the target based on the entire training. The two probabilities are *blended* using a weighting factor, which is a function of the category group size:

$$S_i = \lambda \frac{n_{i(Y=1)}}{n_i} + \left(1 - \lambda_i\right)\frac{n_\lambda}{N}$$

In this formula, n_λ is the total number of cases where the target takes a value of 1, N is the size of the train set, and λ is the weighting factor.

When the category group is large, λ tends to 1, so more weight is given to the first term of the equation. When the category group size is small, then λ tends to 0, so the estimate is mostly driven by the second term of the equation – that is, the target's prior probability. In other words, if the group size is small, knowing the value of the category does not tell us anything about the value of the target.

The weighting factor, λ, is determined differently in different open-source implementations. In Category Encoders, λ is a function of the group size, k, and a smoothing parameter, f, which controls the rate of transition between the first and second term of the preceding equation:

$$\lambda = \frac{1}{1 + e^{-(n-k)/f}}$$

Here, k is half of the minimal size for which we *fully trust* the first term of the equation. The f parameter is selected by the user either arbitrarily or with optimization.

In `scikit-learn` and `feature-engine`, λ is a function of the target variance for the entire dataset and within the category, and is determined as follows:

$$\lambda = \frac{ni \times t}{s + ni \times t}$$

Here, t is the target variance in the entire dataset and s is the target variance within the category. Both implementations are equivalent, but it is important to know the equations because they will help you set up the parameters in the transformers.

> **Note**
>
> Mean encoding was designed to encode highly cardinal categorical variables without expanding the feature space. For more details, check out the following article: Micci-Barreca D. A., *Preprocessing Scheme for High-Cardinality Categorical Attributes in Classification and Prediction Problems*. ACM SIGKDD Explorations Newsletter, 2001.

In this recipe, we will perform mean encoding using `scikit-learn` and `feature-engine`.

How to do it...

Let's begin with this recipe:

1. Import pandas and the data split function:

    ```python
    import pandas as pd
    from sklearn.model_selection import train_test_split
    ```

2. Let's load the Credit Approval dataset and divide it into train and test sets:

    ```python
    data = pd.read_csv("credit_approval_uci.csv")
    X_train, X_test, y_train, y_test = train_test_split(
        data.drop(labels=["target"], axis=1),
        data["target"],
        test_size=0.3,
        random_state=0,
    )
    ```

3. Let's import the transformers from `scikit-learn`:

    ```python
    from sklearn.preprocessing import TargetEncoder
    from sklearn.compose import ColumnTransformer
    ```

4. Let's make a list with the names of the categorical variables:

    ```python
    cat_vars = X_train.select_dtypes(
        include="O").columns.to_list()
    ```

5. Let's set up the encoder to use the target variance to determine the weighting factor, as described at the beginning of the recipe:

    ```python
    enc = TargetEncoder(smooth="auto", random_state=9)
    ```

6. Let's restrict the imputation to categorical variables:

    ```python
    ct = ColumnTransformer(
        [("encoder", enc, cat_vars)],
        remainder="passthrough",
    ).set_output(transform="pandas")
    ```

7. Let's fit the encoder and transform the datasets:

    ```python
    X_train_enc = ct.fit_transform(X_train, y_train)
    X_test_enc = ct.transform(X_test)
    ```

    Check out the result by executing `X_train_enc.head()`.

> **Note**
>
> The `fit_transform()` method of scikit-learn's `TargetEncoder()` is not equivalent to applying `fit().transform()`. With `fit_transform()`, the resulting dataset is encoded based on partial fits over the training folds of a cross-validation scheme. This functionality was intentionally designed to prevent overfitting the machine learning model to the train set.

Now, let's perform target encoding with `feature-engine`:

8. Let's import the encoder:

```
from feature_engine.encoding import MeanEncoder
```

9. Let's set up the target mean encoder to encode all categorical variables while applying smoothing:

```
mean_enc = MeanEncoder(smoothing="auto",
    variables=None)
```

> **Note**
>
> `MeanEncoder()` does not apply smoothing by default. Make sure you set it to `auto` or to an integer to control the blend between prior and posterior target estimates.

10. Let's fit the transformer to the train set so that it learns and stores the mean target value per category per variable:

```
mean_enc.fit(X_train, y_train)
```

11. Finally, let's encode the train and test sets:

```
X_train_enc = mean_enc.transform(X_train)
X_test_enc = mean_enc.transform(X_test)
```

> **Note**
>
> The category-to-number pairs are stored as a dictionary of dictionaries in the `encoder_dict_` attribute. To display the stored parameters, execute `mean_enc.encoder_dict_`.

How it works...

In this recipe, we replaced the categories with the mean target value using `scikit-learn` and `feature-engine`.

To encode with `scikit-learn`, we used `TargetEncoder()`, leaving the `smooth` parameter to its default value of `auto`. Like this, the transformer used the target variance to determine the weighting factor for the blend of probabilities. With `fit()`, the transformer learned the value it should use to replace the categories, and with `transform()`, it replaced the categories.

Note that for `TargetEncoder()`, the `fit()` method followed by `transform()` do not return the same dataset as the `fit_transform()` method. The latter encodes the training set based on mappings found with cross-validation. The idea is to use `fit_transform()` within a pipeline, so the machine learning model does not overfit. However, and here is where it gets confusing, the mappings stored in the `encodings_` attribute are the same after `fit()` and `fit_transform()`, and this is done intentionally so that when we apply `transform()` to a new dataset, we obtain the same result regardless of whether we apply `fit()` or `fit_transform()` to the training set.

> **Note**
>
> Unseen categories are encoded with the target mean by `scikit-learn`'s `TargetEncoder()`. `feature-engine`'s `MeanEncoder()` can either return an error, replace the unseen categories with nan, or with the target mean.

To perform the target encoding with `feature-engine`, we used `MeanEncoder()`, setting the `smoothing` parameter to `auto`. With `fit()`, the transformer found and stored the categorical variables and the values to encode each category. With `transform()`, it replaced the categories with numbers, returning `pandas` DataFrames.

There's more...

If you want to implement target encoding with `pandas` or Category Encoders, check out the notebook in the accompanying GitHub repository: `https://github.com/PacktPublishing/Python-Feature-engineering-Cookbook-Third-Edition/blob/main/ch02-categorical-encoding/Recipe-06-Target-mean-encoding.ipynb`.

There is an alternative way to return *better* target estimates when the category groups are small. The replacement value for each category is determined as follows:

$$S_i = \frac{n_{i(Y=1)} + pY \times m}{n_i + m}$$

Here, $n_{i(Y=1)}$ is the target mean for category i and n_i is the number of observations with category i. The target prior is given by pY and m is the weighting factor. With this adjustment, the only parameter that we have to set is the weight, m. If m is large, then more importance is given to the target's prior probability. This adjustment affects target estimates for all categories but mostly for those with fewer observations because, in such cases, m could be much larger than n_i in the formula's denominator.

> **Note**
>
> This method is a good alternative to Category Encoders' `TargetEncoder()` because, in Category Encoders' implementation of target encoding, we need to optimize two parameters instead of one (as we did with `feature-engine` and `scikit-learn`) to control the smoothing.

For an implementation of this encoding method using `MEstimateEncoder()`, visit this book's GitHub repository: `https://github.com/PacktPublishing/Python-Feature-engineering-Cookbook-Third-Edition/blob/main/ch02-categorical-encoding/Recipe-06-Target-mean-encoding.ipynb`.

Encoding with Weight of Evidence

Weight of Evidence (**WoE**) was developed primarily for credit and financial industries to facilitate variable screening and exploratory analysis and to build more predictive linear models to evaluate the risk of loan defaults.

The WoE is computed from the basic odds ratio:

$$\mathrm{WoE} = \log\left(\frac{proportion\ positive\ cases}{proportion\ negative\ cases}\right)$$

Here, positive and negative refer to the values of the target being *1* or *0*, respectively. The proportion of positive cases per category is determined as the sum of positive cases per category group divided by the total positive cases in the training set. The proportion of negative cases per category is determined as the sum of negative cases per category group divided by the total number of negative observations in the training set.

WoE has the following characteristics:

- WoE = *0* if *p(positive)* / *p(negative)* = *1*; that is, if the outcome is random

- WoE > *0* if *p(positive)* > *p(negative)*

- WoE < *0* if *p(negative)* > *p(positive)*

This allows us to directly visualize the predictive power of the category in the variable: the higher the WoE, the more likely the event will occur. If the WoE is positive, the event is likely to occur.

Logistic regression models a binary response, *Y*, based on *X* predictor variables, assuming that there is a linear relationship between *X* and the log of odds of *Y*:

$$\log\left(\frac{p(Y = 1)}{p(Y = 0)}\right) = b_0 + b_1 X_1 + b_2 X_2 + \ldots + b_n X_n$$

Here, *log (p(Y=1)/p(Y=0))* is the log of odds. As you can see, the WoE encodes the categories in the same scale – that is, the log of odds – as the outcome of the logistic regression.

Therefore, by using WoE, the predictors are prepared and coded on the same scale, and the parameters in the logistic regression model – that is, the coefficients – can be directly compared.

In this recipe, we will perform WoE encoding using `pandas` and `feature-engine`.

How to do it...

Let's begin by making some imports and preparing the data:

1. Import the required libraries and functions:

```python
import numpy as np
import pandas as pd
from sklearn.model_selection import train_test_split
```

2. Let's load the Credit Approval dataset and divide it into train and test sets:

```python
data = pd.read_csv("credit_approval_uci.csv")
X_train, X_test, y_train, y_test = train_test_split(
    data.drop(labels=["target"], axis=1),
    data["target"],
    test_size=0.3,
    random_state=0,
)
```

3. Let's get the inverse of the target values to be able to calculate the negative cases:

```python
neg_y_train = pd.Series(
    np.where(y_train == 1, 0, 1),
    index=y_train.index
)
```

4. Let's determine the number of observations where the target variable takes a value of 1 or 0:

```python
total_pos = y_train.sum()
total_neg = neg_y_train.sum()
```

5. Now, let's calculate the numerator and denominator of the WoE's formula, which we discussed earlier in this recipe:

```python
pos = y_train.groupby(
    X_train["A1"]).sum() / total_pos
neg = neg_y_train.groupby(
    X_train["A1"]).sum() / total_neg
```

6. Now, let's calculate the WoE per category:

```python
woe = np.log(pos/neg)
```

We can display the series with the category to WoE pairs by executing `print(woe)`:

```
A1
Missing    0.203599
a          0.092373
```

```
b            -0.042410
dtype: float64
```

7. Finally, let's replace the categories of A1 with the WoE in a copy of the datasets:

```
X_train_enc = X_train.copy()
X_test_enc = X_test.copy()
X_train_enc["A1"] = X_train_enc["A1"].map(woe)
X_test_enc["A1"] = X_test_enc["A1"].map(woe)
```

You can inspect the encoded variable by executing `X_train_enc["A1"].head()`.

Now, let's perform WoE encoding using `feature-engine`.

8. Let's import the encoder:

```
from feature_engine.encoding import WoEEncoder
```

9. Next, let's set up the encoder to encode three categorical variables:

```
woe_enc = WoEEncoder(variables = ["A1", "A9", "A12"])
```

> **Note**
>
> For rare categories, it might happen that `p(0)=0` or `p(1)=0`, and then the division or the logarithm is not defined. To avoid this, group infrequent categories as shown in the *Grouping rare or infrequent categories* recipe.

10. Let's fit the transformer to the train set so that it learns and stores the WoE of the different categories:

```
woe_enc.fit(X_train, y_train)
```

> **Note**
>
> We can display the dictionaries with the categories to WoE pairs by executing `woe_enc.encoder_dict_`.

11. Finally, let's encode the three categorical variables in the train and test sets:

```
X_train_enc = woe_enc.transform(X_train)
X_test_enc = woe_enc.transform(X_test)
```

`feature-engine` returns pandas DataFrames, which contain the encoded categorical variables ready to use in machine learning models.

How it works...

In this recipe, we encoded categorical variables using the WoE with pandas and `feature-engine`.

We combined the use of pandas' `sum()` and `groupby()` and numpy's `log()` to determine the WoE as we described at the beginning of this recipe.

Next, we automated the procedure with `feature-engine`. We used the `WoEEncoder()`, which learned the WoE per category with the `fit()` method, and then used `transform()` to replace the categories with the corresponding numbers.

See also

For an implementation of WoE with Category Encoders, visit this book's GitHub repository: `https://github.com/PacktPublishing/Python-Feature-engineering-Cookbook-Third-Edition/blob/main/ch02-categorical-encoding/Recipe-07-Weight-of-evidence.ipynb`.

Grouping rare or infrequent categories

Rare categories are those present only in a small fraction of the observations. There is no rule of thumb to determine how small a small fraction is, but typically, any value below 5% can be considered rare.

Infrequent labels often appear only on the train set or only on the test set, thus making the algorithms prone to overfitting or being unable to score an observation. In addition, when encoding categories to numbers, we only create mappings for those categories observed in the train set, so we won't know how to encode new labels. To avoid these complications, we can group infrequent categories into a single category called `Rare` or `Other`.

In this recipe, we will group infrequent categories using `pandas` and `feature-engine`.

How to do it...

First, let's import the necessary Python libraries and get the dataset ready:

1. Import the necessary Python libraries, functions, and classes:

    ```python
    import numpy as np
    import pandas as pd
    from sklearn.model_selection import train_test_split
    from feature_engine.encoding import RareLabelEncoder
    ```

2. Let's load the Credit Approval dataset and divide it into train and test sets:

    ```python
    data = pd.read_csv("credit_approval_uci.csv")
    X_train, X_test, y_train, y_test = train_test_split(
        data.drop(labels=["target"], axis=1),
        data["target"],
        test_size=0.3,
    ```

```
            random_state=0,
    )
```

3. Let's capture the fraction of observations per category in A7 in a variable:

```
freqs = X_train["A7"].value_counts(normalize=True)
```

We can see the percentage of observations per category of A7, expressed as decimals, in the following output after executing `print(freqs)`:

```
v  0.573499
h  0.209110
ff  0.084886
bb  0.080745
z  0.014493
dd  0.010352
j  0.010352
Missing  0.008282
n  0.006211
o  0.002070
Name: A7, dtype: float64
```

If we consider those labels present in less than 5% of the observations as rare, then z, dd, j, Missing, n, and o are rare categories.

4. Let's create a list containing the names of the categories present in more than 5% of the observations:

```
frequent_cat = [
    x for x in freqs.loc[freqs > 0.05].index.values]
```

If we execute `print(frequent_cat)`, we will see the frequent categories of A7:

```
['v', 'h', 'ff', 'bb'].
```

5. Let's replace rare labels – that is, those present in <= 5% of the observations – with the `Rare` string in a copy of the datasets:

```
X_train_enc = X_train.copy()
X_test_enc = X_test.copy()

X_train_enc["A7"] = np.where(X_train["A7"].isin(
    frequent_cat), X_train["A7"], "Rare")

X_test_enc["A7"] = np.where(X_test["A7"].isin(
    frequent_cat), X_test["A7"], "Rare")
```

6. Let's determine the percentage of observations in the encoded variable:

```
X_train["A7"].value_counts(normalize=True)
```

We can see that the infrequent labels have now been re-grouped into the `Rare` category:

```
v         0.573499
h         0.209110
ff        0.084886
bb        0.080745
Rare      0.051760
Name: A7, dtype: float64
```

Now, let's group rare labels using `feature-engine`.

7. Let's create a rare label encoder that groups categories present in less than 5% of the observations, provided that the categorical variable has more than four distinct values:

```
rare_encoder = RareLabelEncoder(tol=0.05,
    n_categories=4)
```

8. Let's fit the encoder so that it finds the categorical variables and then learns their most frequent categories:

```
rare_encoder.fit(X_train)
```

> **Note**
>
> Upon fitting, the transformer will raise warnings, indicating that many categorical variables have less than four categories, thus their values will not be grouped. The transformer just lets you know that this is happening.

We can display the frequent categories per variable by executing `rare_encoder.encoder_dict_`, as well as the variables that will be encoded by executing `rare_encoder.variables_`.

9. Finally, let's group rare labels in the train and test sets:

```
X_train_enc = rare_encoder.transform(X_train)
X_test_enc = rare_encoder.transform(X_test)
```

Now that we have grouped rare labels, we are ready to encode the categorical variables, as we've done in the previous recipes in this chapter.

How it works...

In this recipe, we grouped infrequent categories using `pandas` and `feature-engine`.

We determined the fraction of observations per category of the A7 variable using `pandas`' `value_counts()` by setting the `normalize` parameter to `True`. Using list comprehension, we captured the names of the variables present in more than 5% of the observations. Finally, using NumPy's `where()`, we searched each row of A7, and if the observation was one of the frequent categories in the list, which we checked using `pandas`' `isin()`, its value was kept; otherwise, it was replaced with `Rare`.

We automated the preceding steps for multiple categorical variables using `feature-engine`'s `RareLabelEncoder()`. By setting `tol` to `0.05`, we retained categories present in more than 5% of the observations. By setting `n_categories` to 4, we only grouped categories in variables with more than four unique values. With `fit()`, the transformer identified the categorical variables and then learned and stored their frequent categories. With `transform()`, the transformer replaced infrequent categories with the `Rare` string.

Performing binary encoding

Binary encoding uses binary code – that is, a sequence of zeroes and ones – to represent the different categories of the variable. How does it work? First, the categories are arbitrarily replaced with ordinal numbers, as shown in the intermediate step of the following table. Then, those numbers are converted into binary code. For example, integer `1` can be represented with the sequence of `1-0`, integer `2` with `0-1`, integer `3` with `1-1`, and integer `0` with `0-0`. The digits in the two positions of the binary string become the columns, which are the encoded representations of the original variable:

Color	Intermediate step	1st	2nd
Blue	1	1	0
Red	2	0	1
Green	3	1	1
Yellow	0	0	0

Figure 2.10 – Table showing the steps required for binary encoding the color variable

Binary encoding encodes the data in fewer dimensions than one-hot encoding. In our example, the `Color` variable would be encoded into *k-1* categories by one-hot encoding – that is, three variables – but with binary encoding, we can represent the variable with only two features. More generally, we determine the number of binary features needed to encode a variable as *log2(number of distinct categories)*; in our example, *log2(4) = 2* binary features.

Binary encoding is an alternative method to one-hot encoding where we do not lose information about the variable, yet we obtain fewer features after the encoding. This is particularly useful when we have highly cardinal variables. For example, if a variable contains 128 unique categories, with one-hot encoding, we would need 127 features to encode the variable, whereas with binary encoding, we will only need *7 (log2(128)=7)*. Thus, this encoding prevents the feature space from exploding. In addition, binary-encoded features are also suitable for linear models. On the downside, the derived binary features lack human interpretability, so if we need to interpret the decisions made by our models, this encoding method may not be a suitable option.

In this recipe, we will learn how to perform binary encoding using Category Encoders.

How to do it...

First, let's import the necessary Python libraries and get the dataset ready:

1. Import the required Python libraries, functions, and classes:

```python
import pandas as pd
from sklearn.model_selection import train_test_split
from category_encoders.binary import BinaryEncoder
```

2. Let's load the Credit Approval dataset and divide it into train and test sets:

```python
data = pd.read_csv("credit_approval_uci.csv")
X_train, X_test, y_train, y_test = train_test_split(
    data.drop(labels=["target"], axis=1),
    data["target"],
    test_size=0.3,
    random_state=0,
)
```

3. Let's inspect the unique categories in A7:

```python
X_train["A7"].unique()
```

In the following output, we can see that A7 has 10 different categories:

```
array(['v', 'ff', 'h', 'dd', 'z', 'bb', 'j', 'Missing', 'n',
'o'], dtype=object)
```

4. Let's create a binary encoder to encode A7:

```python
encoder = BinaryEncoder(cols=["A7"],
    drop_invariant=True)
```

> **Note**
>
> `BinaryEncoder()`, as well as other encoders from the Category Encoders package, allow us to select the variables to encode. We simply pass the column names in a list to the `cols` argument.

5. Let's fit the transformer to the train set so that it calculates how many binary variables it needs and creates the variable-to-binary code representations:

```python
encoder.fit(X_train)
```

6. Finally, let's encode A7 in the train and test sets:

```python
X_train_enc = encoder.transform(X_train)
X_test_enc = encoder.transform(X_test)
```

We can display the top rows of the transformed train set by executing `print(X_train_enc.head())`, which returns the following output:

	A1	A2	A3	A4	A5	A6	A7_0	A7_1	A7_2	A7_3	A8	A9	A10	A11	A12	A13	A14	A15
596	a	46.08	3.000	u	g	c	0	0	0	1	2.375	t	t	8	t	g	396.0	4159
303	a	15.92	2.875	u	g	q	0	0	0	1	0.085	f	f	0	f	g	120.0	0
204	b	36.33	2.125	y	p	w	0	0	0	1	0.085	t	t	1	f	g	50.0	1187
351	b	22.17	0.585	y	p	ff	0	0	1	0	0.000	f	f	0	f	g	100.0	0
118	b	57.83	7.040	u	g	m	0	0	0	1	14.000	t	t	6	t	g	360.0	1332

Figure 2.11 – DataFrame with the variables after binary encoding

Binary encoding returned four binary variables for A7, which are A7_0, A7_1, A7_2, and A7_3, instead of the nine that would have been returned by one-hot encoding.

How it works...

In this recipe, we performed binary encoding using the Category Encoders package. We used `BinaryEncoder()` to encode the A7 variable. With the `fit()` method, `BinaryEncoder()` created a mapping from a category to a set of binary columns, and with the `transform()` method, the encoder encoded the A7 variable in both the train and test sets.

3

Transforming Numerical Variables

The statistical methods that are used in data analysis make certain assumptions about the data. For example, in the general linear model, it is assumed that the values of the dependent variable (the target) are independent, that there is a linear relationship between the target and the independent (predictor) variables, and that the residuals – that is, the difference between the predictions and the real values of the target – are normally distributed and centered at 0. When these assumptions are not met, the resulting probabilistic statements might not be accurate. To correct for failure in the assumptions and thus improve the performance of the models, we can transform variables before the analysis.

When we transform a variable, we replace its original values with a function of that variable. Transforming variables with mathematical functions helps reduce variable skewness, improves the value spread, and sometimes unmasks linear and additive relationships between predictors and the target. Commonly used mathematical transformations include the logarithm, reciprocal, power, and square and cube root transformations, as well as the Box-Cox and Yeo-Johnson transformations. This set of transformations is commonly referred to as **variance stabilizing transformations**. Variance stabilizing transformations intend to bring the distribution of the variable to a more symmetric – that is, Gaussian – shape. In this chapter, we will discuss when to use each transformation and then implement them using NumPy, scikit-learn, and Feature-engine.

This chapter contains the following recipes:

- Transforming variables with the logarithm function
- Transforming variables with the reciprocal function
- Using the square root to transform variables
- Using power transformations
- Performing Box-Cox transformations
- Performing Yeo-Johnson transformations

Transforming variables with the logarithm function

The logarithm function is a powerful transformation for dealing with positive data with a right-skewed distribution (observations accumulate at lower values of the variable). A common example is the `income` variable, with a heavy accumulation of values toward lower salaries. The logarithm transformation has a strong effect on the shape of the variable distribution.

In this recipe, we will perform logarithmic transformation using NumPy, scikit-learn, and Feature-engine. We will also create a diagnostic plot function to evaluate the effect of the transformation on the variable distribution.

Getting ready

To evaluate the variable distribution and understand whether a transformation improves value spread and stabilizes the variance, we can visually inspect the data with histograms and **Quantile-Quantile (Q-Q)** plots. A Q-Q plot helps us determine whether two variables show a similar distribution. In a Q-Q plot, we plot the quantiles of one variable against the quantiles of the second variable. If we plot the quantiles of the variable of interest against the expected quantiles of the normal distribution, then we can determine whether our variable is also normally distributed. If the variable is normally distributed, the points in the Q-Q plot will fall along a 45-degree diagonal.

> **Note**
>
> A quantile is the value below which there is a certain fraction of data points in the distribution. Thus, the 20th quantile is the point in the distribution at which 20% of the observations fall below and 80% above that value.

How to do it...

Let's begin by importing the libraries and getting the dataset ready:

1. Import the required Python libraries and dataset:

```
import numpy as np
import pandas as pd
import matplotlib.pyplot as plt
import scipy.stats as stats
from sklearn.datasets import fetch_california_housing
```

2. Let's load the California housing dataset into a pandas DataFrame:

```
X, y = fetch_california_housing(return_X_y=True,
    as_frame=True)
```

3.   Let's explore the distributions of all the variables in the dataset by plotting histograms with pandas:

```
X.hist(bins=30, figsize=(12, 12))
plt.show()
```

In the following output, we can see that the `MedInc` variable shows a mild right-skewed distribution, variables such as `AveRooms` and `Population` are heavily right-skewed, and the `HouseAge` variable shows an even spread of values across its range:

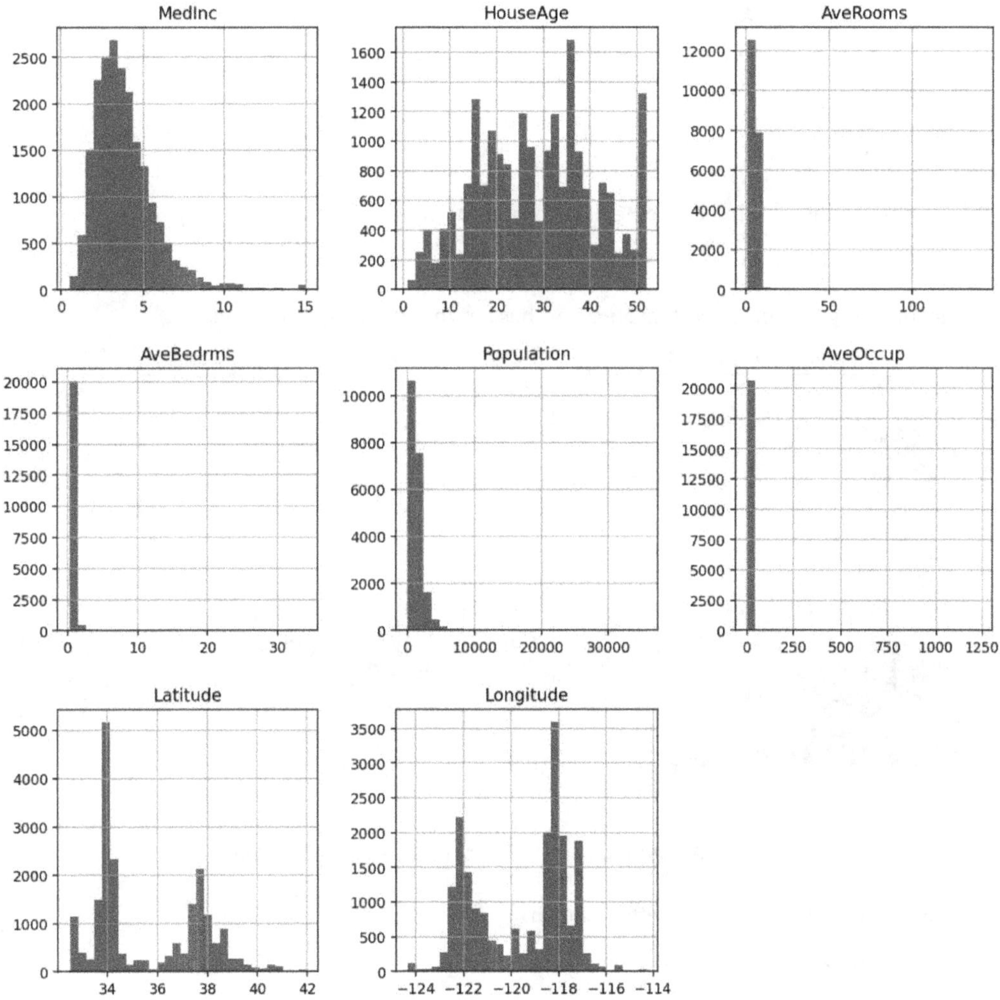

Figure 3.1 – Histograms with the distribution of the numerical variables

4. To evaluate the effect of the transformation on the variable distribution, we'll create a function that takes a DataFrame and a variable name as inputs and plots a histogram next to a Q-Q plot:

```
def diagnostic_plots(df, variable):
    plt.figure(figsize=(15,6))
    plt.subplot(1, 2, 1)
    df[variable].hist(bins=30)
    plt.title(f"Histogram of {variable}")
    plt.subplot(1, 2, 2)
    stats.probplot(df[variable], dist="norm",
        plot=plt)
    plt.title(f"Q-Q plot of {variable}")
    plt.show()
```

5. Let's plot the distribution of the `MedInc` variable with the function from *step 4*:

```
diagnostic_plots(X, "MedInc")
```

The following output shows that `MedInc` has a right-skewed distribution:

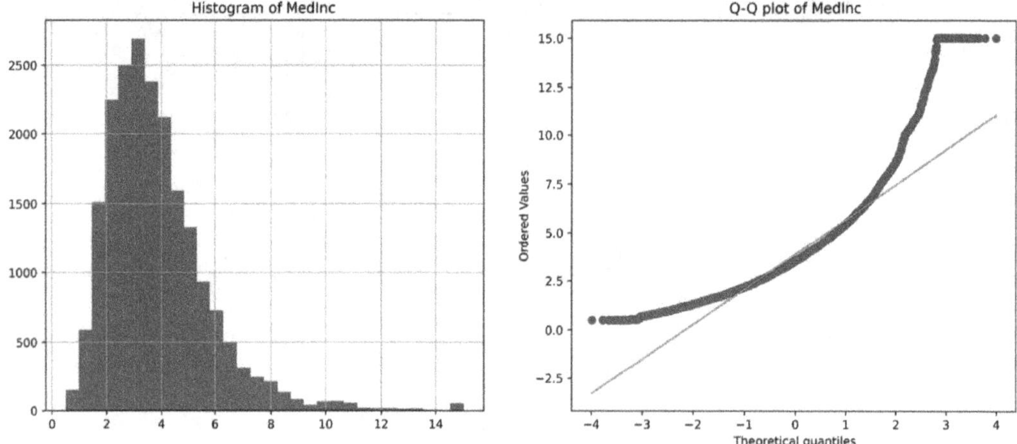

Figure 3.2 – A histogram and Q-Q plot of the MedInc variable

Now, let's transform the data with the logarithm:

6. First, let's make a copy of the original DataFrame:

```
X_tf = X.copy()
```

We've created a copy so that we can modify the values in the copy and not in the original DataFrame, which we need for the rest of this recipe.

> **Note**
>
> If we execute `X_tf = X` instead of using pandas' `copy()` function, `X_tf` will not be a copy of the DataFrame; instead, it will be another view of the same data. Therefore, changes made in `X_tf` will be reflected in `X` as well.

7. Let's make a list with the variables that we want to transform:

```
vars = ["MedInc", "AveRooms", "AveBedrms",
    "Population"]
```

8. Let's apply the logarithmic transformation with NumPy to the variables from *step 7* and capture the transformed variables in the new DataFrame:

```
X_tf[vars] = np.log(X[vars])
```

> **Note**
>
> Remember that the logarithm transformation can only be applied to strictly positive variables. If the variables have zero or negative values, sometimes, it is useful to add a constant to make those values positive. We could add a constant value of `1` using `X_tf[vars] = np.log(X[vars] + 1)`.

9. Let's check the distribution of `MedInc` after the transformation with the diagnostic function from *step 4*:

```
diagnostic_plots(X_tf, "MedInc")
```

In the following output, we can see that the logarithmic transformation returned a more evenly distributed variable that better approximates the theoretical normal distribution in the Q-Q plot:

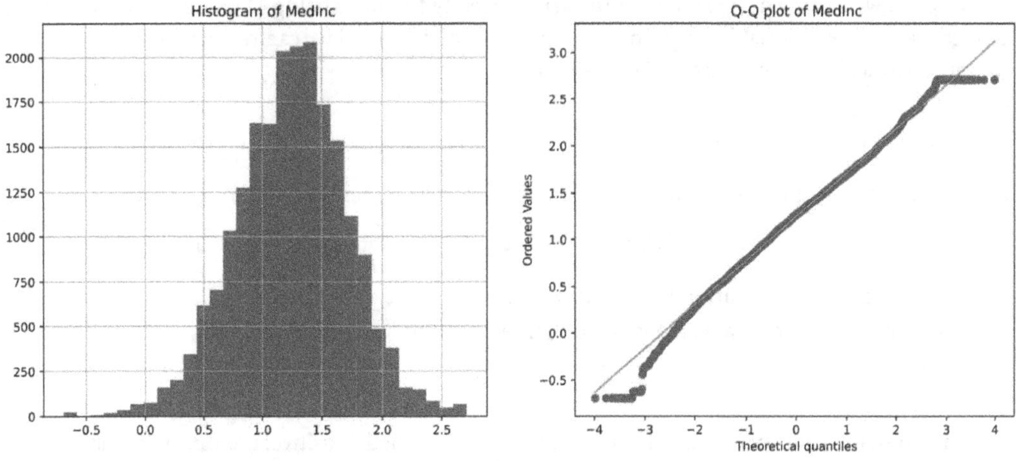

Figure 3.3 – A histogram and Q-Q plot of the MedInc variable after the logarithm transformation

Go ahead and plot the other transformed variables to familiarize yourself with the effect of the logarithm transformation on distributions.

Now, let's apply the logarithmic transformation with `scikit-learn`.

10. Let's import `FunctionTransformer()`:

```
from sklearn.preprocessing import FunctionTransformer
```

Before we proceed, we need to take a copy of the original dataset, as we did in *step 6*.

11. We'll set up the transformer to apply the logarithm and to be able to revert the transformed variable to its original representation:

```
transformer = FunctionTransformer(np.log,
    inverse_func=np.exp)
```

> **Note**
>
> If we set up `FunctionTransformer()` with the default parameter, `validate=False`, we don't need to fit the transformer before transforming the data. If we set `validate` to True, the transformer will check the data input to the `fit` method. The latter is useful when fitting the transformer with a DataFrame so that it learns and stores the variable names.

12. Let's transform the positive variables from *step 7*:

```
X_tf[vars] = transformer.transform(X[vars])
```

> **Note**
>
> Scikit-learn transformers return NumPy arrays and transform the entire DataFrame by default. In this case, we assigned the results of the array directly to our existing DataFrame. We can change the returned format through the `set_output` method and we can restrict the variables to transform with `ColumnTransformer()`.

Check the results of the transformation with the diagnostic function from *step 4*.

13. Let's now revert the transformation to the original variable representation:

```
X_tf[vars] = transformer.inverse_transform(X_tf[vars])
```

If you check the distribution by executing `diagnostic_plots(X_tf, "MedInc")`, you should see a plot that is identical to that returned by *step 5*.

> **Note**
>
> To add a constant value to the variables, in case they are not strictly positive, use `transformer = FunctionTransformer(lambda x: np.log(x + 1))`.

Now, let's apply the logarithm transformation with Feature-engine.

14. Let's import the `LogTransformer()`:

```
from feature_engine.transformation import LogTransformer
```

15. We'll set up the transformer to transform the variables from *step 7* and then fit the transformer to the dataset:

```
lt = LogTransformer(variables = vars)
lt.fit(X)
```

> **Note**
>
> If the `variables` argument is left as `None`, `LogTransformer()` applies the logarithm to all the numerical variables found during `fit()`. Alternatively, we can indicate which variables to modify, as we did in *step 15*.

16. Finally, let's transform the data:

```
X_tf = lt.transform(X)
```

`X_tf` is a copy of the X DataFrame, where the variables from *step 7* are transformed with the logarithm.

17. We can also revert the transformed variables to their original representation:

```
X_tf = lt.inverse_transform(X_tf)
```

If you check the distribution of the variables after *step 17*, they should be identical to those of the original data.

> **Note**
>
> Feature-engine has a dedicated transformer that adds constant values to the variables before the applying the logarithm transformation. Check the *There's more...* section later in this recipe for more details.

How it works...

In this recipe, we applied the logarithm transformation to a subset of positive variables using NumPy, scikit-learn, and Feature-engine.

To compare the effect of the transformation on the variable distribution, we created a diagnostic function to plot a histogram next to a Q-Q plot. To create the Q-Q plot, we used `scipy.stats.probplot()`, which plotted the quantiles of the variable of interest in the *y* axis versus the quantiles of a theoretical normal distribution, which we indicated by setting the `dist` parameter to `norm` in the *x* axis. We used `matplotlib` to display the plot by setting the `plot` parameter to `plt`.

With `plt.figure()` and `figsize`, we adjusted the size of the figure and, with `plt.subplot()`, we organized the two plots in one row with `two` columns – that is, one plot next to the other. The numbers within `plt.subplot()` indicated the number of rows, the number of columns, and the place of the plot in the figure, respectively. We placed the histogram in position 1 and the Q-Q plot in position 2 – that is, left and right, respectively.

To test the function, we plotted a histogram and a Q-Q plot for the `MedInc` variable before the transformation and observed that `MedInc` was not normally distributed. Most observations were at the left of the histogram and the values deviated from the 45-degree line in the Q-Q plot at both ends of the distribution.

Next, using `np.log()`, we applied the logarithm to a slice of the DataFrame with four positive variables. To evaluate the effect of the transformation, we plotted a histogram and Q-Q plot of the transformed `MedInc` variable. We observed that, after the logarithm transformation, the values were more centered in the histogram and that, in the Q-Q plot, they only deviated from the 45-degree line toward the ends of the distribution.

Next, we used the `FunctionTransformer()` from scikit-learn, which applies any user-defined function to a dataset. We passed `np.log()` as an argument to apply the logarithm transformation and NumPy's `exp()` for the inverse transformation to `FunctionTransfomer()`. With the `transform()` method, we transformed a slice of the DataFrame with the positive variables by using the logarithm. With `inverse_transform()`, we reverted the variable values to their original representation.

Finally, we used Feature-engine's `LogTransformer()` and specified the variables to transform in a list using the `variables` argument. With `fit()`, the transformer checked that the variables were numerical and positive, and with `transform()`, it applied `np.log()` under the hood to transform the selected variables. With `inverse_transform()`, we reverted the transformed variables to their original representations.

There's more...

Feature-engine has a dedicated transformer for adding a constant value to variables that are not strictly positive, before applying the logarithm: `LogCpTransformer()`. `LogCpTransformer()` can:

- Add the same constant to all variables

- Automatically identify and add the minimum value required to make the variables positive

- Add different values defined by the user to different variables.

You can find a code implementation of `LogCpTransformer()` in this book's GitHub repository: `https://github.com/PacktPublishing/Python-Feature-Engineering-Cookbook-Third-Edition/blob/main/ch03-variable-transformation/Recipe-1-logarithmic-transformation.ipynb`

Transforming variables with the reciprocal function

The reciprocal function is defined as 1/x. It is often useful when we have ratios – that is, values resulting from the division of two variables. Examples of this are **population density** – that is, people per area – and, as we will see in this recipe, **house occupancy** – that is, the number of occupants per house.

The reciprocal transformation is not defined for the 0 value, and although it is defined for negative values, it is mainly useful for transforming positive variables.

In this recipe, we will implement the reciprocal transformation using NumPy, scikit-learn, and Feature-engine, and compare its effect on variable distribution using histograms and a Q-Q plot.

How to do it...

Let's begin by importing the libraries and getting the dataset ready:

1. Import the required Python libraries and data:

```python
import numpy as np
import pandas as pd
import matplotlib.pyplot as plt
import scipy.stats as stats
from sklearn.datasets import fetch_california_housing
```

2. Let's load the California housing dataset:

```python
X, y = fetch_california_housing(return_X_y=True,
    as_frame=True)
```

3. To evaluate variable distributions, we'll create a function that takes a DataFrame and a variable name as inputs and plots a histogram next to a Q-Q plot:

```python
def diagnostic_plots(df, variable):
    plt.figure(figsize=(15,6))
    plt.subplot(1, 2, 1)
    df[variable].hist(bins=30)
    plt.title(f"Histogram of {variable}")
    plt.subplot(1, 2, 2)
    stats.probplot(df[variable], dist="norm",
        plot=plt)
    plt.title(f"Q-Q plot of {variable}")
    plt.show()
```

4. Now, let's plot the distribution of the AveOccup variable, which specifies the average occupancy of the house:

```python
diagnostic_plots(X, "AveOccup")
```

The `AveOccup` variable shows a very strong right-skewed distribution, as shown in the following output:

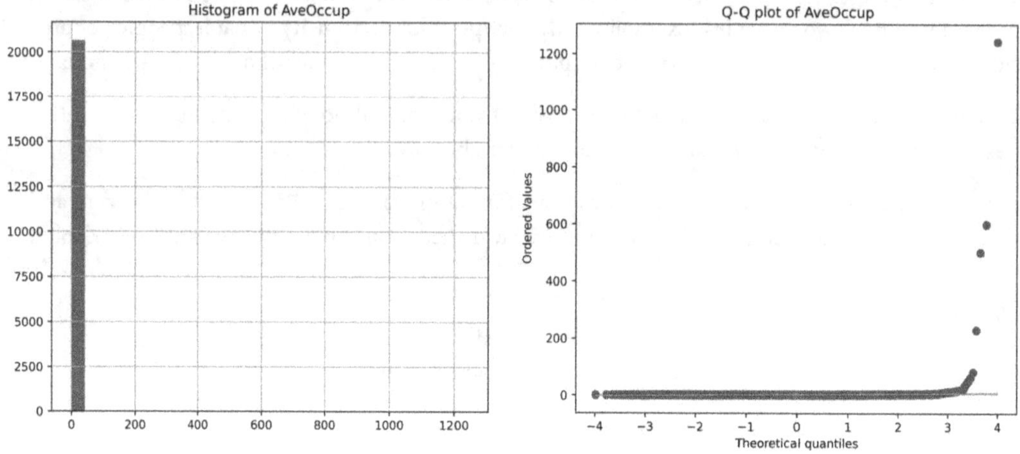

Figure 3.4 – A histogram and Q-Q plot of the AveOccup variable

> **Note**
>
> The `AveOccup` variable refers to the average number of household members – that is, the ratio between the number of people and the number of houses in a certain area. This is a promising variable for a reciprocal transformation. You can find more details about the variables and the dataset by executing `data = fetch_california_housing()` followed by `print(data.DESCR)`.

Now, let's apply the reciprocal transformation with NumPy.

5. First, let's make a copy of the original DataFrame so that we can modify the values in the copy and not in the original one, which we will need for the rest of this recipe:

```
X_tf = X.copy()
```

> **Note**
>
> Remember that executing `X_tf = X` instead of using pandas' `copy()` creates an additional view of the same data. Therefore, changes that are made in `X_tf` will be reflected in X as well.

6. Let's apply the reciprocal transformation to the `AveOccup` variable:

```
X_tf["AveOccup"] = np.reciprocal(X_tf["AveOccup"])
```

7. Let's check the distribution of the `AveOccup` variable after the transformation with the diagnostic function we created in *step 3*:

```
diagnostic_plots(X_tf, "AveOccup")
```

> **Note**
>
> After the transformation, `AveOccup` is now the ratio of the number of houses and the number of people in a certain area – in other words, houses per citizen.

Here, we can see a dramatic change in the distribution of the `AveOccup` variable after the reciprocal transformation:

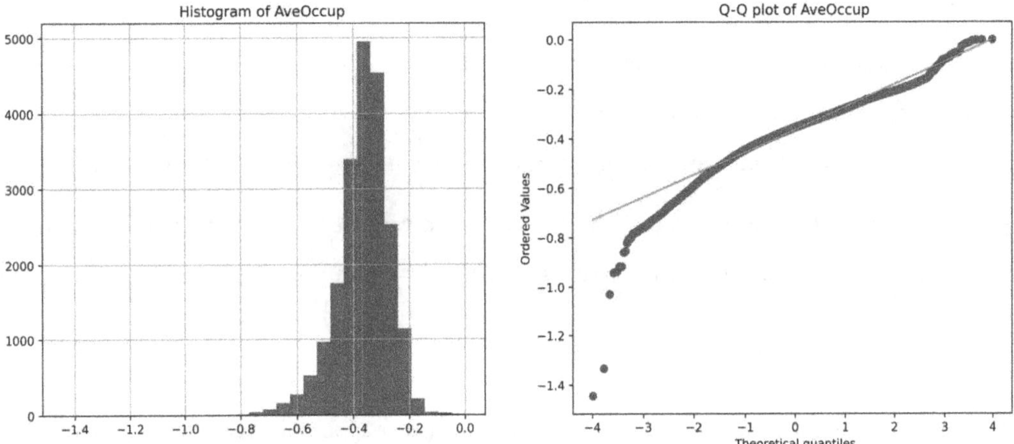

Figure 3.5 – A histogram and Q-Q plot of the AveOccup variable after the reciprocal transformation

Now, let's apply the reciprocal transformation with `scikit-learn`.

8. Let's import the `FunctionTransformer()`:

```
from sklearn.preprocessing import FunctionTransformer
```

9. Let's set up the transformer by passing `np.reciprocal` as an argument:

```
transformer = FunctionTransformer(np.reciprocal)
```

> **Note**
>
> By default, `FunctionTransformer()` does not need to be fit before transforming the data.

10. Now, let's make a copy of the original dataset and transform the variable:

```python
X_tf = X.copy()
X_tf["AveOccup"] = transformer.transform(
    X["AveOccup"])
```

You can check the effect of the transformation using the function from *step 3*.

> **Note**
>
> The inverse transformation of the reciprocal function is also the reciprocal function. Hence, if you re-apply `transform()` to the transformed data, you will revert it to its original representation. A better practice would be to set the `inverse_transform` parameter of the `FunctionTransformer()` to `np.reciprocal` as well.

Now, let's apply the reciprocal transformation with `feature-engine`.

11. Let's import the `ReciprocalTransformer()`:

```python
from feature_engine.transformation import ReciprocalTransformer
```

12. Let's set up the transformer to modify the `AveOccup` variable and then fit it to the dataset:

```python
rt = ReciprocalTransformer(variables=»AveOccup»)
rt.fit(X)
```

> **Note**
>
> If the `variables` argument is set to None, the transformer applies the reciprocal function to *all the numerical variables* in the dataset. If some of the variables contain a 0 value, the transformer will raise an error.

13. Let's transform the selected variable in our dataset:

```python
X_tf = rt.transform(X)
```

`ReciprocalTransformer()` will return a new pandas DataFrame containing the original variables, where the variable indicated in *step 12* is transformed with the reciprocal function.

How it works...

In this recipe, we applied the reciprocal transformation using NumPy, scikit-learn, and Feature-engine.

To evaluate the variable distribution, we used the function to plot a histogram next to a Q-Q plot that we described in the *How it works...* section of the *Transforming variables with the logarithm function* recipe earlier in this chapter.

We plotted the histogram and Q-Q plot of the `AveOccup` variable, which showed a heavy right-skewed distribution; most of its values were at the left of the histogram and they deviated from the 45-degree line toward the right end of the distribution in the Q-Q plot.

To carry out the reciprocal transformation, we applied `np.reciprocal()` to the variable. After the transformation, `AveOccup`'s values were more evenly distributed across the value range and followed the theoretical quantiles of the normal distribution in the Q-Q plot more closely.

Next, we used `np.reciprocal()` with scikit-learn's `FunctionTransformer()`. The `transform()` method applied `np.reciprocal()` to the dataset.

> **Note**
>
> To restrict the effect of `FunctionTransformer()` to a group of variables, use the `ColumnTransformer()`. To change the output to a pandas DataFrame, set the transform output to pandas.

Finally, we used Feature-engine's `ReciprocalTransformer()` to specifically modify one variable. With `fit()`, the transformer checked that the variable was numerical. With `transform()`, the transformer applied `np.reciprocal()` under the hood to transform the variable.

Feature-engine's `ReciprocalTransformer()` provides functionality to revert the variable to its original representation out of the box via the `inverse_transform()` method.

> **Note**
>
> Using the transformers from scikit-learn or Feature-engine, instead of NumPy's `reciprocal()` function, allows us to apply the reciprocal function as an additional step of a feature engineering pipeline within the `Pipeline` object from scikit-learn.

The difference between `FunctionTransformer()` and `ReciprocalTransformer()` is that the first one can apply any user-specified transformation, whereas the latter only applies the reciprocal function. scikit-learn returns NumPy arrays by default and transforms all variables in the dataset. Feature-engine's transformer, on the other hand, returns pandas DataFrames and can modify subsets of variables within the data without using additional classes.

Using the square root to transform variables

The square root transformation, $\sqrt{x}$, as well as its variations, the Anscombe transformation, $\sqrt{(x+3/8)}$, and the Freeman-Tukey transformation, $\sqrt{x} + \sqrt{(x+1)}$, are variance stabilizing transformations that transform a variable with a Poisson distribution into one with an approximately standard Gaussian distribution. The square root transformation is a form of power transformation where the exponent is **1/2** and is only defined for positive values.

The Poisson distribution is a probability distribution that indicates the number of times an event is likely to occur. In other words, it is a count distribution. It is right-skewed and its variance equals its mean. Examples of variables that could follow a Poisson distribution are the number of financial items of a customer, such as the number of current accounts or credit cards, the number of passengers in a vehicle, and the number of occupants in a household.

In this recipe, we will implement square root transformations using NumPy, scikit-learn, and Feature-engine.

How to do it...

We'll start by creating a dataset with two variables whose values are drawn from a Poisson distribution:

1. Let's begin by importing the necessary libraries:

    ```
    import numpy as np import pandas as pd
    import scipy.stats as stats
    ```

2. Let's create a DataFrame with two variables drawn from a Poisson distribution with mean values of 2 and 3, respectively, and `10000` observations:

    ```
    df = pd.DataFrame()
    df["counts1"] = stats.poisson.rvs(mu=3, size=10000)
    df["counts2"] = stats.poisson.rvs(mu=2, size=10000)
    ```

3. Let's create a function that takes a DataFrame and a variable name as inputs and plots a bar graph with the number of observations per value next to a Q-Q plot:

    ```
    def diagnostic_plots(df, variable):
        plt.figure(figsize=(15,6))
        plt.subplot(1, 2, 1)
        df[variable].value_counts().sort_index(). plot.bar()
        plt.title(f"Histogram of {variable}")
        plt.subplot(1, 2, 2)
        stats.probplot(df[variable], dist="norm",
            plot=plt)
        plt.title(f"Q-Q plot of {variable}")
        plt.show()
    ```

4. Let's create a bar plot and a Q-Q plot for one of the variables in the data using the function from *step 3*:

    ```
    diagnostic_plots(df, "counts1")
    ```

Here, we can see the Poisson distribution in the output:

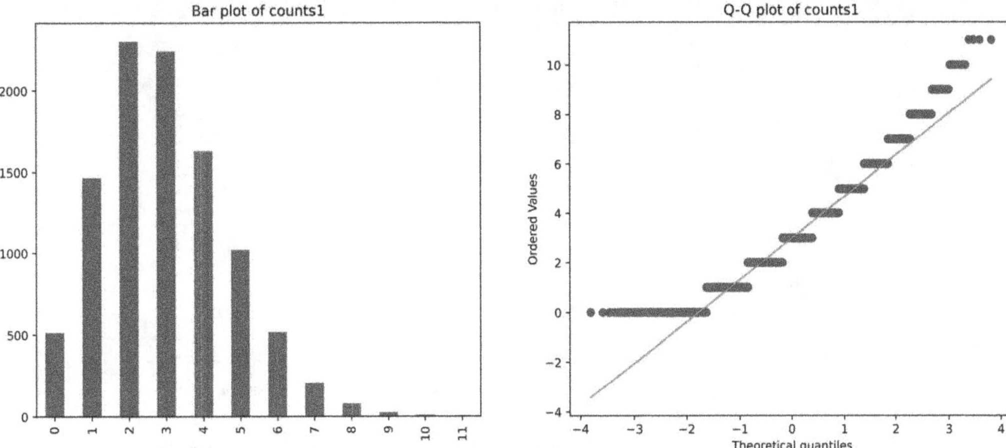

Figure 3.6 – The bar and Q-Q plots of the counts1 variable

5. Now, let's make a copy of the dataset:

```
df_tf = df.copy()
```

6. Let's apply the square root transformation to both variables:

```
df_tf[["counts1", "counts2"]] = np.sqrt(
    df[["counts1","counts2"]])
```

7. Let's round the values to two decimals for a nicer visualization:

```
df_tf[["counts1", "counts2"]] = np.round(
    df_tf[["counts1", "counts2"]], 2)
```

8. Let's plot the distribution of `counts1` after the transformation:

```
diagnostic_plots(df_tf, "counts1")
```

We see a more **stabilized** variance, as the dots in the Q-Q plot follow the 45-degree diagonal more closely:

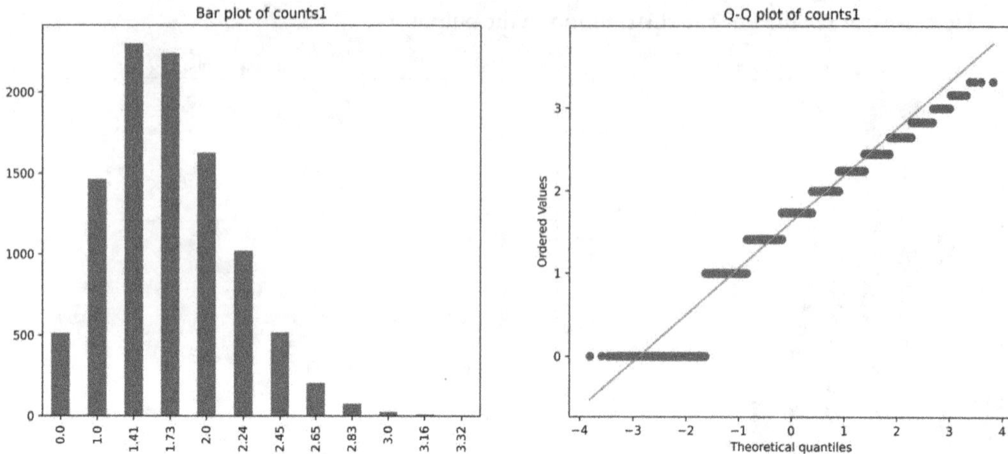

Figure 3.7 – The bar and Q-Q plots of the counts1 variable after the square root transformation

Now, let's apply the square root transformation with `scikit-learn`.

9. Let's import `FunctionTransformer()` and set up it to perform a square root transformation:

```
from sklearn.preprocessing import FunctionTransformer
transformer = FunctionTransformer(
    np.sqrt).set_output(transform="pandas")
```

> **Note**
>
> If we wanted to round the values as we did in *step 7*, we can set up the transformer using `transformer = FunctionTransformer(func=lambda x: np.round(np.sqrt(x), 2))`.

10. Let's make a copy of the data and transform the variables:

```
df_tf = df.copy()
df_tf = transformer.transform(df)
```

Go ahead and check the result of the transformation as we did in *step 8*.

To apply the square root with Feature-engine instead, we use the `PowerTransformer()` with an exponent of 0.5:

```
from feature_engine.transformation import PowerTransformer
root_t = PowerTransformer(exp=1/2)
```

11. Next, we fit the transformer to the data:

```
root_t.fit(df)
```

> **Note**
>
> The transformer automatically identifies the numerical variables, which we can explore by executing `root_t.variables_`.

12. Finally, let's transform the data:

```
df_tf = root_t.transform(df)
```

`PowerTransformer()` returns a pandas DataFrame with the transformed variables.

How it works...

In this recipe, we applied the square root transformation using NumPy, scikit-learn, and Feature-engine.

We used NumPy's `sqrt()` function either directly or within scikit-learn's `FunctionTrasnformer()` to determine the variables' square root. Alternatively, we used Feature-engine's `PowerTransformer()`, setting the exponent to 0.5, that of the square root function. NumPy modified the variables directly. The transformers of scikit-learn and Feature-engine modified the variables when calling the `transform()` method.

Using power transformations

Power functions are mathematical transformations that follow the $X_t = X^{lambda}$ format, where lambda can take any value. The square and cube root transformations are special cases of power transformations where lambda is 1/2 or 1/3, respectively. The challenge resides in finding the value for the lambda parameter. The Box-Cox transformation, which is a generalization of the power transformations, finds the optimal lambda value via maximum likelihood. We will discuss the Box-Cox transformation in the following recipe. In practice, we will try different lambda values and visually inspect the variable distribution to determine which one offers the best transformation. In general, if the data is right-skewed – that is, if observations accumulate toward lower values – we use a lambda value that is smaller than 1, while if the data is left-skewed – that is, there are more observations around higher values – then we use a lambda value that is greater than 1.

In this recipe, we will carry out power transformations using NumPy, scikit-learn, and Feature-engine.

How to do it...

Let's begin by importing the libraries and getting the dataset ready:

1. Import the required Python libraries and classes:

```
import numpy as np
import pandas as pd
from sklearn.datasets import fetch_california_housing
```

```
from sklearn.preprocessing import FunctionTransformer
from feature_engine.transformation import PowerTransformer
```

2. Let's load the California housing dataset into a pandas DataFrame:

```
X, y = fetch_california_housing(
    return_X_y=True, as_frame=True)
```

3. To evaluate variable distributions, we'll create a function that takes a DataFrame and a variable name as inputs and plots a histogram next to a Q-Q plot:

```
def diagnostic_plots(df, variable):
    plt.figure(figsize=(15,6))
    plt.subplot(1, 2, 1)
    df[variable].hist(bins=30)
    plt.title(f"Histogram of {variable}")
    plt.subplot(1, 2, 2)
    stats.probplot(df[variable], dist="norm",
        plot=plt)
    plt.title(f"Q-Q plot of {variable}")
    plt.show()
```

4. Let's plot the distribution of the `Population` variable with the previous function:

```
diagnostic_plots(X, "Population")
```

In the plots returned by the previous command, we can see that `Population` is heavily skewed to the right:

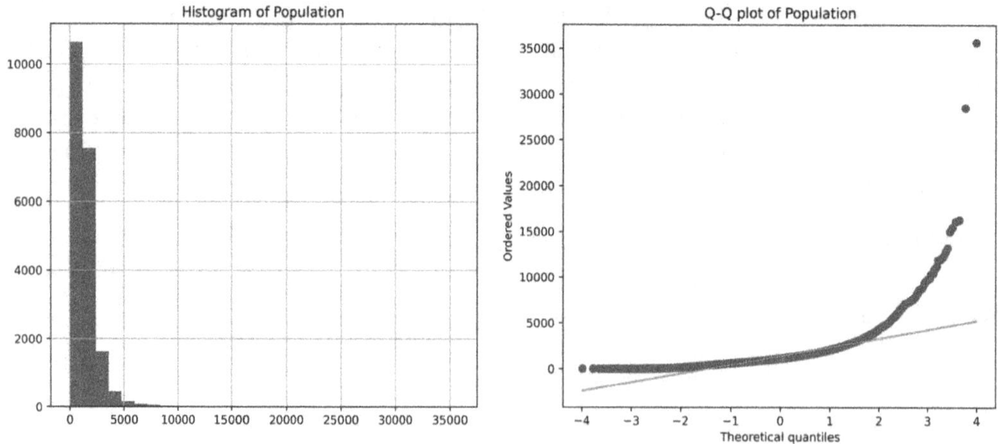

Figure 3.8 – A histogram and Q-Q plot of the Population variable

Now, let's apply a power transformation to the `MedInc` and `Population` variables. As both are skewed to the right, an exponent smaller than *1* might return a better spread of the variable values.

5. Let's capture the variables to transform in a list:

```
variables = ["MedInc", "Population"]
```

6. Let's make a copy of the DataFrame and then apply a power transformation to the variables from *step 5*, where the exponent is 0.3:

```
X_tf = X.copy()
X_tf[variables] = np.power(X[variables], 0.3)
```

> **Note**
>
> With np.power(), we can apply any power transformation by changing the value of the exponent in the second position of the function.

7. Let's examine the change in the distribution of Population:

```
diagnostic_plots(X_tf, "Population")
```

As shown in the plots returned by the previous command, Population is now more evenly distributed across the value range and follows the quantiles of the normal distribution more closely:

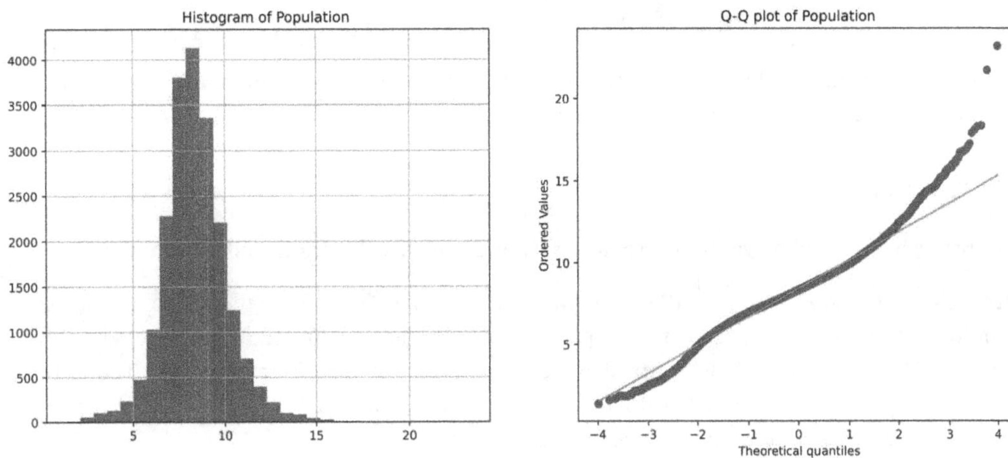

Figure 3.9 – A histogram and Q-Q plot of the Population variable after the transformation

Now, let's apply a power transformation with scikit-learn.

8. Let's set up FunctionTransformer() with a power transformation with an exponent of 0.3:

```
transformer = FunctionTransformer(
    lambda x: np.power(x,0.3))
```

9. Let's make a copy of the DataFrame and transform the variables from *step 5*:

```
X_tf = X.copy()
X_tf[variables] = transformer.transform(X[variables])
```

That's it – we can now examine the variable distribution. Finally, let's perform an exponential transformation with Feature-engine.

10. Let's set up `PowerTransformer()` with an exponent of `0.3` to transform the variables from *step 5*. Then, we'll fit it to the data:

```
power_t = PowerTransformer(variables=variables,
    exp=0.3)
power_t.fit(X)
```

> **Note**
>
> If we don't define the variables to transform, `PowerTransformer()` will select and transform all of the numerical variables in the DataFrame.

11. Finally, let's transform those two variables:

```
X_tf = power_t.transform(X)
```

The transformer returns a DataFrame containing the original variables, where the two variables specified in *step 5* are transformed with the power function.

How it works...

In this recipe, we applied power transformations using NumPy, scikit-learn, and Feature-engine.

To apply power functions with NumPy, we applied the `power()` method to the slice of the dataset containing the variables to transform. To apply this transformation with scikit-learn, we set up the `FunctionTransformer()` with `np.power()` within a `lambda` function, using `0.3` as the exponent. To apply power functions with Feature-engine, we set up the `PowerTransformer()` with a list of the variables to transform and an exponent of `0.3`.

scikit-learn and Feature-engine transformers applied the transformation when we called the `transform()` method. scikit-learn's `FunctionTransformer()` modifies the entire dataset and returns NumPy arrays by default. To return pandas DataFrames, we need to set the transform output to pandas, and to apply the transformation to specific variables, we can use `ColumnTransformer()`. Feature-engine's `PowerTransformer()`, on the other hand, can apply the transformation to a subset of variables out of the box, returning pandas DataFrames by default.

Performing Box-Cox transformations

The Box-Cox transformation is a generalization of the power family of transformations and is defined as follows:

$$y^{(\lambda)} = \frac{(y^{\lambda} - 1)}{\lambda} \; if \, \lambda \neq 0$$

$$y^{(\lambda)} = \log(y) \; if \, \lambda = 0$$

Here, y is the variable and λ is the transformation parameter. It includes important special cases of transformations, such as untransformed ($\lambda = 1$), the logarithm ($\lambda = 0$), the reciprocal ($\lambda = -1$), the square root (when $\lambda = 0.5$, it applies a scaled and shifted version of the square root function), and the cube root.

The Box-Cox transformation evaluates several values of λ using the maximum likelihood and selects the λ parameter that returns the best transformation.

In this recipe, we will perform the Box-Cox transformation using scikit-learn and Feature-engine.

> **Note**
>
> The Box-Cox transformation can only be used on positive variables. If your variables have negative values, try the Yeo-Johnson transformation, which is described in the next recipe, *Performing Yeo-Johnson transformation*. Alternatively, you can shift the variable distribution by adding a constant before the transformation.

How to do it...

Let's begin by importing the necessary libraries and getting the dataset ready:

1. Import the required Python libraries and classes:

```python
import numpy as np
import pandas as pd
import scipy.stats as stats
from sklearn.datasets import fetch_california_housing
from sklearn.preprocessing import PowerTransformer
from feature_engine.transformation import BoxCoxTransformer
```

2. Let's load the California housing dataset into a pandas DataFrame:

```python
X, y = fetch_california_housing(
    return_X_y=True, as_frame=True)
```

3. Let's drop the `Latitude` and `Longitude` variables:

```
X.drop(labels=["Latitude", "Longitude"], axis=1,
    inplace=True)
```

4. Let's inspect the variable distributions with histograms:

```
X.hist(bins=30, figsize=(12, 12), layout=(3, 3))
plt.show()
```

In the following output, we can see that the `MedInc` variable shows a mild right-skewed distribution, variables such as `AveRooms` and `Population` are heavily right-skewed, and the `HouseAge` variable shows an even spread of values across its range:

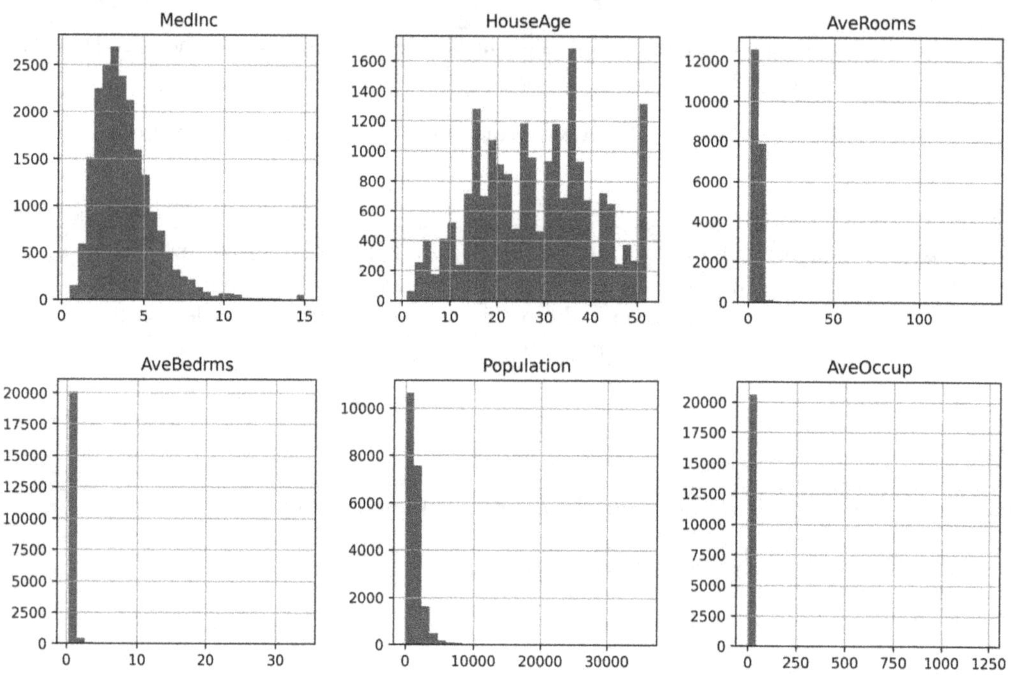

Figure 3.10 – Histograms of the numerical variables

5. Let's capture the variable names in a list since we will use these in the following step:

```
variables = list(X.columns)
```

6. Let's create a function that will plot Q-Q plots for all the variables in the data in two rows with three plots each:

```
def make_qqplot(df):
    plt.figure(figsize=(10, 6),
        constrained_layout=True)
```

```python
for i in range(6):
    # location in figure
    ax = plt.subplot(2, 3, i + 1)
    # variable to plot
    var = variables[i]
    # q-q plot
    stats.probplot((df[var]), dist="norm",
        plot=plt)
    # add variable name as title
    ax.set_title(var)
plt.show()
```

7. Now, let's display the Q-Q plots using the preceding function:

```python
make_qqplot(X)
```

By looking at the following plots, we can corroborate that the variables are not normally distributed:

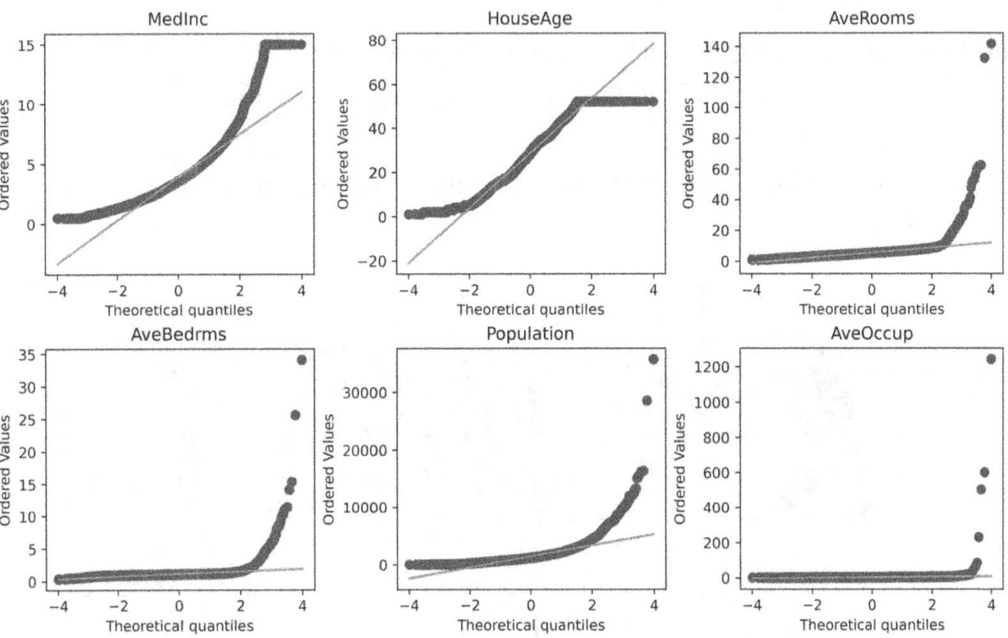

Figure 3.11 – Q-Q plots of the numerical variables

Next, let's carry out the Box-Cox transformation using scikit-learn.

8. Let's set up `PowerTransformer()` to apply the Box-Cox transformation and fit it to the data so that it finds the optimal λ parameter:

```python
transformer = PowerTransformer(
    method="box-cox", standardize=False,
```

```
).set_output(transform="pandas")
transformer.fit(X)
```

> **Note**
>
> To avoid data leakage, the λ parameter should be learned from the train set and then used to transform the train and test sets. Thus, remember to split your data into train and test sets before fitting `PowerTransformer()`.

9. Now, let's transform the dataset:

```
X_tf = transformer.transform(X)
```

> **Note**
>
> scikit-learn's `PowerTransformer()` stores the learned lambdas in its `lambdas_` attribute, which you can display by executing `transformer.lambdas_`.

10. Let's inspect the distributions of the transformed data with histograms:

```
X_tf.hist(bins=30, figsize=(12, 12), layout=(3, 3))
plt.show()
```

In the following output, we can see that the variables' values are more evenly spread across their ranges:

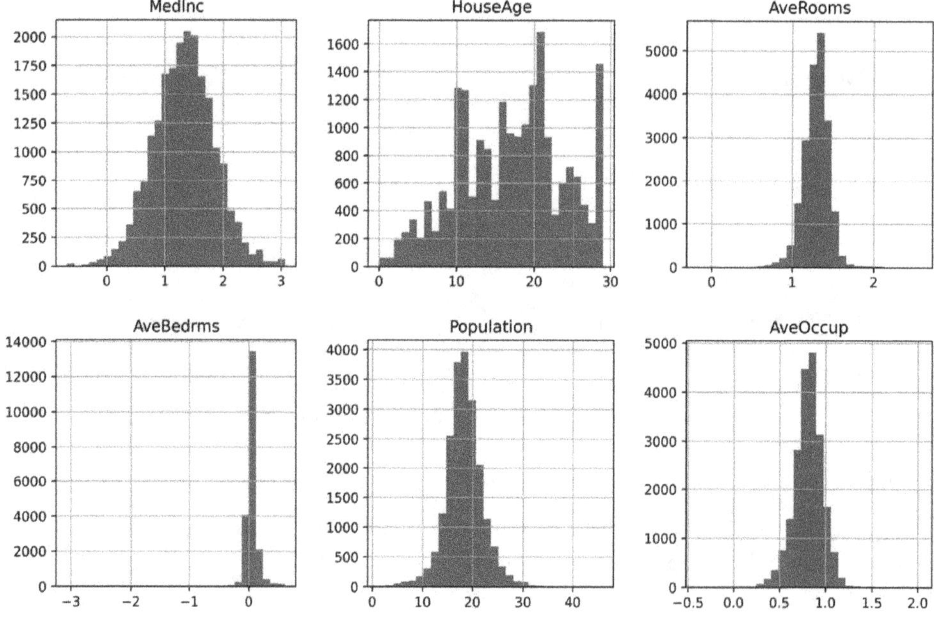

Figure 3.12 – Histograms of the variables after the transformation

11. Now, let's return Q-Q plots of the transformed variables:

```
make_qqplot(X_tf)
```

In the following output, we can see that, after the transformation, the variables follow the theoretical normal distribution more closely:

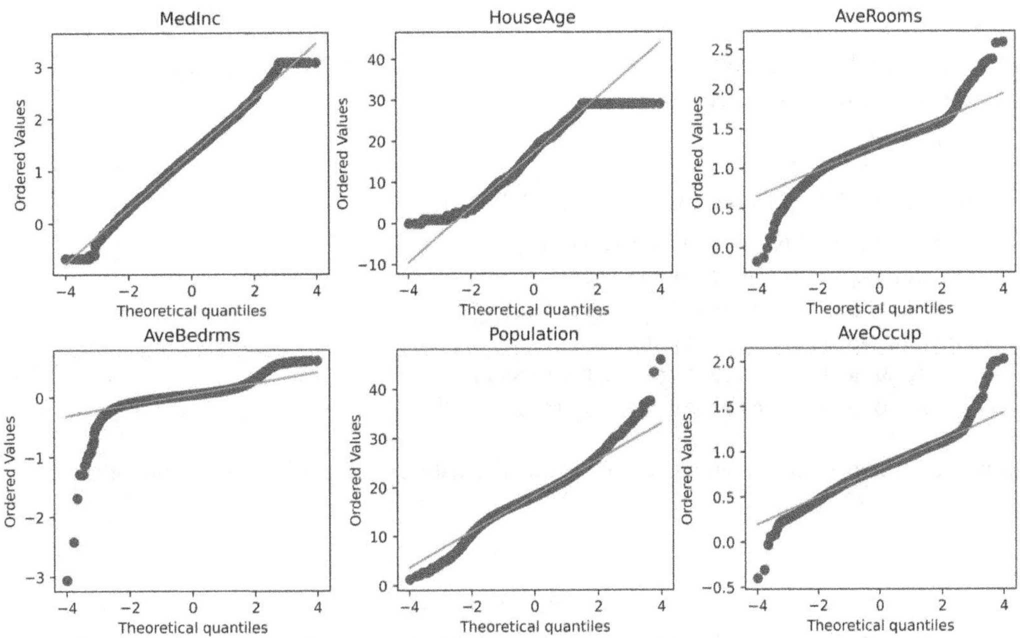

Figure 3.13 – Q-Q plots of the variables after the transformation

Now, let's implement the Box-Cox transformation with Feature-engine.

12. Let's set up `BoxCoxTransformer()` to transform all the variables in the dataset and then fit it to the data:

```
bct = BoxCoxTransformer()
bct.fit(X)
```

13. Now, let's go ahead and transform the variables:

```
X_tf = bct.transform(X)
```

The transformation returns a pandas DataFrame containing the modified variables.

> **Note**
>
> `PowerTransformer()` from scikit-learn will transform the entire dataset. On the other hand, `BoxCoxTransformer()` from Feature-engine can modify a subset of the variables, if we pass their names in a list to the `variables` parameter when setting up the transformer. If the `variables` parameter is set to `None`, the transformer will transform all numerical variables seen during `fit()`.

14. The optimal lambdas for the Box-Cox transformation are stored in the `lambda_dict_` attribute. Let's inspect them:

```
bct.lambda_dict_
```

The output of the previous command is the following:

```
{'MedInc': 0.09085449361507383,
 'HouseAge': 0.8093980940712507,
 'AveRooms': -0.2980048976549959,
 'AveBedrms': -1.6290002625859639,
 'Population': 0.23576757812051324,
 'AveOccup': -0.4763032278973292}
```

Now you know how to implement the Box-Cox transformation with two different Python libraries.

How it works...

scikit-learn's `PowerTransformer()` can apply both Box-Cox and Yeo-Johnson transformations, so we specified the transformation when setting up the transformer by passing the `box-cox` string. Next, we fit the transformer to the data so that the transformer learned the optimal lambdas for each variable. The learned lambdas were stored in the `lambdas_` attribute. Finally, we used the `transform()` method to transform the variables.

> **Note**
>
> Remember that to return DataFrames instead of arrays, you need to specify the transform output through the `set_output()` method. You can apply the transformation to a subset of values by using the `ColumnTransformer()`.

Finally, we applied the Box-Cox transformation using Feature-engine. We initialized `BoxCoxTransformer()`, leaving the parameter `variables` set the `None`. Due to this, the transformer automatically found the numerical variables in the data during `fit()`. We fit the transformer to the data so that it learned the optimal lambdas per variable, which were stored in `lambda_dict_`, and transformed the variables using the `transform()` method. Feature-engine's `BoxCoxTransformer()` can take the entire DataFrame as input and it yet modify only the selected variables.

There's more...

We can apply the Box-Cox transformation with the SciPy library. For a code implementation, visit this book's GitHub repository: `https://github.com/PacktPublishing/Python-Feature-Engineering-Cookbook-Third-Edition/blob/main/ch03-variable-transformation/Recipe-5-Box-Cox-transformation.ipynb`

Performing Yeo-Johnson transformations

The Yeo-Johnson transformation is an extension of the Box-Cox transformation that is no longer constrained to positive values. In other words, the Yeo-Johnson transformation can be used on variables with zero and negative values, as well as positive values. These transformations are defined as follows:

- $\frac{(X+1)^{\lambda}-1}{\lambda}$; if $\lambda \neq 0$ and X >= 0

- $\ln(X + 1)$; if $\lambda = 0$ and X >= 0

- $-\frac{(-X+1)^{2-\lambda}-1}{2-\lambda}$; if $\lambda \neq 2$ and X < 0

- $-\ln(-X + 1)$; if $\lambda = 2$ and X < 0

When the variable has only positive values, then the Yeo-Johnson transformation is like the Box-Cox transformation of the variable plus one. If the variable has only negative values, then the Yeo-Johnson transformation is like the Box-Cox transformation of the negative of the variable plus one, at the power of $2-\lambda$. If the variable has a mix of positive and negative values, the Yeo-Johnson transformation applies different powers to the positive and negative values.

In this recipe, we will perform the Yeo-Johnson transformation using scikit-learn and Feature-engine.

How to do it...

Let's begin by importing the necessary libraries and getting the dataset ready:

1. Import the required Python libraries and classes:

```
import numpy as np import pandas as pd
import scipy.stats as stats
from sklearn.datasets import fetch_california_housing
from sklearn.preprocessing import PowerTransformer
from feature_engine.transformation import YeoJohnsonTransformer
```

2. Let's load the California housing dataset into a pandas DataFrame and then drop the `Latitude` and `Longitude` variables:

```
X, y = fetch_california_housing(
    return_X_y=True, as_frame=True)
```

```
X.drop(labels=[«Latitude», «Longitude»], axis=1,
    inplace=True)
```

> **Note**
>
> We can evaluate the variable distribution with histograms and Q-Q plots, as we did in *steps 4 to 7* of the *Performing Box-Cox transformations* recipe.

Now, let's apply the Yeo-Johnson transformation with scikit-learn.

3. Let's set up `PowerTransformer()` with the `yeo-johnson` transformation:

```
transformer = PowerTransformer(
    method="yeo-johnson", standardize=False,
).set_output(transform="pandas")
```

4. Let's fit the transformer to the data:

```
transformer.fit(X)
```

> **Note**
>
> The λ parameter should be learned from the train set and then used to transform the train and test sets. Thus, remember to separate your data into train and test sets before fitting `PowerTransformer()`.

5. Now, let's transform the dataset:

```
X_tf = transformer.transform(X)
```

> **Note**
>
> `PowerTransformer()` stores the learned parameters in its `lambda_` attribute, which you can return by executing `transformer.lambdas_`.

6. Let's inspect the distributions of the transformed data with histograms:

```
X_tf.hist(bins=30, figsize=(12, 12), layout=(3, 3))
plt.show()
```

In the following output, we can see that the variables' values are more evenly spread across their ranges:

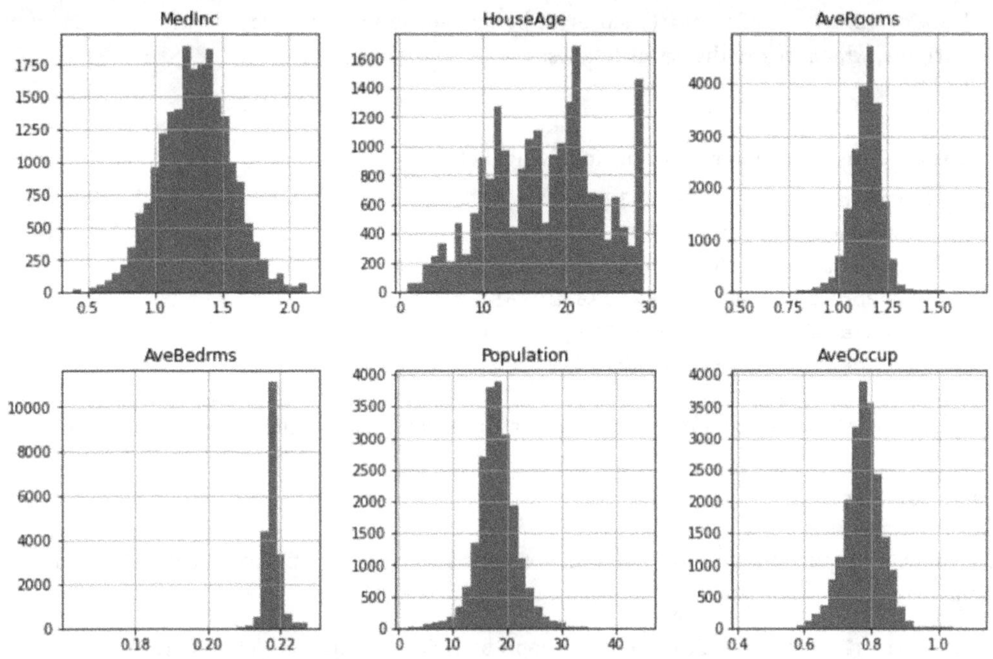

Figure 3.14 – Histograms of the variables after the yeo-Johnson transformation

Finally, let's implement the Yeo-Johnson transformation with Feature-engine.

7. Let's set up `YeoJohnsonTransformer()` to transform all numerical variables and then fit it to the data:

```
yjt = YeoJohnsonTransformer()
yjt.fit(X)
```

> **Note**
>
> If the `variables` argument is left set to `None`, the transformer selects and transforms all the numerical variables in the dataset. Alternatively, we can pass the names of the variables to modify in a list.
>
> Compared to `PowerTransformer()` from scikit-learn, Feature-engine's transformer can take the entire DataFrame as an argument of the `fit()` and `transform()` methods, and yet it will only modify the selected variables.

8. Let's transform the variables:

```
X_tf = yjt.transform(X)
```

9. `YeoJohnsonTransformer()` stores the best parameters per variable in its `lambda_dict_` attribute, which we can display as follows:

```
yjt.lambda_dict_
```

The previous command returns the following dictionary:

```
{'MedInc': -0.1985098937827175,
 'HouseAge': 0.8081480895997063,
 'AveRooms': -0.5536698033957893,
 'AveBedrms': -4.3940822236920365,
 'Population': 0.23352363517075606,
 'AveOccup': -0.9013456270549428}
```

Now you know how to implement the Yeo-Johnson transformation with two different open source libraries.

How it works...

In this recipe, we applied the Yeo-Johnson transformation using `scikit-learn` and `Feature-engine`.

`scikit-learn`'s `PowerTransformer()` can apply both Box-Cox and Yeo-Johnson transformations, so we specified the transformation with the `yeo-johnson` string. The `standardize` argument allowed us to determine whether we wanted to standardize (scale) the transformed values. Next, we fit the transformer to the DataFrame so that it learned the optimal lambdas for each variable. `PowerTransformer()` stored the learned lambdas in its `lambdas_` attribute. Finally, we used the `transform()` method to return the transformed variables. We set the transform output to `pandas` to return DataFrames after the transformation.

After that, we applied the Yeo-Johnson transformation using Feature-engine. We set up `YeoJohnsonTransformer()` so that it transforms all numerical variables seen during `fit()`. We fitted the transformer to the data so that it learned the optimal lambdas per variable, which were stored in `lambda_dict_`, and finally transformed the variables using the `transform()` method. Feature-engine's `YeoJohnnsonTransformer()` can take the entire DataFrame as input, yet it will only transform the selected variables.

There's more...

We can apply the Yeo-Johnson transformation with the SciPy library. For a code implementation, visit this book's GitHub repository: `https://github.com/PacktPublishing/Python-Feature-Engineering-Cookbook-Second-Edition/blob/main/ch03-variable-transformation/Recipe-6-Yeo-Johnson-transformation.ipynb`

4

Performing Variable Discretization

Discretization is the process of transforming continuous variables into discrete features by creating a set of contiguous intervals, also called **bins**, which span the range of the variable values. Subsequently, these intervals are treated as categorical data.

Many machine learning models, such as decision trees and Naïve Bayes, work better with discrete attributes. In fact, decision tree-based models make decisions based on discrete partitions over the attributes. During induction, a decision tree evaluates all possible feature values to find the best cut-point. Therefore, the more values the feature has, the longer the induction time of the tree is. In this sense, discretization can reduce the time it takes to train the models.

Discretization has additional advantages. Data is reduced and simplified; discrete features can be easier to understand by domain experts. Discretization can change the distribution of skewed variables; when sorting observations across bins with equal-frequency, the values are spread more homogeneously across the range. Additionally, discretization can minimize the influence of outliers by placing them at lower or higher intervals, together with the remaining **inlier** values of the distribution. Overall, discretization reduces and simplifies data, making the learning process faster and potentially yielding more accurate results.

Discretization can also lead to a loss of information, for example, by combining values that are strongly associated with different classes or target values into the same bin. Therefore, the aim of a discretization algorithm is to find the minimal number of intervals without incurring a significant loss of information. In practice, many discretization procedures require the user to input the number of intervals into which the values will be sorted. Then, the job of the algorithm is to find the cut points for those intervals. Among these procedures, we find the most widely used equal-width and equal-frequency discretization methods. Discretization methods based on decision trees are, otherwise, able to find the optimal number of partitions, as well as the cut points.

Discretization procedures can be classified as **supervised** and **unsupervised**. Unsupervised discretization methods only use the variable's distribution to determine the limits of the contiguous bins. On the other hand, supervised methods use target information to create the intervals.

In this chapter, we will discuss widely used supervised and unsupervised discretization procedures that are available in established open source libraries. Among these, we will cover equal-width, equal-frequency, arbitrary, k-means, and decision tree-based discretization. More elaborate methods, such as ChiMerge and CAIM, are out of the scope of this chapter, as their implementation is not yet open source available.

This chapter contains the following recipes:

- Performing equal-width discretization
- Implementing equal-frequency discretization
- Discretizing the variable into arbitrary intervals
- Performing discretization with k-means clustering
- Implementing feature binarization
- Using decision trees for discretization

Technical requirements

In this chapter, we will use the numerical computing libraries `pandas`, `numpy`, `matplotlib`, `scikit-learn`, and `feature-engine`. We will also use the `yellowbrick` Python open source library, which you can install with `pip`:

```
pip install yellowbrick
```

For more details about `yellowbrick`, visit the documentation here:

```
https://www.scikit-yb.org/en/latest/index.html
```

Performing equal-width discretization

Equal-width discretization consists of dividing the range of observed values for a variable into k equally sized intervals, where k is supplied by the user. The interval width for the X variable is given by the following:

$$Width = \frac{Max\,(X) - Min(X)}{k}$$

Then, if the values of the variable vary between 0 and 100, we can create five bins like this: *width = (100-0) / 5 = 20*. The bins will be 0–20, 20–40, 40–60, and 80–100. The first and final bins (0–20 and 80–100) can be expanded to accommodate values smaller than 0 or greater than 100 by extending the limits to minus and plus infinity.

In this recipe, we will carry out equal-width discretization using `pandas`, `scikit-learn`, and `feature-engine`.

How to do it...

First, let's import the necessary Python libraries and get the dataset ready:

1. Let's import the libraries and functions:

```python
import numpy as np
import pandas as pd
import matplotlib.pyplot as plt
from sklearn.datasets import fetch_california_housing
from sklearn.model_selection import train_test_split
```

2. Let's load the predictor and target variables of the California housing dataset:

```python
X, y = fetch_california_housing(
    return_X_y=True, as_frame=True)
```

> **Note**
>
> To avoid data leakage, we will find the intervals' limits by using the variables in the train set. Then, we will use these limits to discretize the variables in train and test sets.

3. Let's divide the data into train and test sets:

```python
X_train, X_test, y_train, y_test = train_test_split(
    X, y, test_size=0.3, random_state=0)
```

Next, we will divide the continuous HouseAge variable into 10 intervals using `pandas` and the formula described at the beginning of the recipe.

4. Let's capture the minimum and maximum values of HouseAge:

```python
min_value = int(X_train["HouseAge"].min())
max_value = int(X_train["HouseAge"].max())
```

5. Let's determine the interval width, which is the variable's value range divided by the number of bins:

```python
width = int((max_value - min_value) / 10)
```

If we execute `print(width)`, we will obtain 5, which is the size of the intervals.

6. Now we need to define the interval limits and store them in a list:

```python
interval_limits = [i for i in range(
    min_value, max_value, width)]
```

If we now execute `print(interval_limits)`, we will see the interval limits:

```
[1, 6, 11, 16, 21, 26, 31, 36, 41, 46, 51]
```

7. Let's expand the limits of the first and last intervals to accommodate smaller or greater values that we could find in the test set or in future data sources:

```
interval_limits[0] = -np.inf
interval_limits[-1] = np.inf
```

8. Let's make a copy of the DataFrames so we don't overwrite the original ones, which we will need for later steps in the recipe:

```
train_t = X_train.copy()
test_t = X_test.copy()
```

9. Let's sort the HouseAge variable into the intervals that we defined in *step 6*:

```
train_t["HouseAge_disc"] = pd.cut(
    x=X_train["HouseAge"],
    bins=interval_limits,
    include_lowest=True)
test_t["HouseAge_disc"] = pd.cut(
    x=X_test["HouseAge"],
    bins=interval_limits,
    include_lowest=True)
```

> **Note**
>
> We have set `include_lowest=True` to include the lowest value in the first interval. Note that we used the train set to find the intervals and then used those limits to sort the variable in both datasets.

10. Let's print the top 5 observations of the discretized and original variables:

```
print(train_t[["HouseAge", "HouseAge_disc"]].head(5))
```

In the following output, we can see that the 52 value was allocated to the 46–infinite interval, the 43 value was allocated to the 41–46 interval, and so on:

```
        HouseAge HouseAge_disc
1989       52.0    (46.0, inf]
256        43.0   (41.0, 46.0]
7887       17.0   (16.0, 21.0]
4581       17.0   (16.0, 21.0]
1993       50.0    (46.0, inf]
```

> **Note**
>
> The parentheses and brackets in the intervals indicate whether a value is included in the interval or not. For example, the (41, 46] interval contains all values greater than 41 and smaller than or equal to 46.

Equal-width discretization allocates a different number of observations to each interval.

11. Let's make a bar plot with the proportion of observations across the intervals of `HouseAge` in the train and test sets:

```python
t1 = train_t["HouseAge_disc"].value_counts(
    normalize=True, sort=False)
t2 = test_t["HouseAge_disc"].value_counts(
    normalize=True, sort=False)

tmp = pd.concat([t1, t2], axis=1)
tmp.columns = ["train", "test"]

tmp.plot.bar(figsize=(8, 5))
plt.xticks(rotation=45)
plt.ylabel("Number of observations per bin")
plt.xlabel('Discretized HouseAge')
plt.title("HouseAge")
plt.show()
```

In the following output, we can see that the proportion of observations per interval is approximately the same in the train and test sets, but different across intervals:

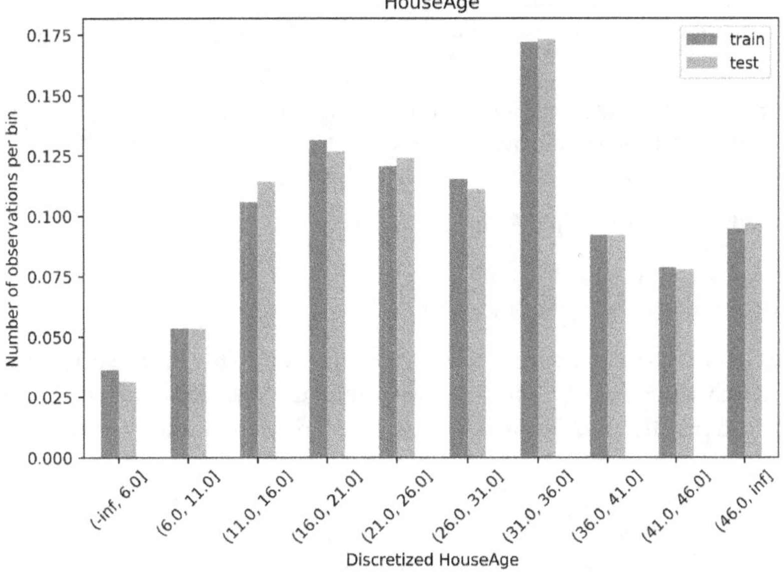

Figure 4.1 – The proportion of observations per interval after the discretization

With `feature-engine`, we can perform equal-width discretization in fewer lines of code and for many variables at a time.

12. First, let's import the discretizer:

```
from feature_engine.discretisation import EqualWidthDiscretiser
```

13. Let's set up the discretizer to sort three continuous variables into eight intervals:

```
variables = ['MedInc', 'HouseAge', 'AveRooms']
disc = EqualWidthDiscretiser(
    bins=8, variables=variables)
```

> **Note**
>
> `EqualWidthDiscretiser()` returns an integer indicating whether the value was sorted into the first, second, or eighth bin by default. That is the equivalent of ordinal encoding, which we described in the *Replacing categories with ordinal numbers* recipe of *Chapter 2, Encoding Categorical Variables*. To carry out a different encoding with the `feature-engine` or `category encoders` Python libraries, cast the returned variables as objects by setting `return_object` to True. Alternatively, make the transformer return the interval limits by setting `return_boundaries` to True.

14. Let's fit the discretizer to the train set so that it learns the cut points for each variable:

```
disc.fit(X_train)
```

After fitting, we can inspect the cut points in the `binner_dict_` attribute by executing `print(disc.binner_dict_)`.

> **Note**
>
> `feature-engine` will automatically extend the limits of the lower and upper intervals to infinite to accommodate potential outliers in future data.

15. Let's discretize the variables in the train and test sets:

```
train_t = disc.transform(X_train)
test_t = disc.transform(X_test)
```

`EqualWidthDiscretiser()` returns a DataFrame where the selected variables are discretized. If we run `test_t.head()`, we will see the following output where the original values of `MedInc`, `HouseAge`, and `AveRooms` are replaced by the interval numbers:

	MedInc	HouseAge	AveRooms	AveBedrms	Population	AveOccup	Latitude	Longitude
14740	2	3	0	1.075472	1551.0	4.180593	32.58	-117.05
10101	2	4	0	0.927739	1296.0	3.020979	33.92	-117.97
20566	2	4	0	1.026217	1554.0	2.910112	38.65	-121.84
2670	1	5	0	1.316901	390.0	2.746479	33.20	-115.60
15709	2	3	0	1.039578	649.0	1.712401	37.79	-122.43

Figure 4.2 – A DataFrame with three discretized variables: HouseAge, MedInc, and AveRooms

16. Now, let's make bar plots with the proportion of observations per interval to better understand the effect of equal-width discretization:

```
plt.figure(figsize=(6, 12), constrained_layout=True)
for i in range(3):
    # location of plot in figure
    ax = plt.subplot(3, 1, i + 1)
    # the variable to plot
    var = variables[i]
    # determine proportion of observations per bin
    t1 = train_t[var].value_counts(normalize=True,
        sort=False)
    t2 = test_t[var].value_counts(normalize=True,
        sort=False)
    # concatenate proportions
    tmp = pd.concat([t1, t2], axis=1)
    tmp.columns = ['train', 'test']
    # sort the intervals
    tmp.sort_index(inplace=True)
    # make plot
    tmp.plot.bar(ax=ax)
    plt.xticks(rotation=0)
    plt.ylabel('Observations per bin')
    ax.set_title(var)
plt.show()
```

The intervals contain a different number of observations, as shown in the following plots:

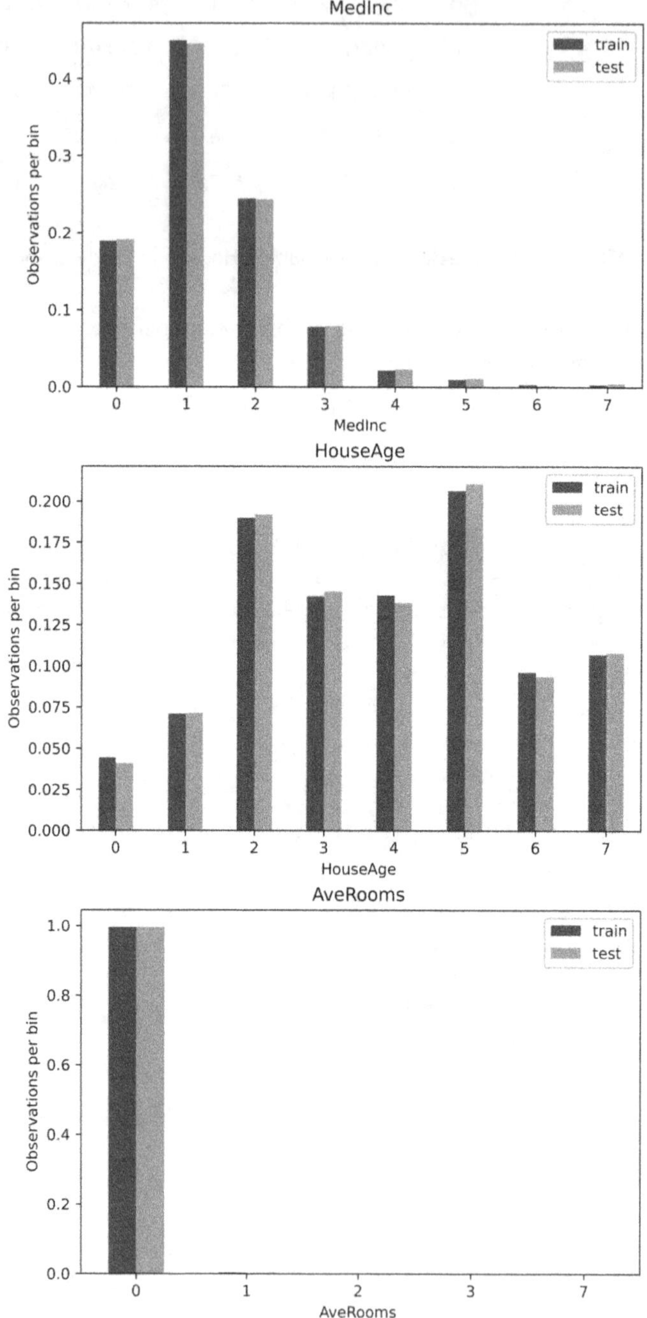

Figure 4.3 – Bar plots with the proportion of observations per interval after the discretization

Now, let's implement equal-width discretization with scikit-learn.

17. Let's import the classes from scikit-learn:

```
from sklearn.compose import ColumnTransformer
from sklearn.preprocessing import kBinsDiscretizer
```

18. Let's set up an equal-width discretizer by setting its `strategy` to `uniform`:

```
disc = KBinsDiscretizer(
    n_bins=8, encode='ordinal', strategy='uniform')
```

> **Note**
>
> `KBinsDiscretiser()` can return the bins as integers by setting encoding to `'ordinal'`
> or one-hot encoded by setting encoding to `'onehot-dense'`.

19. Let's use `ColumnTransformer()` to restrict the discretization to the selected variables from *step 13*:

```
ct = ColumnTransformer(
    [("discretizer", disc, variables)],
    remainder="passthrough",
).set_output(transform="pandas")
```

> **Note**
>
> With `remainder` set to `passthrough`, `ColumnTransformer()` returns all the variables
> in the input DataFrame after the transformation. To return only the transformed variables, set
> `remainder` to drop.

20. Let's fit the discretizer to the train set so that it learns the interval limits:

```
ct.fit(X_train)
```

21. Finally, let's discretize the selected variables in the train and test sets:

```
train_t = ct.transform(X_train)
test_t = ct.transform(X_test)
```

We can inspect the cut points learned by the transformer by executing `ct.named_transformers_["discretizer"].bin_edges_`.

> **Note**
>
> `ColumnTransformer()` will append `discretize` to the variables that were discretized
> and `remainder` to those that were not modified.

We can check the output by executing `test_t.head()`.

How it works...

In this recipe, we sorted the variable values into equidistant intervals. To perform discretization with `pandas`, we first found the maximum and minimum values of the `HouseAge` variable using the `max()` and `min()` methods. Then, we estimated the interval width by dividing the value range by the number of arbitrary bins. With the width and the minimum and maximum values, we determined the interval limits and stored them in a list. We used this list with pandas `cut()` to sort the variable values into the intervals.

> **Note**
>
> Pandas `cut()` sorts the variable into intervals of equal size by default. It will extend the variable range by .1% on each side to include the minimum and maximum values. The reason why we generated the intervals manually is to accommodate potentially smaller or larger values than those seen in the dataset in future data sources when we deploy our model.

After discretization, we normally treat the intervals as categorical values. By default, pandas `cut()` returns the interval values as ordered integers, which is the equivalent of ordinal encoding. Alternatively, we can return the interval limits by setting the `labels` parameter to `None`.

To display the number of observations per interval, we created a bar plot. We used the pandas `value_counts()` function to obtain the fraction of observations per interval, which returns the result in pandas Series, where the index is the interval and the counts are the values. To plot these proportions, first, we concatenated the train and test set series using the pandas `concat()` function in a DataFrame, and then we assigned the `train` and `test` column names to it. Finally, we used `plot.bar()` to display a bar plot. We rotated the labels with Matplotlib's `xticks()` function, and added the x and y legend with `xlabels()` and `ylabel()`, as well as the title with `title()`.

To perform equal-width discretization with `feature-engine`, we used `EqualWidth Discretiser()`, which takes the number of bins and the variables to discretize as arguments. With `fit()`, the discretizer learned the interval limits for each variable. With `transform()`, it sorted the values into each bin.

`EqualWidthDiscretiser()` returns the bins as sorted integers by default, which is the equivalent of ordinal encoding. To follow up the discretization with any other encoding procedure available in the `feature-engine` or `category encoders` libraries, we need to return the bins cast as objects by setting `return_object` to `True` when we set up the transformer.

> **Note**
>
> `EqualWidthDiscretiser()` extends the values of the first and last interval to minus and plus infinity by default to automatically accommodate smaller and greater values than those seen in the training set.

We followed the discretization with bar plots to display the fraction of observations per interval for each of the transformed variables. We could see that if the original variable was skewed, the bar plot was also skewed. Note how some of the intervals of the `MedInc` and `AveRooms` variables, which had skewed distributions, contained very few observations. In particular, even though we wanted to create eight bins for `AveRooms`, there were only enough values to create five, and most values of the variables were allocated to the first interval.

Finally, we discretized three continuous variables into equal-width bins with `KBinsDiscretizer()` from scikit-learn. To create equal-width bins, we set the `strategy` argument to `uniform`. With `fit()`, the transformer learned the limits of the intervals, and with `transform()`, it sorted the values into each interval.

We used the `ColumnTransformer()` to restrict the discretization to the selected variables, setting the transform output to pandas to obtain a DataFrame after the transformation. `KBinsDiscretizer()` can return the intervals as ordinal numbers, as we had it do in the recipe, or as one-hot-encoded variables. The behavior can be modified through the `encode` parameter.

See also

For a comparison of equal-width discretization with more sophisticated methods, see Dougherty J, Kohavi R, Sahami M. *Supervised and unsupervised discretization of continuous features*. In: Proceedings of the 12th international conference on machine learning. San Francisco: Morgan Kaufmann; 1995. p. 194–202.

Implementing equal-frequency discretization

Equal-width discretization is intuitive and easy to compute. However, if the variables are skewed, then there will be many empty bins or bins with only a few values, while most observations will be allocated to a few intervals. This could result in a loss of information. This problem can be solved by adaptively finding the interval cut-points so that each interval contains a similar fraction of observations.

Equal-frequency discretization divides the values of the variable into intervals that carry the same proportion of observations. The interval width is determined by **quantiles**. Quantiles are values that divide data into equal portions. For example, the median is a quantile that divides the data into two halves. Quartiles divide the data into four equal portions, and percentiles divide the data into 100 equal-sized portions. As a result, the intervals will most likely have different widths, but a similar number of observations. The number of intervals is defined by the user.

In this recipe, we will perform equal-frequency discretization using `pandas`, `scikit-learn`, and `feature-engine`.

How to do it...

First, let's import the necessary Python libraries and get the dataset ready:

1. Let's import the required Python libraries and functions:

```
import pandas as pd
import matplotlib.pyplot as plt
from sklearn.datasets import fetch_california_housing
from sklearn.model_selection import train_test_split
```

2. Let's load the California housing dataset into a DataFrame:

```
X, y = fetch_california_housing(
    return_X_y=True, as_frame=True)
```

> **Note**
>
> To avoid data leakage, we will determine the interval boundaries or quantiles from the train set.

3. Let's divide the data into train and test sets:

```
X_train, X_test, y_train, y_test = train_test_split(
    X, y, test_size=0.3, random_state=0)
```

4. Let's make a copy of the DataFrames:

```
train_t = X_train.copy()
test_t = X_test.copy()
```

5. We'll use pandas `qcut()` to obtain a discretized copy of the `HouseAge` variable, which we will store as a new column in the training set, and the limits of eight equal-frequency intervals:

```
train_t["House_disc"], interval_limits = pd.qcut(
    x=X_train["HouseAge"],
    q=8,
    labels=None,
    retbins=True,
)
```

If you execute `print(interval_limits)`, you'll see the following interval limits: `array([ 1., 14., 18., 24., 29., 34., 37., 44., 52.])`.

6. Let's print the top five observations of the discretized and original variables:

```
print(train_t[["HouseAge", "House_disc"]].head(5))
```

In the following output, we see that the 52 value was allocated to the 44–52 interval, the 43 value was allocated to the 37–44 interval, and so on:

```
      HouseAge      House_disc
1989      52.0     (44.0, 52.0]
256       43.0     (37.0, 44.0]
7887      17.0     (14.0, 18.0]
4581      17.0     (14.0, 18.0]
1993      50.0     (44.0, 52.0]
```

7. Now, let's discretize HouseAge in the test set, using pandas cut() with the interval limits determined in *step 5*:

```
test_t["House_disc"] = pd.cut(
    x=X_test["HouseAge"],
    bins=interval_limits,
    include_lowest=True)
```

8. Let's make a bar plot with the proportion of observations per interval in the train and test sets:

```
# determine proportion of observations per bin
t1 = train_t["House_disc"].value_counts(
    normalize=True)
t2 = test_t["House_disc"].value_counts(normalize=True)

# concatenate proportions
tmp = pd.concat([t1, t2], axis=1)
tmp.columns = ["train", "test"]
tmp.sort_index(inplace=True)

# plot
tmp.plot.bar()
plt.xticks(rotation=45)
plt.ylabel("Number of observations per bin")
plt.title("HouseAge")
plt.show()
```

In the following plot, we can see that the bins contain a similar fraction of observations:

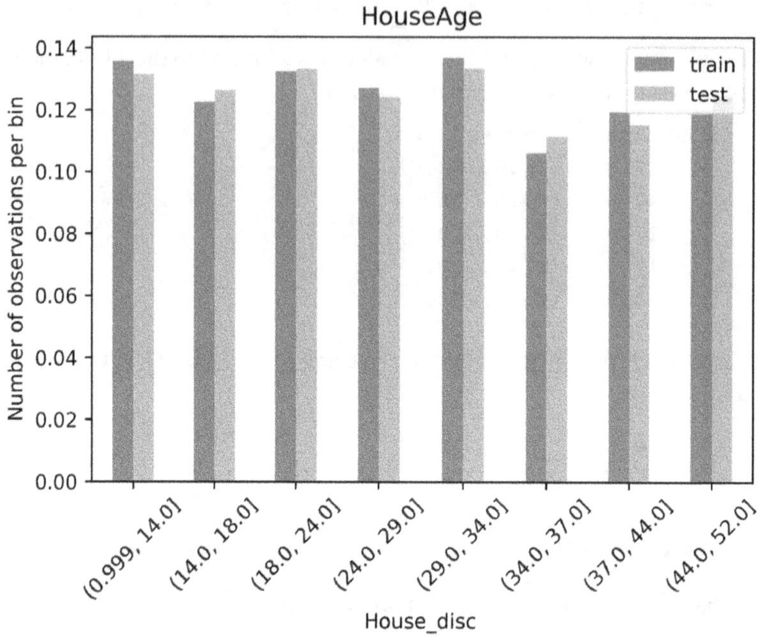

Figure 4.4 – The proportion of observations per interval of HouseAge after equal-frequency discretization

With `feature-engine`, we can apply equal-frequency discretization to multiple variables.

9. Let's import the discretizer:

```
from feature_engine.discretisation import
EqualFrequencyDiscretiser
```

10. Let's set up the transformer to discretize three continuous variables into eight bins:

```
variables = ['MedInc', 'HouseAge', 'AveRooms']
disc = EqualFrequencyDiscretiser(
    q=8, variables=variables, return_boundaries=True)
```

> **Note**
>
> With `return_boundaries=True`, the transformer will return the interval boundaries after the discretization. To return the interval number, set it to `False`.

11. Let's fit the discretizer to the train set so that it learns the interval limits:

```
disc.fit(X_train)
```

The transformer stores the limits of the intervals for each variable in a dictionary in its `disc.binner_dict_` attribute.

> **Note**
>
> `feature-engine` will automatically extend the limits of the lower and upper intervals to infinite to accommodate potential outliers in future data.

12. Let's transform the variables in the train and test sets:

```
train_t = disc.transform(X_train)
test_t = disc.transform(X_test)
```

13. Let's make bar plots with the fraction of observations per interval to better understand the effect of equal-frequency discretization:

```
plt.figure(figsize=(6, 12), constrained_layout=True)
for i in range(3):
    # location of plot in figure
    ax = plt.subplot(3, 1, i + 1)
    # the variable to plot
    var = variables[i]
    # determine proportion of observations per bin
    t1 = train_t[var].value_counts(normalize=True)
    t2 = test_t[var].value_counts(normalize=True)
    # concatenate proportions
    tmp = pd.concat([t1, t2], axis=1)
    tmp.columns = ['train', 'test']
    # sort the intervals
    tmp.sort_index(inplace=True)
    # make plot
    tmp.plot.bar(ax=ax)
    plt.xticks(rotation=45)
    plt.ylabel("Observations per bin")
    # add variable name as title
    ax.set_title(var)
    plt.show()
```

In the following figure, we can see that the intervals have a similar fraction of observations:

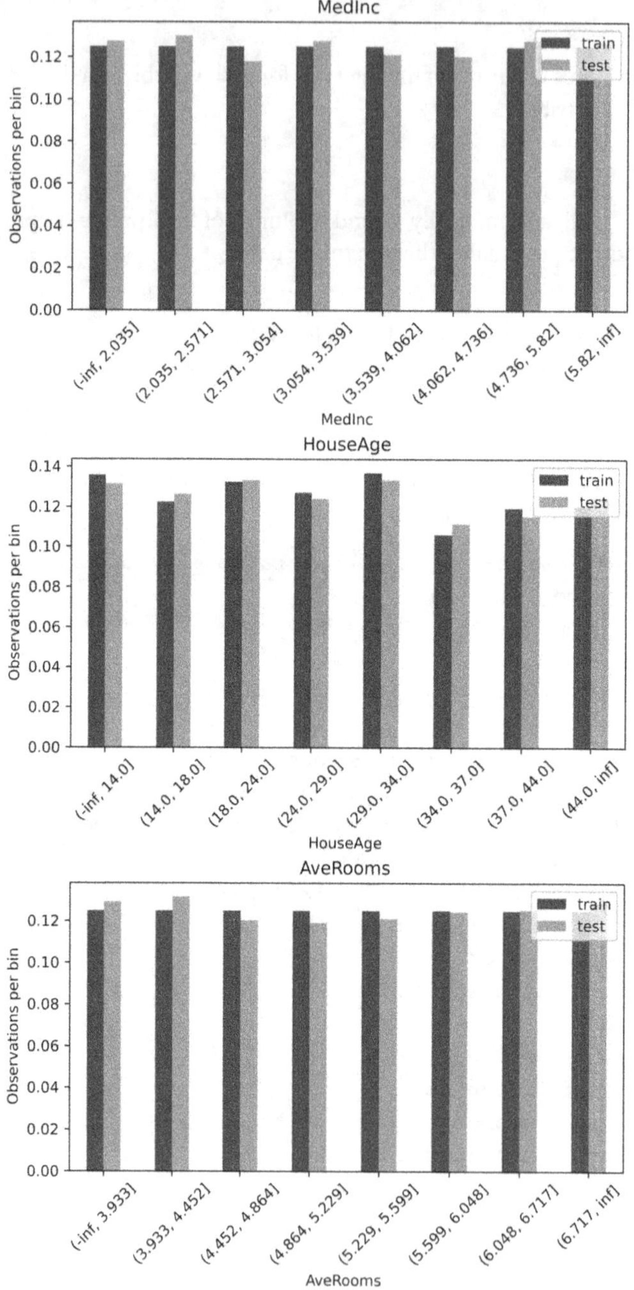

Figure 4.5 – The proportion of observations per interval after
equal-frequency discretization of three variables.

Now, let's carry out equal-frequency discretization with scikit-learn:

14. Let's import the transformer:

```
from sklearn.preprocessing import KBinsDiscretizer
```

15. Let's set up the discretizer to sort variables into eight equal-frequency bins:

```
disc = KBinsDiscretizer(
    n_bins=8, encode='ordinal', strategy='quantile')
```

16. Let's fit the discretizer to a slice of the train set containing the variables from *step 10* so that it learns the interval limits:

```
disc.fit(X_train[variables])
```

> **Note**
>
> scikit-learn's `KBinsDiscretiser()` will discretize all the variables in the dataset. To discretize only a subset, we apply the transformer to the slice of the DataFrame that contains the variables of interest. Alternatively, we can restrict the discretization to a subset of variables by using the `ColumnTransformer()`, as we did in the *Performing equal-width discretization* recipe.

17. Let's make a copy of the DataFrames where we'll store the discretized variables:

```
train_t = X_train.copy()
test_t = X_test.copy()
```

18. Finally, let's transform the variables in both the train and test sets:

```
train_t[variables] = disc.transform(
    X_train[variables])
test_t[variables] = disc.transform(X_test[variables])
```

We can inspect the cut points by executing `disc.bin_edges_`.

How it works...

In this recipe, we sorted the variable values into intervals with a similar proportion of observations.

We used pandas `qcut()` to identify the interval limits from the train set and sort the values of the `HouseAge` variable into those intervals. Next, we passed those interval limits to pandas `cut()` to discretize `HouseAge` in the test set. Note that pandas `qcut()`, like pandas `cut()`, returned the interval values as ordered integers, which is the equivalent of ordinal encoding,

> **Note**
>
> With equal-frequency discretization, many occurrences of values within a small continuous range could cause observations with very similar values, resulting in different intervals. The problem with this is that it can introduce artificial distinctions between data points that are actually quite similar in nature, biasing models or subsequent data analysis.

With Feature-engine's `EqualFrequencyDiscretiser()`, we discretized three variables into eight bins. With `fit()`, the discretizer learned the interval limits and stored them in the `binner_dict_` attribute. With `transform()`, the observations were allocated to the bins.

> **Note**
>
> `EqualFrequencyDiscretiser()` returns an integer indicating whether the value was sorted into the first, second, or eighth bin by default. That is the equivalent of ordinal encoding, which we described in the *Replacing categories with ordinal numbers* recipe in *Chapter 2, Encoding Categorical Variables*.
>
> To follow up the discretization with a different type of encoding, we can return the variables cast as objects by setting `return_object` to True and then use any of the `feature-engine` or `category encoders` transformers. Alternatively, we can return the interval limits, as we did in this recipe.

Finally, we discretized variables into eight equal-frequency bins using `scikit-learn`'s `KBinsDiscretizer()`. With `fit()`, the transformer learned the cut points and stored them in its `bin_edges_` attribute. With `transform()`, it sorted the values into each interval. Note that, differently from `EqualFrequencyDiscretiser()`, `KBinsDiscretizer()` will transform all of the variables in the dataset. To avoid this, we only applied the discretizer on a slice of the data with the variables to modify.

> **Note**
>
> scikit-learn's `KbinsDiscretizer` has the option to return the intervals as ordinal numbers or one-hot encoded. The behavior can be modified through the `encode` parameter.

Discretizing the variable into arbitrary intervals

In various industries, it is common to group variable values into segments that make sense for the business. For example, we might want to group the variable age in intervals representing children, young adults, middle-aged people, and retirees. Alternatively, we might group ratings into bad, good, and excellent. On occasion, if we know that the variable is in a certain scale (for example, logarithmic), we might want to define the interval cut points within that scale.

In this recipe, we will discretize a variable into pre-defined user intervals using `pandas` and `feature-engine`.

How to do it...

First, let's import the necessary Python libraries and get the dataset ready:

1. Import Python libraries and classes:

    ```python
    import numpy as np
    import pandas as pd
    import matplotlib.pyplot as plt
    from sklearn.datasets import fetch_california_housing
    ```

2. Let's load the California housing dataset into a `pandas` DataFrame:

    ```python
    X, y = fetch_california_housing(
        return_X_y=True, as_frame=True)
    ```

3. Let's plot a histogram of the `Population` variable to find out its value range:

    ```python
    X["Population"].hist(bins=30)
    plt.title("Population")
    plt.ylabel("Number of observations")
    plt.show()
    ```

    Population values vary between 0 and approximately 40,000:

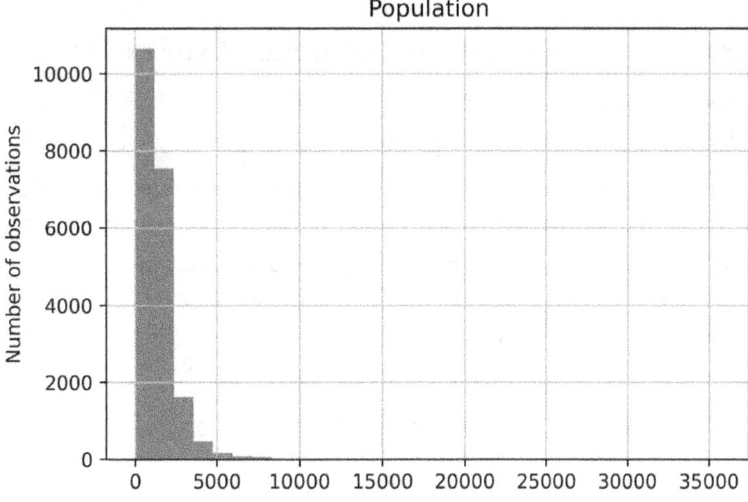

Figure 4.6 – Histogram of the Population variable

4. Let's create a list with arbitrary interval limits, setting the upper limit to infinity to accommodate bigger values:

```
intervals = [0, 200, 500, 1000, 2000, np.inf]
```

5. Let's create a list with the interval limits as strings:

```
labels = ["0-200", "200-500", "500-1000", "1000-2000",
    ">2000"]
```

6. Let's make a copy of the dataset and discretize the Population variable into the pre-defined limits from *step 4*:

```
X_t = X.copy()
X_t[«Population_limits»] = pd.cut(
    X["Population"],
    bins=intervals,
    labels=None,
    include_lowest=True)
```

7. Now, let's discretize Population into pre-defined intervals and name the intervals with the labels that we defined in *step 5* for comparison:

```
X_t[«Population_range»] = pd.cut(
    X[„Population"],
    bins=intervals,
    labels=labels,
    include_lowest=True)
```

8. Let's inspect the first five rows of the original and discretized variables:

```
X_t[['Population', 'Population_range',
    'Population_limits']].head()
```

In the last two columns of the DataFrame, we can see the discretized variables: the first one with the strings that we created in *step 5* as values, and the second one with the interval limits:

	Population	Population_range	Population_limits
0	322.0	200-500	(200.0, 500.0]
1	2401.0	>2000	(2000.0, inf]
2	496.0	200-500	(200.0, 500.0]
3	558.0	500-1000	(500.0, 1000.0]
4	565.0	500-1000	(500.0, 1000.0]

> **Note**
>
> We only need one of the variable versions, either the one with the value range or the one with the interval limits. In this recipe, I created both to highlight the different options offered by pandas.

9. Finally, we can count and plot the number of observations within each interval:

```python
X_t['Population_range'
    ].value_counts().sort_index().plot.bar()
plt.xticks(rotation=0)
plt.ylabel("Number of observations")
plt.title("Population")
plt.show()
```

In the following figure, we can see that the number of observations per interval varies:

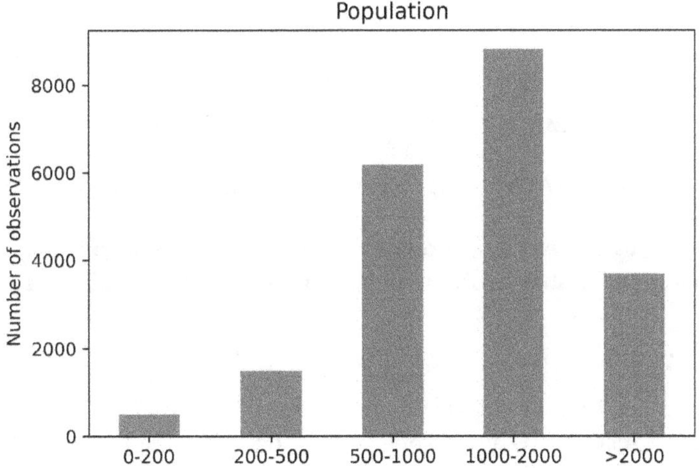

Figure 4.7 – The proportion of observations per interval after the discretization.

To wrap up the recipe, let's discretize multiple variables utilizing `feature-engine`:

10. Let's import the transformer:

```python
from feature_engine.discretisation import
    ArbitraryDiscretiser
```

11. Let's create a dictionary with the variables as keys and the interval limits as values:

```python
intervals = {
    "Population": [0, 200, 500, 1000, 2000, np.inf],
    "MedInc": [0, 2, 4, 6, np.inf]}
```

12. Let's set up the discretizer with the limits from *step 11*:

```python
discretizer = ArbitraryDiscretiser(
    binning_dict=intervals, return_boundaries=True)
```

13. Now, we can go ahead and discretize the variables:

```
X_t = discretizer.fit_transform(X)
```

If we execute `X_t.head()`, we will see the following output, where the `Population` and `MedInc` variables have been discretized:

	MedInc	HouseAge	AveRooms	AveBedrms	Population	AveOccup	Latitude	Longitude
0	(6.0, inf]	41.0	6.984127	1.023810	(200.0, 500.0]	2.555556	37.88	-122.23
1	(6.0, inf]	21.0	6.238137	0.971880	(2000.0, inf]	2.109842	37.86	-122.22
2	(6.0, inf]	52.0	8.288136	1.073446	(200.0, 500.0]	2.802260	37.85	-122.24
3	(4.0, 6.0]	52.0	5.817352	1.073059	(500.0, 1000.0]	2.547945	37.85	-122.25
4	(2.0, 4.0]	52.0	6.281853	1.081081	(500.0, 1000.0]	2.181467	37.85	-122.25

Figure 4.8 – A DataFrame containing the discretized variables

The advantage of using `feature-engine` is that we can discretize multiple variables at the same time and apply arbitrary discretization as part of a scikit-learn `Pipeline`.

How it works...

In this recipe, we sorted the values of a variable into user-defined intervals. First, we plotted a histogram of the `Population` variable to get an idea of its value range. Next, we arbitrarily determined the limits of the intervals and captured them in a list. We created intervals that included 0–200, 200–500, 500–1000, 1000–2000, and more than 2,000 by setting the upper limit to infinite with `np.inf`. Next, we created a list with the interval names as strings. Using pandas `cut()` and passing the list with the interval limits, we sorted the variable values into the pre-defined bins. We executed the command twice; in the first run, we set the `labels` argument to `None`, returning the interval limits as a result. In the second run, we set the `labels` argument to the list of strings. We captured the returned output in two variables: the first one displays the interval limits as values and the second one has strings as values. Finally, we counted the number of observations per variable using pandas `value_counts()`.

Finally, we automated the procedure with `feature-engine`'s `ArbitraryDiscretiser()`. This transformer takes a dictionary with the variables to discretize as keys and the interval limits in a list as values, and then uses pandas `cut()` under the hood to discretize the variables. With `fit()`, the transformer does not learn any parameters but checks that the variables are numerical. With `transform()`, it discretizes the variables.

Performing discretization with k-means clustering

The aim of a discretization procedure is to find a set of cut points that partition a variable into a small number of intervals that have good class coherence. To create partitions that group similar observations, we can use clustering algorithms such as k-means.

In discretization using k-means clustering, the partitions are the clusters identified by the k-means algorithm. The k-means clustering algorithm has two main steps. In the initialization step, k observations are chosen randomly as the initial centers of the k clusters, and the remaining data points are assigned to the closest cluster. The proximity to the cluster is measured by a distance measure, such as the Euclidean distance. In the iteration step, the centers of the clusters are re-computed as the average of all of the observations within the cluster, and the observations are reassigned to the newly created closest cluster. The iteration step continues until the optimal k centers are found.

Discretization with k-means requires one parameter, which is k, the number of clusters. There are a few methods to determine the optimal number of clusters. One of them is the elbow method, which we will use in this recipe. This method consists of training several k-means algorithms over the data using different values of k, and then determining the explained variation returned by the clustering. In the next step, we plot the explained variation as a function of the number of clusters, k, and pick the *elbow* of the curve as the number of clusters to use. The elbow is the inflection point that indicates that increasing the number of k further does not significantly increase the variance explained by the model. There are different metrics to quantify the explained variation. We will use the sum of the square distances from each point to its assigned center.

In this recipe, we will use the Python library `yellowbrick` to determine the optimal number of clusters and then carry out k-means discretization with scikit-learn.

How to do it...

Let's start by importing the necessary Python libraries and get the dataset ready:

1. Import the required Python libraries and classes:

```python
import pandas as pd
from sklearn.cluster import KMeans
from sklearn.datasets import fetch_california_housing
from sklearn.model_selection import train_test_split
from sklearn.preprocessing import KBinsDiscretizer
from yellowbrick.cluster import KElbowVisualizer
```

2. Let's load the California housing dataset into a `pandas` DataFrame:

```
X, y = fetch_california_housing(
    return_X_y=True, as_frame=True)
```

3. The k-means optimal clusters should be determined using the train set, so let's divide the data into train and test sets:

```
X_train, X_test, y_train, y_test = train_test_split(
    X, y, test_size=0.3, random_state=0)
```

4. Let's make a list with the variables to transform:

```
variables = ['MedInc', 'HouseAge', 'AveRooms']
```

5. Let's set up a k-means clustering algorithm:

```
k_means = KMeans(random_state=10)
```

6. Now, using Yellowbrick's visualizer and the elbow method, let's find the optimal number of clusters for each variable:

```
for variable in variables:
    # set up a visualizer
    visualizer = KElbowVisualizer(
        k_means, k=(4,12),
        metric='distortion',
        timings=False)

    visualizer.fit(X_train[variable].to_frame())
    visualizer.show()
```

In the following plots, we see that the optimal number of clusters is six for the first two variables and seven for the third:

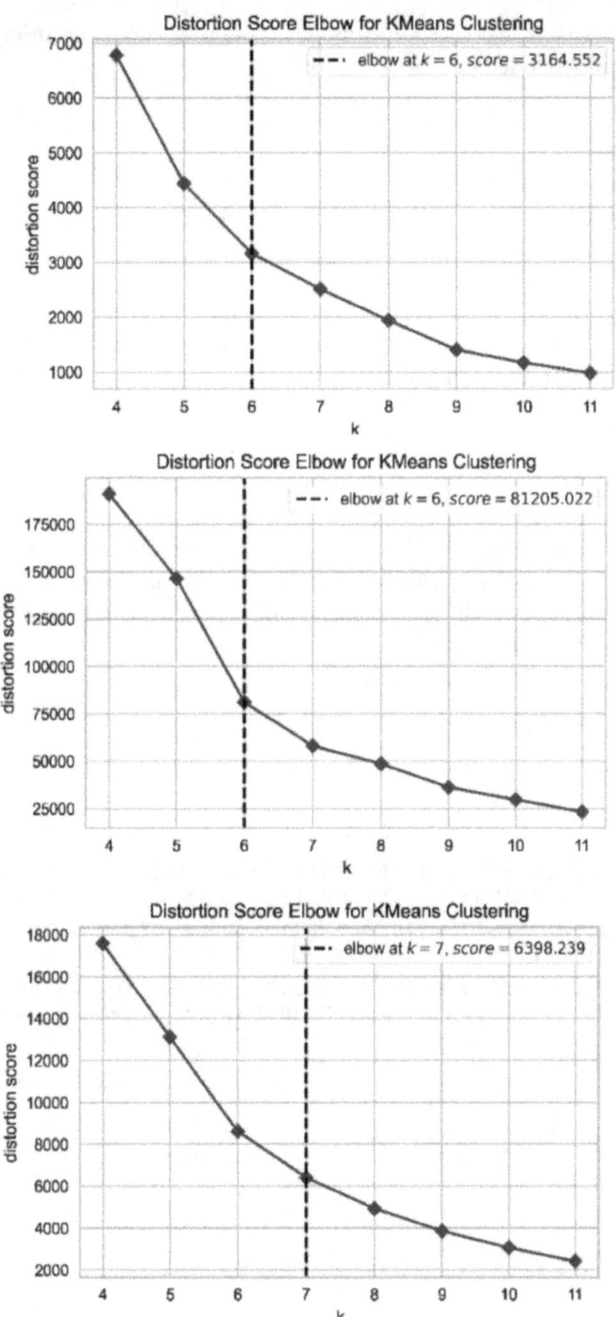

Figure 4.9 – The number of clusters versus the explained variation for the
MedInc, HouseAge, and AveRooms variables, from top to bottom

7. Let's set up a discretizer that uses k-means clustering to create six partitions and returns the clusters as one-hot-encoded variables:

```
disc = KBinsDiscretizer(
    n_bins=6,
    encode="onehot-dense",
    strategy="kmeans",
    subsample=None,
).set_output(transform="pandas")
```

8. Let's fit the discretizer to the slice of the DataFrame that contains the variables to discretize so that it finds the clusters for each variable:

```
disc.fit(X_train[variables])
```

> **Note**
>
> In this recipe, we sort the values of all three of the variables into six clusters. To discretize `MedInc` and `HouseAge` into six partitions and `AveRooms` into seven, we would set up one instance of the discretizer for each variable group and use the `ColumnTransformer()` to restrict the discretization to each group.

9. Let's inspect the cut points:

```
disc.bin_edges_
```

Each array contains the cut points for the six clusters for `MedInc`, `HouseAge`, and `AveRooms`:

```
array([array([0.4999, 2.49587954, 3.66599029, 4.95730115,
6.67700141, 9.67326677, 15.0001]),
array([1., 11.7038878, 19.88430419, 27.81472503, 35.39424098,
43.90930314, 52.]),
array([0.84615385, 4.84568771, 6.62222005, 15.24138445,
37.60664483, 92.4473438, 132.53333333])], dtype=object)
```

10. Let's obtain the discretized form of the variables in the train test sets:

```
train_features = disc.transform(X_train[variables])
test_features = disc.transform(X_test[variables])
```

With `print(test_features)`, we can inspect the DataFrame that is returned by the discretizer. It contains 18 binary variables corresponding to the one-hot-encoded transformation of the six clusters returned for each of the three numerical variables:

```
       MedInc_0.0  MedInc_1.0  MedInc_2.0  MedInc_3.0  \
MedInc_4.0  MedInc_5.0
14740          0.0         0.0         1.0
0.0         0.0         0.0
10101          0.0         0.0         0.0
1.0         0.0         0.0
20566          0.0         0.0         1.0
0.0         0.0         0.0
2670           1.0         0.0         0.0
0.0         0.0         0.0
15709          0.0         0.0         0.0
1.0         0.0         0.0

       HouseAge_0.0  HouseAge_1.0  HouseAge_2.0  HouseAge_3.0  \
HouseAge_4.0
14740           0.0           0.0           1.0
0.0           0.0
10101           0.0           0.0           0.0
1.0           0.0
20566           0.0           0.0           0.0
1.0           0.0
2670            0.0           0.0           0.0
0.0           1.0
15709           0.0           0.0           1.0
0.0           0.0

       HouseAge_5.0  AveRooms_0.0  AveRooms_1.0  AveRooms_2.0  \
AveRooms_3.0
14740           0.0           0.0           1.0
0.0           0.0
10101           0.0           0.0           1.0
0.0           0.0
20566           0.0           0.0           1.0
0.0           0.0
2670            0.0           0.0           1.0
0.0           0.0
15709           0.0           1.0           0.0
0.0           0.0

       AveRooms_4.0  AveRooms_5.0
14740           0.0           0.0
10101           0.0           0.0
20566           0.0           0.0
2670            0.0           0.0
15709           0.0           0.0
```

You can concatenate the result to the original DataFrame using `pandas` and then drop the original numerical variables. Alternatively, use the `ColumnTransformer()` class to restrict the discretization to the selected variables and add the result to the data by setting `remainder` to `"passthrough"`.

How it works...

In this recipe, we performed discretization with k-means clustering. First, we identified the optimal number of clusters utilizing the elbow method by using Yellowbrick's `KElbowVisualizer()`.

To perform k-means discretization, we used scikit-learn's `KBinsDiscretizer()`, setting `strategy` to kmeans and the number of clusters to six in the `n_bins` argument. With `fit()`, the transformer learned the cluster boundaries using the k-means algorithm. With `transform()`, it sorted the variable values to their corresponding cluster. We set `encode` to `"onehot-dense"`; hence, after the discretization, the transformer applied one-hot encoding to the clusters. We also set the output of the discretizer to `pandas`, and with that, the transformer returned the one-hot encoded version of the clustered variables as a DataFrame.

See also

- Discretization with k-means is described in the article found in *Palaniappan and Hong, Discretization of Continuous Valued Dimensions in OLAP Data Cubes*. International Journal of Computer Science and Network Security, VOL.8 No.11, November 2008. `http://paper.ijcsns.org/07_book/200811/20081117.pdf`.

- To learn more about the elbow method, visit Yellowbrick's documentation and references at `https://www.scikit-yb.org/en/latest/api/cluster/elbow.html`.

- For other ways of determining the fit of k-means clustering, check out the additional visualizers in Yellowbrick at `https://www.scikit-yb.org/en/latest/api/cluster/index.html`.

Implementing feature binarization

Some datasets contain sparse variables. Sparse variables are those where the majority of the values are 0. The classical example of sparse variables are those derived from text data through the bag-of-words model, where each variable is a word and each value represents the number of times the word appears in a certain document. Given that a document contains a limited number of words, whereas the feature space contains the words that appear across all documents, most documents, that is, most rows, will show a value of 0 for most columns. However, words are not the sole example. If we think about house details data, the *number of saunas* variable will also be 0 for most houses. In summary, some variables have very skewed distributions, where most observations show the same value, usually 0, and only a few observations show different, usually higher, values.

For a simpler representation of these sparse or highly skewed variables, we can binarize them by clipping all values greater than 1 to 1. In fact, binarization is commonly performed on text count data, where we consider the presence or absence of a feature rather than a quantified number of occurrences of a word.

In this recipe, we will perform binarization using `scikit-learn`.

Getting ready

We will use a dataset consisting of a bag of words, which is available in the UCI Machine Learning Repository (`https://archive.ics.uci.edu/ml/datasets/Bag+of+Words`). It is licensed under CC BY 4.0 (`https://creativecommons.org/licenses/by/4.0/legalcode`).

I downloaded and prepared a small bag of words representing a simplified version of one of those datasets. You will find this dataset in the accompanying GitHub repository:

`https://github.com/PacktPublishing/Python-Feature-Engineering-Cookbook-Third-Edition/tree/main/ch04-discretization`

How to do it...

Let's begin by importing the libraries and loading the data:

1. Let's import the required Python libraries, classes, and datasets:

    ```python
    import pandas as pd
    import matplotlib.pyplot as plt
    from sklearn.model_selection import train_test_split
    from sklearn.preprocessing import Binarizer
    ```

2. Let's load the bag of words dataset, which contains words as columns and different texts as rows:

    ```python
    data = pd.read_csv("bag_of_words.csv")
    ```

3. Let's display histograms to visualize the sparsity of the variables:

    ```python
    data.hist(bins=30, figsize=(20, 20), layout=(3,4))
    plt.show()
    ```

In the following histograms, we can see that the different words appear zero times in most documents:

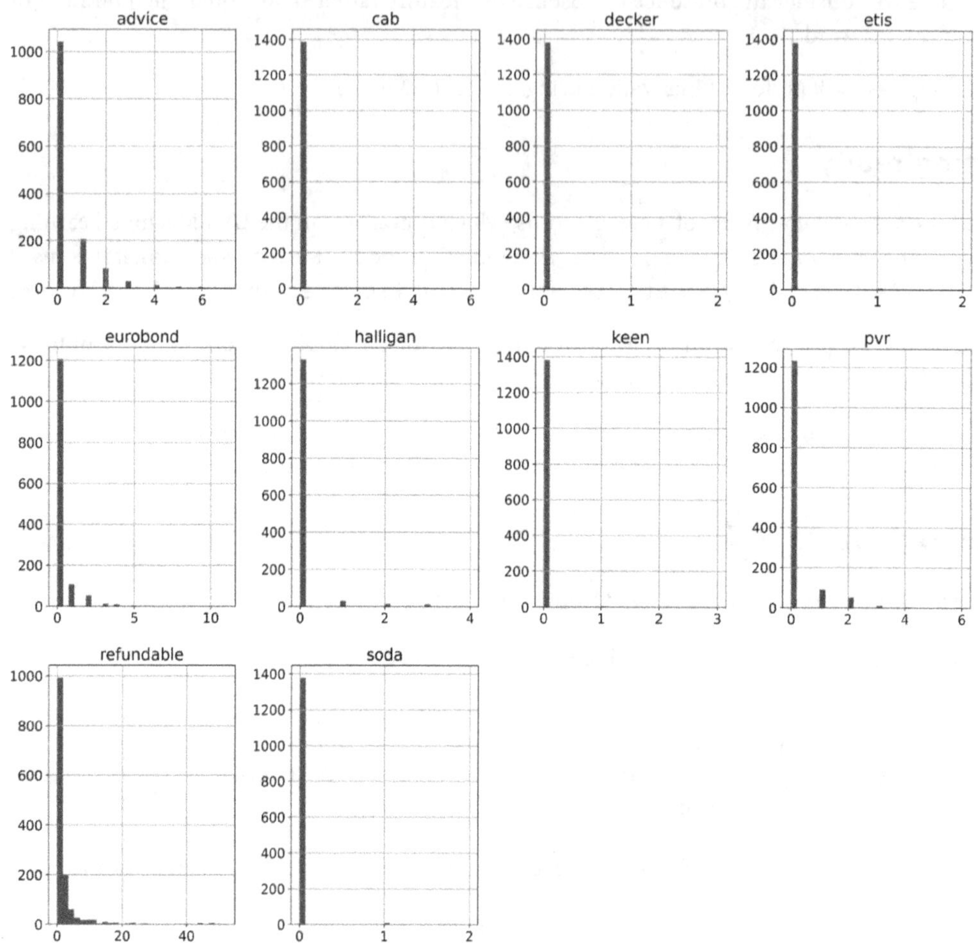

Figure 4.10 – Histograms representing the number of times each word appears in a document

4. Let's set up `binarizer` to clip all values greater than 1 to 1 and return DataFrames as a result:

```
binarizer = Binarizer(threshold = 0) .set_
output(transform="pandas")
```

5. Let's binarize the variables:

```
data_t = binarizer.fit_transform(data)
```

Now we can explore the distribution of the binarized variables by displaying the histograms as in *step 3*, or better, by creating bar plots.

6. Let's create a bar plot with the number of observations per bin per variable:

```
variables = data_t.columns.to_list()
plt.figure(figsize=(20, 20), constrained_layout=True)
for i in range(10):
    ax = plt.subplot(3, 4, i + 1)
    var = variables[i]
    t = data_t[var].value_counts(normalize=True)
    t.plot.bar(ax=ax)
    plt.xticks(rotation=0)
    plt.ylabel("Observations per bin")
    ax.set_title(var)
plt.show()
```

In the following plot, we can see the binarized variables, where most occurrences show the 0 value:

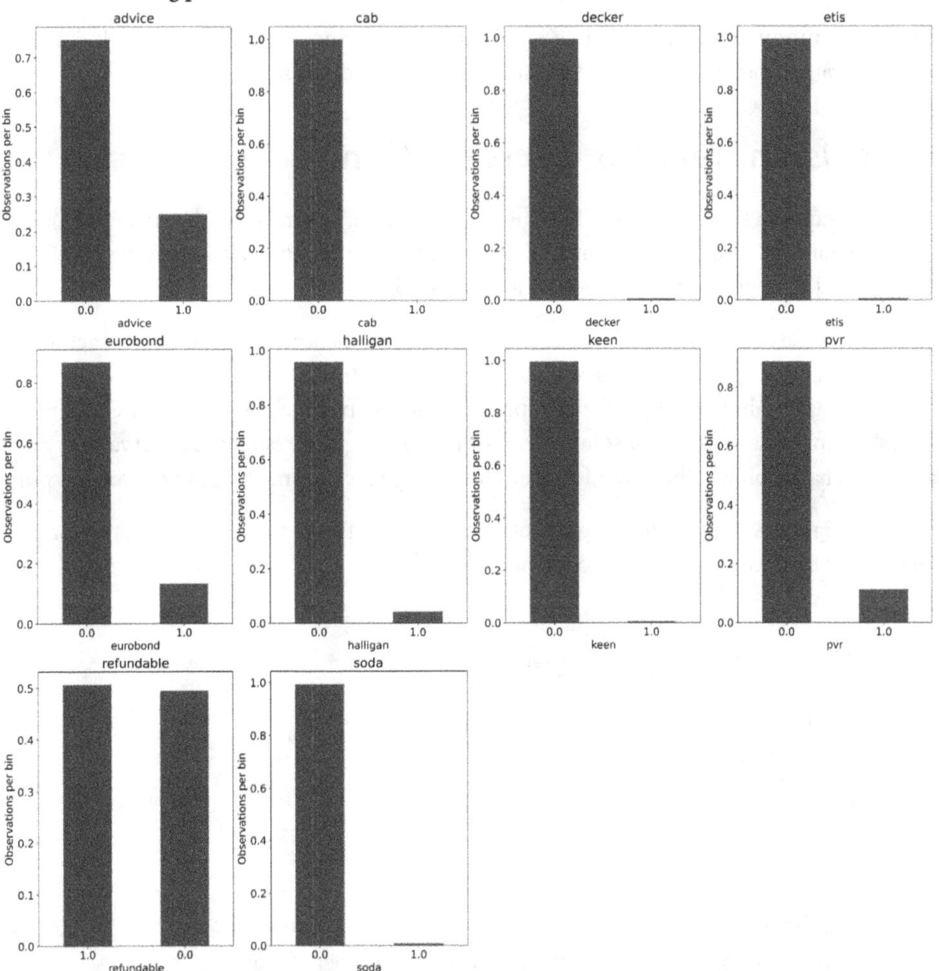

Figure 4.11 – Bar plots containing the number of documents that either show each one of the words or not

That's it; now we have a simpler representation of the data.

How it works...

In this recipe, we changed the representation of sparse variables to consider the presence or absence of an occurrence, which, in our case, is a word. The data consisted of a bag of words, where each variable (column) is a word, each row is a document, and the values represent the number of times the word appears in a document. Most words do not appear in most documents; therefore, most values in the data are 0. We corroborated the sparsity of our data with histograms.

scikit-learn's `Binarizer()` mapped values greater than the threshold, which, in our case, was 0, to the 1 value, while values less than or equal to the threshold were mapped to 0. `Binarizer()` has the `fit()` and `transform()` methods, where `fit()` does not do anything and `transform()` binarizes the variables.

`Binarizer()` modifies all variables in a dataset returning NumPy arrays by default. To return pandas DataFrames instead, we set the transform output to `pandas`.

Using decision trees for discretization

In all previous recipes in this chapter, we determined the number of intervals arbitrarily, and then the discretization algorithm would find the interval limits one way or another. Decision trees can find the interval limits and the optimal number of bins automatically.

Decision tree methods discretize continuous attributes during the learning process. At each node, a decision tree evaluates all possible values of a feature and selects the cut point that maximizes the class separation, or sample coherence, by utilizing a performance metric such as entropy or Gini impurity for classification, or the squared or absolute error for regression. As a result, the observations end up in certain leaves based on whether their feature values are greater or smaller than certain cut points.

In the following figure, we can see the diagram of a decision tree that is trained to predict house prices based on the property's average number of rooms:

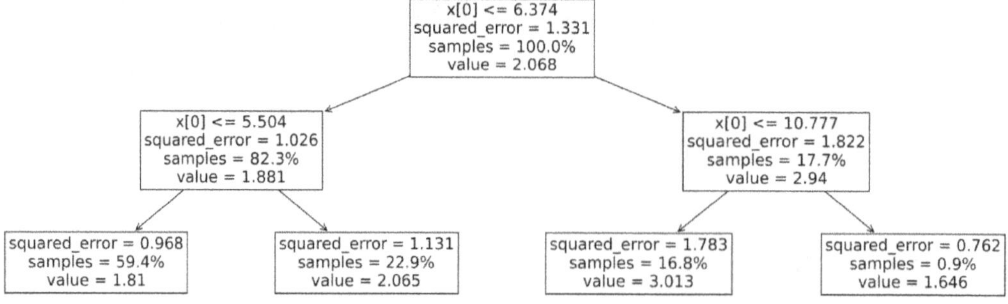

Figure 4.12 – A diagram of a decision tree trained to predict house price based on the property's average number of rooms

Based on this decision tree, houses with a smaller mean number of rooms than 5.5 will go to the first leaf, houses with a mean number of rooms between 5.5 and 6.37 will fall into the second leaf, houses with mean values between 6.37 and 10.77 will end up in the third leaf, and houses with mean values greater than 10.77 will land in the fourth leaf.

As you see, by design, decision trees can find the set of cut points that partition a variable into intervals with good class coherence.

In this recipe, we will perform decision tree-based discretization using Feature-engine.

How to do it...

Let's begin by importing some libraries and loading the data:

1. Let's import the required Python libraries, classes, and datasets:

    ```python
    import pandas as pd
    import matplotlib.pyplot as plt
    from sklearn.datasets import fetch_california_housing
    from sklearn.model_selection import train_test_split
    from sklearn.tree import plot_tree
    from feature_engine.discretisation import
    DecisionTreeDiscretiser
    ```

2. Let's load the California housing dataset into a pandas DataFrame and then split it into train and test sets:

    ```python
    X, y = fetch_california_housing(return_X_y=True,
        as_frame=True)
    X_train, X_test, y_train, y_test = train_test_split(
        X, y, test_size=0.3, random_state=0)
    ```

3. Let's make a list with the names of the variables to discretize:

    ```python
    variables = list(X.columns)[:-2]
    ```

    If we execute `print(variables)`, we'll see the following variable names: `['MedInc', 'HouseAge', 'AveRooms', 'AveBedrms', 'Population', 'AveOccup']`.

4. Let's set up the transformer to discretize the variables from *step 3*. We want the transformer to optimize the hyperparameter's maximum depth and minimum samples per leaf of each tree based on the negative mean square error metric using three-fold cross-validation. As the output of the discretization, we want the limits of the intervals:

    ```python
    disc = DecisionTreeDiscretiser(
        bin_output="boundaries",
        precision=3,
    ```

```
    cv=3,
    scoring="neg_mean_squared_error",
    variables=variables,
    regression=True,
    param_grid={
        "max_depth": [1, 2, 3],
        "min_samples_leaf": [10, 20, 50]},
)
```

5. Let's fit the discretizer using the train set so that it finds the best decision trees for each of the variables:

```
disc.fit(X_train, y_train)
```

> **Note**
>
> You can inspect the limits of the found intervals for each variable in the `binner_dict_` attribute by executing `disc.binner_dict_`. Note how the discretizer appended minus and plus infinity to the limits to accommodate smaller and greater values than those observed in the training set.

6. Let's discretize the variables and then display the first five rows of the transformed training set:

```
train_t = disc.transform(X_train)
test_t = disc.transform(X_test)
train_t[variables].head()
```

In the following output, we can see the limits of the intervals to which each observation was allocated:

	MedInc	HouseAge	AveRooms	AveBedrms	Population	AveOccup
1989	(-inf, 2.234]	(51.5, inf]	(-inf, 2.977]	(-inf, 1.049]	(-inf, 324.5]	(3.86, inf]
256	(2.234, 3.067]	(26.5, 50.5]	(2.977, 5.504]	(1.103, 1.53]	(691.5, 1159.5]	(2.841, 3.136]
7887	(6.087, 7.815]	(4.5, 21.5]	(6.374, 7.392]	(1.049, 1.103]	(1169.5, 11603.5]	(3.548, 3.86]
4581	(-inf, 2.234]	(4.5, 21.5]	(-inf, 2.977]	(1.103, 1.53]	(1169.5, 11603.5]	(2.841, 3.136]
1993	(-inf, 2.234]	(26.5, 50.5]	(2.977, 5.504]	(1.103, 1.53]	(332.5, 691.5]	(3.548, 3.86]

Figure 4.13 – The first five rows of the transformed training set containing the discretized variables

> **Note**
>
> If you choose to return the interval limits and want to use these datasets to train machine learning models, you will need to follow up the discretization with one-hot encoding or ordinal encoding. Check the recipes in *Chapter 2, Encoding Categorical Variables*, for more details.

7. Instead of returning the interval limits, we can return the interval number to which each observation is allocated by setting up the transformer like this:

```python
disc = DecisionTreeDiscretiser(
    bin_output="bin_number",
    cv=3,
    scoring="neg_mean_squared_error",
    variables=variables,
    regression=True,
    param_grid={
        "max_depth": [1, 2, 3],
        "min_samples_leaf": [10, 20, 50]})
```

8. We can now fit and then transform the training and testing sets:

```python
train_t = disc.fit_transform(X_train, y_train)
test_t = disc.transform(X_test)
```

If you now execute `train_t[variables].head()`, you will see integers as a result instead of the interval limits:

	MedInc	HouseAge	AveRooms	AveBedrms	Population	AveOccup
1989	0	5	0	0	0	7
256	1	3	1	2	3	3
7887	5	1	4	1	5	6
4581	0	1	0	2	5	3
1993	0	3	1	2	2	6

Figure 4.14 – The first five rows of the transformed training set containing the discretized variables

To wrap up the recipe, we will make the discretizer return the predictions of the trees as replacement values for the discretized variables:

9. Let's set up the transformer to return the predictions, then fit it to the training set, and finally transform both datasets:

```
disc = DecisionTreeDiscretiser(
    bin_output="prediction",
    precision=1,
    cv=3,
    scoring="neg_mean_squared_error",
    variables=variables,
    regression=True,
    param_grid=
        {"max_depth": [1, 2, 3],
            "min_samples_leaf": [10, 20, 50]},
)


train_t = disc.fit_transform(X_train, y_train)
test_t = disc.transform(X_test)
```

10. Let's explore the number of unique values of the AveRooms variable before and after the discretization:

```
X_test["AveRooms"].nunique(), test_t["AveRooms"].nunique()
```

In the following output, we can see that the predictions of the decision trees are also discrete or finite because the trees contain a finite number of end leaves; 7, while the original variable contained more than 6000 different values:

```
(6034, 7)
```

11. To better understand the structure of the tree, we can capture it into a variable:

```
tree = disc.binner_dict_["AveRooms"].best_estimator_
```

> **Note**
>
> When we set the transformer to return integers or bin limits, we will obtain the bin limits in the `binner_dict_` attribute. If we set the transformer to return the tree predictions, `binner_dict_` will contain the trained tree for each variable.

12. Now, we can display the tree structure:

```
fig = plt.figure(figsize=(20, 6))
plot_tree(tree, fontsize=10, proportion=True)
plt.show()
```

13. In the following figure, we can see the values used by the tree to allocate samples to the different end leaves based on the mean number of rooms:

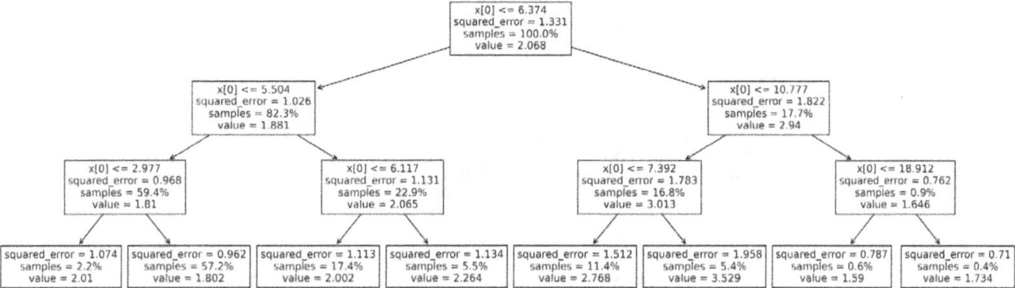

Figure 4.15 – The structure of the decision tree trained to discretize AveRooms

14. To wrap up the recipe, we can plot the number of observations per bin for three of the variables:

```
plt.figure(figsize=(6, 12), constrained_layout=True)
for i in range(3):
    ax = plt.subplot(3, 1, i + 1)
    var = variables[i]
    t1 = train_t[var].value_counts(normalize=True)
    t2 = test_t[var].value_counts(normalize=True)
    tmp = pd.concat([t1, t2], axis=1)
    tmp.columns = ["train", "test"]
    tmp.sort_index(inplace=True)
    tmp.plot.bar(ax=ax)
    plt.xticks(rotation=0)
    plt.ylabel("Observations per bin")
    ax.set_title(var)
plt.show()
```

We can see the number of observations per bin in the following output:

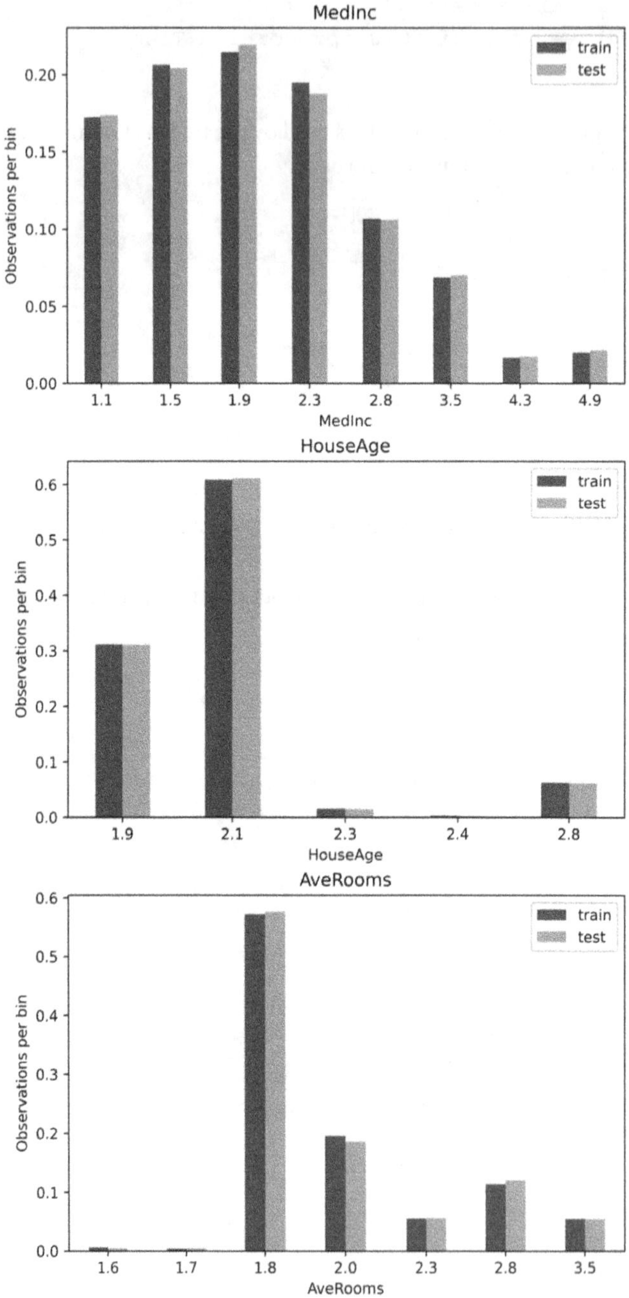

Figure 4.16 – The proportion of observations per bin after discretizing the variables with decision trees

As evidenced in the plots, discretization with decision trees returns a different fraction of observations at each node or bin.

How it works...

To perform discretization with decision trees, we used `feature-engine`'s `DecisionTreeDiscretiser()`. This transformer fitted a decision tree using each variable to discretize as input and optimized the hyperparameters of the model to find the best partitions based on a performance metric. It automatically found the optimal number of intervals, as well as their limits, returning either the limits, the bin number, or the predictions as a result.

There's more...

The implementation of `feature-engine` is inspired by the winning solution of the KDD 2009 data science competition. The winners created new features by obtaining predictions of decision trees based on continuous features. You can find more details in the *Winning the KDD Cup Orange Challenge with Ensemble Selection* article on *page 27* of the article series at `http://www.mtome.com/Publications/CiML/CiML-v3-book.pdf`.

For a review of discretization techniques, you might find the following articles useful:

- Dougherty et al, *Supervised and Unsupervised Discretization of Continuous Features, Machine Learning: Proceedings of the 12th International Conference*, 1995, (`https://ai.stanford.edu/~ronnyk/disc.pdf`).

- Lu et al, *Discretization: An Enabling Technique, Data Mining, and Knowledge Discovery*, 6, 393–423, 2002, (`https://www.researchgate.net/publication/220451974_Discretization_An_Enabling_Technique`).

- Garcia et al, *A Survey of Discretization Techniques: Taxonomy and Empirical Analysis in Supervised Learning, IEEE Transactions on Knowledge in Data Engineering 25 (4)*, 2013, (`https://ieeexplore.ieee.org/document/6152258`).

5

Working with Outliers

An outlier is a data point that diverges notably from other values within a variable. Outliers may stem from the inherent variability of the feature itself, manifesting as extreme values that occur infrequently within the distribution (typically found in the tails). They can be the result of experimental errors or inaccuracies in data collection processes, or they can signal important events. For instance, an unusually high expense in a card transaction may indicate fraudulent activity, warranting flagging and potentially blocking the card to safeguard customers. Similarly, unusually distinct tumor morphologies can suggest malignancy, prompting further examination.

Outliers can exert a disproportionately large impact on a statistical analysis. For example, a small number of outliers can reverse the statistical significance of a test in either direction (think A/B testing) or directly influence the estimation of the parameters of the statistical model (think coefficients). Some machine learning models are well known for being susceptible to outliers, such as linear regression. Other models are known for being robust to outliers, such as decision-tree-based models. AdaBoost is said to be sensitive to outliers in the target variable, and in principle, distance-based models, such as PCA and KNN, could also be affected by the presence of outliers.

There isn't a strict mathematical definition for what qualifies as an outlier, and there is also no consensus on how to handle outliers in statistical or machine learning models. If outliers stem from flawed data collection, discarding them seems like a safe option. However, in many datasets, pinpointing the exact nature of outliers is challenging. Ultimately, detecting and handling outliers remains a subjective exercise, reliant on domain knowledge and an understanding of their potential impact on models.

In this chapter, we will begin by discussing methods to identify potential outliers, or more precisely, observations that significantly deviate from the rest. Then, we'll proceed under the assumption that these observations are not relevant for the analysis, and show how to either remove them or reduce their impact on models through truncation.

This chapter contains the following recipes:

- Visualizing outliers with boxplots and the inter-quartile proximity rule

- Finding outliers using the mean and standard deviation

- Using the median absolute deviation to find outliers

- Removing outliers

- Bringing outliers back within acceptable limits

- Applying winsorization

Technical requirements

In this chapter, we will use the Python numpy, `pandas`, `matplotlib`, `seaborn`, and `feature-engine` libraries.

Visualizing outliers with boxplots and the inter-quartile proximity rule

A common way to visualize outliers is by using boxplots. Boxplots provide a standardized display of the variable's distribution based on quartiles. The box contains the observations within the first and third quartiles, known as the **Inter-Quartile Range (IQR)**. The first quartile is the value below which 25% of the observations lie (equivalent to the 25th percentile), while the third quartile is the value below which 75% of the observations lie (equivalent to the 75th percentile). The IQR is calculated as follows:

$$IQR = 3rd\ quartile - 1st\ quartile$$

Boxplots also display whiskers, which are lines that protrude from each end of the box toward the minimum and maximum values and up to a limit. These limits are given by the minimum or maximum value of the distribution or, in the presence of extreme values, by the following equations:

$$upper\ limit = 3rd\ quartile + IQR \times 1.5$$

$$lower\ limit = 1st\ quartile - IQR \times 1.5$$

According to the **IQR proximity rule**, we can consider a value an outlier if it falls beyond the whisker limits determined by the previous equations. In boxplots, outliers are indicated as dots.

> **Note**
>
> If the variable has a normal distribution, about 99% of the observations will be located within the interval delimited by the whiskers. Hence, we can treat values beyond the whiskers as outliers. Boxplots are, however, non-parametric, which is why we also use them to visualize outliers in skewed variables.

In this recipe, we'll begin by visualizing the variable distribution with boxplots, and then we'll calculate the whisker's limits manually to identify the points beyond which we could consider a value as an outlier.

How to do it...

We will create boxplots utilizing the `seaborn` library. Let's begin by importing the Python libraries and loading the dataset:

1. Let's import the Python libraries and the dataset:

    ```
    import matplotlib.pyplot as plt
    import seaborn as sns
    from sklearn.datasets import fetch_california_housing
    ```

2. Modify the default background from `seaborn` (it makes prettier plots, but that's subjective, of course):

    ```
    sns.set(style="darkgrid")
    ```

3. Load the California house prices dataset from scikit-learn:

    ```
    X, y = fetch_california_housing(
        return_X_y=True, as_frame=True)
    ```

4. Make a boxplot of the `MedInc` variable to visualize its distribution:

    ```
    plt.figure(figsize=(8, 3))
    sns.boxplot(data=X["MedInc"], orient="y")
    plt.title("Boxplot")
    plt.show()
    ```

In the following boxplot, we identify the box containing the observations within the IQR, that is, the observations between the first and third quartiles. We also see the whiskers. On the left, the whisker extends to the minimum value of `MedInc`; on the right, the whisker goes up to the third quartile plus 1.5 times the IQR. Values beyond the right whisker are represented as dots and could constitute outliers:

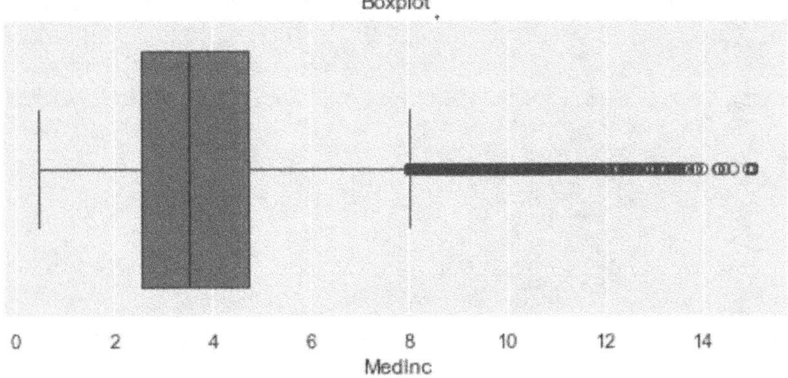

Figure 5.1 – Boxplot of the MedInc variable highlighting potential
outliers on the right tail of the distribution

> **Note**
>
> As shown in *Figure 5.1*, the boxplot returns asymmetric boundaries denoted by the varying lengths of the left and right whiskers. This makes boxplots a suitable method for identifying outliers in highly skewed distributions. As we'll see in the coming recipes, alternative methods to identify outliers create symmetric boundaries around the center of the distribution, which may not be the best option for asymmetric distributions.

5. Let's now create a function to plot a boxplot next to a histogram:

```python
def plot_boxplot_and_hist(data, variable):
    f, (ax_box, ax_hist) = plt.subplots(
        2, sharex=True,
        gridspec_kw={"height_ratios": (0.50, 0.85)})
    sns.boxplot(x=data[variable], ax=ax_box)
    sns.histplot(data=data, x=variable, ax=ax_hist)
    plt.show()
```

6. Let's use the previous function to create the plots for the `MedInc` variable:

```python
plot_boxplot_and_hist(X, "MedInc")
```

In the following figure, we can see the relationship between the boxplot and the variable's distribution shown in the histogram. Note how most of `MedInc`'s observations are located within the IQR box. `MedInc`'s potential outliers lie on the right tail, corresponding to people with unusually high-income salaries:

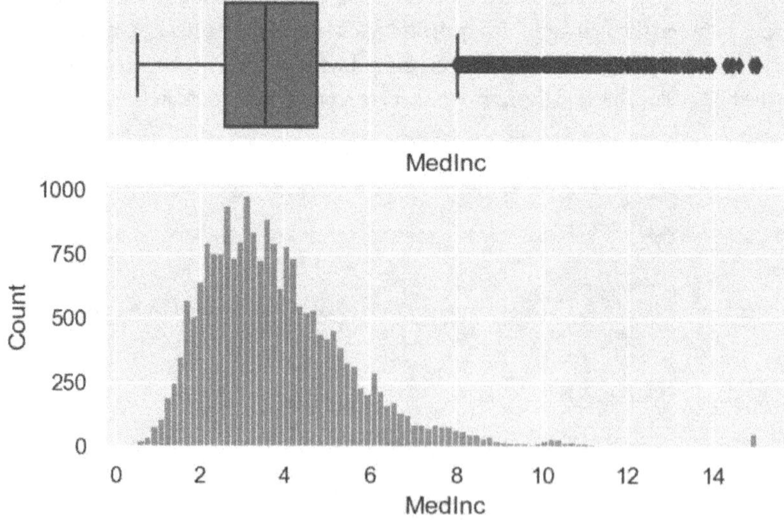

Figure 5.2 – Boxplot and histogram – two ways of displaying a variable's distribution

Now that we've seen how we can visualize outliers, let's see how to calculate the limits beyond which we find outliers at each side of the distribution.

7. Let's create a function that returns the limits based on the IQR proximity rule:

```python
def find_limits(df, variable, fold):
    q1 = df[variable].quantile(0.25)
    q3 = df[variable].quantile(0.75)
    IQR = q3 - q1
    lower_limit = q1 - (IQR * fold)
    upper_limit = q3 + (IQR * fold)
    return lower_limit, upper_limit
```

> **Note**
>
> Remember that the first and third quartiles are equivalent to the 25th and 75th percentiles. That's why we use pandas' `quantile` to determine those values.

8. With the function from *step 7*, we'll calculate the extreme limits for `MedInc`:

```python
lower_limit, upper_limit = find_limits(
    X, "MedInc", 1.5)
```

If we now execute `lower_limit` and `upper_limit`, we will see the values `-0.7063` and `8.013`. The lower limit is beyond `MedInc`'s minimum value, hence in the boxplot, the whisker only goes up to the minimum value. The upper limit, on the other hand, coincides with the right whisker's limit.

> **Note**
>
> Common values to multiply the IQR are `1.5`, which is the default value in boxplots, or `3` if we want to be more conservative.

9. Let's display the box plot and histogram for the `HouseAge` variable:

```python
plot_boxplot_and_hist(X, "HouseAge")
```

We can see that this variable does not seem to contain outliers, and hence the whiskers in the box plot extend to the minimum and maximum values:

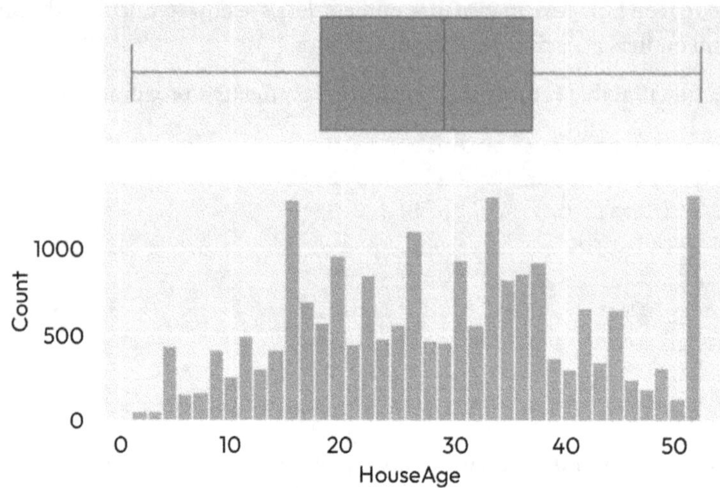

Figure 5.3 – Boxplot and histogram of the HouseAge variable

10. Let's find the variable's limits according to the IQR proximity rule:

```
lower_limit, upper_limit = find_limits(
    X, "HouseAge", 1.5)
```

If we execute `lower_limit` and `upper_limit`, we will see the values `-10.5` and `65.5`, which are beyond the edges of the plots, and hence we don't see any outliers.

How it works...

In this recipe, we used the `boxplot` method from Seaborn to create the boxplots and then we calculated the limits beyond which a value could be considered an outlier based on the IQR proximity rule.

In *Figure 5.2*, we saw that the box in the boxplot for `MedInc` extended from approximately 2 to 5, corresponding to the first and third quantiles (you can determine these values precisely by executing `X["MedInc"].quantile(0.25)` and `X["MedInc"].quantile(0.75)`). We also saw that the whiskers start at `MedInc`'s minimum on the left and extend up to `8.013` on the right (we know this value exactly because we calculated it in *step 8*). `MedInc` showed values greater than `8.013`, which were displayed in the boxplot as dots. Those are the values that could be considered outliers.

In *Figure 5.3*, we displayed the boxplot for the `HouseAge` variable. The box included values ranging from approximately 18 to 35 (you can determine the precise values by executing `X["HouseAge"].quantile(0.25)` and `X["HouseAge"].quantile(0.75)`). The whiskers extended to the minimum and maximum values of the distribution. The limits of the whiskers in the plot did not coincide with those based on the IQR proximity rule (which we calculated in *step 10*) because these limits were far beyond the value range observed for this variable.

Finding outliers using the mean and standard deviation

In normally distributed variables, around 99.8% of the observations lie within the interval comprising the mean plus and minus three times the standard deviation. Thus, values beyond those limits can be considered outliers; they are rare.

> **Note**
>
> Using the mean and standard deviation to detect outliers has some drawbacks. Firstly, it assumes a normal distribution, including outliers. Secondly, outliers strongly influence the mean and standard deviation. Therefore, a recommended alternative is the **Median Absolute Deviation (MAD)**, which we'll discuss in the next recipe.

In this recipe, we will identify outliers as those observations that lie outside the interval delimited by the mean plus and minus three times the standard deviation.

How to do it...

Let's begin the recipe by importing the Python libraries and loading the dataset:

1. Let's import the Python libraries and dataset:

```python
import numpy as np
import matplotlib.pyplot as plt
import seaborn as sns
from sklearn.datasets import load_breast_cancer
```

2. Load the breast cancer dataset from scikit-learn:

```python
X, y = load_breast_cancer(
    return_X_y=True, as_frame=True)
```

3. Create a function to plot a boxplot next to a histogram:

```python
def plot_boxplot_and_hist(data, variable):
    f, (ax_box, ax_hist) = plt.subplots(
        2, sharex=True,
        gridspec_kw={"height_ratios": (0.50, 0.85)})
    sns.boxplot(x=data[variable], ax=ax_box)
    sns.histplot(data=data, x=variable, ax=ax_hist)
    plt.show()
```

> **Note**
>
> We discussed the function from *step 3* in the previous recipe, *Visualizing outliers with boxplots and the inter-quartile proximity rule*.

4. Let's plot the distribution of the `mean  smoothness` variable:

```
plot_boxplot_and_hist(X, "mean smoothness")
```

In the following boxplot, we see that the variable's values show a distribution like the normal distribution, and it has six outliers – one on the left and five on the right tail:

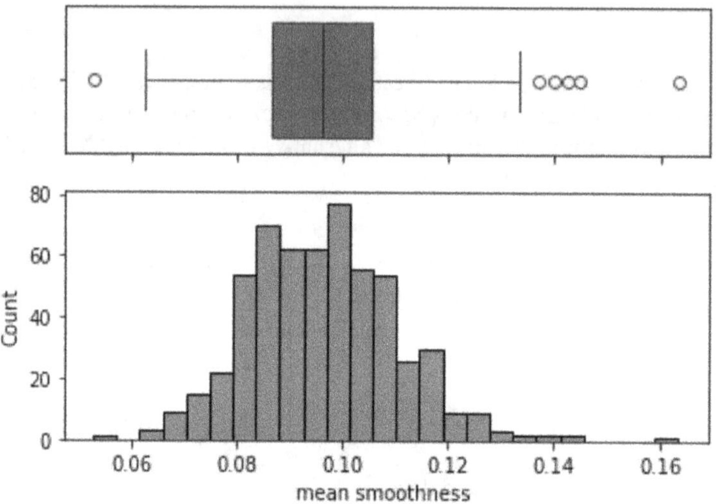

Figure 5.4 – Boxplot and histogram of the variable mean smoothness

5. Create a function that returns the mean plus and minus `fold` times the standard deviation, where `fold` is a parameter to the function:

```
def find_limits(df, variable, fold):
    var_mean = df[variable].mean()
    var_std = df[variable].std()
    lower_limit = var_mean - fold * var_std
    upper_limit = var_mean + fold * var_std
    return lower_limit, upper_limit
```

6. Use the function to identify the extreme limits of the `mean  smoothness` variable:

```
lower_limit, upper_limit = find_limits(
    X, "mean smoothness", 3)
```

If we now execute `lower_limit` or `upper_limit`, we will see the values `0.0541` and `0.13855`, corresponding to the limits beyond which we can consider a value an outlier.

> **Note**
>
> The interval between the mean plus and minus three times the standard deviation encloses 99.87% of the observations if the variable is normally distributed. For less conservative limits, we could multiply the standard deviation by 2 or 2.5, which would produce intervals that enclose 95.4% and 97.6% of the observations, respectively.

7. Create a Boolean vector that flags observations with values beyond the limits determined in *step 6*:

```python
outliers = np.where(
    (X[«mean smoothness»] > upper_limit) |
    (X[«mean smoothness»] < lower_limit),
    True,
    False
)
```

If we now execute `outliers.sum()`, we will see the value 5, indicating that there are five outliers or observations that are smaller or greater than the extreme values found with the mean and the standard deviation. According to these limits, we'd identify one outlier less compared to the IQR rule.

8. Let's add red vertical lines to the histogram from *step 3* to highlight the limits determined by using the mean and the standard deviation:

```python
def plot_boxplot_and_hist(data, variable):
    f, (ax_box, ax_hist) = plt.subplots(
        2, sharex=True,
        gridspec_kw={"height_ratios": (0.50, 0.85)})
    sns.boxplot(x=data[variable], ax=ax_box)
    sns.histplot(data=data, x=variable, ax=ax_hist)
    plt.vlines(
        x=lower_limit, ymin=0, ymax=80, color='r')
    plt.vlines(
        x=upper_limit, ymin=0, ymax=80, color='r')
    plt.show()
```

9. And now let's make the plots:

```python
plot_boxplot_and_hist(X, "mean smoothness")
```

In the following plot, we see that the limits observed by the IQR proximity rule in the box plot are less conservative than those identified by the mean and the standard deviation. Hence why we observe six potential outliers in the boxplot, but only five based on the mean and standard deviation calculations:

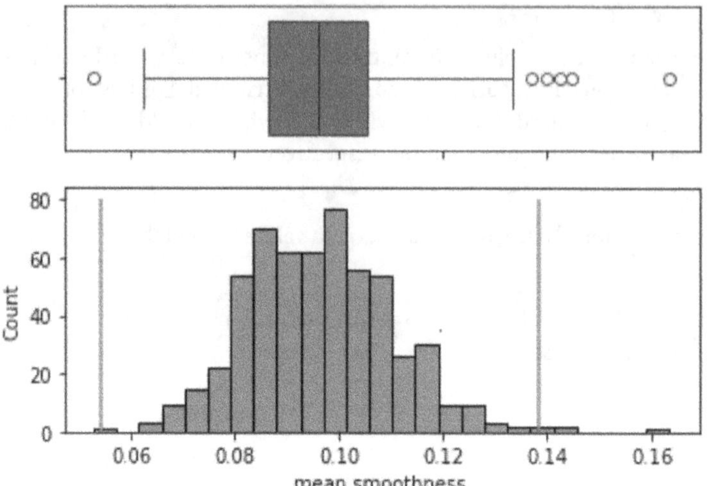

Figure 5.5 – Comparison of the limits between the whiskers in the boxplot and those
determined by using the mean and the standard deviation (vertical lines in the histogram)

The boundaries derived from the mean and standard deviation are symmetric. They extend
equidistantly from the center of the distribution toward both tails. As previously mentioned,
these boundaries are only suitable for normally distributed variables.

How it works...

With pandas' `mean()` and `std()`, we captured the mean and standard deviation of the variable. We
determined the limits as the mean plus and minus three times the standard deviation. To highlight
the outliers, we used NumPy's `where()`. The `where()` function scanned the rows of the variable,
and if the value was greater than the upper limit or smaller than the lower limit, it was assigned `True`,
and alternatively `False`. Finally, we used pandas' `sum()` over this Boolean vector to calculate the
total number of outliers.

Finally, we compared the boundaries to determine outliers returned by the IQR proximity rule, which
we discussed in the previous recipe, *Visualizing outliers with boxplots and the inter-quartile proximity
rule*, and the mean and the standard deviation. We observed that the limits of the IQR rule are less
conservative. That means that with the IQR rule, we'd flag more outliers in this particular variable.

Using the median absolute deviation to find outliers

The mean and the standard deviation are heavily impacted by outliers. Hence, using these parameters
to identify outliers can defeat the purpose. A better way to identify outliers is by using MAD. MAD is
the median of the absolute deviation between each observation and the median value of the variable:

$$MAD = b \times Median(|xi - Median(X)|)$$

In the previous equation, x_i is each observation in the X variable. The beauty of MAD is that it uses the median instead of the mean, which is robust to outliers. The b constant is used to estimate the standard deviation from MAD, and if we assume normality, then $b = 1.4826$.

> **Note**
>
> If the variable is assumed to have a different distribution, b is then calculated as 1 divided by the 75th percentile. In the case of normality, 1/75th percentile = 1.4826.

After computing MAD, we use the median and MAD to establish distribution limits, designating values beyond these limits as outliers. The limits are set as the median plus and minus a multiple of MAD, typically ranging from 2 to 3.5. The multiplication factor we choose reflects how stringent we want to be (the higher, the more conservative). In this recipe, we will identify outliers using MAD.

How to do it...

Let's begin the recipe by importing the Python libraries and loading the dataset:

1. Let's import the Python libraries and dataset:

```python
import numpy as np
import matplotlib.pyplot as plt
import seaborn as sns
from sklearn.datasets import load_breast_cancer
```

2. Load the breast cancer dataset from scikit-learn:

```python
X, y = load_breast_cancer(
    return_X_y=True, as_frame=True)
```

3. Create a function that returns the limits based on MAD:

```python
def find_limits(df, variable, fold):
    median = df[variable].median()
    center = df[variable] - median
    MAD = center.abs().median() * 1.4826
    lower_limit = median - fold * MAD
    upper_limit = median + fold * MAD
    return lower_limit, upper_limit
```

4. Let's use the function to capture the extreme limits of the mean smoothness variable:

```python
lower_limit, upper_limit = find_limits(
    X, "mean smoothness", 3)
```

If we execute `lower_limit` or `upper_limit`, we will see the values `0.0536` and `0.13812`, corresponding to the limits beyond which we can consider a value an outlier.

5. Let's create a Boolean vector that flags observations with values beyond the limits:

```python
outliers = np.where(
    (X[«mean smoothness»] > upper_limit) |
    (X[«mean smoothness»] < lower_limit),
    True,
    False
)
```

If we now execute `outliers.sum()`, we will see the value 5, indicating that there are five outliers or observations that are smaller or greater than the extreme values found with MAD.

6. Let's make a function to plot a boxplot next to a histogram of a variable, highlighting in the histogram the limits calculated in *step 4*:

```python
def plot_boxplot_and_hist(data, variable):
    f, (ax_box, ax_hist) = plt.subplots(
        2, sharex=True,
        gridspec_kw={"height_ratios": (0.50, 0.85)})
    sns.boxplot(x=data[variable], ax=ax_box)
    sns.histplot(data=data, x=variable, ax=ax_hist)
    plt.vlines(
        x=lower_limit, ymin=0, ymax=80, color='r')
    plt.vlines(
        x=upper_limit, ymin=0, ymax=80, color='r')
    plt.show()
```

7. And now let's make the plots:

```python
plot_boxplot_and_hist(X, "mean smoothness")
```

In the following plot, we see that the limits observed by the IQR proximity rule in the box plot are less conservative than those identified by using MAD. MAD returns symmetric boundaries, while the boxplot generates asymmetric boundaries, which are more suitable for highly skewed distributions:

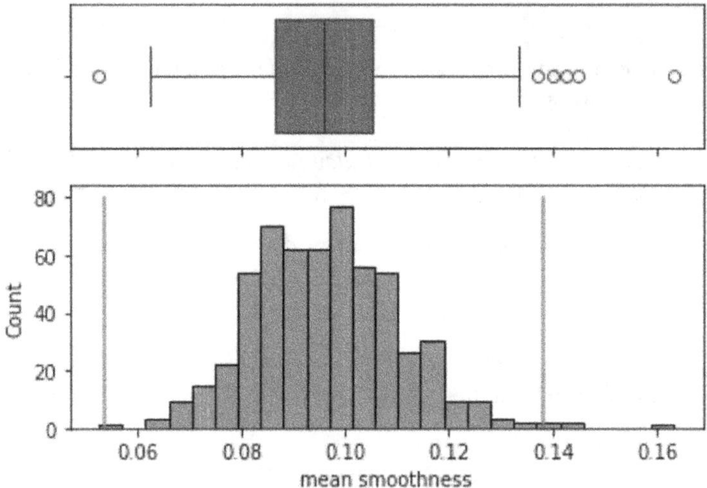

Figure 5.6 – Comparison of the limits between the whiskers in the
boxplot and those determined by using MAD

> **Note**
>
> Detecting outliers with MAD requires that the variable has certain variability. If more than 50% of the values in a variable are identical, the median coincides with the most frequent value, and MAD=0. This means that all values different from the median will be flagged as outliers. This constitutes another limitation of using MAD in outlier detection.

That's it! You now know how to identify outliers using the median and MAD.

How it works...

We determined the median with pandas' `median()` and the absolute difference with pandas' `abs()`. Next, we used the NumPy `where()` function to create a Boolean vector with `True` if a value was greater than the upper limit or smaller than the lower limit, otherwise `False`. Finally, we used pandas' `sum()` over this Boolean vector to calculate the total number of outliers.

Finally, we compared the boundaries to determine outliers returned by the IQR proximity rule, which we discussed in the *Visualizing outliers with boxplots and the inter-quartile range proximity rule* recipe, and those returned by using MAD. The limits returned by the IQR rule were less conservative. This behavior can be changed by multiplying the IQR by 3 instead of 1.5, which is the default value in boxplots. In addition, we noted that MAD returns symmetric boundaries, whereas the boxplot provided asymmetric limits, which could be better suited for asymmetric distributions.

See also

For a thorough discussion of the advantages and limitations of the different methods to detect outliers, check out the following resources:

- Rousseeuw PJ, Croux C. *Alternatives to the Median Absolute deviation.* Journal of the American Statistical Association, 1993. `http://www.jstor.org/stable/2291267`.

- Leys C, et. al. *Detecting outliers: Do not use standard deviation around the mean, use absolute deviation around the median.* Journal of Experimental Social Psychology, 2013. `http://dx.doi.org/10.1016/j.jesp.2013.03.013`.

- Thériault R, et. al. *Check your outliers! An introduction to identifying statistical outliers in R with easystats.* Behavior Research Methods, 2024. `https://doi.org/10.3758/s13428-024-02356-w`.

Removing outliers

Recent studies distinguish three types of outliers: error outliers, interesting outliers, and random outliers. Error outliers are likely due to human or methodological errors and should be either corrected or removed from the data analysis. In this recipe, we'll assume outliers are errors (you don't want to remove interesting or random outliers) and remove them from the dataset.

How to do it...

We'll use the IQR proximity rule to find the outliers and then remove them from the data using pandas and Feature-engine:

1. Let's import the Python libraries, functions, and classes:

```python
import matplotlib.pyplot as plt
import seaborn as sns
from sklearn.datasets import fetch_california_housing
from sklearn.model_selection import train_test_split
from feature_engine.outliers import OutlierTrimmer
```

2. Load the California housing dataset from scikit-learn and separate it into train and test sets:

```python
X, y = fetch_california_housing(
    return_X_y=True, as_frame=True)
X_train, X_test, y_train, y_test = train_test_split(
    X, y, test_size=0.3, random_state=0)
```

3. Let's create a function to find the limits beyond which we'll consider a data point an outlier using the IQR proximity rule:

```python
def find_limits(df, variable, fold):
    q1 = df[variable].quantile(0.25)
    q3 = df[variable].quantile(0.75)
    IQR = q3 - q1
    lower_limit = q1 - (IQR * fold)
    upper_limit = q3 + (IQR * fold)
    return lower_limit, upper_limit
```

> **Note**
>
> In *step 3*, we use the IQR proximity rule to find the limits beyond which data points will be considered outliers, which we discussed in the *Visualizing outliers with boxplots and the inter-quartile proximity rule* recipe. Alternatively, you can identify outliers with the mean and the standard deviation or MAD, as we covered in the *Finding outliers using the mean and standard deviation* and *Using the median absolute deviation to find outliers* recipes.

4. Using the function from *step 3*, let's determine the limits of the `MedInc` variable:

```python
lower, upper = find_limits(X_train, "MedInc", 3)
```

If you execute `print(lower_limit, upper_limit)`, you'll see the result of the previous command: `(-3.925900000000002, 11.232600000000001)`.

5. Let's retain the observations in the train and test sets whose values are greater than or equal to (`ge`) the lower limit:

```python
inliers = X_train["MedInc"].ge(lower)
train_t = X_train.loc[inliers]
inliers = X_test["MedInc"].ge(lower)
test_t = X_test.loc[inliers]
```

6. Let's retain the observations whose values are lower than or equal to (`le`) the upper limit:

```python
inliers = X_train["MedInc"].le(upper)
train_t = X_train.loc[inliers]
inliers = X_test["MedInc"].le(upper)
test_t = X_test.loc[inliers]
```

Go ahead and execute `X_train.shape` followed by `train_t.shape` to corroborate that the transformed DataFrame contains fewer observations than the original one after removing the outliers.

We can remove outliers across multiple variables simultaneously with `feature-engine`.

7.   Set up a transformer to identify outliers in three variables by using the IQR rule:

```python
trimmer = OutlierTrimmer(
    variables = ["MedInc", "HouseAge", "Population"],
    capping_method="iqr",
    tail="both",
    fold=1.5,
)
```

> **Note**
>
> `OutlierTrimmer` can identify boundaries using the IQR, as we show in this recipe, as well as by using the mean and standard deviation, or MAD. You need to change `capping_method` to gaussian or mad, respectively.

8.   Fit the transformer to the training set so that it learns those limits:

```python
trimmer.fit(X_train)
```

> **Note**
>
> By executing `trimmer.left_tail_caps_`, we can visualize the lower limits for the three variables: `{'MedInc': -0.6776500000000012, 'HouseAge': -10.5, 'Population': -626.0}`. By executing `trimmer.right_tail_caps_`, we can see the variables' upper limits: `{'MedInc': 7.984350000000001, 'HouseAge': 65.5, 'Population': 3134.0}`.

9.   Finally, let's remove outliers from the train and test sets:

```python
X_train_t = trimmer.transform(X_train)
X_test_t = trimmer.transform(X_test)
```

To finish with the recipe, let's compare the distribution of a variable before and after removing outliers.

10.   Let's create a function to display a boxplot on top of a histogram:

```python
def plot_boxplot_and_hist(data, variable):
    f, (ax_box, ax_hist) = plt.subplots(
        2, sharex=True,
        gridspec_kw={"height_ratios": (0.50, 0.85)}
    )
    sns.boxplot(x=data[variable], ax=ax_box)
    sns.histplot(data=data, x=variable, ax=ax_hist)
    plt.show()
```

> **Note**
>
> We discussed the code in *step 10* in the *Visualizing outliers with boxplots* recipe earlier in this chapter.

11. Let's plot the distribution of `MedInc` before removing the outliers:

```
plot_boxplot_and_hist(X_train, "MedInc")
```

In the following plot, we see that `MedInc` is skewed and observations greater than 8 are marked as outliers:

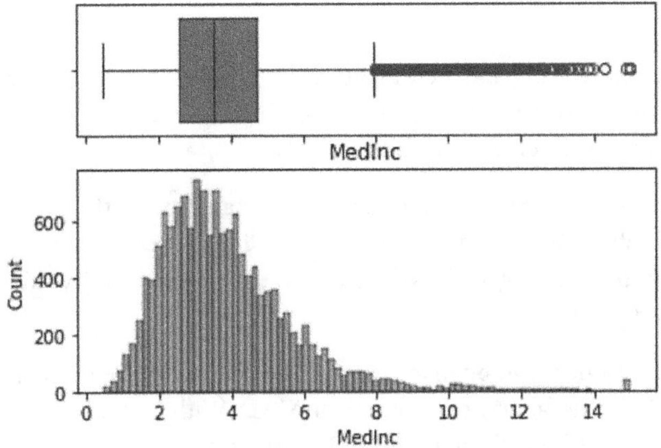

Figure 5.7– Boxplot and the histogram of MedInc before removing outliers.

12. Finally, let's plot the distribution of `MedInc` after removing the outliers:

```
plot_boxplot_and_hist(train_t, "MedInc")
```

After removing outliers, `MedInc` seems less skewed and its values more evenly distributed:

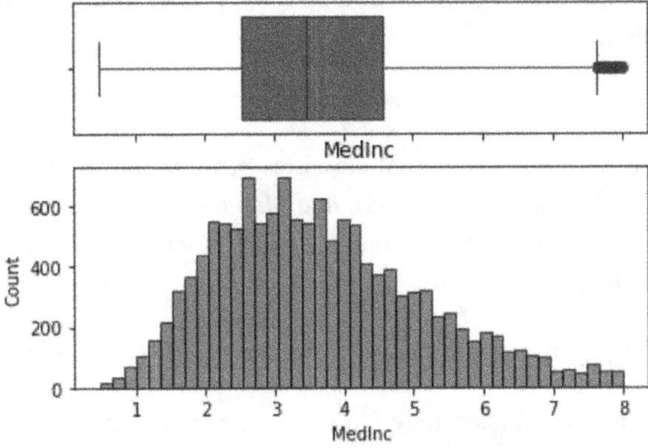

Figure 5.8 – Boxplot and the histogram of MedInc after removing outliers

> **Note**
>
> Using the IQR rule over the transformed variable reveals new outliers. This is not surprising; removing observations at the extremes of the distribution alters parameters such as the median and quartile values, which in turn determine the length of the whiskers, potentially identifying additional observations as outliers. The tools that we use to identify outliers are just that: tools. To unequivocally identify outliers, we need to support these tools with additional data analysis.

If thinking of removing error outliers from the dataset, make sure to compare and report the results with and without outliers, to see the extent of their impact on the models.

How it works...

The `ge()` and `le()` methods from pandas created Boolean vectors identifying observations exceeding or falling below thresholds set by the IQR proximity rule. We used these vectors with pandas `loc` to retain observations within the interval defined by the IQR.

The `feature-engine` library's `OutlierTrimmer()` automates the procedure of removing outliers for multiple variables. `OutlierTrimmer()` can identify outliers based on the mean and standard deviation, IQR proximity rule, MAD, or quantiles. We can modify this behavior through the `capping_method` parameter.

The methods to identify outliers can be made more or less conservative by changing the factor by which we multiply the IQR, the standard deviation, or MAD. With `OutlierTrimmer()`, we can control the strength of the methods through the `fold` parameter.

With `tails` set to `"both"`, `OutlierTrimmer()` found and removed outliers at both ends of the variables' distribution. To remove outliers just on one of the tails, we can pass `"left"` or `"right"` to the `tails` parameter.

`OutlierTrimmer()` adopts the scikit-learn functionality with the `fit()` method, to learn parameters, and `transform()` to modify the dataset. With `fit()`, the transformer learned and stored the limits for each variable. With `transform()`, it removed the outliers from the data, returning pandas DataFrames.

See also

This is the study that I mentioned earlier that classifies outliers into errors; it is interesting and random: Leys C, et.al. 2019. *How to Classify, Detect, and Manage Univariate and Multivariate Outliers, with Emphasis on Pre-Registration*. International Review of Social Psychology. `https://doi.org/10.5334/irsp.289`.

Bringing outliers back within acceptable limits

Removing error outliers can be a valid strategy. However, this approach can reduce statistical power, in particular when there are outliers across many variables, because we end up removing big parts of the dataset. An alternative way to handle error outliers is by bringing outliers back within acceptable limits. In practice, what this means is replacing the value of the outliers with some thresholds identified with the IQR proximity rule, the mean and standard deviation, or MAD. In this recipe, we'll replace outlier values using `pandas` and `feature-engine`.

How to do it...

We'll use the mean and standard deviation to find outliers and then replace their values using `pandas` and `feature-engine`:

1. Let's import the required Python libraries and functions:

    ```python
    from sklearn.datasets import load_breast_cancer
    from sklearn.model_selection import train_test_split
    from feature_engine.outliers import Winsorizer
    ```

2. Load the breast cancer dataset from scikit-learn and separate it into train and test sets:

    ```python
    X, y = load_breast_cancer(
        return_X_y=True, as_frame=True)
    X_train, X_test, y_train, y_test = train_test_split(
        X, y, test_size=0.3, random_state=0)
    ```

3. Let's create a function to find outliers using the mean and standard deviation:

    ```python
    def find_limits(df, variable, fold):
        var_mean = df[variable].mean()
        var_std = df[variable].std()
        lower_limit = var_mean - fold * var_std
        upper_limit = var_mean + fold * var_std
        return lower_limit, upper_limit
    ```

> **Note**
>
> In *step 3*, we use the mean and standard deviation to find the limits beyond which data points will be considered outliers, as discussed in the *Finding outliers using the mean and standard deviation* recipe. Alternatively, you can identify outliers with the IQR rule or MAD, as we covered in the *Visualizing outliers with boxplots and the inter-quartile proximity rule* and *Using the median absolute deviation to find outliers* recipes.

4. Using the function from *step 3*, let's determine the limits of the mean smoothness variable, which follows approximately a Gaussian distribution:

    ```python
    var = "worst smoothness"
    lower_limit, upper_limit = find_limits(
        X_train, var, 3)
    ```

5. Let's make a copy of the original datasets:

```
train_t = X_train.copy()
test_t = X_test.copy()
```

6. Now, replace outliers with the lower or upper limits from *step 4* in the new DataFrames:

```
train_t[var] = train_t[var].clip(
    lower=lower_limit, upper=upper_limit)
test_t[var] = test_t[var].clip(
    lower=lower_limit, upper=upper_limit)
```

To corroborate that the outliers were replaced with the values determined in *step 4*, execute `train_t["worst smoothness"].agg(["min", "max"])` to obtain the new maximum and minimum values. They should coincide with the minimum and maximum values of the variable, or the limits returned in *step 4*.

We can replace outliers in multiple variables simultaneously by utilizing `feature-engine`.

7. Let's set up a transformer to replace outliers in two variables, using limits determined with the mean and standard deviation:

```
capper = Winsorizer(
    variables=[«worst smoothness», «worst texture»],
    capping_method="gaussian",
    tail="both",
    fold=3,
)
```

> **Note**
>
> `Winsorizer` can identify boundaries using the mean and standard deviation, as we show in this recipe, as well as the IQR proximity rule and MAD. You need to change `capping_method` to `iqr` or `mad`, respectively.

8. Let's fit the transformer to the data so that it learns those limits:

```
capper.fit(X_train)
```

By executing `capper.left_tail_caps_`, we can visualize the lower limits for the two variables: `{'worst smoothness': 0.06364743973736293, 'worst texture': 7.115307053129349}`. By executing `capper.right_tail_caps_`, we can see the variables' upper limits: `{'worst smoothness': 0.20149734880520967, 'worst texture': 43.97692158753917}`.

9. Finally, let's replace the outliers with the limits from *step 8*:

```
X_train = capper.transform(X_train)
X_test = capper.transform(X_test)
```

If we now execute `train_t[capper.variables_].agg(["min", "max"])`, we'll see that the maximum and minimum values of the transformed DataFrame coincide with either the maximum and minimum values of the variables or the identified limits, whatever comes first:

```
     worst smoothness  worst texture
min          0.071170      12.020000
max          0.201411      43.953738
```

If you are planning to cap variables, make sure you compare the performance of your models or the results of your analysis before and after replacing outliers.

How it works...

The `clip()` function from pandas is used to cap values at lower or upper specified limits. In this recipe, we found those limits using the mean and standard deviation, and then clipped the variable so that all observations took values within those limits. The minimum value of the `worst smoothness` variable was actually greater than the lower limit we found in *step 4*, so no values were replaced at the left of its distribution. However, there were values greater than the upper limit from *step 4*, and those were replaced with the limit. This means that the minimum value of the transformed variable and the original variable coincide, but the maximum values do not.

We used `feature-engine` to replace outliers in multiple variables simultaneously. `Winsorizer()` can identify outliers based on the mean and standard deviation, the IQR proximity rule, MAD, or by using percentiles. We can modify this behavior through the `capping_method` parameter.

The methods to identify outliers can be made more or less conservative by changing the factor by which we multiply the IQR, the standard deviation, or MAD. With `Winsorizer()`, we can control the strength of the methods through the `fold` parameter.

With `tails` set to `"both"`, `Winsorizer()` found and replaced outliers at both ends of the variables' distribution. To replace outliers at either end, we can pass `"left"` or `"right"` to the `tails` parameter.

`Winsorizer()` adopts the scikit-learn functionality with the `fit()` method, to learn parameters, and `transform()` to modify the dataset. With `fit()`, the transformer learned and stored the limits for each variable. With `transform()`, it replaced the values of the outliers, returning pandas DataFrames.

See also

`feature-engine` has `ArbitraryOutlierCapper()`, which caps variables at arbitrary minimum and maximum values: `https://feature-engine.readthedocs.io/en/latest/api_doc/outliers/ArbitraryOutlierCapper.html`.

Applying winsorization

Winsorizing, or winsorization, consists of replacing extreme, poorly known observations, that is, outliers, with the magnitude of the next largest (or smallest) observation. It's similar to the procedure described in the previous recipe, *Bringing outliers back within acceptable limits*, but not exactly the same. Winsorization involves replacing the *same number of outliers* at both ends of the distribution, which makes Winsorization a symmetric process. This guarantees that the **Winsorized mean**, that is, the mean estimated after replacing outliers, remains a robust estimator of the central tendency of the variable.

In practice, to remove a similar number of observations at both tails, we'd use percentiles. For example, the 5th percentile is the value below which 5% of the observations lie and the 95th percentile is the value beyond which 5% of the observations lie. Using these values as replacements might result in replacing a similar number of observations on both tails, but it's not guaranteed. If the dataset contains repeated values, obtaining reliable percentiles is challenging and can lead to an uneven replacement of values at each tail. If this happens, then the winsorized mean is not a good estimator of the central tendency. In this recipe, we will apply winsorization.

How to do it...

We will cap all variables of the breast cancer dataset at their 5th and 95th percentiles:

1. Let's import the required Python libraries and functions:

    ```python
    import matplotlib.pyplot as plt
    import seaborn as sns
    from sklearn.datasets import load_breast_cancer
    from sklearn.model_selection import train_test_split
    ```

2. Load the breast cancer dataset from scikit-learn:

    ```python
    X, y = load_breast_cancer(
        return_X_y=True, as_frame=True)
    ```

3. Separate the data into a train and test sets:

    ```python
    X_train, X_test, y_train, y_test = train_test_split(
        X,
        y,
        test_size=0.3,
        random_state=0,
    )
    ```

4. Capture the 5th and 95th percentiles of each variable in dictionaries:

```
q05 = X_train.quantile(0.05).to_dict()
q95 = X_train.quantile(0.95).to_dict()
```

5. Let's now replace values beyond those percentiles with the respective percentiles for all variables at once:

```
train_t = X_train.clip(lower=q05, upper=q95)
test_t = X_test.clip(lower=q05, upper=q95)
```

6. Let's display the minimum, maximum, and mean values of one variable before winsorization:

```
var = 'worst smoothness'
X_train[var].agg(["min", "max", "mean"])
```

We can see the values in the following output:

```
min           0.071170
max           0.222600
mean          0.132529
Name: worst smoothness, dtype: float64
```

7. Display the minimum, maximum, and mean values of the same variable after winsorization:

```
train_t[var].agg([„min", „max"])
```

In the following output, we can see that the minimum and maximum values correspond to the percentiles. However, the mean is quite similar to the original mean of the variable:

```
min           0.096053
max           0.173215
mean          0.132063
Name: worst smoothness, dtype: float64
```

> **Note**
>
> If you want to use winsorization as part of a scikit-learn pipeline, you can use the `feature-engine` library's `Winsorizer()`, by setting it up as follows:
>
> ```
> capper = Winsorizer(
>
>     capping_method="quantiles",
>
>     tail="both",
>
>     fold=0.05,
>
> )
> ```
>
> After this, proceed with the `fit()` and `transform()` methods as described in the *Bringing outliers back within acceptable limits* recipe.

It's worth noting that despite employing percentiles, the procedure didn't precisely replace the same number of observations on both sides of the distribution. If you intend to winsorize your variables, compare the outcomes of your analyses before and after winsorization.

How it works...

We used pandas' `quantiles()` to obtain the 5th and 95th percentiles of all the variables in the dataset, and combined it with `to_dict()` to retain those percentiles in dictionaries, where the keys were the variables and the values were the percentiles. We then passed these dictionaries to pandas' `clip()` to replace values smaller or larger than those percentiles by the percentiles. By using dictionaries, we capped multiple variables at once.

See also

For more details about how winsorization affects the mean and standard deviation in symmetric and asymmetric replacements, check out the original article:

Dixon W. *Simplified Estimation from Censored Normal Samples. The Annals of Mathematical Statistics*, 1960. `http://www.jstor.org/stable/2237953`

6

Extracting Features from Date and Time Variables

Date and time variables contain information about dates, times, or both, and in programming, we refer to them collectively as `datetime` features. Date of birth, the time of an event, and the date and time of the last payment are examples of `datetime` variables.

Because of their nature, `datetime` features typically exhibit high cardinality. This means that they contain a huge number of unique values, each corresponding to a specific date and/or time combination. We don't normally use `datetime` variables for machine learning models in their raw format. Instead, we enrich the dataset by extracting multiple features from these variables. These new features will typically have reduced cardinality, and allow us to capture meaningful information, such as trends, seasonality, and important events and tendencies.

In this chapter, we will explore how to extract features from dates and time by utilizing the `pandas` `dt` module, and then automate this procedure with `feature-engine`.

This chapter will cover the following recipes:

- Extracting features from dates with `pandas`
- Extracting features from time with `pandas`
- Capturing elapsed time between `datetime` variables
- Working with time in different time zones
- Automating `datetime` feature extraction with `feature-engine`

Technical requirements

In this chapter, we will use the `pandas`, `numpy`, and `feature-engine` Python libraries.

Extracting features from dates with pandas

The values of datetime variables can be dates, time, or both. We'll begin by focusing on those variables that contain dates. We rarely use raw dates with machine learning algorithms. Instead, we extract simpler features, such as the year, month, or day of the week, that allow us to capture insights such as seasonality, periodicity, and trends.

The pandas Python library is great for working with date and time. Utilizing the pandas dt module, we can access the datetime properties of a pandas Series to extract many features. However, to leverage this functionality, the variables need to be cast into a data type that supports these operations, such as datetime or timedelta.

> **Note**
>
> The datetime variables can be cast as objects, particularly when we load the data from a CSV file. To extract the date and time features that we will discuss throughout this chapter, it is necessary to recast the variables as datetime.

In this recipe, we will learn how to extract features from dates by utilizing pandas.

Getting ready

The following are some of the features that we can extract from the date part of the datetime variable off the shelf using pandas:

- pandas.Series.dt.year
- pandas.Series.dt.quarter
- pandas.Series.dt.month
- pandas.Series.dt.isocalendar().week
- pandas.Series.dt.day
- pandas.Series.dt.day_of_week
- pandas.Series.dt.weekday
- pandas.Series.dt.dayofyear
- pandas.Series.dt.day_of_year

We can use the features we've obtained with pandas to create even more features, such as the semester or whether it is a weekend. We will learn how to do this in the next section.

How to do it...

To proceed with the recipe, let's import `pandas` and `numpy`, and create a sample DataFrame:

1. Let's import the libraries:

```
import numpy as np
import pandas as pd
```

2. We'll start by creating 20 `datetime` values beginning from `2024-05-17` at midnight and followed by increments of 1 day. Then, we'll capture those values in a `DataFrame` instance and display the top five rows:

```
rng_ = pd.date_range(
    "2024-05-17", periods=20, freq="D")
data = pd.DataFrame({"date": rng_})
data.head()
```

In the following output, we see the variable containing dates that we created in *Step 2*:

	date
0	2024-05-17
1	2024-05-18
2	2024-05-19
3	2024-05-20
4	2024-05-21

Figure 6.1 – Top rows of a DataFrame with a datetime variable containing only dates

> **Note**
>
> We can check the data format of the variable by executing `data["date"].dtypes`. If the variable is cast as an object, we can convert it into `datetime` format by executing `data["date_dt"] = pd.to_datetime(data["date"])`.

3. Let's extract the year part of the date in a new column and display the top five rows of the resulting DataFrame:

```
data["year"] = data["date"].dt.year
data.head()
```

We see the new `year` variable in the following output:

	date	year
0	2024-05-17	2024
1	2024-05-18	2024
2	2024-05-19	2024
3	2024-05-20	2024
4	2024-05-21	2024

Figure 6.2 – First five rows of the DataFrame with the year variable extracted from the date

4. Let's extract the quarter of the year out of the date into a new column and display the top five rows:

```python
data["quarter"] = data["date"].dt.quarter
data[["date", "quarter"]].head()
```

We see the new `quarter` variable in the following output:

	date	quarter
0	2024-05-17	2
1	2024-05-18	2
2	2024-05-19	2
3	2024-05-20	2
4	2024-05-21	2

Figure 6.3 – The first five rows of a DataFrame with the quarter variable extracted from the date

5. With `quarter`, we can now create the `semester` feature:

```python
data["semester"] = np.where(data["quarter"] < 3, 1, 2)
```

> **Note**
>
> You can explore the distinct values of the new variables utilizing pandas' `unique()`, for example, by executing `df["quarter"].unique()` or `df["semester"].unique()`.

6. Let's extract the `month` part of the date in a new column and display the top five rows of the DataFrame:

```
data["month"] = data["date"].dt.month
data[["date", "month"]].head()
```

We see the new `month` variable in the following output:

	date	month
0	2024-05-17	5
1	2024-05-18	5
2	2024-05-19	5
3	2024-05-20	5
4	2024-05-21	5

Figure 6.4 – The first five rows of a DataFrame with the new month variable

7. Let's extract the week number (a year has 52 weeks) from the date:

```
data["week"] = data["date"].dt.isocalendar().week
data[["date", "week"]].head()
```

We see the `week` variable in the following output:

	date	week
0	2024-05-17	20
1	2024-05-18	20
2	2024-05-19	20
3	2024-05-20	21
4	2024-05-21	21

Figure 6.5 – The first five rows of a DataFrame with the new week variable

8. Let's extract the day of the month, which can take values between 1 and 31, into a new column:

```
data["day_mo"] = data["date"].dt.day
data[["date", "day_mo"]].head()
```

We see the day_mo variable in the following output:

	date	day_mo
0	2024-05-17	17
1	2024-05-18	18
2	2024-05-19	19
3	2024-05-20	20
4	2024-05-21	21

Figure 6.6 – The top rows of a DataFrame with the new variable capturing the day of the month

9. Let's extract the day of the week, with values between 0 and 6 (from Monday to Sunday), in a new column, then display the top rows:

```
data["day_week"] = data["date"].dt.dayofweek
data[["date", "day_mo", "day_week"]].head()
```

We see the day_week variable in the following output:

	date	day_mo	day_week
0	2024-05-17	17	4
1	2024-05-18	18	5
2	2024-05-19	19	6
3	2024-05-20	20	0
4	2024-05-21	21	1

Figure 6.7 – The top rows of a DataFrame with a new variable representing days of a week

10. With the variable from *Step 9*, we can create a binary variable that indicates whether it was a weekend:

```
data["is_weekend"] = (
    data[«date»].dt.dayofweek > 4).astype(int)
data[["date", "day_week", "is_weekend"]].head()
```

We see the new `is_weekend` variable in the following output:

	date	day_week	is_weekend
0	2024-05-17	4	0
1	2024-05-18	5	1
2	2024-05-19	6	1
3	2024-05-20	0	0
4	2024-05-21	1	0

Figure 6.8 – The first five rows of a DataFrame with the new is_weekend variable

> **Note**
> We can automate the extraction of all these features by using `feature-engine`. Check out the *Automating datetime feature extraction with feature-engine* recipe in this chapter for more details.

With that, we have extracted many new features from the date part of a `datetime` variable using `pandas`. These features are useful for data analysis, visualization, and predictive modelling.

How it works...

In this recipe, we extracted many date-related features from a `datetime` variable by using the `dt` module from `pandas`. First, we created a sample DataFrame with a variable that contained dates. We used `pandas'` `date_range()` to create a range of values starting from an arbitrary date and increasing the time by intervals of 1 day. With the `periods` argument, we indicated the number of values to create in the range – that is, the number of dates. With the `freq` argument, we indicated the size of the steps between the dates. We used D for days in our example. Finally, we transformed the date range into a DataFrame with `pandas` `DataFrame()`.

To extract the different parts of a date, we used `pandas'` `dt` to access the `datetime` properties of a `pandas` Series and then utilized the different properties. We used `year`, `month`, and `quarter` to capture the year, month, and quarter into new columns of the DataFrame. To find the semester, we created a Boolean using NumPy's `where()` in combination with the newly created `quarter` variable. NumPy's `where()` scanned the values of the `quarter` variable; if they were smaller than 3, it returned the value of 1 for the first semester; otherwise, it returned the value of 2, corresponding to the second semester.

To extract the different representations of days and weeks, we used the `isocalender().week`, day, and `dayofweek` properties. With the day of the week, we went ahead and created a binary variable to indicate whether it was a weekend. We used `where()` to scan the day of the week, and if the value was greater than 4, which corresponds to Saturday and Sunday, the function returned `True` and otherwise `False`. Finally, we cast this Boolean vector as an integer to have a binary variable with 1s and 0s. With that, we created multiple features from dates that we can use for data analysis and predictive modelling.

There's more...

Using pandas' `dt` module, we can extract many more features from dates out of the box. For example, we can extract the beginning and end of a month, quarter, or year, whether it is a leap year, and the number of days in a month. These are the functions that allow you to do so:

- `pandas.Series.dt.is_month_start`

- `pandas.Series.dt.is_month_end`

- `pandas.Series.dt.is_quarter_start`

- `pandas.Series.dt.is_quarter_end`

- `pandas.Series.dt.is_year_start`

- `pandas.Series.dt.is_year_end`

- `pandas.Series.dt.is_leap_year`

- `pandas.Series.dt.days_in_month`

We can also return the number of days in a specific month with `pd.dt.days_in_month` and the day in a year (from 1 to 365) with `pd.dt.dayofyear`.

For more details, visit the pandas' `datetime` documentation: `https://pandas.pydata.org/pandas-docs/stable/user_guide/timeseries.html#time-date-components`.

See also

To learn how to create different `datetime` ranges with pandas' `date_ranges()`, visit `https://pandas.pydata.org/pandas-docs/stable/user_guide/timeseries.html#off-set-aliases`.

To learn more about pandas' `dt`, visit `https://pandas.pydata.org/pandas-docs/stable/reference/series.html#datetime-properties`.

Extracting features from time with pandas

Some events occur more often at certain times of the day – for example, fraudulent activity is more likely to occur during the night or early morning. Air pollutant concentration also changes with the time of the day, with peaks at rush hour when there are more vehicles on the streets. Therefore, deriving time features is extremely useful for data analysis and predictive modelling. In this recipe, we will extract different time parts of a `datetime` variable by utilizing `pandas` and NumPy.

Getting ready

We can extract hours, minutes, and seconds using the following pandas' `datetime` properties:

- `pandas.Series.dt.hour`
- `pandas.Series.dt.minute`
- `pandas.Series.dt.second`

How to do it...

In this recipe, we'll extract the `hour`, `minute`, and `second` part of a `time` variable. Let's begin by importing the libraries and creating a sample dataset:

1. Let's import pandas and numpy:

    ```
    import numpy as np
    import pandas as pd
    ```

2. Let's begin by creating 20 `datetime` observations, starting on `2024-05-17` at midnight and followed by increments of 1 hour, 15 minutes, and 10 seconds. Next, we'll capture the time range in a DataFrame and display the top five rows:

    ```
    rng_ = pd.date_range(
        "2024-05-17", periods=20, freq="1h15min10s")
    df = pd.DataFrame({"date": rng_})
    df.head()
    ```

    In the following output, we see the variable from *Step 2*, with a `date` part and a `time` part, and the values increasing by intervals of 1 hour, 15 minutes, and 10 seconds:

	date
0	2024-05-17 00:00:00
1	2024-05-17 01:15:10
2	2024-05-17 02:30:20
3	2024-05-17 03:45:30
4	2024-05-17 05:00:40

Figure 6.9 – The first five rows of a sample DataFrame with a datetime variable

3. Let's extract the `hour`, `minute`, and `second` part and capture them into three new columns, then display the DataFrame's top five rows:

```
df["hour"] = df["date"].dt.hour
df["min"] = df["date"].dt.minute
df["sec"] = df["date"].dt.second
df.head()
```

In the following output, we see the three `time` features that we extracted in *Step 3*:

	date	hour	min	sec
0	2024-05-17 00:00:00	0	0	0
1	2024-05-17 01:15:10	1	15	10
2	2024-05-17 02:30:20	2	30	20
3	2024-05-17 03:45:30	3	45	30
4	2024-05-17 05:00:40	5	0	40

Figure 6.10 – The first five rows of a DataFrame with three variables derived from time

> **Note**
>
> Remember that pandas' dt needs a `datetime` object to work. You can change the data type of an object variable into `datetime` by using pandas `to_datetime()`.

4. Let's perform the same operations that we did in *Step 3* but now in one line of code:

```
df[["h", "m", "s"]] = pd.DataFrame(
    [(x.hour, x.minute, x.second) for x in df["date"]]
)
df.head()
```

We see the newly created variables in the following output:

	date	hour	min	sec	h	m	s
0	2024-05-17 00:00:00	0	0	0	0	0	0
1	2024-05-17 01:15:10	1	15	10	1	15	10
2	2024-05-17 02:30:20	2	30	20	2	30	20
3	2024-05-17 03:45:30	3	45	30	3	45	30
4	2024-05-17 05:00:40	5	0	40	5	0	40

Figure 6.11 – The first five rows of a DataFrame with the variables derived from time

> **Note**
>
> You can inspect the unique values of the new variables with pandas' `unique()`, for example, by executing `df['hour'].unique()`.

5. Finally, let's create a binary variable that flags events that occurred in the morning, between 6 A.M. and 12 P.M.:

```python
df["is_morning"] = np.where(
    (df[«hour»] < 12) & (df[«hour»] > 6), 1, 0 )
df.head()
```

We see the `is_morning` variable in the following output:

	date	hour	min	sec	h	m	s	is_morning
0	2024-05-17 00:00:00	0	0	0	0	0	0	0
1	2024-05-17 01:15:10	1	15	10	1	15	10	0
2	2024-05-17 02:30:20	2	30	20	2	30	20	0
3	2024-05-17 03:45:30	3	45	30	3	45	30	0
4	2024-05-17 05:00:40	5	0	40	5	0	40	0

Figure 6.12 – The top rows of a DataFrame with the new variables derived from time

With that, we extracted multiple features from the time part of a `datetime` variable. These features can be used for data analysis and predictive modelling.

How it works...

In this recipe, we created features that capture representations of time. First, we created a sample DataFrame with a `datetime` variable. We used pandas `date_range()` to create a range of 20 values starting from an arbitrary date and increasing by intervals of 1 hour, 15 minutes, and 10 seconds. We used the `1h15min10s` string as the frequency term for the `freq` argument to indicate the desired increments. Next, we transformed the date range into a DataFrame with pandas' `DataFrame()`.

To extract the different time parts, we used pandas' `dt` to access the `hour`, `minute`, and `second` `time` properties. After extracting `hour` from `time`, we used it to create a new feature that indicated whether it was morning by using NumPy's `where()`. NumPy's `where()` scanned the `hour` variable; if its values were smaller than 12 and greater than 6, it assigned a value of 1; otherwise, it assigned a value of 0. With these operations, we added several features to the DataFrame that can be used for data analysis and to train machine learning models.

There's more...

We can also extract microseconds and nanoseconds with the following `pandas` properties:

- `pandas.Series.dt.microsecond`

- `pandas.Series.dt.nanosecond`

For more details, visit `https://pandas.pydata.org/pandas-docs/stable/user_guide/timeseries.html#time-date-components`.

Capturing the elapsed time between datetime variables

We can extract powerful features from each `datetime` variable individually, as we did in the previous two recipes. We can create additional features by combining multiple `datetime` variables. A common example consists of extracting the **age** at the time of an event by comparing the **date of birth** with the **date of the event**.

In this recipe, we will learn how to capture the time between two `datetime` variables by utilizing `pandas` and `feature-engine`.

How to do it...

To proceed with this recipe, we'll create a DataFrame containing two `datatime` variables:

1. Let's begin by importing `pandas`, `numpy`, and `datetime`:

    ```
    import datetime
    import numpy as np
    import pandas as pd
    ```

2. We'll start by creating two `datetime` variables with 20 values each; the values start from `2024-05-17` and increase in intervals of `1` hour for the first variable, and `1` month for the second. Then, we'll capture the variables in a DataFrame, add column names, and display the top rows:

    ```
    date = "2024-05-17"
    rng_hr = pd.date_range(date, periods=20, freq="h")
    rng_month = pd.date_range(date, periods=20, freq="ME")
    df = pd.DataFrame(
        {"date1": rng_hr, "date2": rng_month})
    df.head()
    ```

We see the first five rows of the DataFrame from *Step 2* in the following output:

	date1	date2
0	2024-05-17 00:00:00	2024-05-31
1	2024-05-17 01:00:00	2024-06-30
2	2024-05-17 02:00:00	2024-07-31
3	2024-05-17 03:00:00	2024-08-31
4	2024-05-17 04:00:00	2024-09-30

Figure 6.13 – The first five rows of a DataFrame with two datetime variables

3. Let's capture the difference in days between the two variables in a new feature, and then display the DataFrame's top rows:

```
df["elapsed_days"] = (
    df["date2"] - df["date1"]).dt.days
df.head()
```

We see the difference in days in the following output:

	date1	date2	elapsed_days
0	2024-05-17 00:00:00	2024-05-31	14
1	2024-05-17 01:00:00	2024-06-30	43
2	2024-05-17 02:00:00	2024-07-31	74
3	2024-05-17 03:00:00	2024-08-31	105
4	2024-05-17 04:00:00	2024-09-30	135

Figure 6.14 – Top rows of a DataFrame with a new variable capturing
the time difference between the two datetime features

4. Let's capture the difference in weeks between the two datetime variables and then display the DataFrame's top rows:

```
df["weeks_passed"] = (
    (df[«date2»] - df[«date1»]) / np.timedelta64(1, "W"))
df.head()
```

We see the difference in weeks between the variables in the following screenshot:

	date1	date2	elapsed_days	weeks_passed
0	2024-05-17 00:00:00	2024-05-31	14	2.000000
1	2024-05-17 01:00:00	2024-06-30	43	6.279762
2	2024-05-17 02:00:00	2024-07-31	74	10.702381
3	2024-05-17 03:00:00	2024-08-31	105	15.125000
4	2024-05-17 04:00:00	2024-09-30	135	19.404762

Figure 6.15 – A DataFrame with the time difference between the datetime
variables expressed in number of days and number of weeks

5. Now, let's calculate the time in between the variables in minutes and seconds and then display
   the DataFrame's top rows:

```
df["diff_seconds"] = (
    df[«date2»] - df[«date1»])/np.timedelta64(1, «s»)
df["diff_minutes"] = (
    df[«date2»] - df[«date1»])/ np.timedelta64(1,»m»)
df.head()
```

We see the new variables in the following output:

	date1	date2	elapsed_days	weeks_passed	diff_seconds	diff_minutes
0	2024-05-17 00:00:00	2024-05-31	14	2.000000	1209600.0	20160.0
1	2024-05-17 01:00:00	2024-06-30	43	6.279762	3798000.0	63300.0
2	2024-05-17 02:00:00	2024-07-31	74	10.702381	6472800.0	107880.0
3	2024-05-17 03:00:00	2024-08-31	105	15.125000	9147600.0	152460.0
4	2024-05-17 04:00:00	2024-09-30	135	19.404762	11736000.0	195600.0

Figure 6.16 – A DataFrame with the time difference between the two
datetime variables expressed in different time units

6. Finally, let's calculate the difference between one variable and the current day, expressed in
   number of days, and then display the first five rows of the DataFrame:

```
df["to_today"] = (
    datetime.datetime.today() - df["date1"])
df.head()
```

We can find the new variable in the final column of the DataFrame in the following output:

	date1	date2	elapsed_days	weeks_passed	diff_seconds	diff_minutes	to_today
0	2024-05-17 00:00:00	2024-05-31	14	2.000000	1209600.0	20160.0	0
1	2024-05-17 01:00:00	2024-06-30	43	6.279762	3798000.0	63300.0	0
2	2024-05-17 02:00:00	2024-07-31	74	10.702381	6472800.0	107880.0	0
3	2024-05-17 03:00:00	2024-08-31	105	15.125000	9147600.0	152460.0	0
4	2024-05-17 04:00:00	2024-09-30	135	19.404762	11736000.0	195600.0	0

Figure 6.17 – A DataFrame with the new variable containing the difference
between date1 and the day this code was executed

> **Note**
>
> The `to_today` variable on your computer will be different from the one in this book, due to the difference between the current date (at the time of writing) and when you execute the code.

That's it! We've now enriched our dataset with new features that were created by comparing two `datetime` variables.

How it works...

In this recipe, we captured different representations of the time between two `datetime` variables. To proceed with this recipe, we created a sample DataFrame with two variables, each with 20 dates starting at an arbitrary date. The first variable increased in intervals of 1 hour, while the second variable increased in intervals of 1 month. We created the variables with `pandas`' `date_range()`, which we discussed in the previous two recipes in this chapter.

To determine the difference between the variables – that is, to determine the time between them – we directly subtracted one `datetime` variable from the other – that is, one `pandas` Series from the other. The difference between the two `pandas` Series returned a new `pandas` Series. To capture the difference in days, we used `pandas`' `dt`, followed by `days`. To convert the time difference into months, we used `timedelta()` from NumPy, indicating that we wanted the difference in weeks by passing `W` in the second argument of the method. To capture the difference in seconds and minutes, we passed the `s` and `m` strings to `timedelta()`, respectively.

> **Note**
>
> The arguments for NumPy's `timedelta` are a number, – 1, in our example, to represent the number of units, and a `datetime` unit, such as day (D), week (W), hours (h), minutes (m), or seconds (s).

Finally, we captured the difference from one `datetime` variable to today's date. We obtained the date and time of today (at the time of writing) by using `today()` from the built-in `datetime` Python library.

There's more...

We can automate the creation of features that capture the time between variables by using the `feature-engine`'s transformer `DatetimeSubstraction()`.

1. Let's import pandas and `feature-engine`'s transformer:

```python
import pandas as pd
from feature_engine.datetime import (
    DatetimeSubtraction
)
```

2. Let's re-create the sample dataset that we described in *Step 2* of the *How to do it...* section:

```python
date = "2024-05-17"
rng_hr = pd.date_range(date, periods=20, freq="h")
rng_month = pd.date_range(date, periods=20, freq="ME")
df = pd.DataFrame(
    {"date1": rng_hr, "date2": rng_month})
```

3. Let's set up `DatetimeSubstraction()` to return the time difference between the second date and the first date expressed in days:

```python
ds = DatetimeSubtraction(
    variables="date2",
    reference="date1",
    output_unit="D",
)
```

> **Note**
>
> We can obtain the difference between more than two variables by passing variable lists in the `variables` and `reference` parameters.

4. Let's create and then display the new feature:

```python
dft = ds.fit_transform(df)
dft.head()
```

In the following output, we see the variable that captures the time difference between the two `datetime` variables in days:

	date1	date2	date2_sub_date1
0	2024-05-17 00:00:00	2024-05-31	14.000000
1	2024-05-17 01:00:00	2024-06-30	43.958333
2	2024-05-17 02:00:00	2024-07-31	74.916667
3	2024-05-17 03:00:00	2024-08-31	105.875000
4	2024-05-17 04:00:00	2024-09-30	135.833333

Figure 6.18 – A DataFrame with the new variable containing the difference between the two datetime variables

For more details, check out `https://feature-engine.trainindata.com/en/latest/api_doc/datetime/DatetimeSubtraction.html`.

See also

To learn more about NumPy's `timedelta`, visit `https://numpy.org/devdocs/reference/arrays.datetime.html#datetime-and-timedelta-arithmetic`.

Working with time in different time zones

Some organizations operate internationally; therefore, the information they collect about events may be recorded alongside the time zone of the area where the event took place. To be able to compare events that occurred across different time zones, we typically have to set all of the variables within the same zone. In this recipe, we will learn how to unify the time zones of a `datetime` variable and how to reassign a variable to a different time zone using `pandas`.

How to do it...

To proceed with this recipe, we'll create a sample DataFrame containing two variables in different time zones:

1. Let's import `pandas`:

    ```
    import pandas as pd
    ```

2. Let's create a DataFrame containing one variable with values in different time zones:

    ```
    df = pd.DataFrame()
    df['time1'] = pd.concat([
        pd.Series(
    ```

```
            pd.date_range(
                start='2024-06-10 09:00',
                freq='h',
                periods=3,
                tz='Europe/Berlin')),
        pd.Series(
            pd.date_range(
                start='2024-09-10 09:00',
                freq='h',
                periods=3,
                tz='US/Central'))
    ], axis=0)
```

3. Let's add another `datetime` variable to the DataFrame, which also contains values in different time zones:

```
df['time2'] = pd.concat([
    pd.Series(
        pd.date_range(
            start='2024-07-01 09:00',
            freq='h',
            periods=3,
            tz='Europe/Berlin')),
    pd.Series(
        pd.date_range(
            start='2024-08-01 09:00',
            freq='h',
            periods=3,
            tz='US/Central'))
    ], axis=0)
```

If we now execute `df`, we'll see the DataFrame with the variables in the different time zones like in the following output:

	time1	time2
0	2024-06-10 09:00:00+02:00	2024-07-01 09:00:00+02:00
1	2024-06-10 10:00:00+02:00	2024-07-01 10:00:00+02:00
2	2024-06-10 11:00:00+02:00	2024-07-01 11:00:00+02:00
0	2024-09-10 09:00:00-05:00	2024-08-01 09:00:00-05:00
1	2024-09-10 10:00:00-05:00	2024-08-01 10:00:00-05:00
2	2024-09-10 11:00:00-05:00	2024-08-01 11:00:00-05:00

Figure 6.19 – A DataFrame with two datetime variables in different time zones

> **Note**
>
> The time zone is indicated with the +02 and -05 values, respectively, which indicates the time difference to the **Coordinated Universal Time (UTC)**.

4. To work with different time zones, we typically set the variables in the same time zone, in this case, we chose the UTC:

```
df['time1_utc'] = pd.to_datetime(
    df['time1'], utc=True)
df['time2_utc'] = pd.to_datetime(
    df['time2'], utc=True)
```

If we now execute df, we'll see the new variables, which have a difference of 00 hours with respect to UTC:

	time1	time2	time1_utc	time2_utc
0	2024-06-10 09:00:00+02:00	2024-07-01 09:00:00+02:00	2024-06-10 07:00:00+00:00	2024-07-01 07:00:00+00:00
1	2024-06-10 10:00:00+02:00	2024-07-01 10:00:00+02:00	2024-06-10 08:00:00+00:00	2024-07-01 08:00:00+00:00
2	2024-06-10 11:00:00+02:00	2024-07-01 11:00:00+02:00	2024-06-10 09:00:00+00:00	2024-07-01 09:00:00+00:00
0	2024-09-10 09:00:00-05:00	2024-08-01 09:00:00-05:00	2024-09-10 14:00:00+00:00	2024-08-01 14:00:00+00:00
1	2024-09-10 10:00:00-05:00	2024-08-01 10:00:00-05:00	2024-09-10 15:00:00+00:00	2024-08-01 15:00:00+00:00
2	2024-09-10 11:00:00-05:00	2024-08-01 11:00:00-05:00	2024-09-10 16:00:00+00:00	2024-08-01 16:00:00+00:00

Figure 6.20 – A DataFrame containing the new variables in the UTC

1. Let's calculate the difference in days between the variables and then display the first five rows of the DataFrame:

```
df['elapsed_days'] = (
    df[<time2_utc>] - df[<time1_utc>]). dt.days
df['elapsed_days'].head()
```

We see the time difference between the variables in the following output:

```
0        21
1        21
2        21
0       -40
1       -40
Name: elapsed_days, dtype: int64
```

2. Finally, let's change the time zone of the `datetime` variables to the `London` and `Berlin` time zones, and then display the resulting variables:

```
df['time1_london'] = df[
    <time1_utc>].dt.tz_convert('Europe/London')
df['time2_berlin'] = df[
    <time1_utc>].dt.tz_convert('Europe/Berlin')
df[['time1_london', 'time2_berlin']]
```

We see the variables in their respective time zones in the following output:

	time1_london	time2_berlin
0	2024-06-10 08:00:00+01:00	2024-06-10 09:00:00+02:00
1	2024-06-10 09:00:00+01:00	2024-06-10 10:00:00+02:00
2	2024-06-10 10:00:00+01:00	2024-06-10 11:00:00+02:00
0	2024-09-10 15:00:00+01:00	2024-09-10 16:00:00+02:00
1	2024-09-10 16:00:00+01:00	2024-09-10 17:00:00+02:00
2	2024-09-10 17:00:00+01:00	2024-09-10 18:00:00+02:00

Figure 6.21 – Variables reformatted into different time zones

When changing time zones, not only do the values of the zone change – that is, the `+01` and `+02` values in the previous image – but the value of the hour changes as well.

How it works...

In this recipe, we changed time zones and performed operations between variables in different time zones. To begin, we created a DataFrame with two variables, the values of which started at an arbitrary date and increased hourly; these were set in different time zones. To combine the different time zone variables in one DataFrame column, we concatenated the series returned by `pandas`' `date_range()` by utilizing `pandas`' `concat()`. We set the `axis` argument to 0 to indicate we wanted to concatenate the series vertically in one column. We covered the arguments of `pandas`' `date_range()` extensively in former recipes in this chapter; see the *Extracting features from dates with pandas* and *Extracting features from time with pandas* recipes for more details.

To reset the time zone of the variables to the central zone, we used `pandas`' `to_datetime()`, passing `utc=True`. Finally, we determined the time difference between the variables by subtracting one series from the other and capturing the difference in days. To reassign a different time zone, we used `pandas`' `tz_convert()`, indicating the new time zone as an argument.

See also

To learn more about pandas' `to_datetime()`, visit `https://pandas.pydata.org/pandas-docs/stable/reference/api/pandas.to_datetime.html`.

To learn more about pandas' `tz_convert()`, visit `https://pandas.pydata.org/pandas-docs/stable/reference/api/pandas.Series.dt.tz_convert.html`.

Automating the datetime feature extraction with Feature-engine

`feature-engine` is a Python library for feature engineering and selection that is well suited to working with `pandas` DataFrames. The `DatetimeFeatures()` class can extract features from date and time automatically by using `pandas`' `dt` under the hood. `DatetimeFeatures()` allows you to extract the following features:

- Month
- Quarter
- Semester
- Year
- Week
- Day of the week
- Day of the month
- Day of the year
- Weekend
- Month start
- Month end
- Quarter start
- Quarter end
- Year start
- Year end
- Leap year
- Days in a month
- Hour

- Minute

- Second

In this recipe, we will automatically create features from date and time by utilizing `feature-engine`.

How to do it...

To showcase `feature-engine`'s functionality, we'll create a sample DataFrame with a `datetime` variable:

1. Let's begin by importing `pandas` and `DatetimeFeatures()`:

    ```
    import pandas as pd
    from feature_engine.datetime import DatetimeFeatures
    ```

2. Let's create a `datetime` variable with 20 values, beginning from `2024-05-17` at midnight and followed by increments of 1 day. Then, we store this variable in a DataFrame:

    ```
    rng_ = pd.date_range(
        '2024-05-17', periods=20, freq='D')
    data = pd.DataFrame({'date': rng_})
    ```

3. We'll start by setting up the transformer to extract all supported `datetime` features:

    ```
    dtfs = DatetimeFeatures(
        variables=None,
        features_to_extract= "all",
    )
    ```

> **Note**
>
> `DatetimeFeatures()` automatically finds the variables of the `datetime` type, or that could be parsed as `datetime` when the `variables` parameter is set to None. Alternatively, you can pass a list with the names of the variables from which you want to extract `date` and `time` features.

4. Let's add the `date` and `time` features to the data:

    ```
    dft = dtfs.fit_transform(data)
    ```

> **Note**
>
> By default, `DatetimeFeatures()` extracts the following features from each `datetime` variable: `month`, `year`, `day_of_week`, `day_of_month`, `hour`, `minute`, and `second`. We can modify this behavior through the `features_to_extract` parameter as we did in *Step 3*.

5. Let's capture the names of the new variables in a list:

```
vars_ = [v for v in dft.columns if "date" in v]
```

> **Note**
>
> `DatetimeFeatures()` names the new variables with the original variable name (in this case, `date`) followed by an underscore and then the type of feature created, for example, `date_day_of_week` contains the day of the week extracted from the `date` variable.

If we execute `vars_`, we'll see the names of the features that were created:

```
['date_month',
 'date_quarter',
 'date_semester',
 'date_year',
 'date_week',
 'date_day_of_week',
 'date_day_of_month',
 'date_day_of_year',
 'date_weekend',
 'date_month_start',
 'date_month_end',
 'date_quarter_start',
 'date_quarter_end',
 'date_year_start',
 'date_year_end',
 'date_leap_year',
 'date_days_in_month',
 'date_hour',
 'date_minute',
 'date_second']
```

To visualize the resulting DataFrame, go ahead and execute `dft[vars_].head()`. We can't show the resulting DataFrame in the book because it is too big.

> **Note**
>
> We can create specific features by passing their names to the `features_to_extract` parameter.
>
> For example, to extract `week` and `year`, we set the transformer like this: `dtfs = DatetimeFeatures(features_to_extract=["week", "year"])`. We can also extract all supported features by setting the `features_to_extract` parameter to `"all"`.

`DatetimeFeatures()` can also create features from variables in different time zones. Let's learn how to correctly set up the transformer in this situation.

6. Let's create a sample DataFrame with a variable's values in different time zones:

```python
df = pd.DataFrame()
df["time"] = pd.concat(
    [
        pd.Series(
            pd.date_range(
            start="2024-08-01 09:00",
            freq="h",
            periods=3,
            tz="Europe/Berlin"
            )
        ),
        pd.Series(
            pd.date_range(
                start="2024-08-01 09:00",
                freq="h",
                periods=3, tz="US/Central"
            )
        ),
    ],
    axis=0,
)
```

If we execute `df`, we will see the DataFrame from *Step 6*, as shown in the following output:

	time
0	2024-08-01 09:00:00+02:00
1	2024-08-01 10:00:00+02:00
2	2024-08-01 11:00:00+02:00
0	2024-08-01 09:00:00-05:00
1	2024-08-01 10:00:00-05:00
2	2024-08-01 11:00:00-05:00

Figure 6.22 – A DataFrame with a variable's values in different time zones

7. We'll set the transformer to extract three specific features from this variable after setting it to the UTC:

```python
dfts = DatetimeFeatures(
    features_to_extract=
        ["day_of_week", "hour","minute"],
```

```
        drop_original=False,
        utc=True,
    )
```

8. Let's create the new features:

```
dft = dfts.fit_transform(df)
```

`DatetimeFeatures()` will set all variables into UTC before deriving the features. With `dft.head()`, we can see the resulting DataFrame:

	time	time_day_of_week	time_hour	time_minute
0	2024-08-01 09:00:00+02:00	3	7	0
1	2024-08-01 10:00:00+02:00	3	8	0
2	2024-08-01 11:00:00+02:00	3	9	0
0	2024-08-01 09:00:00-05:00	3	14	0
1	2024-08-01 10:00:00-05:00	3	15	0

Figure 6.23 – A DataFrame with the original and new variables

With that, we've created multiple date and time-related features in a few lines of code. `feature-engine` offers a great alternative to manually creating features per feature with `pandas`. In addition, `DatetimeFeatures()` can be integrated into scikit-learn's `Pipeline` and `GridSearchCV`, among other classes.

How it works...

`DatetimeFeatures()` extracts several date and time features from `datetime` variables automatically by utilizing `pandas'` `dt` under the hood. It works with variables whose original data types are `datetime`, as well as with object-like and categorical variables, provided that they can be parsed into a `datetime` format.

`DatetimeFeatures()` extracts the following features by default: `month`, `year`, `day_of_week`, `day_of_month`, `hour`, `minute` and `second`. We can make the transformer return all the features it supports by setting the parameter `features_to_extract` to `all`. In addition, we can extract a specific subset of features by passing the feature names in a list, as we did in *Step 7*.

`DatetimeFeatures()` automatically finds `datetime` variables or variables that can be parsed as `datetime` in the DataFrame passed to the `fit()` method. To extract features from a selected variable or group of variables, we can pass their name in a list to the `variables` parameter when we set up the transformer.

With `fit()`, `DatetimeFeatures()` does not learn any parameters; instead, it checks that the variables entered by the user are, or can be, parsed into a `datetime` format. If the user does not indicate variable names, `DatetimeFeatures()` finds the `datetime` variables automatically. With `transform()`, the transformer adds the date and time-derived variables to the DataFrame.

7

Performing Feature Scaling

Many machine learning algorithms are sensitive to the variable scale. For example, the coefficients of linear models depend on the scale of the feature – that is, changing the feature scale will change the coefficient's value. In linear models, as well as in algorithms that depend on distance calculations such as clustering and principal component analysis, features with larger value ranges tend to dominate over features with smaller ranges. Therefore, having features on a similar scale allows us to compare feature importance and may help algorithms converge faster, improving performance and training times.

Scaling techniques, in general, divide the variables by some constant; therefore, it is important to highlight that the shape of the variable distribution does not change when we rescale the variables. If you want to change the distribution shape, check out *Chapter 3, Transforming Numerical Variables.*

In this chapter, we will describe different methods to set features on a similar scale.

This chapter will cover the following recipes:

- Standardizing the features
- Scaling to the maximum and minimum values
- Scaling with the median and quantiles
- Performing mean normalization
- Implementing maximum absolute scaling
- Scaling to vector unit length

Technical requirements

The main libraries that we use in this chapter are scikit-learn (`sklearn`) for scaling, `pandas` to handle the data, and `matplotlib` for plotting.

Standardizing the features

Standardization is the process of centering the variable at 0 and standardizing the variance to 1. To standardize features, we subtract the mean from each observation and then divide the result by the standard deviation:

$$x_{scaled} = \frac{x - mean(x)}{std(x)}$$

The result of the preceding transformation is called the **z-score** and represents how many standard deviations a given observation *deviates* from the mean.

Standardization is generally useful when models require the variables to be centered at zero and data is not sparse (centering sparse data will destroy its sparse nature). On the downside, standardization is sensitive to outliers and the z-score does not keep the symmetric properties if the variables are highly skewed, as we discuss in the following section.

Getting ready

With standardization, the variable distribution does not change; what changes is the magnitude of their values, as we see in the following figure:

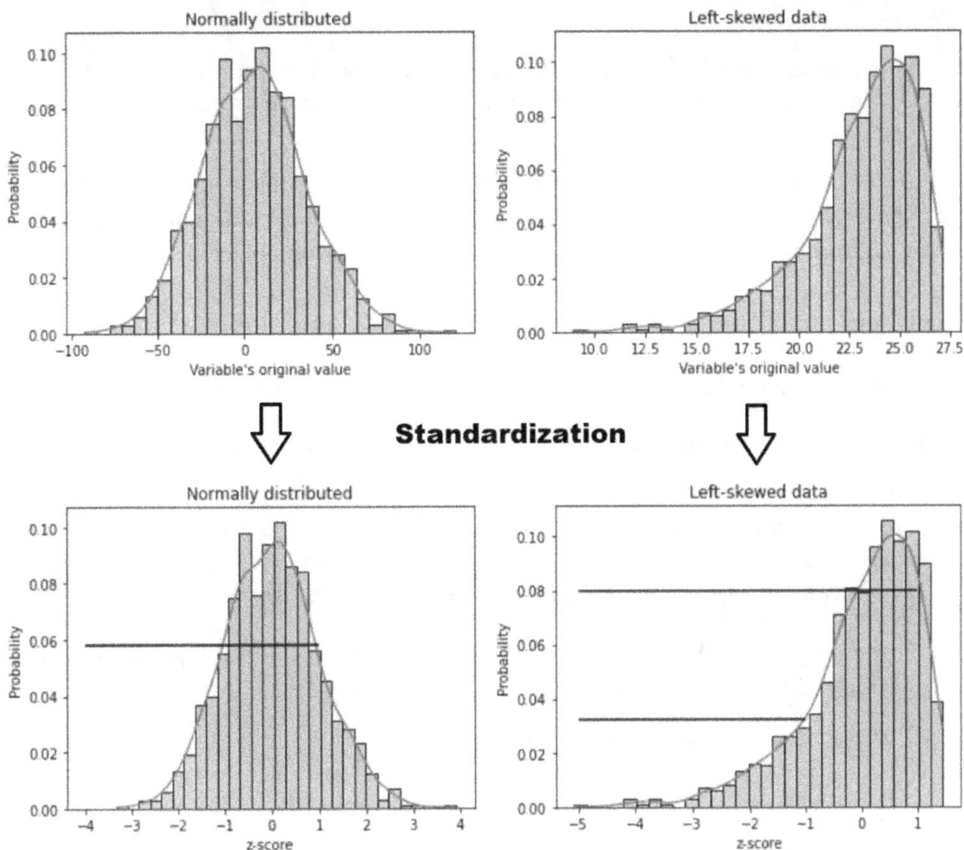

Figure 7.1 – Distribution of a normal and skewed variable before and after standardization.

The z-score (x axis in the bottom panels) indicates how many standard deviations an observation deviates from the mean. When the z-score is 1, the observation lies 1 standard deviation to the right of the mean, whereas when the z-score is -1, the sample is 1 standard deviation to the left of the mean.

In normally distributed variables, we can estimate the probability of a value being greater or smaller than a given z-score, and this probability distribution is symmetric. The probability of an observation being smaller than a z-score of -1 is equivalent to the probability of a value being greater than 1 (horizontal line in the bottom-left panel). This symmetry is fundamental to many statistical tests. In skewed distributions, this symmetry does not hold. As illustrated in the bottom-right panel of *Figure 7.1* (horizontal lines), the probability of a value being smaller than -1 is different from that of being greater than 1.

> **Note**
>
> The mean and the standard deviation are sensitive to outliers; therefore, the features may scale differently from each other in the presence of outliers when using standardization.

In practice, we often apply standardization ignoring the shape of the distribution. However, keep in mind that if the models or tests you are using make assumptions about the data's distribution, you might benefit from transforming the variables before standardization, or trying a different scaling method.

How to do it...

In this recipe, we'll apply standardization to the variables of the California housing dataset:

1. Let's begin by importing the required Python packages, classes, and functions:

```python
import pandas as pd
from sklearn.datasets import fetch_california_housing
from sklearn.model_selection import train_test_split
from sklearn.preprocessing import StandardScaler
```

2. Let's load the California housing dataset from scikit-learn into a DataFrame and drop the `Latitude` and `Longitude` variables:

```python
X, y = fetch_california_housing(
    return_X_y=True, as_frame=True)
X.drop(labels=["Latitude", "Longitude"], axis=1,
    inplace=True)
```

3. Now, let's divide the data into train and test sets:

```python
X_train, X_test, y_train, y_test = train_test_split(
    X, y, test_size=0.3, random_state=0)
```

4. Next, we'll set up the `StandardScaler()` function from scikit-learn and fit it to the train set so that it learns each variable's mean and standard deviation:

```python
scaler = StandardScaler().set_output(
    transform="pandas")
scaler.fit(X_train)
```

> **Note**
>
> Scikit-learn scalers, like any scikit-learn transformer, return NumPy arrays by default. To return `pandas` or `polars` DataFrames, we need to specify the output container with the `set_output()` method, as we did in *Step 4*.

5. Now, let's standardize the train and test sets with the trained scaler:

```
X_train_scaled = scaler.transform(X_train)
X_test_scaled = scaler.transform(X_test)
```

`StandardScaler()` stores the mean and standard deviation learned from the training set during `fit()`. Let's visualize the learned parameters.

6. First, we'll print the mean values that were learned by `scaler`:

```
scaler.mean_
```

We see the mean values of each variable in the following output:

```
array([3.86666741e+00, 2.86187016e+01,
5.42340368e+00,                1.09477484e+00,1.42515732e+03,
3.04051776e+00])
```

7. Now, let's print the standard deviation values that were learned by `scaler`:

```
scaler.scale_
```

We see the standard deviation of each variable in the following output:

```
array([1.89109236e+00, 1.25962585e+01,
2.28754018e+00,                4.52736275e-01,
1.14954037e+03, 6.86792905e+00])
```

Let's compare the transformed data with the original data to understand the changes.

8. Let's print the descriptive statistics from the original variables in the test set:

```
X_test.describe()
```

In the following output, we see that the variables' mean values are different from zero and the variance varies:

	MedInc	HouseAge	AveRooms	AveBedrms	Population	AveOccup
count	6192.000000	6192.000000	6192.000000	6192.000000	6192.000000	6192.000000
mean	3.880013	28.687984	5.442057	1.101109	1426.222061	3.140976
std	1.920007	12.560416	2.862733	0.519956	1091.567168	15.796292
min	0.499900	1.000000	1.465753	0.500000	8.000000	0.692308
25%	2.552150	18.000000	4.414452	1.006494	796.000000	2.436452
50%	3.529600	29.000000	5.227365	1.048741	1169.500000	2.825041
75%	4.768750	37.000000	6.064257	1.098434	1727.250000	3.285501
max	15.000100	52.000000	141.909091	25.636364	16305.000000	1243.333333

Figure 7.2 – Descriptive statistical parameters of the variables before scaling

9. Let's now print the descriptive statistical values from the transformed variables:

```
X_test_scaled.describe()
```

In the following output, we see that the variables' mean is now centered at 0 and the variance is approximately 1:

	MedInc	HouseAge	AveRooms	AveBedrms	Population	AveOccup
count	6192.000000	6192.000000	6192.000000	6192.000000	6192.000000	6192.000000
mean	0.007057	0.005500	0.008154	0.013991	0.000926	0.014627
std	1.015290	0.997154	1.251446	1.148474	0.949568	2.300008
min	-1.780329	-2.192612	-1.730090	-1.313734	-1.232803	-0.341909
25%	-0.695110	-0.843004	-0.441064	-0.194995	-0.547312	-0.087955
50%	-0.178240	0.030271	-0.085698	-0.101679	-0.222400	-0.031374
75%	0.477017	0.665380	0.280150	0.008082	0.262794	0.035671
max	5.887302	1.856210	59.664826	54.207251	12.944167	180.591967

Figure 7.3 – Descriptive statistical parameters of the scaled variables showing a mean of 0 and variance of approximately 1

> **Note**
>
> The `AveRooms`, `AveBedrms`, and `AveOccup` variables are highly skewed, which can lead to observed values in the test set that are much greater or much smaller than those in the training set, and hence we see that the variance deviates from 1. This is to be expected because standardization is sensitive to outliers and very skewed distributions.

We mentioned, in the *Getting ready* section, that the shape of the distribution does not change with standardization. Go ahead and corroborate that by executing `X_test.hist()` and then `X_test_scaled.hist()` to compare the variables' distribution before and after the transformation.

How it works...

In this recipe, we standardized the variables of the California housing dataset by utilizing scikit-learn. We split the data into train and test sets because the parameters for the standardization should be learned from the train set. This is to avoid leaking data from the test to the train set during the preprocessing steps and to ensure the test set remains naïve to all feature transformation processes.

To standardize these features, we used scikit-learn's `StandardScaler()` function, which is able to learn and store the parameters utilized in the transformation. Using `fit()`, the scaler learned each variable's mean and standard deviation and stored them in its `mean_` and `scale_` attributes. Using `transform()`, the scaler standardized the variables in the train and test sets. The default output of `StandardScaler()` is a NumPy array, but through the `set_output()` parameter, we can change the output container to a `pandas` DataFrame, as we did in *Step 4*, or to `polars`, by setting `transform="polars"`.

> **Note**
>
> `StandardScaler()` will subtract the mean and divide it by the standard deviation by default. If we want to just center the distributions without standardizing the variance, we can do so by setting `with_std=False` when initializing the transformer. If we want to set the variance to 1, without cantering the distribution, we can do so by setting `with_mean=False` in *Step 4*.

Scaling to the maximum and minimum values

Scaling to the minimum and maximum values squeezes the values of the variables between 0 and 1. To implement this scaling method, we subtract the minimum value from all the observations and divide the result by the value range – that is, the difference between the maximum and minimum values:

$$x_{scaled} = \frac{x - \min(x)}{\max(x) - \min(x)}$$

Scaling to the minimum and maximum is suitable for variables with very small standard deviations, when the models do not require data to be centered at zero, and when we want to preserve zero entries in sparse data, such as in one-hot encoded variables. On the downside, it is sensitive to outliers.

Getting ready

Scaling to the minimum and maximum value does not change the distribution of the variables, as illustrated in the following figure:

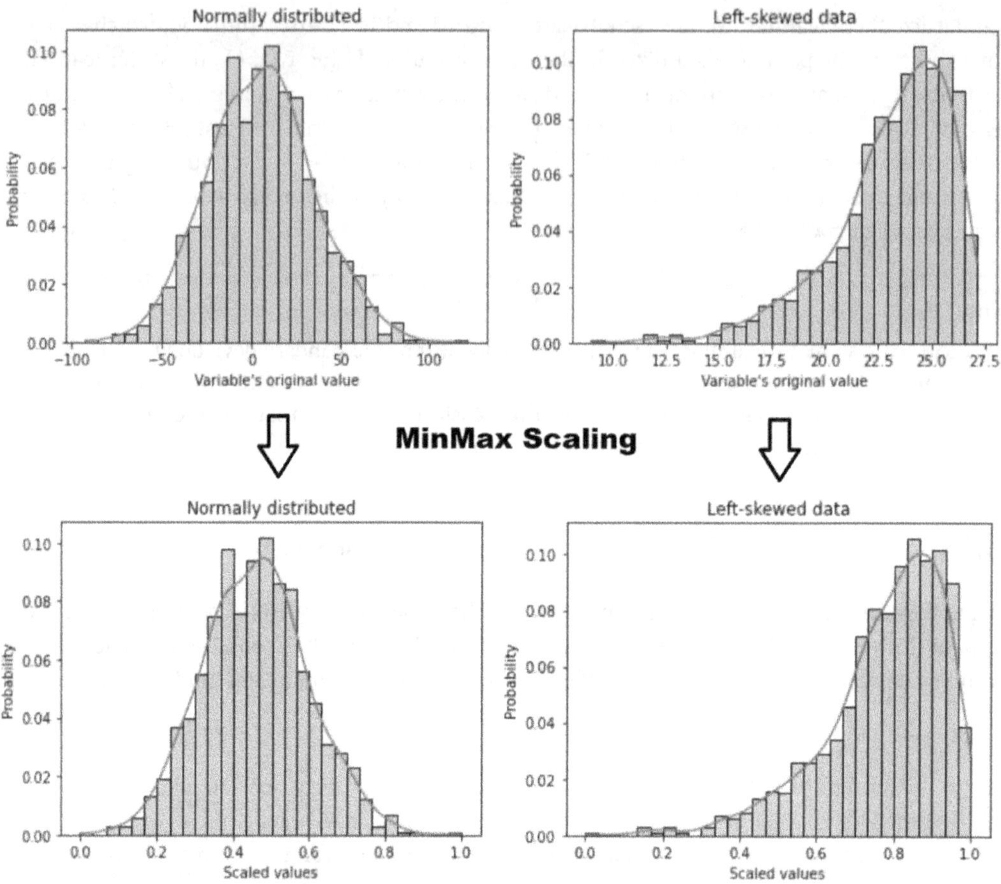

Figure 7.4 – Distribution of a normal and skewed variable before and
after scaling to the minimum and maximum value

This scaling method standardizes the maximum value of the variables to a unit size. Scaling to the minimum and maximum value tends to be the preferred alternative to standardization, and it is suitable for variables with very small standard deviations and when we want to preserve zero entries in sparse data, such as in one-hot encoded variables, or variables derived from counts, such as bag of words. However, this procedure does not center the variables at zero, so if the algorithm has that requirement, this method might not be the best choice.

> **Note**
>
> Scaling to the minimum and maximum values is sensitive to outliers. If outliers are present in the training set, the scaling will squeeze the values toward one of the tails. If, on the contrary, outliers are in the test set, the variable will show values greater than 1 or smaller than 0 after scaling, depending on whether the outlier is on the left or right tail.

How to do it...

In this recipe, we'll scale the variables of the California housing dataset to values between 0 and 1:

1. Let's start by importing `pandas` and the required classes and functions:

    ```
    import pandas as pd
    from sklearn.datasets import fetch_california_housing
    from sklearn.model_selection import train_test_split
    from sklearn.preprocessing import MinMaxScaler
    ```

2. Let's load the California housing dataset from scikit-learn into a `pandas` DataFrame, dropping the `Latitude` and `Longitude` variables:

    ```
    X, y = fetch_california_housing(
        return_X_y=True, as_frame=True)
    X.drop(labels=["Latitude", "Longitude"], axis=1,
        inplace=True)
    ```

3. Let's divide the data into training and test sets:

    ```
    X_train, X_test, y_train, y_test = train_test_split(
        X, y, test_size=0.3, random_state=0)
    ```

4. Let's set up the scaler and then fit it to the train set so that it learns each variable's minimum and maximum values and the value range:

    ```
    scaler = MinMaxScaler().set_output(
        transform="pandas"")
    scaler.fit(X_train)
    ```

5. Finally, let's scale the variables in the train and test sets with the trained scaler:

    ```
    X_train_scaled = scaler.transform(X_train)
    X_test_scaled = scaler.transform(X_test)
    ```

> **Note**
>
> `MinMaxScaler()` stores the maximum and minimum values and the value ranges in its `data_max_`, `min_`, and `data_range_` attributes, respectively.

We can corroborate the minimum values of the transformed variables by executing `X_test_scaled.min()`, which will return the following output:

```
MedInc          0.000000
HouseAge        0.000000
AveRooms        0.004705
AveBedrms       0.004941
```

```
Population       0.000140
AveOccup        -0.000096
dtype: float64
```

By executing `X_test_scaled.max()`, we see that the maximum values of the variables are around 1:

```
MedInc           1.000000
HouseAge         1.000000
AveRooms         1.071197
AveBedrms        0.750090
Population        0.456907
AveOccup         2.074553
dtype: float64
```

> **Note**
>
> If you check the maximum values of the variables in the train set after the transformation, you'll see that they are exactly 1. Yet, in the test set, we see values greater and smaller than 1. This occurs because, in the test set, there are observations with larger or smaller magnitudes than those in the train set. In fact, we see the greatest differences in the variables that deviate the most from the normal distribution (the last four variables in the dataset). This behavior is expected because scaling to the minimum and maximum values is sensitive to outliers and very skewed distributions.

Scaling to the minimum and maximum value does not change the shape of the variable's distribution. You can corroborate that by displaying the histograms before and after the transformation.

How it works...

In this recipe, we scaled the variables of the California housing dataset to values between 0 and 1.

`MinMaxScaler()` from scikit-learn learned the minimum and maximum values and the value range of each variable when we called the `fit()` method and stored these parameters in its `data_max_`, `min_`, and `data_range_` attributes. By using `transform()`, we made the scaler remove the minimum value from each variable in the train and test sets and divide the result by the value range.

> **Note**
>
> `MinMaxScaler()` will scale all variables by default. To scale only a subset of the variables in the dataset, you can use `ColumnTransformer()` from scikit-learn or `SklearnTransformerWrapper()` from `Feature-engine`.

`MinMaxScaler()` will scale the variables between 0 and 1 by default. However, we have the option to scale to a different range by adjusting the tuple passed to the `feature_range` parameter.

By default, `MinMaxScaler()` returns NumPy arrays, but we can modify this behavior to return pandas DataFrames with the `set_output()` method, as we did in *Step 4*.

Scaling with the median and quantiles

When scaling variables to the median and quantiles, the median value is removed from the observations, and the result is divided by the **Inter-Quartile Range (IQR)**. The IQR is the difference between the 3rd quartile and the 1st quartile, or, in other words, the difference between the 75th percentile and the 25th percentile:

$$x\_scaled = \frac{x - median(x)}{3rd\ quaritle(x) - 1st\ quartile(x)}$$

This method is known as **robust scaling** because it produces more robust estimates for the center and value range of the variable. Robust scaling is a suitable alternative to standardization when models require the variables to be centered and the data contains outliers. It is worth noting that robust scaling will not change the overall shape of the variable distribution.

How to do it...

In this recipe, we will implement scaling with the median and IQR by utilizing scikit-learn:

1. Let's start by importing pandas and the required scikit-learn classes and functions:

    ```python
    import pandas as pd
    from sklearn.datasets import fetch_california_housing
    from sklearn.model_selection import train_test_split
    from sklearn.preprocessing import RobustScaler
    ```

2. Let's load the California housing dataset into a pandas DataFrame and drop the `Latitude` and `Longitude` variables:

    ```python
    X, y = fetch_california_housing(
        return_X_y=True, as_frame=True)
    X.drop(labels=[    "Latitude", "Longitude"], axis=1,
        inplace=True)
    ```

3. Let's divide the data into train and test sets:

    ```python
    X_train, X_test, y_train, y_test = train_test_split(
        X, y, test_size=0.3, random_state=0)
    ```

4. Let's set up scikit-learn's `RobustScaler()` and fit it to the train set so that it learns and stores the median and IQR:

    ```python
    scaler = RobustScaler().set_output(
        transform="pandas")
    scaler.fit(X_train)
    ```

5. Finally, let's scale the variables in the train and test sets with the trained scaler:

```
X_train_scaled = scaler.transform(X_train)
X_test_scaled = scaler.transform(X_test)
```

6. Let's print the variable median values learned by `RobustScaler()`:

```
scaler.center_
```

We see the parameters learned by `RobustScaler()` in the following output:

```
array([3.53910000e+00, 2.90000000e+01,
5.22931763e+00,                 1.04878049e+00, 1.16500000e+03,
2.81635506e+00])
```

7. Now, let's display the IQR learned by `RobustScaler()`:

```
scaler.scale_
```

We can see the IQR for each variable in the following output:

```
array([2.16550000e+00, 1.90000000e+01,
1.59537022e+00,                 9.41284380e-02, 9.40000000e+02,
8.53176853e-01])
```

This scaling procedure does not change the variable distributions. Go ahead and compare the distribution of the variables before and after the transformation by using histograms.

How it works...

To scale the features using the median and IQR, we created an instance of `RobustScaler()`. With `fit()`, the scaler learned the median and IQR for each variable from the train set. With `transform()`, the scaler subtracted the median from each variable in the train and test sets and divided the result by the IQR.

After the transformation, the median values of the variables were centered at 0, but the overall shape of the distributions did not change. You can corroborate the effect of the transformation by displaying the histograms of the variables before and after the transformation and by printing out the main statistical parameters through `X_test.describe()` and `X_test_scaled.b()`.

Performing mean normalization

In mean normalization, we center the variable at 0 and rescale the distribution to the value range, so that its values lie between -1 and 1. This procedure involves subtracting the mean from each observation and then dividing the result by the difference between the minimum and maximum values, as shown here:

$$x_{scaled} = \frac{x - mean(x)}{max(x) - min(x)}$$

> **Note**
>
> Mean normalization is an alternative to standardization. In both cases, the variables are centered at 0. In mean normalization, the variance varies, while the values lie between -1 and 1. On the other hand, in standardization, the variance is set to 1 and the value range varies.

Mean normalization is a suitable alternative for models that need the variables to be centered at zero. However, it is sensitive to outliers and not a suitable option for sparse data, as it will destroy the sparse nature.

How to do it...

In this recipe, we will implement mean normalization with `pandas`:

1. Let's import `pandas` and the required scikit-learn class and function:

```
import pandas as pd
from sklearn.datasets import fetch_california_housing
from sklearn.model_selection import train_test_split
```

2. Let's load the California housing dataset from scikit-learn into a `pandas` DataFrame, dropping the `Latitude` and `Longitude` variables:

```
X, y = fetch_california_housing(
    return_X_y=True, as_frame=True)
X.drop(labels=[
    "Latitude", "Longitude"], axis=1, inplace=True)
```

3. Let's divide the data into train and test sets:

```
X_train, X_test, y_train, y_test = train_test_split(
    X, y, test_size=0.3, random_state=0)
```

4. Let's learn the mean values from the variables in the train set:

```
means = X_train.mean(axis=0)
```

> **Note**
>
> We set `axis=0` to take the mean of the rows – that is, of the observations in each variable. If we set `axis=1` instead, `pandas` will calculate the mean value per observation across all the columns.

By executing `print(mean)`, we display the mean values per variable:

```
MedInc              3.866667
HouseAge           28.618702
AveRooms            5.423404
AveBedrms           1.094775
Population       1425.157323
AveOccup            3.040518
dtype: float64
```

5. Now, let's determine the difference between the maximum and minimum values per variable:

```
ranges = X_train.max(axis=0)-X_train.min(axis=0)
```

By executing `print(ranges)`, we display the value ranges per variable:

```
MedInc             14.500200
HouseAge           51.000000
AveRooms          131.687179
AveBedrms          33.733333
Population      35679.000000
AveOccup          598.964286
dtype: float64
```

> **Note**
>
> The pandas `mean()`, `max()`, and `min()` methods return a pandas series.

6. Now, we'll apply mean normalization to the train and test sets by utilizing the learned parameters:

```
X_train_scaled = (X_train - means) / ranges
X_test_scaled = (X_test - means) / ranges
```

> **Note**
>
> In order to transform future data, you will need to store these parameters, for example, in a `.txt` or `.csv` file.

Step 6 returns pandas DataFrames with the transformed train and test sets. Go ahead and compare the variables before and after the transformations. You'll see that the distributions did not change, but the variables are centered at 0, and their values lie between -1 and 1.

How it works...

To implement mean normalization, we captured the mean values of the numerical variables in the train set using `mean()` from `pandas`. Next, we determined the difference between the maximum and minimum values of the numerical variables in the train set by utilizing `max()` and `min()` from `pandas`. Finally, we used the `pandas` series returned by these functions containing the mean values and the value ranges to normalize the train and test sets. We subtracted the mean from each observation in our train and test sets and divided the result by the value ranges. This returned the normalized variables in a `pandas` DataFrame.

There's more...

There is no dedicated scikit-learn transformer to implement mean normalization, but we can combine the use of two transformers to do so.

To do this, we need to import `pandas` and load the data, just like we did in *Steps 1 to 3* in the *How to do it...* section of this recipe. Then, follow these steps:

1. Import the scikit-learn transformers:

    ```python
    from sklearn.preprocessing import (
        StandardScaler, RobustScaler
    )
    ```

2. Let's set up `StandardScaler()` to learn and subtract the mean without dividing the result by the standard deviation:

    ```python
    scaler_mean = StandardScaler(
        with_mean=True, with_std=False,
    ).set_output(transform="pandas")
    ```

3. Now, let's set up `RobustScaler()` so that it does not remove the median from the values but divides them by the value range – that is, the difference between the maximum and minimum values:

    ```python
    scaler_minmax = RobustScaler(
        with_centering=False,
        with_scaling=True,
        quantile_range=(0, 100)
    ).set_output(transform="pandas")
    ```

> **Note**
>
> To divide by the difference between the minimum and maximum values, we need to specify `(0, 100)` in the `quantile_range` argument of `RobustScaler()`.

4. Let's fit the scalers to the train set so that they learn and store the mean, maximum, and minimum values:

```
scaler_mean.fit(X_train)
scaler_minmax.fit(X_train)
```

5. Finally, let's apply mean normalization to the train and test sets:

```
X_train_scaled = scaler_minmax.transform(
    scaler_mean.transform(X_train)
)
X_test_scaled = scaler_minmax.transform(
    scaler_mean.transform(X_test)
)
```

We transformed the data with `StandardScaler()` to remove the mean and then transformed the resulting DataFrame with `RobustScaler()` to divide the result by the range between the minimum and maximum values. We described the functionality of `StandardScaler()` in this chapter's *Standardizing the features* recipe and `RobustScaler()` in the *Scaling with the median and quantiles* recipe of this chapter.

Implementing maximum absolute scaling

Maximum absolute scaling scales the data to its maximum value – that is, it divides every observation by the maximum value of the variable:

$$x_{scaled} = \frac{x}{\max(x)}$$

As a result, the maximum value of each feature will be `1.0`. Note that maximum absolute scaling does not center the data, and hence, it's suitable for scaling sparse data. In this recipe, we will implement maximum absolute scaling with scikit-learn.

> **Note**
>
> Scikit-learn recommends using this transformer on data that is centered at 0 or on sparse data.

Getting ready

Maximum absolute scaling was specifically designed to scale sparse data. Thus, we will use a bag-of-words dataset that contains sparse variables for the recipe. In this dataset, the variables are words, the observations are documents, and the values are the number of times each word appears in the document. Most entries in the data are 0.

We will use a dataset consisting of a bag of words, which is available in the UCI Machine Learning Repository (`https://archive.ics.uci.edu/ml/datasets/Bag+of+Words`), which is licensed under CC BY 4.0 (`https://creativecommons.org/licenses/by/4.0/legalcode`).

I downloaded and prepared a small bag of words representing a simplified version of one of those datasets. You will find this dataset in the accompanying GitHub repository: `https://github.com/PacktPublishing/Python-Feature-Engineering-Cookbook-Third-Edition/tree/main/ch07-scaling`.

How to do it...

Let's begin by importing the required packages and loading the dataset:

1. Let's import the required libraries and the scaler:

    ```
    import matplotlib.pyplot as plt
    import pandas as pd
    from sklearn.preprocessing import MaxAbsScaler
    ```

2. Let's load the bag-of-words dataset:

    ```
    data = pd.read_csv("bag_of_words.csv")
    ```

    If we execute `data.head()`, we will see the DataFrame consisting of the words as columns, the documents as rows, and the number of times each word appeared in a document as values:

	advice	cab	decker	etis	eurobond	halligan	keen	pvr	refundable	soda
0	0.0	0.0	2.0	0.0	0.0	0.0	0.0	0.0	0.0	0.0
1	0.0	0.0	2.0	0.0	0.0	0.0	0.0	0.0	0.0	0.0
2	1.0	0.0	0.0	0.0	0.0	0.0	0.0	0.0	0.0	0.0
3	0.0	0.0	0.0	0.0	0.0	0.0	0.0	0.0	1.0	0.0
4	0.0	0.0	2.0	0.0	0.0	0.0	0.0	0.0	0.0	0.0

Figure 7.5 – DataFrame with the bag of words

> **Note**
>
> Although we omit this step in the recipe, remember that the maximum absolute values should be learned from a training dataset only. Split the dataset into train and test sets when carrying out your analysis.

3. Let's set up `MaxAbsScaler()` and fit it to the data so that it learns the variables' maximum values:

```
scaler = MaxAbsScaler().set_output(
    transform="pandas")
scaler.fit(data)
```

4. Now, let's scale the variables by utilizing the trained scaler:

```
data_scaled = scaler.transform(data)
```

> **Note**
>
> `MaxAbsScaler ()` stores the maximum values in its `max_abs_` attribute.

5. Let's display the maximum values stored by the scaler:

```
scaler.max_abs_
```

In the following output, we see the maximum number of times each word appeared in a document:

```
array([ 7.,   6.,   2.,   2., 11.,   4.,   3.,   6., 52.,   2.])
```

To follow up, let's plot the distributions of the original and scaled variables.

6. Let's make a histogram with the bag of words before the scaling:

```
data.hist(bins=20, figsize=(20, 20))
plt.show()
```

In the following output, we see histograms with the number of times each word appears in a document:

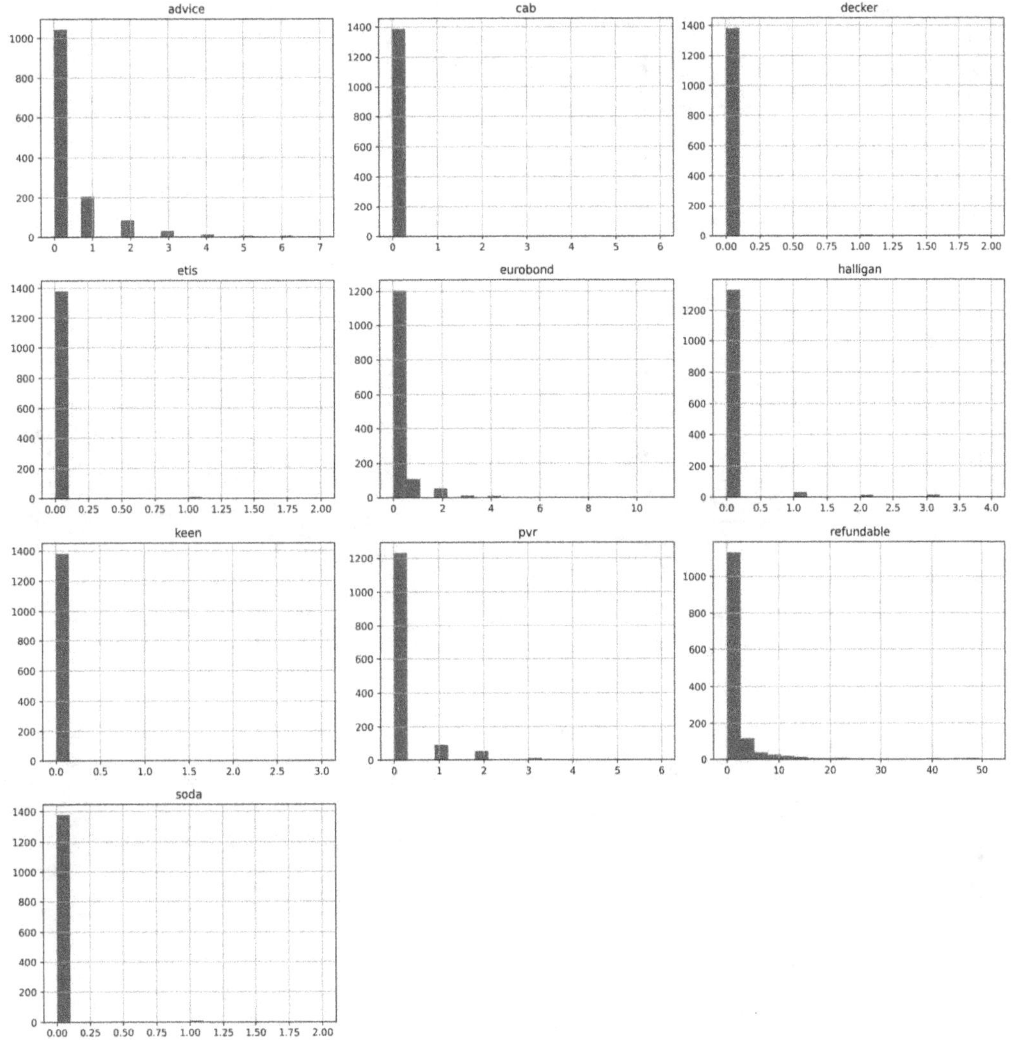

Figure 7.6 – Histograms with different word counts

7. Now, let's make a histogram with the scaled variables:

```
data_scaled.hist(bins=20, figsize=(20, 20))
plt.show()
```

In the following output, we can corroborate the change of scale of the variables, but their distribution shape remains the same:

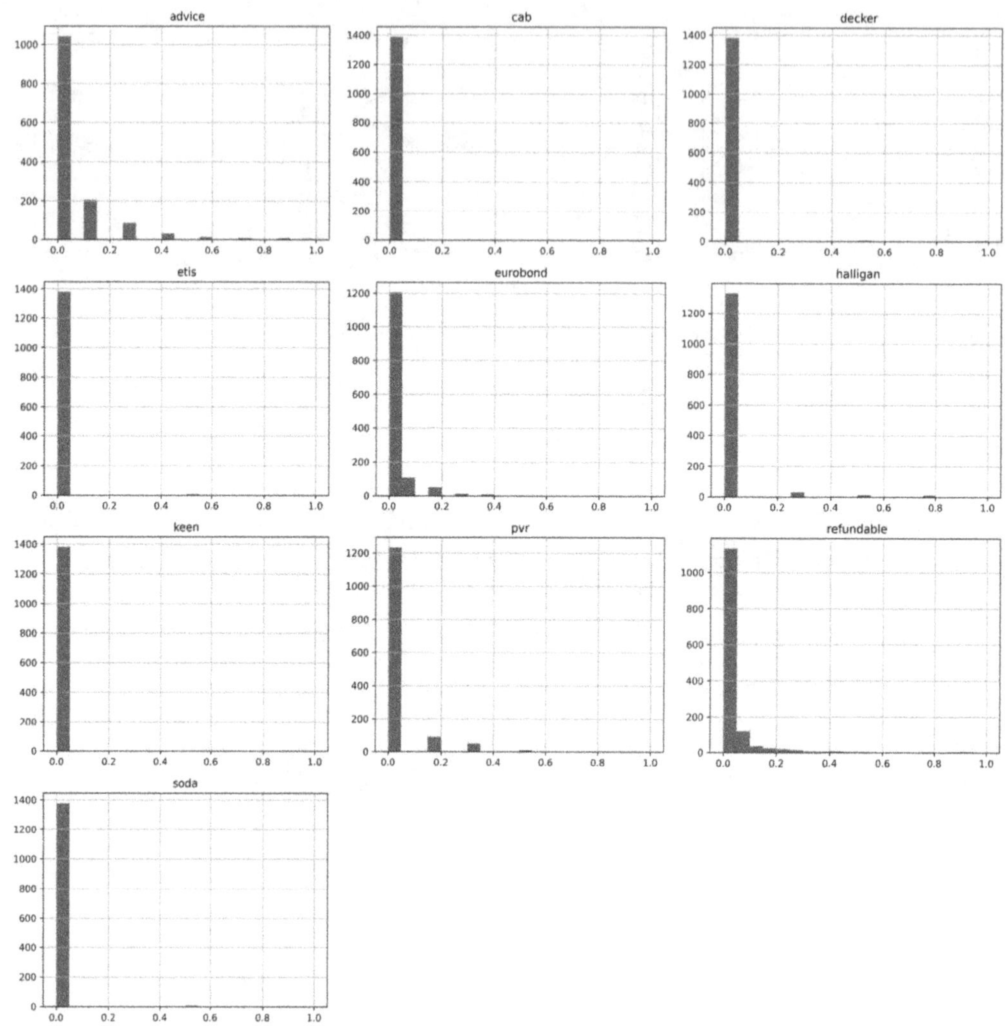

Figure 7.7 – Histograms of the word counts after the scaling

With scaling to the maximum absolute value, we linearly scale down the magnitude of the features.

How it works...

In this recipe, we scaled the sparse variables of a bag of words to their absolute maximum values by using `MaxAbsScaler()`. With `fit()`, the scaler learned the maximum absolute values for each variable and stored them in its `max_abs_` attribute. With `transform()`, the scaler divided the variables by their absolute maximum values, returning a `pandas` DataFrame.

> **Note**
>
> Remember that you can change the output container to a NumPy array or a `polars` DataFrame through the `set_output()` method of the scikit-learn library's transformers.

There's more...

If you want to center the variables' distribution at 0 and then scale them to their absolute maximum, you can do so by combining the use of two scikit-learn transformers within a pipeline:

1. Let's import the required libraries, transformers, and functions:

```python
import pandas as pd
from sklearn.datasets import fetch_california_housing
from sklearn.model_selection import train_test_split
from sklearn.preprocessing import (
    MaxAbsScaler, StandardScaler)
from sklearn.pipeline import Pipeline
```

2. Let's load the California housing dataset and split it into train and test sets:

```python
X, y = fetch_california_housing(
    return_X_y=True, as_frame=True)
X.drop( labels=[ "Latitude",
    "Longitude"], axis=1, inplace=True)
X_train, X_test, y_train, y_test = train_test_split(
    X, y, test_size=0.3, random_state=0)
```

3. Let's set up `StandardScaler()` from scikit-learn so that it learns and subtracts the mean but does not divide the result by the standard deviation:

```python
scaler_mean = StandardScaler(
    with_mean=True, with_std=False)
```

4. Now, let's set up `MaxAbsScaler()` with its default parameters:

```python
scaler_maxabs = MaxAbsScaler()
```

5. Let's include both scalers within a pipeline that returns pandas DataFrames:

```
scaler = Pipeline([
    ("scaler_mean", scaler_mean),
    ("scaler_max", scaler_maxabs),
]).set_output(transform="pandas")
```

6. Let's fit the scalers to the train set so that they learn the required parameters:

```
scaler.fit(X_train)
```

7. Finally, let's transform the train and test sets:

```
X_train_scaled = scaler.transform(X_train)
X_test_scaled = scaler.transform(X_test)
```

The pipeline applies `StandardScaler()` and `MaxAbsScaler()` in sequence to first remove the mean and then scale the resulting variables to their maximum values.

Scaling to vector unit length

Scaling to the vector unit length involves scaling individual observations (not features) to have a unit norm. Each sample (that is, each row of the data) is rescaled independently of other samples so that its norm equals one. Each row constitutes a **feature vector** containing the values of every variable for that row. Hence, with this scaling method, we rescale the feature vector.

The norm of a vector is a measure of its magnitude or length in a given space and it can be determined by using the Manhattan (*l1*) or the Euclidean (*l2*) distance. The Manhattan distance is given by the sum of the absolute components of the vector:

$$l1(x) = \left|x_1\right| + \left|x_2\right| + \ldots + \left|x_n\right|$$

The Euclidean distance is given by the square root of the square sum of the component of the vector:

$$l2(x) = \sqrt{x_1^2 + x_2^2 + \ldots + x_n^2}$$

Here, x_1, x_2, and x_n are the values of variables *1*, *2*, and *n* for each observation. Scaling to unit norm consists of dividing each feature vector's value by either *l1* or *l2*, so that after the scaling, the norm of the feature vector is *1*. To be clear, we divide each of x_1, x_2, and x_n, by *l1* or *l2*.

This scaling procedure changes the variables' distribution, as illustrated in the following figure:

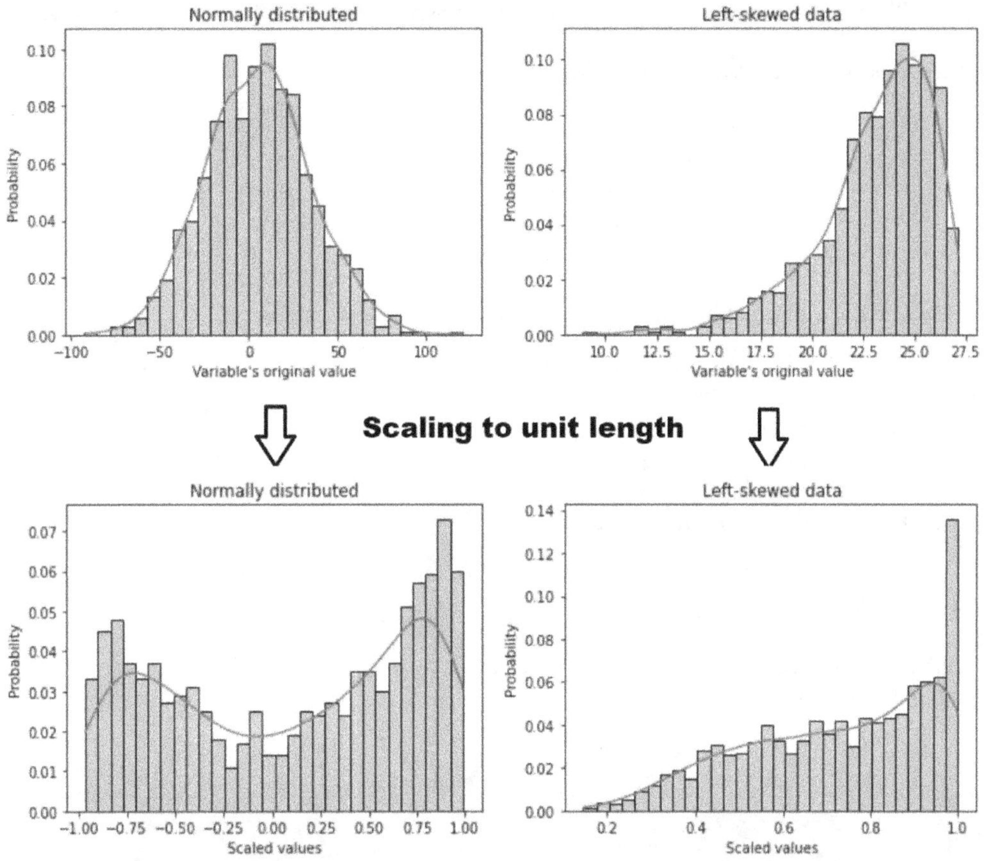

Figure 7.8 – Distribution of a normal and skewed variable before and after scaling each observation's feature vector to its norm

> **Note**
>
> This scaling technique scales each observation and not each variable. The scaling methods that we discussed so far in this chapter aimed at shifting and resetting the scale of the variables' distribution. When we scale to the unit length, however, we normalize each observation individually, contemplating their values across all features.

Scaling to the unit norm can be used when utilizing kernels to quantify similarity for text classification and clustering. In this recipe, we will scale each observation's feature vector to a unit length of 1 using scikit-learn.

How to do it...

To begin, we'll import the required packages, load the dataset, and prepare the train and test sets:

1. Let's import the required Python packages, classes, and functions:

```python
import numpy as np
import pandas as pd
from sklearn.datasets import fetch_california_housing
from sklearn.model_selection import train_test_split
from sklearn.preprocessing import Normalizer
```

2. Let's load the California housing dataset into a `pandas` DataFrame:

```python
X, y = fetch_california_housing(
    return_X_y=True, as_frame=True)
X.drop(labels=[
    "Latitude", "Longitude"], axis=1, inplace=True)
```

3. Let's divide the data into train and test sets:

```python
X_train, X_test, y_train, y_test = train_test_split(
    X, y, test_size=0.3, random_state=0)
```

4. Let's set up the scikit-learn library's `Normalizer()` transformer to scale each observation to the Manhattan distance or `l1`:

```python
scaler = Normalizer(norm='l1')
```

> **Note**
>
> To normalize to the Euclidean distance, you need to set the norm to `l2` using `scaler = Normalizer(norm='l2')`.

5. Let's transform the train and test sets – that is, we'll divide each observation's feature vector by its norm:

```python
X_train_scaled = scaler.fit_transform(X_train)
X_test_scaled = scaler.transform(X_test)
```

We can calculate the length (that is, the Manhattan distance of each observation's feature vector) using `linalg()` from NumPy.

6. Let's calculate the norm (Manhattan distance) before scaling the variables:

```python
np.round(np.linalg.norm(X_train, ord=1, axis=1), 1)
```

As expected, the norm of each observation varies:

```
array([ 255.3,   889.1, 1421.7, ...,   744.6, 1099.5,
           1048.9])
```

7. Let's now calculate the norm after the scaling:

```
np.round(np.linalg.norm(
    X_train_scaled, ord=1, axis=1), 1)
```

> **Note**
>
> You need to set `ord=1` for the Manhattan distance and `ord=2` for the Euclidean distance as arguments of NumPy's `linalg()` function, depending on whether you scaled the features to the l1 or l2 norm.

We see that the Manhattan distance of each feature vector is 1 after scaling:

```
array([1., 1., 1., ..., 1., 1., 1.])
```

Based on the scikit-learn library's documentation, this scaling method can be useful when using a quadratic form such as the dot-product or any other kernel to quantify the similarity of a pair of samples.

How it works...

In this recipe, we scaled the observations from the California housing dataset to their feature vector unit norm by utilizing the Manhattan or Euclidean distance. To scale the feature vectors, we created an instance of `Normalizer()` from scikit-learn and set the norm to l1 for the Manhattan distance. For the Euclidean distance, we set the norm to l2. Then, we applied the `fit()` method, although there were no parameters to be learned, as this normalization procedure depends exclusively on the values of the features for each observation. Finally, with the `transform()` method, the scaler divided each observation's feature vector by its norm. This returned a NumPy array with the scaled dataset. After the scaling, we used NumPy's `linalg.norm` function to calculate the norm (l1 and l2) of each vector to confirm that after the transformation, it was 1.

8

Creating New Features

Adding new features to a dataset can help machine learning models learn patterns and important details in the data. For example, in finance, the **disposable income**, which is the *total income* minus the *acquired debt* for any one month, might be more relevant for credit risk than just the income or the acquired debt. Similarly, the *total acquired debt* of a person across financial products, such as a car loan, a mortgage, and credit cards, might be more important to estimate the credit risk than any debt considered individually. In these examples, we use domain knowledge to craft new variables, and these variables are created by adding or subtracting existing features.

In some cases, a variable may not have a linear or monotonic relationship with the target, but a polynomial combination might. For example, if our variable has a quadratic relationship with the target, $y = x^2$, we can convert that into a linear relationship by squaring the original variable. We can also help linear models better understand the relationships between variables and targets by transforming the predictors through splines, or by using decision trees.

The advantage of crafting additional features to train simpler models, such as linear or logistic regression, is that both the features and the models remain interpretable. We can explain the reasons driving a model's output to management, clients, and regulators, adding a layer of transparency to our machine learning pipelines. In addition, simpler models tend to be faster to train and easier to deploy and maintain.

In this chapter, we will create new features by transforming or combining variables with mathematical functions, splines, and decision trees.

This chapter will cover the following recipes:

- Combining features with mathematical functions
- Comparing features to reference variables
- Performing polynomial expansion
- Combining features with decision trees
- Creating periodic features from cyclical variables
- Creating spline features

Technical requirements

In this chapter, we will use the `pandas`, `numpy`, `matplotlib`, `scikit-learn`, and `feature-engine` Python libraries.

Combining features with mathematical functions

New features can be created by combining existing variables with mathematical and statistical functions. Taking an example from the finance industry, we can calculate the total debt of a person by summing up their debt across individual financial products, such as car loan, mortgage, or credit card debt:

Total debt = car loan debt + credit card debt + mortgage debt

We can also derive other insightful features using alternative statistical operations. For example, we can determine the maximum debt of a customer across financial products or the average time a user spends on a website:

maximum debt = max(car loan balance, credit card balance, mortgage balance)

average time on website = mean(time spent on homepage, time spent on about page, time spent on FAQ page)

We can, in principle, use any mathematical or statistical operation to create new features, such as the product, mean, standard deviation, or maximum or minimum values. In this recipe, we will implement these mathematical operations using `pandas` and `feature-engine`.

> **Note**
>
> While, in the recipe, we can show you how to combine features with mathematical functions, we can't do justice to the use of domain knowledge in deciding which function to apply, as that varies with every domain. So, we will leave that with you.

Getting ready

In this recipe, we will use the breast cancer dataset from `scikit-learn`. The features are computed from digitized images of breast cells and describe the characteristics of their cell nuclei, in terms of smoothness, concavity, symmetry, and compactness, among others. Each row contains information about the morphology of cell nuclei in a tissue sample. The target variable indicates whether the tissue sample corresponds to cancerous cells. The idea is to predict whether the tissue samples belong to benign or malignant breast cells, based on their cell nuclei morphology.

To become familiar with the dataset, run the following commands in a Jupyter notebook or Python console:

```
from sklearn.datasets import load_breast_cancer
data = load_breast_cancer()
print(data.DESCR)
```

The preceding code block should print out a description of the dataset and an interpretation of its variables.

How to do it...

In this recipe, we will create new features by combining variables using multiple mathematical operations:

1. Let's begin by loading the necessary libraries, classes, and data:

```
import pandas as pd
from feature_engine.creation import MathFeatures
from sklearn.datasets import load_breast_cancer
```

2. Next, load the breast cancer dataset into a pandas DataFrame:

```
data = load_breast_cancer()
df = pd.DataFrame(data.data,
    columns=data.feature_names)
```

In the following code lines, we will create new features by combining variables using multiple mathematical operations.

3. Let's begin by creating a list with the subset of the features that we want to combine:

```
features = [
    «mean smoothness",
    «mean compactness",
    «mean concavity",
    «mean concave points",
    «mean symmetry",
]
```

The features in *step 3* represent the mean characteristics of cell nuclei in the images. It might be useful to obtain the mean across all examined characteristics.

4. Let's get the mean value of the features and then display the resulting feature:

```
df["mean_features"] = df[features].mean(axis=1)
df["mean_features"].head()
```

The following output shows the mean value of the features from *step 3*:

```
0      0.21702
1      0.10033
2      0.16034
3      0.20654
4      0.14326
Name: mean_features, dtype: float64
```

5. Similarly, to capture the general variability of the cell nuclei, let's determine the standard deviation of the mean characteristics, and then display the resulting feature:

```
df["std_features"] = df[features].std(axis=1)
df["std_features"].head()
```

The following output shows the standard deviation of the features from step 3:

```
0        0.080321
1        0.045671
2        0.042333
3        0.078097
4        0.044402
Name: std_features, dtype: float64
```

> **Note**
>
> When we craft new features based on domain knowledge, we know exactly how we want to combine the variables. We could also combine features with multiple operations and then evaluate whether they are predictive, using, for example, a feature selection algorithm or deriving feature importance from the machine learning model.

6. Let's make a list containing mathematical functions that we want to use to combine the features:

```
math_func = [
    "sum", "prod", "mean", "std", "max", "min"]
```

7. Now, let's apply the functions from *step 6* to combine the features from *step 3*, capturing the resulting variables in a new DataFrame:

```
df_t = df[features].agg(math_func, axis="columns")
```

If we execute df_t.head(), we will see the DataFrame with the newly created features:

	sum	prod	mean	std	max	min
0	1.08510	0.000351	0.21702	0.080321	0.3001	0.11840
1	0.50165	0.000007	0.10033	0.045671	0.1812	0.07017
2	0.80170	0.000092	0.16034	0.042333	0.2069	0.10960
3	1.03270	0.000267	0.20654	0.078097	0.2839	0.10520
4	0.71630	0.000050	0.14326	0.044402	0.1980	0.10030

Figure 8.1 – A DataFrame with the newly created features

> **Note**
>
> `pandas agg` can apply multiple functions to combine features. It can take a list of strings with the function names, as we did in *step 7*; a list of NumPy functions, such as `np.log`; and Python functions that you create.

We can create the same features that we created with `pandas` automatically by using `feature-engine`.

8. Let's create a list by using the name of the output features:

```
new_feature_names = [
    "sum_f", "prod_f", "mean_f",
    „std_f", „max_f", „min_f"]
```

9. Let's set up `MathFeatures()` to apply the functions in *step 6* to the features from *step 3*, naming the new features with the strings from *step 8*:

```
create = MathFeatures(
    variables=features,
    func=math_func,
    new_variables_names=new_feature_names,
)
```

10. Let's add the new features to the original DataFrame, capturing the result in a new variable:

```
df_t = create.fit_transform(df)
```

We can display the input and output features by executing `df_t[features + new_feature_names].head()`:

	mean smoothness	mean compactness	mean concavity	mean concave points	mean symmetry	sum_f	prod_f	mean_f	std_f	max_f	min_f
0	0.11840	0.27760	0.3001	0.14710	0.2419	1.08510	0.000351	0.21702	0.080321	0.3001	0.11840
1	0.08474	0.07864	0.0869	0.07017	0.1812	0.50165	0.000007	0.10033	0.045671	0.1812	0.07017
2	0.10960	0.15990	0.1974	0.12790	0.2069	0.80170	0.000092	0.16034	0.042333	0.2069	0.10960
3	0.14250	0.28390	0.2414	0.10520	0.2597	1.03270	0.000267	0.20654	0.078097	0.2839	0.10520
4	0.10030	0.13280	0.1980	0.10430	0.1809	0.71630	0.000050	0.14326	0.044402	0.1980	0.10030

Figure 8.2 – DataFrame with the input features and the newly created variables

While `pandas agg` returns a DataFrame with the features resulting from the operation, `feature-engine` goes one step further, by concatenating the new features to the original DataFrame.

How it works...

`pandas` has many built-in operations to apply mathematical and statistical computations to a group of variables. To combine features mathematically, we first made a list containing the names of the features we wanted to combine. Then, we determined the mean and standard deviation of those features by using `pandas mean()` and `std()`. We could also apply any of the `sum()`, `prod()`, `max()`, and `min()` methods, which return the sum, product, maximum, and minimum values of those features, respectively. To perform these operations across the columns, we added the `axis=1` argument within the methods.

With pandas `agg()`, we applied several mathematical functions simultaneously. It takes as arguments a list of strings, corresponding to the functions to apply and the `axis` that the functions should be applied to, which can be either `1` for columns or `0` for rows. As a result, pandas `agg()` returned a `pandas` DataFrame, resulting from applying the mathematical functions to the groups of features.

Finally, we created the same features by combining variables with `feature-engine`. We used the `MathFeatures()` transformer, which takes the features to combine and the functions to apply as input; it also has the option to indicate the names of the resulting features. When we used `fit()`, the transformer did not learn parameters but checked that the variables were indeed numerical. The `transform()` method triggered the use of `pandas.agg` under the hood, applying the mathematical functions to create the new variables.

See also

To find out more about the mathematical operations supported by pandas, visit `https://pandas.pydata.org/pandas-docs/stable/reference/frame.html#computations-descriptive-stats`.

To learn more about `pandas aggregate`, check out `https://pandas.pydata.org/pandas-docs/stable/reference/api/pandas.DataFrame.aggregate.html`.

Comparing features to reference variables

In the previous recipe, *Combining features with mathematical functions*, we created new features by applying mathematical or statistical functions, such as the sum or the mean, to a group of variables. Some mathematical operations, however, such as subtraction or division, are performed *between* features. These operations are useful to derive ratios, such as the *debt-to-income ratio*:

$$debt\text{-}to\text{-}income\ ratio = total\ debt\ /\ total\ income$$

These operations are also useful to compute differences, such as the *disposable income*:

$$disposable\ income = income - total\ debt$$

In this recipe, we will learn how to create new features by subtracting or dividing variables with `pandas` and `feature-engine`.

> **Note**
>
> In the recipe, we will show you how to create features with subtraction and division. We hope that the examples, relating to the financial sector, shed some light on how to use domain knowledge to decide which features to combine and how.

How to do it...

Let's begin by loading the necessary Python libraries and the breast cancer dataset from scikit-learn:

1. Load the necessary libraries, classes, and data:

    ```python
    import pandas as pd
    from feature_engine.creation import RelativeFeatures
    from sklearn.datasets import load_breast_cancer
    ```

2. Load the breast cancer dataset into a pandas DataFrame:

    ```python
    data = load_breast_cancer()
    df = pd.DataFrame(data.data,
        columns=data.feature_names)
    ```

    In the breast cancer dataset, some features capture the worst and the mean characteristics of the cell nuclei of breast cells. For example, for each image (that is, for each row), we have the worst compactness observed in all nuclei and the mean compactness of all nuclei. A feature that captures the difference between the worst and the mean value could predict malignancy.

3. Let's capture the difference between two features, the `worst compactness` and `mean compactness` of cell nuclei, in a new variable and display its values:

    ```python
    df["difference"] = df["worst compactness"].sub(
        df["mean compactness"])
    df["difference"].head()
    ```

    In the following output, we can see the difference between these feature values:

    ```
    0    0.38800
    1    0.10796
    2    0.26460
    3    0.58240
    4    0.07220
    Name: difference, dtype: float64
    ```

> **Note**
>
> We can perform the same calculation by executing `df["difference"] = df["worst compactness"] - (df["mean compactness"])`.

Similarly, the ratio between the worst and the average characteristic of the cell nuclei might be indicative of malignancy.

4. Let's create a new feature with the ratio between the worst and mean radius of the nuclei, and then display its values:

```
df["quotient"] = df["worst radius"].div(
    df["mean radius"])
df["quotient"].head()
```

In the following output, we can see the values corresponding to the ratio between the features:

```
0    1.410784
1    1.214876
2    1.197054
3    1.305604
4    1.110892
Name: quotient, dtype: float64
```

> **Note**
>
> We can calculate the ratio by executing an alternative command, df["quotient"] = df["worst radius"] / (df["mean radius"]).

We can also capture the ratio and difference between every nuclei morphology characteristic and the mean radius or mean area of the nuclei. Let's begin by capturing these subsets of variables into lists.

5. Let's make a list of the features in the numerator:

```
features = [
    "mean smoothness",
    «mean compactness",
    "mean concavity",
    "mean symmetry"
]
```

6. Let's make a list of the features in the denominator:

```
reference = ["mean radius", "mean area"]
```

> **Note**
>
> We can create features by dividing the features in *step 5* by one of the features in *step 6* with pandas, by executing df[features].div(df["mean radius"]). For subtraction, we'd execute df[features].sub(df["mean radius"]).

7. Let's set up the `feature-engine` library's `RelativeFeatures()` so that it subtracts or divides every feature from *step 5* with respect to the features from *step 6*:

```python
creator = RelativeFeatures(
    variables=features,
    reference=reference,
    func=["sub", "div"],
)
```

> **Note**
>
> Subtracting the features from *step 5* and *step 6* does not make biological sense, but we will do it anyway to demonstrate the use of the `RelativeFeatures()` transformer.

8. Let's add the new features to the DataFrame and capture the result in a new variable:

```python
df_t = creator.fit_transform(df)
```

9. Let's capture the names of the new features in a list:

```python
all_feat = creator.feature_names_in_
new_features = [
    f for f in df_t.columns if f not in all_feat]
```

> **Note**
>
> `feature_names_in_` is a common attribute in `scikit-learn` and `feature-engine` transformers and stores the name of the variables from the DataFrame used to fit the transformer. In other words, it stores the names of the input features. When using `transform()`, the transformers check that the features from the new input dataset match those used during training. In *step 9*, we leverage this attribute to find the additional variables added to the data after the transformation.

If we execute `print(new_features)`, we will see a list with the names of the features created by `ReferenceFeatures()`. Note that the features contain the variables on the left- and right-hand sides of the mathematical equation, plus the function that was applied to them to create the new feature:

```python
['mean smoothness_sub_mean radius',
 'mean compactness_sub_mean radius',
 'mean concavity_sub_mean radius',
 'mean symmetry_sub_mean radius',
 'mean smoothness_sub_mean area',
 'mean compactness_sub_mean area',
 'mean concavity_sub_mean area',
 'mean symmetry_sub_mean area',
```

```
'mean smoothness_div_mean radius',
'mean compactness_div_mean radius',
'mean concavity_div_mean radius',
'mean symmetry_div_mean radius',
'mean smoothness_div_mean area',
'mean compactness_div_mean area',
'mean concavity_div_mean area',
'mean symmetry_div_mean area']
```

Finally, we can display the first five rows of the resulting variables by executing `df_t[new_features].head()`:

	mean smoothness_sub_mean radius	mean compactness_sub_mean radius	mean concavity_sub_mean radius	mean symmetry_sub_mean radius	mean smoothness_sub_mean area	mean compactness_sub_mean area
0	-17.87160	-17.71240	-17.6899	-17.7481	-1000.88160	-1000.72240
1	-20.48526	-20.49136	-20.4831	-20.3888	-1325.91526	-1325.92136
2	-19.58040	-19.53010	-19.4926	-19.4831	-1202.89040	-1202.84010
3	-11.27750	-11.13610	-11.1786	-11.1603	-385.95750	-385.81610
4	-20.18970	-20.15720	-20.0920	-20.1091	-1296.89970	-1296.86720

Figure 8.3 – A DataFrame with the newly created features

`feature-engine` adds new features as columns at the right of the original DataFrame and automatically adds variable names to those features. By doing so, `feature-engine` automates much of the manual work that we would do with `pandas`.

How it works...

`pandas` has many built-in operations to compare a feature or a group of features to a reference variable. In this recipe, we used pandas `sub()` and `div()` to determine the difference or the ratio between two variables, or a subset of variables and one reference feature.

To subtract one variable from another, we applied `sub()` to a `pandas` series with the first variable, passing the `pandas` series with the second variable as an argument to `sub()`. This operation returned a third `pandas` series with the difference between the first and second variables. To divide one variable from another, we used `div()`, which works identically to `sub()` – that is, it divides the variable on the left by the variable passed as an argument of `div()`.

Then, we combined several variables with two reference variables automatically via subtraction or division, by utilizing `ReferenceFeatures()` from Feature-engine. The `ReferenceFeatures()` transformer takes the variables to be combined, the reference variables, and the functions to use to combine them. When using `fit()`, the transformer did not learn about parameters but checked that the variables were numerical. Executing `transform()` added the new features to the DataFrame.

> **Note**
>
> `ReferenceFeatures()` can also add, multiply, get the modulo, or get the power of a group of variables relating to a second group of reference variables. You can find out more in its documentation: `https://feature-engine.readthedocs.io/en/latest/api_doc/creation/RelativeFeatures.html`.

See also

To learn more about the binary operations supported by `pandas`, visit `https://pandas.pydata.org/pandas-docs/stable/reference/frame.html#binary-operator-functions`.

Performing polynomial expansion

Simple models, such as linear and logistic regression, can capture complex patterns if we feed them the right features. Sometimes, we can create powerful features by combining the variables in our datasets with themselves or with other variables. For example, in the following figure, we can see that the target, y, has a quadratic relation with the variable, x, and as shown in the left panel, a linear model is not able to capture that relationship accurately:

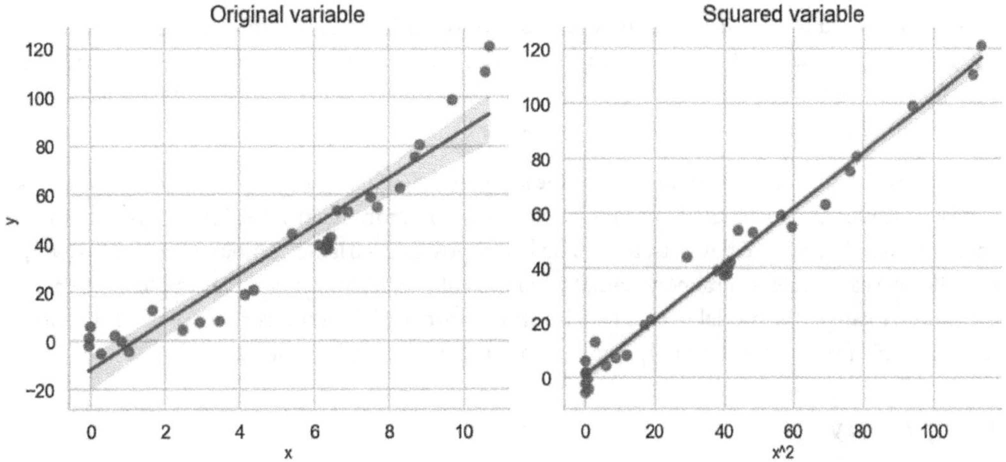

Figure 8.4 – A linear model fit to predict a target, y, from a feature, x, which has a quadratic relationship to the target, before and after squaring x. In the left panel: the model offers a poor fit by using the original variable; in the right panel, the model offers a better fit, based on the square of the original variable

This linear model has a quadratic relationship to the target, before and after squaring x. However, if we square x, or, in other words, if we create a second-degree polynomial of the feature, the linear model can accurately predict the target, y, from the square of x, as we see in the right panel.

Another classical example in which a simple feature can make a simple model, such as logistic regression, understand the underlying relationship in the data is the **XOR** situation. In the left panel of the following diagram, we see how the target class is distributed across the values of *x1* and *x2* (the class is highlighted with different color shades):

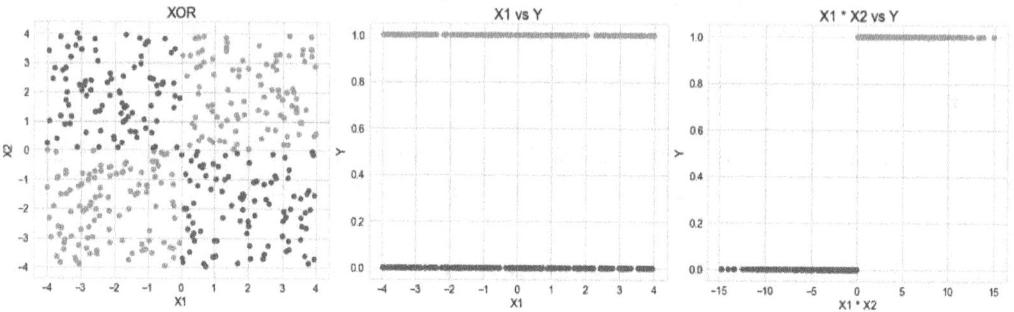

Figure 8.5 – An illustration of the XOR relationship and how combining features allows a full class separation

If both features are positive, or both features are negative, then the class is 1, but if the features take different signs, then the class is 0 (left panel). Logistic regression will not be able to pick this pattern from each individual feature because, as we can see in the middle panel, there is significant class overlap across the values of the feature – in this case, x1. However, multiplying x1 by x2 creates a feature that allows a logistic regression to predict the classes accurately because x3, as can we see in the right panel, allows the classes to be clearly separated.

With similar logic, polynomial combinations of the same or different variables can return new variables that convey additional information and capture feature interaction thereby resulting in useful inputs for linear models. With huge datasets, analyzing every possible variable combination is not always possible. But we can create several polynomial variables automatically, using, for example, `scikit-learn`, and we can let the model decide which variables are useful. In this recipe, we will learn how to create multiple features through polynomial combinations using scikit-learn.

Getting ready

Polynomial expansion serves to automate the creation of new features, capture feature interaction, and potential non-linear relationships between the original variables and the target. To create polynomial features, we need to determine which features to combine and which polynomial degree to use.

> **Note**
>
> While determining the features to combine or the degree of the polynomial combination is not an easy task, keep in mind that high polynomial degrees will result in a lot of new features and may lead to overfitting. In general, we keep the degree low, to a maximum of 2 or 3.

The `PolynomialFeatures()` transformer from `scikit-learn` creates polynomial combinations of the features with a degree less than or equal to a user-specified degree, automatically.

To follow up easily with this recipe, let's first understand the output of `PolynomialFeatures()` when used to create second- and third-degree polynomial combinations of three variables.

Second-degree polynomial combinations of three variables – a, b, and c – will return the following new features:

$$1, a, b, c, ab, ac, bc, a2, b2, c2$$

From the previous features, a, b, and c are the original variables; ab, ac, and bc are the products of those features; and $a2$, $b2$, and $c2$ are the squared values of the original features. `PolynomialFeatures()` also returns the bias term 1, which we would probably exclude when creating features.

> **Note**
>
> The resulting features – ab, ac, and bc – are called **interactions** or feature interactions of **degree 2**. The degree reflects the number of variables combined. The result combines a maximum of two variables because we indicated a second-degree polynomial as the maximum allowed combination.

Third-degree polynomial combinations of the three variables – a, b, and c – will return the following new features:

$$1, a, b, c, ab, ac, bc, abc, a2b, a2c, b2a, b2c, c2a, c2b, a3, b3, c3$$

Among the returned features, in addition to those returned by the second-degree polynomial combination, we now have the third-degree combinations of the features with themselves ($a3$, $b3$, and $c3$), the squared values of every feature combined linearly with a second feature ($a2b$, $a2c$, $b2a$, $b2c$, $c2a$, and $c2b$), and the product of the three features (abc). Note how we have all possible interactions of degrees 1, 2, and 3 and the bias term 1.

Now that we understand the output of the polynomial expansion implemented by `scikit-learn`, let's jump into the recipe.

How to do it...

In this recipe, we will create features with polynomial expansion using a toy dataset to become familiar with the resulting variables. Creating features with the polynomial expansion of a real dataset is identical to what we will discuss in this recipe:

1. Let's import the required libraries, classes, and data:

```
import numpy as np
import pandas as pd
import matplotlib.pyplot as plt
```

```
from sklearn import set_config
from sklearn.preprocessing import PolynomialFeatures
```

2. Let's set `scikit-learn` library's `set_output` API globally so that all transformers return a DataFrame as a result of the `transform()` method:

```
set_config(transform_output="pandas")
```

3. Let's create a DataFrame containing one variable, with values from 1 to 10:

```
df = pd.DataFrame(np.linspace(
    0, 10, 11), columns=["var"])
```

4. Let's set up `PolynomialFeatures()` to create all possible combinations up to a third-degree polynomial of the single variable and exclude the bias term from the result – that is, we will exclude the value *1*:

```
poly = PolynomialFeatures(
    degree=3,
    interaction_only=False,
    include_bias=False)
```

5. Now, let's create the polynomial combinations:

```
dft = poly.fit_transform(df)
```

If we execute `dft`, we'll see a DataFrame with the original feature, followed by its values squared, and then its values to the power of three:

	var	var^2	var^3
0	0.0	0.0	0.0
1	1.0	1.0	1.0
2	2.0	4.0	8.0
3	3.0	9.0	27.0
4	4.0	16.0	64.0
5	5.0	25.0	125.0
6	6.0	36.0	216.0
7	7.0	49.0	343.0
8	8.0	64.0	512.0
9	9.0	81.0	729.0
10	10.0	100.0	1000.0

Figure 8.6 – A DataFrame with the polynomial expansion of the third degree of a single variable

If, instead of returning a DataFrame, `PolynomialFeatures()` returns a NumPy array and you want to obtain the names of the features in the array, you can do so by executing `poly.get_feature_names_out()`, which returns `array(['var', 'var^2', 'var^3'], dtype=object)`.

6. Now, let's plot the new feature values against the original variable:

```python
dft = pd.DataFrame(
    dft, columns=poly.get_feature_names_out())
plt.plot(df["var"], dft)
plt.legend(dft.columns)
plt.xlabel("original variable")
plt.ylabel("new variables")
plt.show()
```

In the following diagram, we can see the relationship between the polynomial features and the original variable:

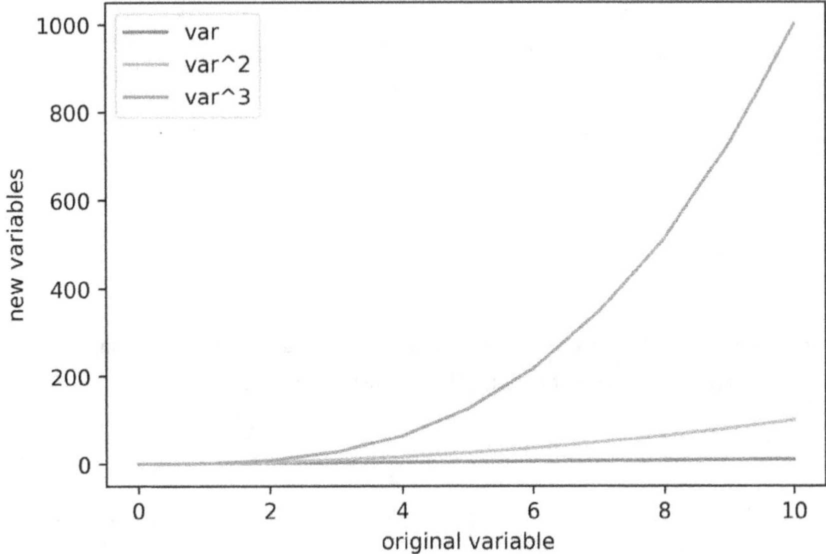

Figure 8.7 – The relationship between the features resulting from polynomial expansion and the original variable

7. Let's add two additional variables to our toy dataset, with values from 1 to 10:

```python
df["col"] = np.linspace(0, 5, 11)
df["feat"] = np.linspace(0, 5, 11)
```

8. Next, let's combine the three features in the dataset with polynomial expansion up to the second degree, but this time, we will only return features produced by combining at least two different variables – that is, the interaction features:

```
poly = PolynomialFeatures(
    degree=2, interaction_only=True,
    include_bias=False)
dft = poly.fit_transform(df)
```

If we execute `dft`, we will see the features resulting from the polynomial expansion, which contain the original features, plus all possible combinations of the three variables but without the quadratic terms, as we set the transformer to return only the interaction between features:

	var	col	feat	var col	var feat	col feat
0	0.0	0.0	0.0	0.0	0.0	0.00
1	1.0	0.5	0.5	0.5	0.5	0.25
2	2.0	1.0	1.0	2.0	2.0	1.00
3	3.0	1.5	1.5	4.5	4.5	2.25
4	4.0	2.0	2.0	8.0	8.0	4.00
5	5.0	2.5	2.5	12.5	12.5	6.25
6	6.0	3.0	3.0	18.0	18.0	9.00
7	7.0	3.5	3.5	24.5	24.5	12.25
8	8.0	4.0	4.0	32.0	32.0	16.00
9	9.0	4.5	4.5	40.5	40.5	20.25
10	10.0	5.0	5.0	50.0	50.0	25.00

Figure 8.8 – A DataFrame with the result of creating features with polynomial expansion but retaining only the interaction between variables

> **Note**
>
> Go ahead and create third-degree polynomial combinations of the features, returning only the interactions or all possible features to get a better sense of the output of `PolynomialFeatures()`.

With that, we've learned how to create new features by combining existing variables with themselves or other features in data. Creating features via polynomial expansion using a real dataset is, in essence, identical.

If you want to combine only a subset of features, you can select the features to combine by utilizing `ColumnTransformer()`, as we will demonstrate in the *There's more...* section ahead in this recipe, or by using `SklearnTransformerWrapper()` from `feature-engine`, as you can see in the accompanying GitHub repository: `https://github.com/PacktPublishing/Python-Feature-Engineering-Cookbook-Third-Edition/blob/main/ch08-creation/Recipe3-PolynomialExpansion.ipynb`.

How it works...

In this recipe, we created features by using polynomial combinations of a feature with itself or among three variables. To create these polynomial features, we used `PolynomialFeatures()` from `scikit-learn`. By default, `PolynomialFeatures()` generates a new feature matrix consisting of all polynomial combinations of the features in the data, with a degree less than or equal to the user-specified `degree`. By setting `degree` to 3, we created all possible polynomial combinations of a degree of 3 or smaller. To retain the combination of a feature with itself, we set the `interaction_only` parameter to `False`. To avoid returning the bias term, we set the `include_bias` parameter to `False`.

> **Note**
>
> Setting the `interaction_only` parameter to `True` returns the interaction terms only – that is, the variables resulting from combinations of two or more variables.

The `fit()` method determined all of the possible feature combinations based on the parameters specified. At this stage, the transformer did not perform actual mathematical computations. The `transform()` method performed the mathematical computations with the features to create the new variables. With the `get_feature_names()` method, we could identify the terms of the expansion – that is, how each new feature was calculated.

In *step 2*, we set `scikit-learn` library's `set_output` API **globally** to return pandas DataFrames as a result of the `transform()` method. scikit-learn transformers return NumPy arrays by default. The new `set_output` API allows us to change the container of the result to a pandas or a polars DataFrame. We can set the output individually every time we set up a transformer – for example, by using `poly = PolynomialFeatures().set_output(transform="pandas")`. Alternatively, as we did in this recipe, we can set the global configuration, and then every time we set up a new transformer, it will return a pandas DataFrame.

There's more...

Let's create features by performing polynomial expansion on a subset of variables in the breast cancer dataset:

1. First, import the necessary libraries, classes, and data:

    ```python
    import pandas as pd
    from sklearn.datasets import load_breast_cancer
    from sklearn.compose import ColumnTransformer
    ```

```python
from sklearn.model_selection import train_test_split
from sklearn.preprocessing import PolynomialFeatures
```

2. Then, load the data and separate it into train and test sets:

```python
data = load_breast_cancer()
df = pd.DataFrame(data.data,
    columns=data.feature_names)
X_train, X_test, y_train, y_test = train_test_split(
    df, data.target, test_size=0.3, random_state=0
)
```

3. Make a list with the features to combine:

```python
features = [
    "mean smoothness",
    "mean compactness",
    "mean concavity"]
```

4. Set up `PolynomialFeatures()` to create all possible combinations up to the third degree:

```python
poly = PolynomialFeatures(
    degree=3,
    interaction_only=False,
    include_bias=False)
```

5. Set up the column transformer to create features only from those specified in *step 3*:

```python
ct = ColumnTransformer([("poly", poly, features)])
```

6. Create the polynomial features:

```python
train_t = ct.fit_transform(X_train)
test_t = ct.transform(X_test)
```

And that's it. By executing `ct.get_feature_names_out()`, we obtain the names of the new features.

> **Note**
>
> `ColumnTransformer()` will append the word `poly` to the resulting variables, which is the name we gave to the step within `ColumnTransformer()` in *step 5*. I am not a huge fan of this behavior because it makes data analysis harder, as you need to keep track of the variable name changes. To avoid variable name changes, you can use `feature-engine`'s `SklearnTransformerWrapper()` instead.

Combining features with decision trees

In the winning solution of the **Knowledge Discovery and Data** Mining **(KDD)** competition in 2009, the authors created new features by combining two or more variables using decision trees. When examining the variables, they noticed that some features had a high level of mutual information with the target yet low correlation, indicating that the relationship with the target was not linear. While these features were predictive when used in tree-based algorithms, linear models could not take advantage of them. Hence, to use these features in linear models, they replaced the features with the outputs of decision trees trained on the individual features, or combinations of two or three variables, to return new features with a monotonic relationship with the target.

In short, combining features with decision trees is useful for creating features that show a monotonic relationship with the target, which is useful for making accurate predictions using linear models. The procedure consists of training a decision tree using a subset of the features – typically, one, two, or three at a time – and then using the prediction of the tree as a new feature.

> **Note**
>
> You can find more details about this procedure and the overall winning solution of the 2009 KDD data competition in this article: `http://proceedings.mlr.press/v7/niculescu09/niculescu09.pdf`.

The good news is that we can automate the creation of features using trees, using `feature-engine`, and in this recipe, we will learn how to do so.

How to do it...

In this recipe, we'll combine features with decision trees, using the California housing dataset:

1. Let's begin by importing `pandas` and the required functions, classes, and dataset:

    ```python
    import numpy as np
    import pandas as pd
    import matplotlib.pyplot as plt
    from sklearn.datasets import fetch_california_housing
    from sklearn.model_selection import train_test_split
    from feature_engine.creation, import DecisionTreeFeatures
    ```

2. Let's load the California housing dataset into a `pandas` DataFrame and remove the `Latitude` and `Longitude` variables:

    ```python
    X, y = fetch_california_housing(
        return_X_y=True, as_frame=True)
    X.drop(labels=[
        "Latitude", "Longitude"], axis=1, inplace=True)
    ```

3. Separate the dataset into train and test sets:

```
X_train, X_test, y_train, y_test = train_test_split(
    X, y, test_size=0.3, random_state=0)
```

4. Check out Pearson's correlation coefficient between the features and the target, which is a measure of a linear relationship:

```
for var in X_train.columns:
    pearson = np.corrcoef(X_train[var], y_train)[0, 1]
    pearson = np.round(pearson, 2)
    print(
        f"corr {var} vs target: {pearson}")
```

In the following output, we can see that, apart from `MedInc`, most variables do not show a strong linear relationship with the target; the correlation coefficient is smaller than 0.5:

```
corr MedInc vs target: 0.69
corr HouseAge vs target: 0.1
corr AveRooms vs target: 0.16
corr AveBedrms vs target: -0.05
corr Population vs target: -0.03
corr AveOccup vs target: -0.03
```

The `feature-engine` library's `DecisionTreeFeatures()` selects the best tree by using cross-validation.

5. Create a grid of hyperparameters to optimize each decision tree:

```
param_grid = {"max_depth": [2, 3, 4, None]}
```

The `feature-engine` library's `DecisionTreeFeatures()` allows us to add features resulting from the predictions of a decision tree, trained on one or more features. There are many ways in which we can instruct the transformer to combine the features. We'll start by creating all possible combinations between two variables.

6. Make a list with the two features that we want to use as inputs:

```
variables = ["AveRooms", "AveBedrms"]
```

7. Set up `DecisionTreeFeatures()` to create all possible combinations between the features from *step 6*:

```
dtf = DecisionTreeFeatures(
    variables=variables,
    features_to_combine=None,
    cv=5,
    param_grid=param_grid,
    scoring="neg_mean_squared_error",
```

```
        regression=True,
    )
```

> **Note**
>
> We set `regression` to `True` because the target in this dataset is continuous. If you have a binary target or are performing classification, set it to `False`. Make sure to select an evaluation metric (`scoring`) that is suitable for your model.

8. Fit the transformer so that it trains the decision trees on the input features:

    ```
    dtf.fit(X_train, y_train)
    ```

9. If you wonder which features have been used to train decision trees, you can inspect them like this:

    ```
    dtf.input_features_
    ```

    In the following output, we can see that `DecisionTreeFeatures()` has trained three decision trees – two by using the single features, `AveRooms` and `AveBedrms`, and one by using both features:

    ```
    ['AveRooms', 'AveBedrms', ['AveRooms', 'AveBedrms']]
    ```

> **Note**
>
> `DecisionTreeFeatures()` also stores the decision trees. You can check them out by executing `dtf.estimators_`.

10. Now, add the features to the training and testing sets:

    ```
    train_t = dtf.transform(X_train)
    test_t = dtf.transform(X_test)
    ```

11. Make a list with the name of the new features (the transformer appends the word `tree` to the feature names):

    ```
    tree_features = [
        var for var in test_t.columns if "tree" in var ]
    ```

12. Finally, display the features that were added to the test set:

    ```
    test_t[tree_features].head()
    ```

In the following output, we can see the first five rows of the new features, resulting from the decision trees trained in *step 8*:

	tree(AveRooms)	tree(AveBedrms)	tree(['AveRooms', 'AveBedrms'])
14740	1.999776	2.080254	2.099977
10101	1.999776	2.165554	2.438937
20566	1.999776	2.165554	2.099977
2670	1.786777	1.882763	1.728401
15709	1.786777	2.165554	1.821467

Figure 8.9 – A portion of the testing set containing the features derived from the decision trees

13. To check the power of this transformation, calculate Pearson's correlation coefficient between the new features and the target:

```
for var in tree_features:
    pearson = np.corrcoef(test_t[var], y_test)[0, 1]
    pearson = np.round(pearson, 2)
    print(
        f"corr {var} vs target: {pearson}")
```

In the following output, we can see that the correlation between the new variables and the target is greater than the correlation shown by the original features (compare these values with those of *step 4*):

```
corr tree(AveRooms) vs target: 0.37
corr tree(AveBedrms) vs target: 0.12
corr tree(['AveRooms', 'AveBedrms']) vs target: 0.47
```

If you want to combine specific features instead of getting all possible combinations between variables, you can do so by specifying the input features in tuples.

14. Create a tuple of tuples with the different features that we want to use as input for decision trees:

```
features = (('Population'), ('Population','AveOccup'),
    ('Population', 'AveOccup', 'HouseAge'))
```

15. Now, we need to pass these tuples to the `features_to_combine` parameter of `DecisionTreeFeatures()`:

```
dtf = DecisionTreeFeatures(
    variables=None,
    features_to_combine=features,
    cv=5,
```

```
        param_grid=param_grid,
        scoring="neg_mean_squared_error"
    )
dtf.fit(X_train, y_train)
```

16. We fitted the transformer in the previous step, so we can go ahead and add the features to training and test sets:

```
train_t = dtf.transform(X_train)
test_t = dtf.transform(X_test)
```

17. Display the new features:

```
tree_features = [
    var for var in test_t.columns if "tree" in var]
test_t[tree_features].head()
```

In the following output, we can see the new features derived from predictions of decision trees in the test set:

	tree(Population)	tree(['Population', 'AveOccup'])	tree(['Population', 'AveOccup', 'HouseAge'])
14740	2.007490	1.484939	1.443097
10101	2.007490	2.059187	2.257968
20566	2.007490	2.059187	2.257968
2670	2.148072	2.235743	2.257968
15709	2.148072	2.747390	3.111251

Figure 8.10 – A portion of the testing set containing the features derived from the decision trees

To wrap up the recipe, we'll compare the performance of a Lasso linear regression model trained using the original features with one using the features derived from the decision trees.

18. Import Lasso and the `cross_validate` function from `scikit-learn`:

```
from sklearn.linear_model import Lasso
from sklearn.model_selection import cross_validate
```

19. Set up a Lasso regression model:

```
lasso = Lasso(random_state=0, alpha=0.0001)
```

20. Train and evaluate the model using the original data with cross-validation, and then print out the resulting r-squared:

```
cv_results = cross_validate(lasso, X_train, y_train,
    cv=3)
```

```python
    mean = cv_results['test_score'].mean()
    std = cv_results['test_score'].std()
    print(f"Results: {mean} +/- {std}")
```

In the following output, we can see the *r*-squared of the Lasso regression model trained using the original features:

```
Results: 0.5480403481478856 +/- 0.004214649109293269
```

21. Finally, train a Lasso regression model with the features derived from the decision trees and evaluate it with cross-validation:

```python
    variables = ["AveRooms", "AveBedrms", "Population"]
    train_t = train_t.drop(variables, axis=1)
    cv_results = cross_validate(lasso, train_t, y_train,
        cv=3)
    mean = cv_results['test_score'].mean()
    std = cv_results['test_score'].std()
    print(f"Results: {mean} +/- {std}")
```

In the following output, we can see that the performance of the Lasso regression model trained based of the tree-derived features is better; the *r*-square is greater than that from *step 20*:

```
Results: 0.5800993721099441 +/- 0.002845475651622909
```

I hope I've given you a flavor of the power of combining features with decision trees and how to do so with `feature-engine`.

How it works...

In this recipe, we created new features based on the predictions of decision trees trained on one or more variables. We used `DecisionTreeFeatures()` from `Feature-engine` to automate the process of training the decision trees with cross-validation and hyperparameter optimization.

`DecisionTreeFeatures()` trains decision trees using grid-search under the hood. Hence, you can pass a grid of hyperparameters to optimize the tree, or the transformer will optimize just the depth, which, in any case, is the most important parameter in a decision tree. You can also change the metric you want to optimize through the `scoring` parameter and the cross-validation scheme you want to use through the cv parameter.

The most exciting feature of `DecisionTreeFeatures()` is its ability to infer the feature combinations to create tree-derived features, which is regulated through the `features_to_combine` parameter. If you pass an integer to this parameter – say, for example, 3, `DecisionTreeFeatures()` will create all possible combinations of 1, 2, and 3 features and use these to train the decision trees. Instead of an integer, you can pass a list of integers – say, [2, 3] – in which case, `DecisionTreeFeatures()` will create all possible combinations of 2 and 3 features. You can also specify which features you want to combine and how by passing the feature combinations in tuples, as we did in *step 14*.

With `fit()`, `DecisionTreeFeatures()` finds the feature combinations and trains the decision trees. With `transform()`, `DecisionTreeFeatures()` adds the features resulting from the decision trees to the DataFrame.

> **Note**
>
> If you are training regression or multi-class classification, the new features will be either the prediction of the continuous target or the class. If you are training a binary classification model, the new features will result from the probability of class 1.

After adding the new features, we compared their relationship to the target by analyzing Pearson's correlation coefficient, which returned a measure of linear association. We saw that the features derived from trees had a greater correlation coefficient.

See also

If you want to know more about what mutual information is and how to calculate it, check out this article: `https://www.blog.trainindata.com/mutual-information-with-python/`.

Creating periodic features from cyclical variables

Some features are periodic – for example, the hours in a day, the months in a year, and the days in a week. They all start at a certain value (say, January), go up to a certain other value (say, December), and then start over from the beginning. Some features are numeric, such as the hours, and some can be represented with numbers, such as the months, with values of 1 to 12. Yet, this numeric representation does not capture the periodicity or cyclical nature of the variable. For example, December (12) is closer to January (1) than June (6); however, this relationship is not captured by the numerical representation of the feature. But we could change it if we transformed these variables with the sine and cosine, two naturally periodic functions.

Encoding cyclical features with the sine and cosine functions allows linear models to leverage the cyclical nature of features and reduce their modeling error. In this recipe, we will create new features from periodic variables that capture the cyclical nature of time.

Getting ready

Trigonometric functions, such as sine and cosine, are periodic, with values cycling between -1 and 1 every 2π cycles, as shown here:

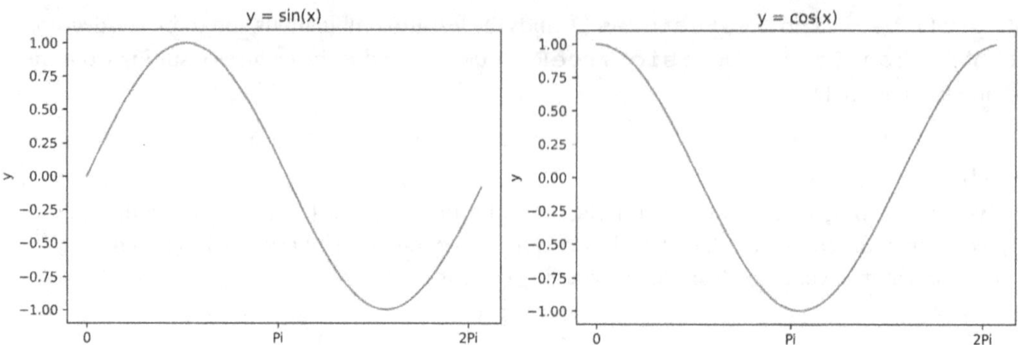

Figure 8.11 – Sine and cosine functions

We can capture the periodicity of a cyclical variable by applying a trigonometric transformation after normalizing the variable values between 0 and 2π:

$$\sin(x) = \sin\left(2\pi\frac{X}{X_{max}}\right)$$

Dividing the variable's values by its maximum will normalize it between 0 and 1 (assuming that the minimum value is 0), and multiplying it by 2π will rescale the variable between 0 and 2π.

Should we use sine? Or should we use cosine? The thing is, we need to use both to encode all the values of the variables unequivocally. Since sine and cosine circle between 0 and 1, they will take a value of 0 for more than one value of x. For example, the sine of 0 returns 0, and so does the sine of π. So, if we encode a variable with just the sine, we wouldn't be able to distinguish between the values 0 and π anymore. However, because the sine and the cosine are out of phase, the cosine of 0 returns 1, whereas the cosine of π returns -1. Hence, by encoding the variable with the two functions, we are now able to distinguish between 0 and 1, which would take (0,1) and (0,-1) as values for the sine and cosine functions, respectively.

How to do it...

In this recipe, we will first transform the `hour` variable in a toy DataFrame with the sine and the cosine to get a sense of the new variable representation. Then, we will automate feature creation from multiple cyclical variables using `feature-engine`:

1. Begin by importing the necessary libraries:

```
import numpy as np
import pandas as pd
import matplotlib.pyplot as plt
```

2. Create a toy DataFrame with one variable – `hour` – with values between 0 and 23:

```
df = pd.DataFrame([i for i in range(24)],
    columns=["hour"])
```

3. Next, create two features using the sine and cosine transformations, after normalizing the variable values between 0 and 2π:

```python
df["hour_sin"] = np.sin(
    df["hour"] / df["hour"].max() * 2 * np.pi)
df["hour_cos"] = np.cos(
    df["hour"] / df["hour"].max() * 2 * np.pi)
```

If we execute `df.head()`, we will see the original and new features:

	hour	hour_sin	hour_cos
0	0	0.000000	1.000000
1	1	0.269797	0.962917
2	2	0.519584	0.854419
3	3	0.730836	0.682553
4	4	0.887885	0.460065

Figure 8.12 – A DataFrame with the hour variable and the new features obtained through the sine and cosine transformations

4. Make a scatter plot between the hour and its sine-transformed values:

```python
plt.scatter(df["hour"], df["hour_sin"])
plt.ylabel("Sine of hour")
plt.xlabel("Hour")
plt.title("Sine transformation")
```

In the following plot, we can see how the values of the hour circle between -1 and 1, just like the sine function after the transformation:

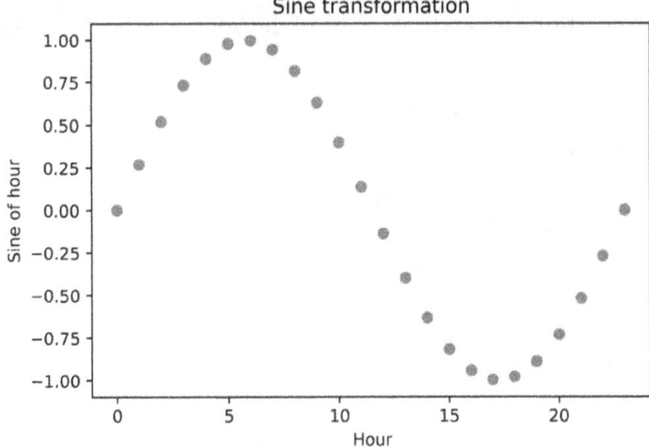

Figure 8.13 – A scatter plot of the hour versus its sine transformed values

5. Now, make a scatter plot between the hour and its cosine transformation:

```python
plt.scatter(df["hour"], df["hour_cos"])
plt.ylabel("Cosine of hour")
plt.xlabel("Hour")
plt.title("Cosine transformation")
```

In the following plot, we can see how the values of the hour circle between -1 and 1, just like the cosine function after the transformation:

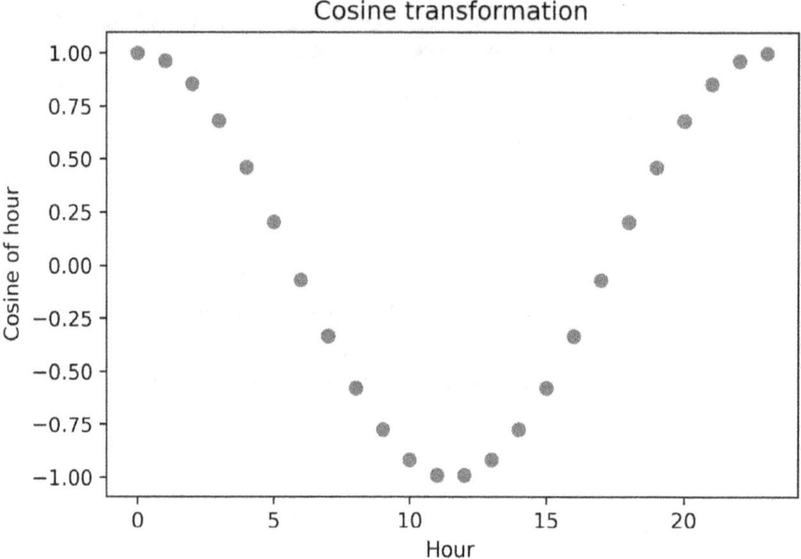

Figure 8.14 – A scatter plot of the hour versus its cosine-transformed values

Finally, we can reconstitute the cyclical nature of the hour, which is now captured by the two new features.

6. Plot the values of the sine versus the cosine of the hour, and overlay the original values of the hour using a color map:

```python
fig, ax = plt.subplots(figsize=(7, 5))
sp = ax.scatter(
    df["hour_sin"], df["hour_cos"], c=df["hour"])
ax.set(
    xlabel="sin(hour)",
    ylabel="cos(hour)",
)
_ = fig.colorbar(sp)
```

In the following plot, we can see how the two trigonometric transformations of the hour reflect the cyclical nature of the hour, in a plot that reminds us of a clock:

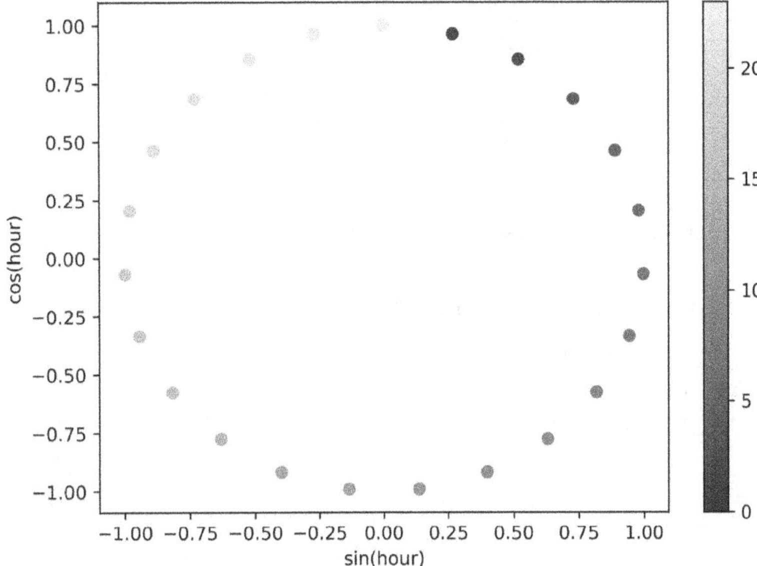

Figure 8.15 – A scatter plot of the trigonometric transformation of the hour

> **Note**
>
> The code implementation and idea for this plot were taken from scikit-learn's documentation: `https://scikit-learn.org/stable/auto_examples/applications/plot_cyclical_feature_engineering.html#trigonometric-features`.

Now that we understand the nature and effect of the transformation, let's create new features using the sine and cosine transformations from multiple variables automatically. We will use the `feature-engine` library's `CyclicalFeatures()`.

7. Import `CyclicalFeatures()`:

```python
from feature_engine.creation import CyclicalFeatures
```

8. Let's create a toy DataFrame that contains the `hour`, `month`, and `week` variables, whose values vary between 0 and 23, 1 and 12, and 0 and 6, respectively:

```python
df = pd.DataFrame()
df["hour"] = pd.Series([i for i in range(24)])
df["month"] = pd.Series([i for i in range(1, 13)]*2)
df["week"] = pd.Series([i for i in range(7)]*4)
```

If we execute `df.head()`, we will see the first five rows of the toy DataFrame:

	hour	month	week
0	0	1	0
1	1	2	1
2	2	3	2
3	3	4	3
4	4	5	4

Figure 8.16 – The toy DataFrame with three cyclical features

9. Set up the transformer to create the sine and cosine features from these variables:

```
cyclic = CyclicalFeatures(
    variables=None,
    drop_original=False,
)
```

> **Note**
>
> By setting `variables` to `None`, `CyclicalFeatures()` will create trigonometric features from all numerical variables. To create trigonometric features from a subset of variables, we can pass the variables' names in a list to the `variables` parameter. We can retain or drop the original variables after creating the cyclical features using the `drop_original` parameter.

10. To finish, add the features to the DataFrame and capture the result in a new variable:

```
dft = cyclic.fit_transform(df)
```

If we execute `dft.head()`, we will see the original and new features:

	hour	month	week	hour_sin	hour_cos	month_sin	month_cos	week_sin	week_cos
0	0	1	0	0.000000	1.000000	0.500000	8.660254e-01	0.000000e+00	1.0
1	1	2	1	0.269797	0.962917	0.866025	5.000000e-01	8.660254e-01	0.5
2	2	3	2	0.519584	0.854419	1.000000	6.123234e-17	8.660254e-01	-0.5
3	3	4	3	0.730836	0.682553	0.866025	-5.000000e-01	1.224647e-16	-1.0
4	4	5	4	0.887885	0.460065	0.500000	-8.660254e-01	-8.660254e-01	-0.5

Figure 8.17 – DataFrame with cyclical features plus the features
created through the sine and cosine functions

And that's it – we've created features by using the sine and cosine transformation automatically from multiple variables and added them directly to the original DataFrame.

How it works...

In this recipe, we encoded cyclical features with values obtained from the sine and cosine functions, applied to the normalized values of the variable. First, we normalized the variable values between 0 and 2 π. To do this, we divided the variable values by the variable maximum value, which we obtained with `pandas.max()`, to scale the variables between 0 and 1. Then, we multiplied those values by 2π, using `numpy.pi`. Finally, we used `np.sin` and `np.cos` to apply the sine and cosine transformations, respectively.

To automate this procedure for multiple variables, we used the `Feature-engine` library's `CyclicalFeatures()`. With `fit()`, the transformer learned the maximum values of each variable, and with `transform()`, it added the features resulting from the sine and cosine transformations to the DataFrame.

> **Note**
>
> In theory, to apply the sine and cosine transformation, we need to scale the original variable between 0 and 1. Dividing by the maximum of the variable will only result in this scaling if the minimum value is 0. scikit-learn's documentation and `Feature-engine`'s current implementation divide the variable by its maximum value (or an arbitrary period), without paying too much attention to whether the variable starts at 0. In practice, you won't see a big difference in the resulting variables if you divide the hour feature by 23 or 24, or the month feature by 12 or 11. Discussions are underway on whether Feature-engine's implementation should be updated, so the default behavior might change by the time this book is published. Check out the documentation for more details.

Creating spline features

Linear models expect a linear relationship between the predictor variables and the target. However, we can use linear models to model non-linear effects if we first transform the features. In the *Performing polynomial expansion* recipe, we saw how we can unmask linear patterns by creating features with polynomial functions. In this recipe, we will discuss the use of splines.

Splines are used to mathematically reproduce flexible shapes. They consist of piecewise low-degree polynomial functions. To create splines, we must place knots at several values of x. These knots indicate where the pieces of the function join. Then, we fit low-degree polynomials to the data between two consecutive knots.

There are several types of splines, such as smoothing splines, regression splines, and B-splines. scikit-learn supports the use of B-splines to create features. The procedure to fit and, therefore, return the spline values for a certain variable, based on a polynomial degree and the number of knots, exceeds the scope of this recipe. For more details, check out the resources in the *See also* section of this recipe. In this recipe, we'll get a sense of what splines are and how we can use them to improve the performance of linear models.

Getting ready

Let's get a sense of what splines are. In the following figure, on the left, we can see a spline with a degree of 1. It consists of two linear pieces – one from 2.5 to 5 and the other from 5 to 7.5. There are three knots – 2.5, 5, and 7.5. Outside the interval between 2.5 and 7.5, the spline takes a value of 0. The latter is characteristic of splines; they are only non-negative between certain values. On the right panel of the figure, we can see three splines of degree 1. We can construct as many splines as we want by introducing more knots:

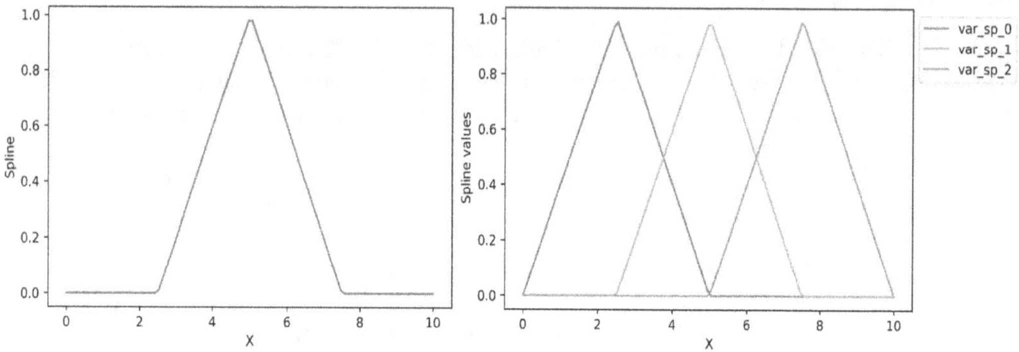

Figure 8.18 – The splines with a degree of 1

In the following figure, on the left, we can see a quadratic spline, also known as a spline with a degree of 2. It is based on four adjacent knots – 0, 2.5, 5, and 7.5. On the right-hand side of the figure, we can see several splines of degree 2:

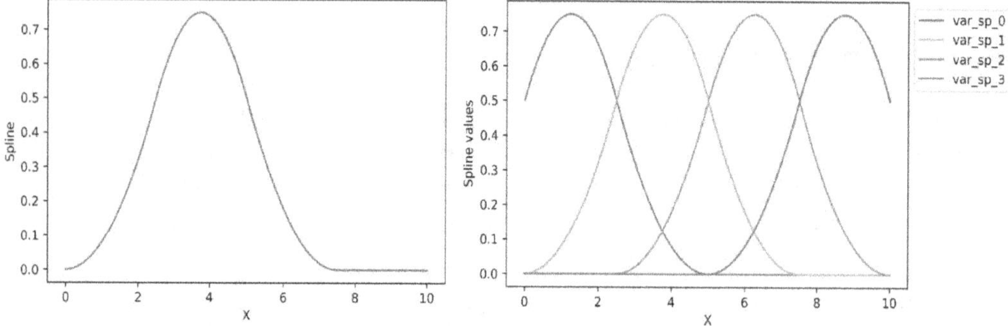

Figure 8.19 – The splines with a degree of 2

We can use splines to model non-linear functions, and we will learn how to do this in the next section.

How to do it...

In this recipe, we will use splines to model the sine function. Once we get a sense of what splines are and how we can use them to fit non-linear relationships through a linear model, we will use splines for regression in a real dataset:

> **Note**
>
> The idea to model the sine function with splines was taken from scikit-learn's documentation: `https://scikit-learn.org/stable/auto_examples/linear_model/plot_polynomial_interpolation.html`.

1. Let's begin by importing the necessary libraries and classes:

```python
import numpy as np
import pandas as pd
import matplotlib.pyplot as plt
from sklearn.linear_model import Ridge
from sklearn.preprocessing import SplineTransformer
```

2. Create a training set, X, with 20 values between -1 and 11, and the target variable, y, which is the sine of X:

```python
X = np.linspace(-1, 11, 20)
y = np.sin(X)
```

3. Plot the relationship between X and y:

```python
plt.plot(X, y)
plt.ylabel("y")
plt.xlabel("X")
```

In the following plot, we can see the sine function of X:

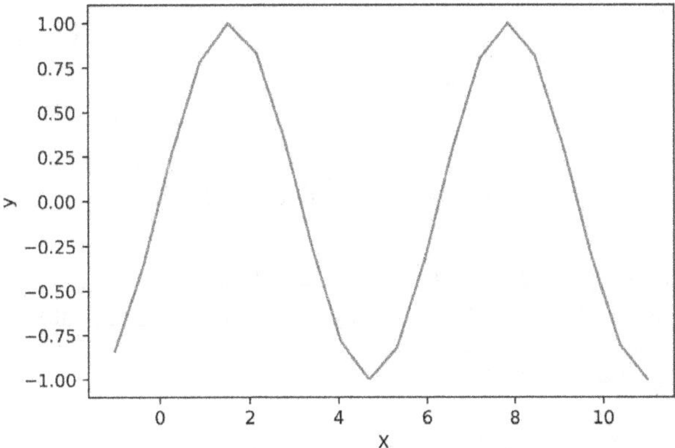

Figure 8.20 – The relationship between the predictor and the target variable, where y = sine(x)

4. Fit a linear model to predict y from X by utilizing a Ridge regression, and then obtain the predictions of the model:

```
linmod = Ridge(random_state=10)
linmod.fit(X.reshape(-1, 1), y)
pred = linmod.predict(X.reshape(-1, 1))
```

5. Now, plot the relationship between X and y, and overlay the predictions:

```
plt.plot(X, y)
plt.plot(X, pred)
plt.ylabel("y")
plt.xlabel("X")
plt.legend(
    ["y", "linear"],
    bbox_to_anchor=(1, 1),
    loc="upper left")
```

In the following figure, we can see that the linear model makes a very poor fit of the non-linear relationship between X and y:

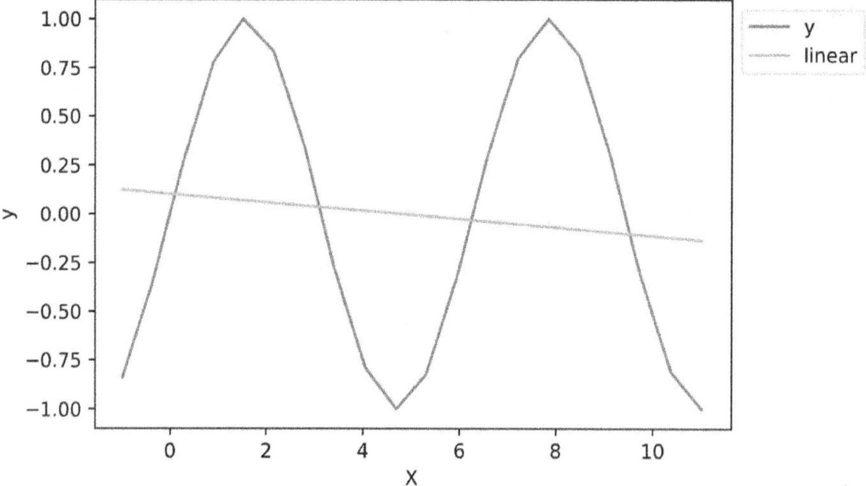

Figure 8.21 – The linear fit between X and y

6. Now, set up `SplineTransformer()` to obtain spline features from X, by utilizing third-degree polynomials and five knots at equidistant places within the values of X:

```
spl = SplineTransformer(degree=3, n_knots=5)
```

7. Obtain the spline features and convert the NumPy array into a `pandas` DataFrame, adding the names of the spline basis functions:

```
X_t = spl.fit_transform(X.reshape(-1, 1))
X_df = pd.DataFrame(
    X_t,
    columns=spl.get_feature_names_out(["var"])
)
```

By executing `X_df.head()`, we can see the spline features:

	var_sp_0	var_sp_1	var_sp_2	var_sp_3	var_sp_4	var_sp_5	var_sp_6
0	0.166667	0.666667	0.166667	0.000000	0.0	0.0	0.0
1	0.082009	0.627011	0.289425	0.001555	0.0	0.0	0.0
2	0.032342	0.526705	0.428512	0.012441	0.0	0.0	0.0
3	0.008335	0.393741	0.555936	0.041989	0.0	0.0	0.0
4	0.000656	0.256111	0.643704	0.099529	0.0	0.0	0.0

Figure 8.22 – A DataFrame with the splines

> **Note**
>
> `SplineTransformer()` returns a feature matrix consisting of `n_splines` = `n_knots` + `degree` - 1.

8. Now, plot the splines against the values of X:

```
plt.plot(X, X_t)
plt.legend(
    spl.get_feature_names_out(["var"]),
    bbox_to_anchor=(1, 1),
    loc="upper left")
plt.xlabel("X")
plt.ylabel("Splines values")
plt.title("Splines")
plt.show()
```

In the following figure, we can see the relationship between the different splines and the values of the predictor variable, X:

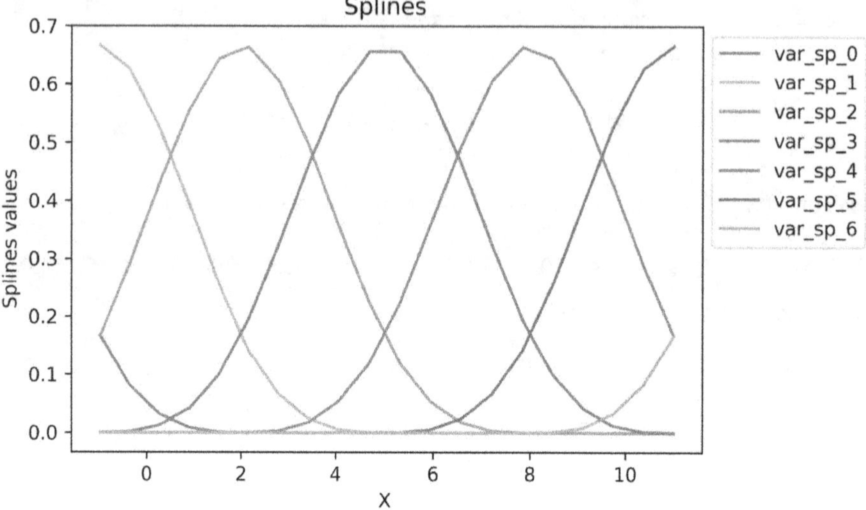

Figure 8.23 – Splines plotted against the values of the predictor variable, X

9. Now, fit a linear model to predict y from the spline features obtained from X, by utilizing a Ridge regression, and then obtain the predictions of the model:

```
linmod = Ridge(random_state=10)
linmod.fit(X_t, y)
pred = linmod.predict(X_t)
```

10. Now, plot the relationship between X and y, and overlay the predictions:

```
plt.plot(X, y)
plt.plot(X, pred)
plt.ylabel("y")
plt.xlabel("X")
plt.legend(
    ["y", "splines"],
    bbox_to_anchor=(1, 1),
    loc="upper left")
```

In the following figure, we can see that by utilizing spline features as input, the Ridge regression can better predict the shape of y:

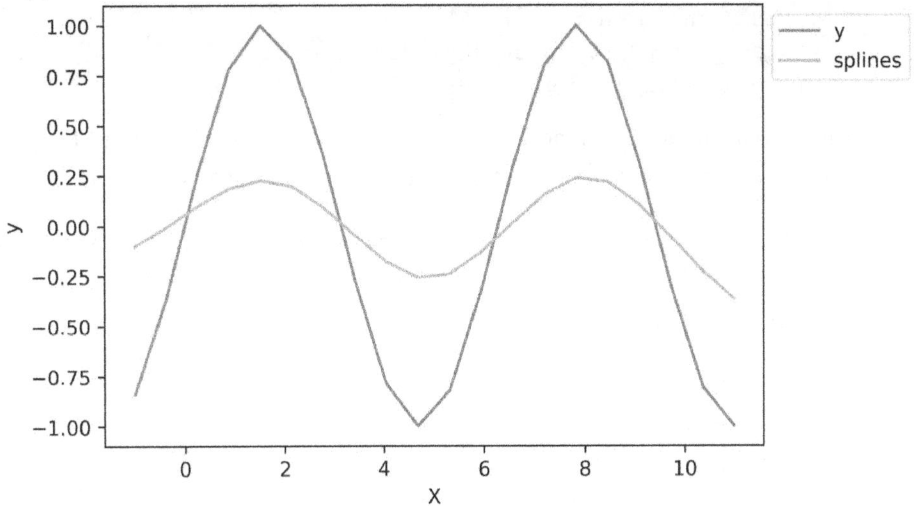

Figure 8.24 – The predictions of a linear model, based on splines
overlaid over the true relationship between X and y

> **Note**
>
> Increasing the number of knots or the degree of the polynomial increases the flexibility of the spline curves. Try creating splines from higher polynomial degrees and see how the Ridge regression predictions change.

Now that we understand what the spline features are and how we can use them to predict non-linear effects, let's try them out on a real dataset.

11. Import some additional classes and functions from `scikit-learn`:

```
from sklearn.datasets import fetch_california_housing
from sklearn.compose import ColumnTransformer
from sklearn.model_selection import cross_validate
```

12. Load the California housing dataset and drop two of the variables, which we won't use for modeling:

```
X, y = fetch_california_housing(
    return_X_y=True, as_frame=True)
X.drop(["Latitude", "Longitude"], axis=1,
    inplace=True)
```

13. First, we will fit a Ridge regression to predict house prices based on the existing variables, by utilizing cross-validation, and then obtain the performance of the model to set up the benchmark:

```
linmod = Ridge(random_state=10)
cv = cross_validate(linmod, X, y)
```

```
mean_, std_ = np.mean(
    cv[«test_score"]), np.std(cv["test_score"])
print(f"Model score: {mean_} +- {std_}")
```

In the following output, we can see the model performance, where the values are the *R*-squared:

```
Model score: 0.490618615960575 +- 0.03617289854929812
```

14. Now, set up `SplineTransformer()` to obtain spline features from four variables by utilizing third-degree polynomials and 50 knots, and then fit the pipeline to the data:

```
spl = SplineTransformer(degree=3, n_knots=50)
ct = ColumnTransformer(
    [("splines", spl, [
        "AveRooms", "AveBedrms", "Population",
        "AveOccup"]
    )],
    remainder="passthrough",
)
ct.fit(X, y)
```

> **Note**
>
> Remember that we need to use `ColumnTransformer()` to obtain features from a subset of variables in the data. With `remainder=passthrough`, we ensure that the variables that are not used as templates for the splines – that is, `MedInc` and `HouseAge` – are also returned in the resulting DataFrame. To check out the features resulting from this step, execute `ct.get_feature_names_out()`.

15. Now, fit a Ridge regression to predict house prices based on `MedInc`, `HouseAge`, and the spline features, using cross-validation, and then obtain the performance of the model:

```
cv = cross_validate(linmod, ct.transform(X), y)
mean_, std_ = np.mean(
    cv[«test_score"]), np.std(cv["test_score"])
print(f"Model score: {mean_} +- {std_}")
```

In the following output, we can see the model performance, where the values are the *R*-squared:

```
Model score: 0.5553526813919297 +- 0.02244513992785257
```

As we can see, by using splines in place of some of the original variables, we can improve the performance of the linear regression model.

How it works...

In this recipe, we created new features based on splines. First, we used a toy variable, with values from -1 to 11, and then we obtained splines from a real dataset. The procedure in both cases was identical – we used `SplineTransformer()` from `scikit-learn`. The `SplineTransformer()` transformer takes the `degree` property of the polynomial and the number of knots (`n_knots`) as input and returns the splines that better fit the data. The knots are placed at equidistant values of `X` by default, but through the `knots` parameter, we can choose to uniformly distribute them to the quantiles of `X` instead, or we can pass an array with the specific values of `X` that should be used as knots.

> **Note**
>
> The number, spacing, and position of the knots are arbitrarily set by the user and are the parameters that influence the shape of the splines the most. When using splines in regression models, we can optimize these parameters in a randomized search with cross-validation.

With `fit()`, the transformer computes the knots of the splines. With `transform()`, it returns the array of B-splines. The transformer returns `n_splines=n_knots + degree - 1`.

Remember that, like most scikit-learn transformers, `SplineTransformer()` also now has the option to return `pandas` and polars DataFrames in addition to NumPy arrays, a behavior that can be modified through the `set_output()` method.

Finally, we used `ColumnTransformer()` to derive splines from a subset of features. Because we set `remainder` to `passthrough`, `ColumnTransformer()` concatenated the features that were not used to obtain splines to the resulting matrix of splines. By doing this, we fitted a Ridge regression with the splines, plus the `MedInc` and `HouseAge` variables, and managed to improve the linear model's performance.

See also

To find out more about the math underlying B-splines, check out the following articles:

- Perperoglou, et al. *A review of spline function procedures in R* (`https://bmcmedresmethodol.biomedcentral.com/articles/10.1186/s12874-019-0666-3`). BMC Med Res Methodol 19, 46 (2019).

- Eilers and Marx. *Flexible Smoothing with B-splines and Penalties* (`https://projecteuclid.org/journals/statistical-science/volume-11/issue-2/Flexible-smoothing-with-B-splines-and-penalties/10.1214/ss/1038425655.full`).

- For an example of how to use B-splines to model time series data, check out the following page in the `scikit-learn` library's documentation: `https://scikit-learn.org/stable/auto_examples/applications/plot_cyclical_feature_engineering.html#periodic-spline-features`.

9

Extracting Features from Relational Data with Featuretools

In previous chapters, we worked with data organized in rows and columns, where the columns are the variables, the rows are the observations, and each observation is independent. In this chapter, we will focus on creating features from relational datasets. In relational datasets, data is structured across various tables, which can be joined together via unique identifiers. These unique identifiers indicate relationships that exist between the different tables.

A classic example of relational data is that held by retail companies. One table contains information about customers, such as names and addresses. A second table has information about the purchases made by the customers, such as the type and number of items bought per purchase. A third table contains information about the customers' interactions with the company's website, variables such as session duration, the mobile device used, and pages visited. Customers, purchases, and sessions are identified with unique identifiers. These unique identifiers allow us to put these tables together, and in this way, we can get information about customers' purchases or sessions.

If we want to know more about the types of customers we have (that is, customer segmentation) or make predictions about whether they would buy a product, we can create features that aggregate or summarize information across different tables at the customer level. For example, we can create features that capture the maximum amount spent by a customer on a purchase, the number of purchases they have made, the time between sessions, or the average session duration. The number of features we can create and the various ways we can aggregate data across tables are abundant. In this chapter, we will discuss some common ways of creating aggregated views of relational data utilizing the `featuretools` Python library. We will begin by setting up various data tables and their relationships and automatically creating features, and next, we will follow up with more detail on the different features we can create.

In this chapter, we will cover the following recipes:

- Setting up an entity set and creating features automatically
- Creating features with general and cumulative operations
- Combining numerical features
- Extracting features from date and time
- Extracting features from text
- Creating features with aggregation primitives

Technical requirements

In this chapter, we will use `pandas`, `matplotlib`, and `featuretools` open source Python libraries. You can install `featuretools` with `pip`:

```
pip install featuretools
```

Additionally, you can do so with `conda`:

```
conda install -c conda-forge featuretools
```

These commands install the basic `featuretools` functionality, but we can install add-ons for creating features with **natural language processing** (**NLP**) or for using `dask` as the backend instead of `pandas`. For more information on how to install `featuretools` add-ons, including `graphviz`, check out their documentation here: `https://docs.featuretools.com/en/v0.16.0/getting_started/install.html`.

We will work with the *Online Retail II* dataset from the UCI Machine Learning Repository, which is available at `https://archive.ics.uci.edu/ml/datasets/Online+Retail+II` and licensed under a **Creative Commons Attribution 4.0 International** (**CC BY 4.0**) license: `https://creativecommons.org/licenses/by/4.0/legalcode`. The corresponding citation for this data is provided here: *Chen, Daqing (2019). Online Retail II. UCI Machine Learning Repository* (`https://doi.org/10.24432/C5CG6D`).

I downloaded and modified the data as shown in this notebook: `https://github.com/PacktPublishing/Python-Feature-engineering-Cookbook-Third-Edition/blob/main/ch09-featuretools/prepare-retail-dataset.ipynb`

You'll find a copy of the modified dataset in the accompanying GitHub repository: `https://github.com/PacktPublishing/Python-Feature-engineering-Cookbook-Third-Edition/blob/main/ch09-featuretools/retail.csv`

Setting up an entity set and creating features automatically

Relational datasets or databases contain data spread across multiple tables, and the relationships between tables are dictated by a unique identifier that tells us how we can join those tables. To automate feature creation with `featuretools`, we first need to enter the different data tables and establish their relationships within what is called an **entity set**. The entity set then informs `featuretools` how these tables are connected so that the library can automatically create features based on those relationships.

We will work with a dataset containing information about customers, invoices, and products. First, we will set up an entity set highlighting the relationships between these three items. This entity set will be the starting point for the remaining recipes in this chapter. Next, we will create features automatically by aggregating the data at the customer, invoice, and product levels, utilizing the default parameters from `featuretools`.

In this recipe, you will learn how to correctly set up an entity set and extract a bunch of features automatically for each entity. In the upcoming recipes, we will dig deeper into the different types of features that we can create with `featuretools`.

Getting ready

In this recipe, we will use the *Online Retail II* dataset from the UCI Machine Learning Repository. In this table, there are customers, which are businesses that buy in bulk from the retail company. Customers are identified with a `customer_id` unique identifier. Each customer makes one or more purchases, which are flagged by an `invoice` unique identifier, containing the invoice number. In each invoice, there are one or more items that have been bought by the customer. Each item or product sold by the company is also identified with a unique stock code.

Thus, the data has the following relations:

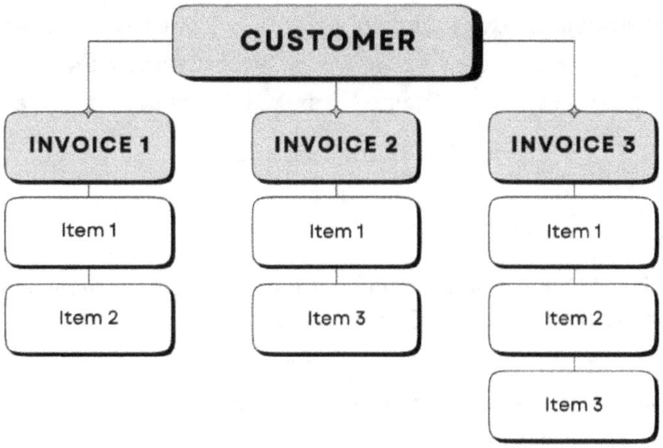

Figure 9.1 – Diagram showing the relationships in the data

Each customer made one or more purchases, identified by the invoice number. Each invoice contains one or more items, identified by the stock code. Each item can be bought by one or more customers and is therefore present in several invoices. With these relationships in mind, let's proceed to the recipe.

How to do it...

In this recipe, we will set up an entity set with the data, and then highlight the different relationships in the dataset. Finally, we will create features by aggregating information in the dataset at the customer, invoice, and product levels:

1. Let's import the required libraries:

    ```
    import pandas as pd
    import featuretools as ft
    from woodwork.logical_types import Categorical
    ```

2. Let's load the retail dataset described in the *Getting ready* section and display its first five rows:

    ```
    df = pd.read_csv(
        «retail.csv», parse_dates=[«invoice_date»])
    df.head()
    ```

    In the following screenshot, we see the unique identifiers for customers (`customer_id`) and invoices (`invoice`), and additional information about the items bought in each invoice, such as the item's code (`stock_code`), description, quantity, and unit price, as well as the date of the invoice:

	customer_id	invoice	invoice_date	stock_code	description	quantity	price
0	13085.0	489434	2009-12-01 07:45:00	85048	15CM CHRISTMAS GLASS BALL 20 LIGHTS	12	6.95
1	13085.0	489434	2009-12-01 07:45:00	79323P	PINK CHERRY LIGHTS	12	6.75
2	13085.0	489434	2009-12-01 07:45:00	79323W	WHITE CHERRY LIGHTS	12	6.75
3	13085.0	489434	2009-12-01 07:45:00	22041	RECORD FRAME 7" SINGLE SIZE	48	2.10
4	13085.0	489434	2009-12-01 07:45:00	21232	STRAWBERRY CERAMIC TRINKET BOX	24	1.25

Figure 9.2 – Online Retail II dataset

> **Note**
>
> Use pandas' `unique()` function to identify the number of unique items, customers, and invoices – for example, by executing `df["customer_id"].nunique()`.

3. Let's initialize an entity set with an arbitrary name, such as `data`:

    ```
    es = ft.EntitySet(id="data")
    ```

4. Let's add a DataFrame to the entity set; we give the DataFrame a name (`data`). We need to add a unique identifier for each row, which we call `rows`, and since we do not have a unique row identifier in this dataset, we will create it as an additional column by setting `make_index=True`. Finally, we indicate that `invoice_date` is of the `datetime` type and `customer_id` should be handled as `Categorical`:

```
es = es.add_dataframe(
    dataframe=df,
    dataframe_name=»data»,
    index="rows",
    make_index=True,
    time_index=»invoice_date»,
    logical_types={ «customer_id»: Categorical},
)
```

5. Next, we add the relationship between the original `data` DataFrame and `invoices`. To do this, we indicate the original or base DataFrame, which we called `data` in *step 4*, we give the new DataFrame a name, `invoices`, we add the unique identifier for invoices, and we add the column containing `customer_id` to this DataFrame:

```
es.normalize_dataframe(
    base_dataframe_name=»data»,
    new_dataframe_name=»invoices»,
    index="invoice",
    copy_columns=[«customer_id»],
)
```

> **Note**
>
> We copy the `customer_id` variable to the `invoices` data because we want to create a subsequent relationship between customers and invoices.

6. Now, we add a second relationship, which is between customers and invoices. To do this, we indicate the base DataFrame, which we named `invoices` in *step 5*, then we give the new DataFrame a name, `customers`, and add the unique customer identifier:

```
es.normalize_dataframe(
    base_dataframe_name=»invoices»,
    new_dataframe_name=»customers»,
    index=»customer_id»,
)
```

7. We can add a third relationship between the original data and the products:

```
es.normalize_dataframe(
    base_dataframe_name=»data»,
    new_dataframe_name=»items»,
    index=»stock_code»,
)
```

8. Let's display the information in the entity set:

```
es
```

In the following output, we see that the entity set contains four DataFrames: the original data, the `invoices` DataFrame, the `customers` DataFrame, and the product or `items` DataFrame. The entity also contains the relationships between invoices or items with the original data, as well as between customers and invoices:

```
Entityset: data
  DataFrames:
    data [Rows: 741301, Columns: 8]
    invoices [Rows: 40505, Columns: 3]
    customers [Rows: 5410, Columns: 2]
    items [Rows: 4631, Columns: 2]
  Relationships:
    data.invoice -> invoices.invoice
    invoices.customer_id -> customers.customer_id
    data.stock_code -> items.stock_code
```

9. Let's display the `invoices` DataFrame:

```
es["invoices"].head()
```

We see in the following output that `featuretools` automatically created a DataFrame containing the invoice's unique identifier, followed by the customer's unique identifier and the first date registered for each invoice:

	invoice	customer_id	first_data_time
489434	489434	13085.0	2009-12-01 07:45:00
489435	489435	13085.0	2009-12-01 07:46:00
489436	489436	13078.0	2009-12-01 09:06:00
489437	489437	15362.0	2009-12-01 09:08:00
489438	489438	18102.0	2009-12-01 09:24:00

Figure 9.3 – DataFrame with information at the invoice level

10. Let's now display the `customers` DataFrame:

```
es["customers"].head()
```

We can see in the following output that `featuretools` automatically created a DataFrame containing the customer's unique identifier, followed by the date of the first invoice for this customer:

	customer_id	first_invoices_time
13085.0	13085.0	2009-12-01 07:45:00
13078.0	13078.0	2009-12-01 09:06:00
15362.0	15362.0	2009-12-01 09:08:00
18102.0	18102.0	2009-12-01 09:24:00
18087.0	18087.0	2009-12-01 09:43:00

Figure 9.4 – DataFrame with information at the customer level

> **Note**
>
> Go ahead and display the DataFrame containing the products by executing `es["items"].head()`. You can also evaluate the size of the different DataFrames using `pandas`' shape function. You will notice that the number of rows in each DataFrame coincides with the number of unique invoices, customers, and products.

11. We can also display the relationships between these data tables as follows:

```
es.plot()
```

> **Note**
>
> To visualize the data relationships, you need to have `graphviz` installed. If you don't, follow the instructions in the `featuretools` documentation to install it: `https://featuretools.alteryx.com/en/stable/install.html#installing-graphviz`.

In the following output, we can see the relational datasets and their relationships:

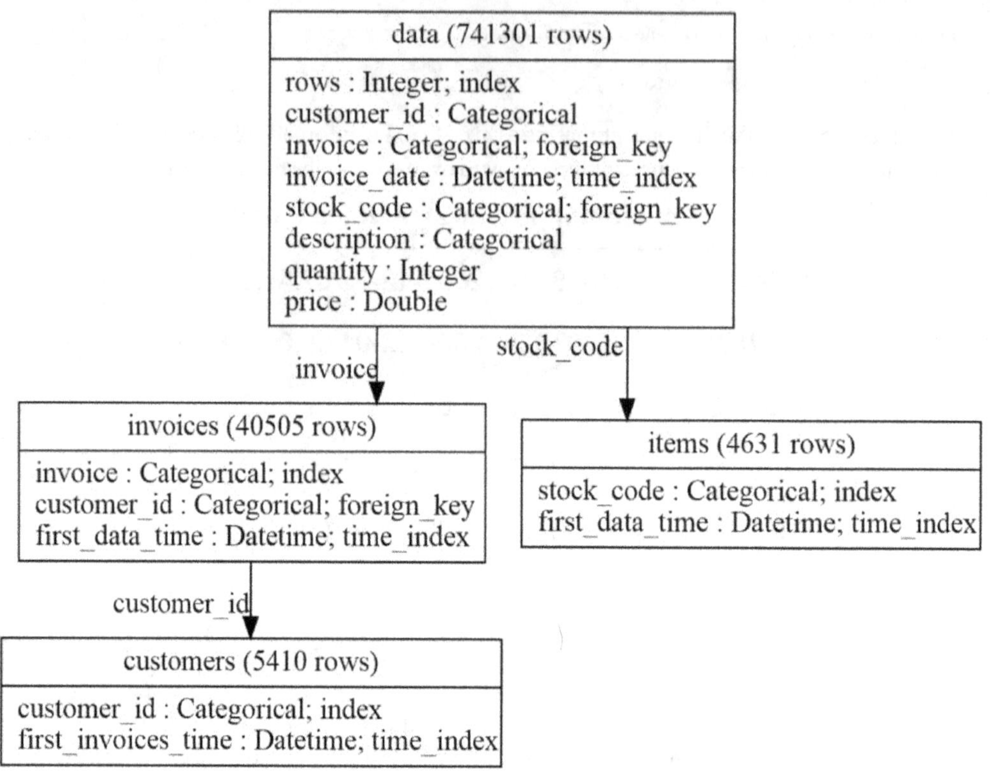

Figure 9.5 – Relationships between the tables containing invoices, customers, and products

After entering the data and their relationships, we can start automatically creating features for each one of our new DataFrames – that is, customers, invoices, and products – using the default parameters from `featuretools`.

12. Let's create features by aggregating the data at the customer level. To do this, we set up the **deep feature synthesis** (**dfs**) class from `featuretools`, indicating `customers` as the target DataFrame. When creating features, we want to ignore the two columns with unique identifiers:

```
feature_matrix, feature_defs = ft.dfs(
    entityset=es,
    target_dataframe_name=»customers»,
    ignore_columns={
        «invoices»:[«invoice»],
        «invoices»:[«customer_id»],
    }
)
```

> **Note**
>
> The command from *step 12* triggered the creation of 114 features with different aggregations of data at the customer level. The `feature_matrix` variable is a DataFrame with the feature values, and `feature_defs` is a list with the names of the new features. Go ahead and execute `feature_defs` or visit our accompanying GitHub repository (`https://github.com/PacktPublishing/Python-Feature-Engineering-Cookbook-Third-Edition/blob/main/ch09-featuretools/Recipe1-Setting-up-an-entity-set.ipynb`) to check the names of the created features. You will find more details about these features in the *How it works...* section.

13. For reasons of space, we can't print out all the features in the book, so instead, let's display the names of five of the created features:

```
feature_defs[5:10]
```

In the following output, we see 5 of the 114 features created by `featuretools`:

```
[<Feature: MIN(data.price)>,
 <Feature: MIN(data.quantity)>,
 <Feature: MODE(data.description)>,
 <Feature: MODE(data.stock_code)>,
 <Feature: NUM_UNIQUE(data.description)>]
```

> **Note**
>
> The `featuretools` library names the new features with the function used to create them, followed by the DataFrame that was used to perform the aggregation, followed by the aggregated variable name. Thus, `MIN(data.quantity)` is equivalent to `df.groupby(["customer_id"])["quantity"].min()`, if you are familiar with `pandas`. We will give more details in the *How it works...* section.

14. Let's display the first five rows of the DataFrame containing five of the created features:

```
feature_matrix[feature_matrix.columns[5:10]].head()
```

In the following output, we can see the first five rows containing the values of the five new features:

customer_id	MIN(data.price)	MIN(data.quantity)	MODE(data.description)	MODE(data.stock_code)	NUM_UNIQUE(data.description)
13085.0	0.55	-48.0	RECORD FRAME 7" SINGLE SIZE	22041	52
13078.0	0.19	-14.0	AREA PATROLLED METAL SIGN	82582	165
15362.0	0.21	1.0	BLUE PADDED SOFT MOBILE	20703	38
18102.0	0.27	-324.0	CREAM HEART CARD HOLDER	22189	415
18087.0	0.36	-96.0	WHITE HANGING HEART T-LIGHT HOLDER	85123A	48

Figure 9.6 – DataFrame with five features created by aggregating the data at the customer level

15. Similarly, we can create features automatically by aggregating information at the invoice level:

```
feature_matrix, feature_defs = ft.dfs(
    entityset=es,
    target_dataframe_name=»invoices»,
    ignore_columns = {«data»: [«customer_id»]},
    max_depth = 1,
)
```

16. The previous step returns 24 features – let's display their names:

```
feature_defs
```

We can see the names of the features in the following output:

```
[<Feature: customer_id>,
<Feature: COUNT(data)>,
<Feature: MAX(data.price)>,
<Feature: MAX(data.quantity)>,
<Feature: MEAN(data.price)>,
<Feature: MEAN(data.quantity)>,
<Feature: MIN(data.price)>,
<Feature: MIN(data.quantity)>,
<Feature: MODE(data.description)>,
<Feature: MODE(data.stock_code)>,
<Feature: NUM_UNIQUE(data.description)>,
<Feature: NUM_UNIQUE(data.stock_code)>,
<Feature: SKEW(data.price)>,
<Feature: SKEW(data.quantity)>,
<Feature: STD(data.price)>,
<Feature: STD(data.quantity)>,
<Feature: SUM(data.price)>,
<Feature: SUM(data.quantity)>,
<Feature: DAY(first_data_time)>,
<Feature: MONTH(first_data_time)>,
<Feature: WEEKDAY(first_data_time)>,
<Feature: YEAR(first_data_time)>]
```

> **Note**
>
> Go ahead and display the DataFrame containing the new features by executing `feature_matrix.head()` or check our accompanying GitHub repository for the result.

To wrap up, by using the code from *step 16* and changing the target DataFrame name from `invoices` to `items`, go ahead and create features automatically at the product level.

How it works...

In this recipe, we set up an entity set containing the data and the relationships between some of its variables (unique identifiers). After that, we automatically created features by aggregating the information in the dataset for each of the unique identifiers. We used two main classes from `featuretools`, `EntitySet` and `dfs`, to create the features. Let's discuss each of these in more detail.

The `EntitySet` class stores the data, the logical types of the variables, and the relationships between the variables. The variable types (whether numeric or categorical) are automatically assigned by `featuretools`. We can also set up specific variable types when adding a DataFrame to the entity set. In *step 4*, we added the data to the entity set and set the logical type of `customer_id` to `Categorical`.

> **Note**
>
> To inspect the datatypes inferred by `featuretools`, you can execute `es["data"].ww`, where `es` is the entity set and `data` is the name of the DataFrame.

The `EntitySet` class has the `add_dataframe` method, which we used in *step 4* to add a new DataFrame. When using this method, we need to specify the unique identifier, and if there is none, then we need to create one, as we did in *step 4*, by setting `make_index` to `True`. Note that in the `index` parameter from `add_dataframe`, we passed the `"rows"` string. With this configuration, `EntitySet` added a `rows` column containing the unique identifier for each row to the DataFrame, which is a new sequence of integers starting at 0.

> **Note**
>
> Instead of using the `add_dataframe` method to add a DataFrame to an entity set, we can add it by executing `es["df_name"]=df`, where `"df_name"` is the name we want to give to the DataFrame and `df` is the DataFrame we want to add.

The `EntitySet` class has the `normalize_dataframe` method, which is used to create a new DataFrame and relationship from the unique values of an existing column. The method takes the name of the DataFrame to which the new DataFrame will be related and a name for the new DataFrame. We also need to indicate the unique identifier for the new DataFrame in the `index` parameter. By default, this method creates a new DataFrame containing the unique identifier, followed by a `datetime` column containing the first date each unique identifier was registered. We can add more columns to this DataFrame by using the `copy_columns` parameters, as we did in *step 5*. Adding more columns to the new DataFrame is useful if we want to follow up with relationships to this new DataFrame, as we did in *step 6*.

The `EntitySet` class also has the `plot()` method, which displays existing relationships in the entity set. In *Figure 9.5*, we saw the relationships between our data tables; the `invoices` and `items` (products) tables were related to the original data, whereas the `customers` table was related to the `invoices` table, which was, in turn, related to the original data.

> **Note**
>
> The relationship between the tables dictates how features will be created. The `invoices` and `items` tables are related to the original data. Thus, we can only create features with depth 1. The `customers` table is, on the other hand, related to invoices, which is related to data. Thus, we can create features with depth 2. That means that new features will consist of aggregations from the entire dataset or aggregations for invoices first, which will then be subsequently aggregated for customers. We can regulate the features to create with the `max_depth` parameter in `dfs`.

After setting up the data and the relationships, we used `dfs` from `featuretools` to automatically create features. When creating features with `dfs`, we need to set the target DataFrame – that is, the data table for which the features should be created. The `dfs` class creates features by *transforming* and *aggregating* existing variables, through what are called **transform** and **aggregate primitives**.

A transform primitive transforms variables. For example, from datetime variables, using a transform primitive, `dfs` extracts the `month`, `year`, `day`, and `week` values.

An aggregate primitive aggregates information for a unique identifier. It uses mathematical operations such as the mean, standard deviation, maximum and minimum values, the sum, and the skew coefficient for numerical variables. For categorical variables, aggregate primitives use the mode and the count of unique items. For unique identifiers, they count the number of occurrences.

With the functionality of transform and aggregate primitives in mind, let's try to understand the features that we created in this recipe. We used the default parameters of `dfs` to create the default features.

> **Note**
>
> For more details on the default features returned by `featuretools`, visit `https://featuretools.alteryx.com/en/stable/generated/featuretools.dfs.html#featuretools.dfs`.

We first created features for each customer. `featuretools` returned 114 features for each customer. Because the `customers` data is related to the `invoices` data, which is related to the entire dataset, the features were created by aggregating data at two levels. First, the data was aggregated for each customer using the entire dataset. Next, it was aggregated for each invoice first, and then the pre-aggregated data was aggregated again for each customer.

The `featuretools` library names the new features with the function used to aggregate the data – for example, COUNT, MEAN, STD, and SKEW, among others. Next, it uses the data that was used for the aggregation and follows it with the variable that was aggregated. For example, the MEAN(`data.quantity`) feature contains the mean quantity of items bought by the customer calculated from the entire dataset, which is the equivalent of `df.groupby("customer_id")` `["quantity"].mean()`, if you are familiar with `pandas`. On the other hand, the MEAN(`invoices.` MEAN(`data.quantity`)) feature first takes the mean quantity of items for each invoice – that is, `df.groupby("invoice")["quantity"].mean()` – and from the resulting series, it takes the mean value, considering the invoices for a particular customer.

For categorical features, `featuretools` determines the mode and the unique values. For example, from the `description` variable, we've got the `NUM_UNIQUE(data.description)` and `MODE(data.description)` features. The description is just the name of the item. Thus, these features highlight the number of unique items the customer bought and the item the customer bought the most times.

> **Note something interesting**
>
> The `NUM_UNIQUE(data.description)` and `MODE(data.description)` variables are numeric after the aggregation of the categorical features. The `featuretools` library creates more features by using numerical aggregations of these newly created variables. In this way, the `MAX(invoices.NUM_UNIQUE(data.description)` feature first finds the number of unique items per invoice and then returns the maximum from those values for a particular customer, considering all the customer's invoices.

From datetime features, `featuretools` extracts date components by default. Remember that the `customers` DataFrame contains the `customer_id` variable and the date of the first invoice for each customer, as we saw in the output of *step 10*. From this datetime feature, `featuretools` created `DAY(first_invoices_time)`, `MONTH(first_invoices_time)`, `WEEKDAY(first_invoices_time)`, and `YEAR(first_invoices_time)` features containing the different date parts.

Finally, `featuretools` also returned the total number of invoices per customer (`COUNT(invoices)`) and the total number of rows (`COUNT(data)`) per customer.

See also

For more details into what inspired `featuretools`, check the original article *Deep Feature Synthesis: Towards Automating Data Science Endeavors* by Kanter and Veeramachaneni at `https://www.jmaxkanter.com/papers/DSAA_DSM_2015.pdf`.

Creating features with general and cumulative operations

The `featuretools` library uses what are called **transform primitives** to create features. Transform primitives take one or more columns in a dataset as input and return one or more columns as output. They are applied to a *single* DataFrame.

The `featuretools` library divides its transform primitives into various categories depending on the type of operation they perform or the type of variable they modify. For example, **general transform primitives** apply mathematical operations, such as the square root, the sine, and the cosine. **Cumulative transform primitives** create new features by comparing a row's value to the previous row's value. For example, the cumulative sum, cumulative mean, and cumulative minimum and maximum values belong to this category, as well as the difference between row values. There is another cumulative transformation that can be applied to datetime variables, which is the **time since previous** transformation, which determines the time passed between two consecutive timestamps.

In this recipe, we will create features using the general and cumulative transform primitives from `featuretools`.

Getting ready

Variable transformations such as the square root or the logarithm are useful when we want to change the distribution of a variable, as we saw in *Chapter 3, Transforming Numerical Variables*. Other mathematical derivations such as the sine and cosine help to capture underlying data patterns, as we described in the *Creating periodic features from cyclical variables* recipe in *Chapter 8, Creating New Features*. From the transformations described in those chapters, `featuretools` supports the square root and the logarithm transformation and the sine and cosine (but without the normalization between 0 and 2π).

With a cumulative transformation, we can, for example, get the total number of items bought per invoice by adding up the item's quantity on each row at the invoice level. To understand the features that we will create in this recipe, let's create them with `pandas` first:

1. Let's import `pandas` and `numpy`:

    ```
    import numpy as np
    import pandas as pd
    ```

2. Let's load the retail dataset described in the *Technical requirements* section:

    ```
    df = pd.read_csv(
        «retail.csv», parse_dates=[«invoice_date»])
    ```

3. Let's capture the two numerical variables, `price` and `quantity`, in a list:

    ```
    numeric_vars = ["quantity", "price"]
    ```

4. Let's capture the names of the cumulative functions in a list:

    ```
    func = ["cumsum", "cummax", "diff"]
    ```

5. Let's create a list with new names for the variables that we will create:

    ```
    new_names = [f"{var}_{function}"
        for function in func for var in numeric_vars]
    ```

6. Let's create new variables using the cumulative functions from *step 4*, applied to the variables from *step 3*, and add them to the DataFrame:

    ```
    df[new_names] = df.groupby(
        "invoice")[numeric_vars].agg(func)
    ```

The previous step returns the cumulative sum, cumulative maximum value, and the difference between rows, within each invoice. As soon as it encounters a new invoice number, it starts afresh.

7. Let's display the original and new features for one particular invoice:

```
df[df["invoice"] == "489434"][
    numeric_vars + new_names]
```

In the following output, we can see that `quantity_cumsum` is the cumulative sum for the variable quantity and `price_diff` is the price difference row after row:

	quantity	price	quantity_cumsum	price_cumsum	quantity_cummax	price_cummax	quantity_diff	price_diff
0	12	6.95	12	12	NaN	6.95	6.95	NaN
1	12	6.75	24	12	0.0	13.70	6.95	-0.20
2	12	6.75	36	12	0.0	20.45	6.95	0.00
3	48	2.10	84	48	36.0	22.55	6.95	-4.65
4	24	1.25	108	48	-24.0	23.80	6.95	-0.85

Figure 9.7 – DataFrame showing cumulative functions applied
to numerical features in a single entity (invoice)

Let's now apply the sine and cosine transformation to the entire DataFrame.

8. Let's create a list with names for the new variables:

```
new_names = [
    f"{var}_{function}"
    for function in ["sin", "cos"]
    for var in numeric_vars]
```

9. Let's transform the price and quantity with the sine and cosine:

```
df[new_names] = df[numeric_vars].agg(
    [np.sin, np.cos])
```

The transformation in *step 9* was applied to the entire dataset, irrespective of the invoice number, which is fine because it maps from one row to the same row, as opposed to from one row to the next, as with cumulative functions. You can inspect the result by executing `df[new_names].head()`.

Now that we understand the types of features we want to create, let's automate the process with `featuretools`.

How to do it...

We will apply cumulative transformations for each invoice and general transformations to the entire dataset:

1. First, we'll import `pandas`, `featuretools`, and the `Categorical` logical type:

```
import pandas as pd
import featuretools as ft
from woodwork.logical_types import Categorical
```

2. Let's load the dataset described in the *Technical requirements* section:

```python
df = pd.read_csv(
    «retail.csv», parse_dates=[«invoice_date»])
```

3. Let's set up an entity set:

```python
es = ft.EntitySet(id="data")
```

4. Let's add the DataFrame to the entity set:

```python
es = es.add_dataframe(
    dataframe=df,
    dataframe_name=»data»,
    index="rows",
    make_index=True,
    time_index=»invoice_date»,
    logical_types={
        "customer_id": Categorical,
        "invoice": Categorical,
    }
)
```

> **Note**
>
> By default, `featuretools` only retains categorical, numeric, and Boolean features in the feature matrix that is generated *after* creating new features. The type of the `invoice` variable is not accurately inferred, so we need to enforce it as categorical by setting its logical type as we do in *step 4*, if we want `featuretools` to retain it in the dataset containing the new features. To learn the datatypes inferred by `featuretools`, you can execute `es["data"].ww`.

5. Let's create a new DataFrame with a relationship to the DataFrame from *step 4*:

```python
es.normalize_dataframe(
    base_dataframe_name=»data»,
    new_dataframe_name=»invoices»,
    index="invoice",
    copy_columns=[«customer_id»],
)
```

> **Note**
>
> For more details about *steps 4* and *5*, visit the *Setting up an entity set and creating features automatically* recipe.

6. Let's make a list with the cumulative transformations that we'll use to create features:

```python
cum_primitives = [
    "cum_sum",
    "cum_max",
    "diff",
    "time_since_previous"]
```

> **Note**
>
> You can find `featuretools`-supported cumulative transformations at this link: https://featuretools.alteryx.com/en/stable/api_reference.html#cumulative-transform-primitives

7. Let's make a list of the general transformations to carry out:

```python
general_primitives = ["sine", " cosine "]
```

> **Note**
>
> You can find `featuretools`-supported general transformations at this link: https://featuretools.alteryx.com/en/stable/api_reference.html#general-transform-primitives

8. Finally, let's create the features. We use the `dfs` class, setting the original DataFrame as the target DataFrame – that is, the one whose variables we'll use as a template for the new features. Note that we pass an empty list to the `agg_primitives` parameter; this is to avoid returning the default aggregation primitives. We pass the general primitives from *step 7* to the `trans_primitives` parameter and the cumulative primitives from *step 6* to the `groupby_trans_primitives` parameter:

```python
feature_matrix, feature_defs = ft.dfs(
    entityset=es,
    target_dataframe_name=»data»,
    agg_primitives=[],
    trans_primitives=general_primitives,
    groupby_trans_primitives = cum_primitives,
    ignore_dataframes = [«invoices»],
)
```

> **Note**
>
> *Step 8* triggers the creation of features, which may take some time depending on how big the data is, how many aggregation levels it has, and the number of features to create. You can check out the output features *before* creating them, by setting the `features_only` parameter to `True`. This will return just the feature names; you can check them out, make sure they show what you need, and only then trigger the feature synthesis by setting that parameter back to `False`.

9. Let's now display the names of the created features:

```
feature_defs
```

In the following output, we see the names of the features that we created, including the sine and cosine of the price and quantity, and the cumulative transformations of these variables after grouping them by invoice number:

```
[<Feature: customer_id>,
<Feature: invoice>,
<Feature: stock_code>,
<Feature: description>,
<Feature: quantity>,
<Feature: price>,
<Feature: COSINE(price)>,
<Feature: COSINE(quantity)>,
<Feature: SINE(price)>,
<Feature: SINE(quantity)>,
<Feature: CUM_MAX(price) by invoice>,
<Feature: CUM_MAX(quantity) by invoice>,
<Feature: CUM_SUM(price) by invoice>,
<Feature: CUM_SUM(quantity) by invoice>,
<Feature: DIFF(price) by invoice>,
<Feature: DIFF(quantity) by invoice>,
<Feature: TIME_SINCE_PREVIOUS(invoice_date) by invoice>]
```

> **Note**
>
> The sine and cosine transformation of price and quantity will probably not add much value because these are not cyclical features. I kept these transformations in the recipe to show you how to apply transformation primitives in general, if you ever need them.

As you can see from the previous list, the new features were appended as new columns to the original DataFrame. You can display the final DataFrame by executing `feature_matrix. head()`:

rows	customer_id	invoice	stock_code	description	quantity	price	COSINE(price)	COSINE(quantity)	SINE(price)	SINE(quantity)	CUM_MAX(price) by invoice
0	13085.0	489434	85048	15CM CHRISTMAS GLASS BALL 20 LIGHTS	12	6.95	0.785796	0.843854	0.618486	-0.536573	6.95
1	13085.0	489434	79323P	PINK CHERRY LIGHTS	12	6.75	0.893006	0.843854	0.450044	-0.536573	6.95
2	13085.0	489434	79323W	WHITE CHERRY LIGHTS	12	6.75	0.893006	0.843854	0.450044	-0.536573	6.95
3	13085.0	489434	22041	RECORD FRAME 7" SINGLE SIZE	48	2.10	-0.504846	-0.640144	0.863209	-0.768255	6.95
4	13085.0	489434	21232	STRAWBERRY CERAMIC TRINKET BOX	24	1.25	0.315322	0.424179	0.948985	-0.905578	6.95

CUM_MAX(price) by invoice	CUM_MAX(quantity) by invoice	CUM_SUM(price) by invoice	CUM_SUM(quantity) by invoice	DIFF(price) by invoice	DIFF(quantity) by invoice	TIME_SINCE_PREVIOUS(invoice_date) by invoice
6.95	12.0	6.95	12.0	NaN	NaN	NaN
6.95	12.0	13.70	24.0	-0.20	0.0	0.0
6.95	12.0	20.45	36.0	0.00	0.0	0.0
6.95	48.0	22.55	84.0	-4.65	36.0	0.0
6.95	48.0	23.80	108.0	-0.85	-24.0	0.0

Figure 9.8 – DataFrame resulting from the deep feature synthesis,
containing the original variables and the new features

For more details about the created features, check the *How it works…* section.

How it works...

To create features using general and cumulative transformations with `featuretools`, we first need to set up an entity set with the data and define the relationships between its variables. We described how to set up an entity set in the *Setting up an entity set and creating features automatically* recipe.

To apply cumulative and general transforms, we used the `dfs` class from `featuretools`. General transformations are applied to the entire DataFrame without grouping by a specific variable. To perform general transformations, we passed a list of strings with the transformation names to the `trans_primitives` parameter from `dfs`.

We applied cumulative transformation after grouping by `invoice`. To do this, we passed a list of strings with the names of the cumulative transformation to the `groupby_trans_primitives` parameter from `dfs`. The `featuretools` library knows it should group by invoice because we established this unique identifier by using the `normalize_dataframe` method from `EntitySet` in *step 5*.

Finally, we did not want features created from the variables in the `invoices` DataFrame; thus, we set `dfs` to ignore this DataFrame by setting `ignore_dataframes = ["invoices"]`.

The `dfs` class returned two variables, the DataFrame with the original and new features, and the name of the features in a list. The new features are named with the operations applied to create them, such as `SINE`, `COSINE`, `CUM_MAX`, or `DIFF`, followed by the variable to which the transformation was applied and, when corresponding, the variable that was used for grouping.

Note that `featuretools` automatically recognizes and selects the variables over which the transformations should be applied. The sine, cosine, cumulative sum, maximum, and difference were applied to numerical variables, whereas the `time_since_previous` transformation was applied to the datetime variable.

Combining numerical features

In *Chapter 8, Creating New Features*, we saw that we can create new features by combining variables with mathematical operations. The `featuretools` library supports several operations for combining variables, including addition, division, modulo, and multiplication. In this recipe, we will learn how to combine these features with `featuretools`.

How to do it...

Let's begin by importing the libraries and getting the dataset ready:

1. First, we'll import `pandas`, `featuretools`, and the `Categorical` logical type:

```
import pandas as pd
import featuretools as ft
from woodwork.logical_types import Categorical
```

2. Let's load the dataset that described in the *Technical requirements* section:

```
df = pd.read_csv(
    «retail.csv», parse_dates=[«invoice_date»])
```

3. Let's set up an entity set:

```
es = ft.EntitySet(id="data")
```

4. Let's add the DataFrame to the entity set:

```
es = es.add_dataframe(
    dataframe=df,
    dataframe_name=»data»,
    index="rows",
    make_index=True,
```

```
        time_index=»invoice_date»,
        logical_types={«customer_id»: Categorical},
    )
```

5. Let's create a new DataFrame with a relationship to the DataFrame from *step 4*:

```
es.normalize_dataframe(
    base_dataframe_name=»data»,
    new_dataframe_name=»invoices»,
    index="invoice",
    copy_columns=[«customer_id»],
)
```

> **Note**
>
> For more details about *steps 4* and *5*, visit the *Setting up an entity set and creating features automatically* recipe.

6. We will multiply the `quantity` and `price` variables, which reflect the number of items bought and the unit price, respectively, to obtain the total amount paid:

```
feature_matrix, feature_defs = ft.dfs(
    entityset=es,
    target_dataframe_name=»data»,
    agg_primitives=[],
    trans_primitives=[«multiply_numeric»],
    primitive_options={
        («multiply_numeric»): {
            ‹include_columns›: {
                'data': ["quantity", "price"]
            }
        }
    },
    ignore_dataframes=[«invoices»],
)
```

> **Note**
>
> We set `agg_primitives` to an empty list to avoid the creation of default primitives.

7. Let's now display the name of the new features:

```
feature_defs
```

In the following output, we see the feature names, the last one of which corresponds to the combination of the `price` and `quantity` variables:

```
[<Feature: customer_id>,
 <Feature: stock_code>,
 <Feature: description>,
 <Feature: quantity>,
 <Feature: price>,
 <Feature: price * quantity>]
```

8. To finish off, let's inspect the new DataFrame created in *step 6*:

    ```
    feature_matrix.head()
    ```

    In the following output, we can see that the new feature was appended to the right of the original DataFrame:

rows	customer_id	stock_code	description	quantity	price	price * quantity
0	13085.0	85048	15CM CHRISTMAS GLASS BALL 20 LIGHTS	12	6.95	83.4
1	13085.0	79323P	PINK CHERRY LIGHTS	12	6.75	81.0
2	13085.0	79323W	WHITE CHERRY LIGHTS	12	6.75	81.0
3	13085.0	22041	RECORD FRAME 7" SINGLE SIZE	48	2.10	100.8
4	13085.0	21232	STRAWBERRY CERAMIC TRINKET BOX	24	1.25	30.0

Figure 9.9 – DataFrame with the new feature resulting from the product of price with quantity

Combining features with `featuretools` may seem like a lot of work compared to the `df["price"].mul(df["quantity"])` pandas functionality. The real power comes in when we create new features in this way and follow it up with aggregations at the invoice or customer level. We will discuss aggregation functions in the *Creating features with aggregation primitives* recipe.

How it works...

To multiply features, we used the `MultiplyNumeric` primitive from `featuretools`, which can be accessed from `dfs` using the `multiply_numeric` string. We passed the former string to the `trans_primitive` parameter and then used the `primitive_options` parameter to specify which variables to multiply. Note that in addition, we passed an empty list to the `agg_primitives` parameter to avoid returning the default aggregation primitives, and we ignored the features coming from the `invoices` DataFrame.

To check out other functions that allow you to combine variables, visit `https://featuretools.alteryx.com/en/stable/api_reference.html#binary-transform-primitives`. At the time of writing, I noticed that `MultiplyNumeric` and `DivideNumeric` are not in the documentation. You can always double-check which functions are supported by inspecting the source code: `https://github.com/alteryx/featuretools/tree/main/featuretools/primitives/standard/transform/binary`. You can also check out which operations you can perform on your data by running the following command after you set up the entity set and its relationships: `ft.get_valid_primitives(es, target_dataframe_name="data", max_depth=2)`. Here, `es` is the entity set resulting from *step 5*.

Extracting features from date and time

In *Chapter 6*, *Extracting Features from Date and Time Variables*, we discussed how we can enrich our datasets by extracting features from the date and time parts of datetime variables, such as the year, the month, the day of the week, the hour, and much more. We can extract those features automatically utilizing `featuretools`.

The `featuretools` library supports the creation of various features from datetime variables using its **datetime transform primitives**. These primitives include common variables such as year, month, and day, and other features such as *is it lunch time* or *is it weekday*. In addition, we can extract features indicating if the date was a federal or bank holiday (as they call it in the UK) or features that determine the distance in time to a certain date. For a retail company, the proximity to dates such as Boxing Day, Black Fridays, or Christmas normally signals an increase in sales, and if they are forecasting demand, these will make useful variables.

> **Note**
>
> For more details on the features that can be created from datetime variables, visit `https://featuretools.alteryx.com/en/stable/api_reference.html#datetime-transform-primitives`.

In this recipe, we will automatically create multiple features from a datetime variable with `featuretools`.

How to do it...

Let's begin by importing the libraries and getting the dataset ready:

1. First, we'll import `pandas`, `featuretools`, and some special datetime primitives:

    ```python
    import pandas as pd
    import featuretools as ft
    from featuretools.primitives import (
        IsFederalHoliday, DistanceToHoliday)
    from woodwork.logical_types import Categorical
    ```

2. Let's load the dataset described in the *Technical requirements* section:

```
df = pd.read_csv(
    «retail.csv», parse_dates=[«invoice_date»])
```

3. Let's set up an entity set:

```
es = ft.EntitySet(id="data")
```

4. Let's add the DataFrame to the entity set:

```
es = es.add_dataframe(
    dataframe=df,
    dataframe_name=»data»,
    index="rows",
    make_index=True,
    time_index=»invoice_date»,
    logical_types={«customer_id»: Categorical},
)
```

5. Let's create a new DataFrame with a relationship to the DataFrame from *step 4*:

```
es.normalize_dataframe(
    base_dataframe_name=»data»,
    new_dataframe_name=»invoices»,
    index="invoice",
    copy_columns=[«customer_id»],
)
```

> **Note**
>
> For more details about *steps 4* and *5*, visit the *Setting up an entity set and creating features automatically* recipe.

6. Let's create a primitive that returns a Boolean vector indicating if the date coincides with a UK bank holiday (that is, a non-working day):

```
is_bank_hol = IsFederalHoliday(country="UK")
```

> **Note**
>
> When setting up the primitive to determine bank holidays, it is important to choose the right country. For a list of supported countries, visit `https://github.com/dr-prodigy/python-holidays#available-countries`.

7. Let's check out which bank holidays are included in this primitive:

```
hols = is_bank_hol.holidayUtil.federal_holidays.values()
available_hols = list(set(hols))
```

If we execute `available_hols`, we'll see a list of bank holidays supported for the UK:

```
['May Day',
 'Good Friday',
 'Wedding of William and Catherine',
 'Coronation of Charles III',
 'Christmas Day',
 'Wedding of Charles and Diana',
 'Christmas Day (observed)',
 'State Funeral of Queen Elizabeth II',
 'Silver Jubilee of Elizabeth II',
 'Spring Bank Holiday',
 'Diamond Jubilee of Elizabeth II',
 'Boxing Day (observed)',
 'Platinum Jubilee of Elizabeth II',
 "New Year's Day (observed)",
 'Boxing Day',
 'Golden Jubilee of Elizabeth II',
 'Millennium Celebrations',
 "New Year's Day"]
```

8. Let's create another primitive that determines the days to a certain date – in this case, the distance to Boxing Day:

```
days_to_boxing = DistanceToHoliday(
    holiday="Boxing Day", country="UK")
```

9. Now, let's make a list containing strings that identify common features that we can get from `datetime` and include the primitives from *steps 6* and *8*:

```
date_primitives = [
    "day", "year", "month", "weekday",
    "days_in_month", "part_of_day",
    "hour", "minute",
    is_bank_hol,
    days_to_boxing
]
```

10. Let's now create date and time features from *step 9* based on the `invoice_date` date variable:

```
feature_matrix, feature_defs = ft.dfs(
    entityset=es,
```

```
    target_dataframe_name=»invoices»,
    agg_primitives=[],
    trans_primitives=date_primitives,
)
```

> **Note**
>
> In *step 4*, we entered the `invoice_date` variable as a time variable. Thus, `featuretools` will use this variable to create date- and time-related features.

11. Let's display the names of the created features:

```
feature_defs
```

In the following output, we see the names of the original and time features:

```
[<Feature: customer_id>,
<Feature: DAY(first_data_time)>,
<Feature: DAYS_IN_MONTH(first_data_time)>,
<Feature: DISTANCE_TO_HOLIDAY(
    first_data_time, holiday=Boxing Day, country=UK)>,
<Feature: HOUR(first_data_time)>,
<Feature: IS_FEDERAL_HOLIDAY(
    first_data_time, , country=UK)>,
<Feature: MINUTE(first_data_time)>,
<Feature: MONTH(first_data_time)>,
<Feature: PART_OF_DAY(first_data_time)>,
<Feature: WEEKDAY(first_data_time)>,
<Feature: YEAR(first_data_time)>]
```

Go ahead and execute `feature_matrix.head()` to take a look at the resulting DataFrame with the features created from the invoice date. The DataFrame is quite big, so for reasons of space, we'll only display a few columns in the book.

12. Let's display the resulting DataFrame containing three of the new features:

```
columns = [
    "DISTANCE_TO_HOLIDAY(first_data_time,
        holiday=Boxing Day, country=UK)",
    "HOUR(first_data_time)",
    "IS_FEDERAL_HOLIDAY(first_data_time,
        country=UK)",
]
feature_matrix[columns].head()
```

In the following output, we see the DataFrame with the new features:

invoice	DISTANCE_TO_HOLIDAY(first_data_time, holiday=Boxing Day, country=UK)	HOUR(first_data_time)	IS_FEDERAL_HOLIDAY(first_data_time, country=UK)
489434	25.0	7	False
489435	25.0	7	False
489436	25.0	9	False
489437	25.0	9	False
489438	25.0	9	False

Figure 9.10 – DataFrame with some of the features derived from datetime

Note that some of the created features are numeric, such as HOUR or DAY, some are Booleans, such as IS_FEDERAL_HOLIDAY, and some are categorical, such as PART_OF_DAY. To take a look at the values of PART_OF_DAY, execute `feature_matrix["PART_OF_DAY(first_data_time)"].unique()`.

How it works...

To create features from datetime variables, we used datetime transform primitives from `featuretools` (`https://featuretools.alteryx.com/en/stable/api_reference.html#datetime-transform-primitives`). These primitives can be accessed from `dfs` using the strings and functions we specified in *steps 6* to *9* through the `trans_primitive` parameter. Note that in addition, we passed an empty list to the `agg_primitives` parameter not to return the default aggregation primitives that would have been otherwise applied to our datetime features. We also ignored the features coming from the `invoices` DataFrame.

> **Note**
>
> We set `agg_primitives` to an empty list and ignored the `invoices` DataFrame to keep the outputs simple and be able to focus on datetime features. However, note that the real power of `featuretools` consists in creating primitives from `datetime` and then aggregating them further at different entity levels.

Extracting features from text

In *Chapter 11, Extracting Features from Text Variables*, we will discuss various features that we can extract from text pieces utilizing `pandas` and `scikit-learn`. We can also extract multiple features from text automatically by utilizing `featuretools`.

The `featuretools` library supports the creation of several basic features from text as part of its default functionality, such as the number of characters, the number of words, the mean character count per word, and the median word length in a piece of text, among others.

> **Note**
>
> For a full list of the default text primitives, visit `https://featuretools.alteryx.com/en/stable/api_reference.html#naturallanguage-transform-primitives`.

In addition, there is an accompanying Python library, `nlp_primitives`, which contains additional primitives to create more advanced features based on NLP. Among these functions, we find primitives for determining the diversity score, the polarity score, or the count of stop words.

> **Note**
>
> There is no documentation at the time of writing to learn more about the primitives supported by the `nlp_primitives` library, so to find out more, you need to check the source code: `https://github.com/alteryx/nlp_primitives/tree/6243ef2379501bfec2c3f19e35a30b5954605e57/nlp_primitives`.

In this recipe, we will first create multiple features from a text variable utilizing `featuretools'` default functionality and then highlight how to use primitives from the `nlp_primitives` library.

Getting ready

To follow along with this recipe, you need to install the `nlp_primitives` library, which you can do with `pip`:

```
pip install nlp_primitives
```

Otherwise, you can use `conda`:

```
conda install -c conda-forge nlp-primitives
```

> **Note**
>
> For more details, visit the `nlp_primitives` GitHub repository: `https://github.com/alteryx/nlp_primitives`

How to do it...

Let's begin by importing the libraries and getting the dataset ready:

1. First, we'll import `pandas`, `featuretools`, and the logical types:

    ```
    import pandas as pd
    import featuretools as ft
    from woodwork.logical_types import (
        Categorical, NaturalLanguage)
    ```

2. Let's load the dataset described in the *Technical requirements* section:

```
df = pd.read_csv(
    «retail.csv», parse_dates=[«invoice_date»])
```

3. Let's set up an entity set:

```
es = ft.EntitySet(id="data")
```

4. Let's add the DataFrame to the entity set, highlighting that the `description` variable is a text variable:

```
es = es.add_dataframe(
    dataframe=df,
    dataframe_name=»data»,
    index="rows",
    make_index=True,
    time_index=»invoice_date»,
    logical_types={
        «customer_id»: Categorical,
        "invoice": Categorical,
        «description»: NaturalLanguage,
    }
)
```

> **Note**
>
> For the `featuretools` library's text primitives to work, we need to indicate which variables are text by using the `NaturalLanguage` logical type.

5. Let's create a new DataFrame with a relationship to the DataFrame from *step 4*:

```
es.normalize_dataframe(
    base_dataframe_name=»data»,
    new_dataframe_name=»invoices»,
    index="invoice",
    copy_columns=[«customer_id»],
)
```

> **Note**
>
> For more details about *steps 4* and *5*, visit the *Setting up an entity set and creating features automatically* recipe.

6. Let's make a list with strings corresponding to the text features we want to create:

```python
text_primitives = [
    "num_words",
    "num_characters",
    "MeanCharactersPerWord" ,
    "PunctuationCount"]
```

7. Let's now extract the text features from the `description` variable:

```python
feature_matrix, feature_defs = ft.dfs(
    entityset=es,
    target_dataframe_name=»data»,
    agg_primitives=[],
    trans_primitives=text_primitives,
    ignore_dataframes=[«invoices»],
)
```

8. Let's display the names of the created features:

```python
feature_defs
```

In the following output, we see the names of the original features, followed by those created from the `description` variable:

```python
[<Feature: customer_id>,
<Feature: invoice>,
<Feature: stock_code>,
<Feature: quantity>,
<Feature: price>,
<Feature: MEAN_CHARACTERS_PER_WORD(description)>,
<Feature: NUM_CHARACTERS(description)>,
<Feature: NUM_WORDS(description)>,
<Feature: PUNCTUATION_COUNT(description)>]
```

Go ahead and inspect the result by executing `feature_matrix.head()`.

9. Let's display a slice of the DataFrame containing the text-derived features:

```python
text_f = [
    "NUM_CHARACTERS(description)",
    "NUM_WORDS(description)",
    "PUNCTUATION_COUNT(description)",
]
feature_matrix[text_f].head()
```

In the following output, we see a DataFrame with the features created from the text:

rows	NUM_CHARACTERS(description)	NUM_WORDS(description)	PUNCTUATION_COUNT(description)
0	35	6	0
1	18	3	0
2	20	3	0
3	28	5	1
4	30	4	0

Figure 9.11 – DataFrame with the features created from text

> **Note**
> The `featuretools` library removes the original text variable, `description`, and in its place, it returns the new features.

To create features using the primitives from the `nlp_primitives` package, you need to import them first – for example, by executing from `nlp_primitives import DiversityScore` – and then add the primitives to the text primitive list that we created in *step 6*. Note that these are complex functions, so they may take some time to create the features.

How it works...

To create features from text variables, we used the default text primitives from `featuretools`. These primitives can be accessed from `dfs` by passing a list with strings corresponding to the primitive names, such as those from *step 6*, to the `trans_primitives` parameter.

For more advanced primitives, you need to import the primitive functions from the `nlp_primitives` library and then pass them on to the `trans_primitives` parameter from `dfs`. With this, `dfs` can tap into the functionality of these primitives to create new features from the text. The `nlp_primitives` library uses the `nltk` Python library under the hood.

Creating features with aggregation primitives

Throughout this chapter, we've created features automatically by mapping existing variables into new features through various functions. For example, we extracted date and time parts from datetime variables, counted the number of words, characters, and punctuation in texts, combined numerical features into new variables, and transformed features with functions such as sine and cosine. To create these features, we worked with transform primitives.

The `featuretools` library also supports **aggregation primitives**, and here is where it gets interesting. These primitives take related observations as input and return a single value as output. For example, if we have a numerical variable, `price`, related to an invoice, an aggregation primitive would take all the price observations for a single invoice and return a single value, such as the mean price or the sum (that is, the total amount paid), for that invoice.

> **Note**
>
> The `featuretools` aggregation functionality is the equivalent of `groupby` in `pandas`, followed by `pandas` functions such as `mean`, `sum`, `std`, and `count`, among others.

Some aggregation primitives work with numerical variables, such as the mean, sum, or maximum and minimum values. Other aggregation primitives are specific to categorical variables, such as the number of unique values and the most frequent value (mode).

> **Note**
>
> For a complete list of supported aggregation primitives, visit `https://featuretools.alteryx.com/en/stable/api_reference.html#aggregation-primitives`.

In this recipe, we will first create multiple features by aggregating existing variables. After that, we will combine the use of transform and aggregation primitives to highlight the true power of `featuretools`.

Getting ready

In this recipe, we will use the *Online Retail II* dataset from the UCI Machine Learning Repository. This dataset has information about products (items), invoices, and customers. To follow along with this recipe, it is important to understand the nature of and the relationships between these entities and how to correctly set up an entity set with `featuretools`, which we described in the *Setting up an entity set and creating features automatically* recipe. Make sure you checked that recipe out before proceeding with the next section.

How to do it...

Let's begin by importing the libraries and getting the dataset ready:

1. First, we'll import `pandas`, `featuretools`, and the logical types:

    ```python
    import pandas as pd
    import featuretools as ft
    from woodwork.logical_types import (
        Categorical, NaturalLanguage)
    ```

2. Let's load the dataset described in the *Technical requirements* section:

```
df = pd.read_csv(
    «retail.csv», parse_dates=[«invoice_date»])
```

3. Let's set up an entity set:

```
es = ft.EntitySet(id="data")
```

4. Let's add the DataFrame to the entity set, highlighting that the `description` variable is a text variable, `customer_id` is categorical, and `invoice_date` is a datetime feature:

```
es = es.add_dataframe(
    dataframe=df,
    dataframe_name=»data»,
    index="rows",
    make_index=True,
    time_index=»invoice_date»,
    logical_types={
        «customer_id»: Categorical,
        «description»: NaturalLanguage,
    }
)
```

5. Let's create a new DataFrame with a relationship to the DataFrame from *step 4*:

```
es.normalize_dataframe(
    base_dataframe_name=»data»,
    new_dataframe_name=»invoices»,
    index="invoice",
    copy_columns=[«customer_id»],
)
```

6. Now, we add the second relationship, which is between customers and invoices. To do this, we indicate the base DataFrame, which we called `invoices` in *step 5*, we give the new DataFrame a name, `customers`, and we add a unique customer identifier:

```
es.normalize_dataframe(
    base_dataframe_name=»invoices»,
    new_dataframe_name=»customers»,
    index=»customer_id»,
)
```

> **Note**
>
> For more details about *steps 4 to 5*, visit the *Setting up an entity set and creating features automatically* recipe.

7. Let's make a list with string names that identify the aggregation primitives we want to use:

```
agg_primitives = ["mean", "max", "min", "sum"]
```

8. Let's create features by aggregating the data at the customer level. To do this, we set up the `dfs` class from `featuretools`, indicating `customers` as the target DataFrame and passing the aggregation primitives from *step 7* and an empty list to the `trans_primitives` parameter to prevent `dfs` from returning the default transformations:

```
feature_matrix, feature_defs = ft.dfs(
    entityset=es,
    target_dataframe_name=»customers»,
    agg_primitives=agg_primitives,
    trans_primitives=[],
)
```

9. Let's display the names of the created features:

```
feature_defs
```

In the following output, we see the name features that were aggregated at the customer level:

```
[<Feature: MAX(data.price)>,
 <Feature: MAX(data.quantity)>,
 <Feature: MEAN(data.price)>,
 <Feature: MEAN(data.quantity)>,
 <Feature: MIN(data.price)>,
 <Feature: MIN(data.quantity)>,
 <Feature: SUM(data.price)>,
 <Feature: SUM(data.quantity)>,
 <Feature: MAX(invoices.MEAN(data.price))>,
 <Feature: MAX(invoices.MEAN(data.quantity))>,
 <Feature: MAX(invoices.MIN(data.price))>,
 <Feature: MAX(invoices.MIN(data.quantity))>,
 <Feature: MAX(invoices.SUM(data.price))>,
 <Feature: MAX(invoices.SUM(data.quantity))>,
 <Feature: MEAN(invoices.MAX(data.price))>,
 <Feature: MEAN(invoices.MAX(data.quantity))>,
 <Feature: MEAN(invoices.MEAN(data.price))>,
 <Feature: MEAN(invoices.MEAN(data.quantity))>,
 <Feature: MEAN(invoices.MIN(data.price))>,
 <Feature: MEAN(invoices.MIN(data.quantity))>,
 <Feature: MEAN(invoices.SUM(data.price))>,
 <Feature: MEAN(invoices.SUM(data.quantity))>,
 <Feature: MIN(invoices.MAX(data.price))>,
 <Feature: MIN(invoices.MAX(data.quantity))>,
```

```
<Feature: MIN(invoices.MEAN(data.price))>,
<Feature: MIN(invoices.MEAN(data.quantity))>,
<Feature: MIN(invoices.SUM(data.price))>,
<Feature: MIN(invoices.SUM(data.quantity))>,
<Feature: SUM(invoices.MAX(data.price))>,
<Feature: SUM(invoices.MAX(data.quantity))>,
<Feature: SUM(invoices.MEAN(data.price))>,
<Feature: SUM(invoices.MEAN(data.quantity))>,
<Feature: SUM(invoices.MIN(data.price))>,
<Feature: SUM(invoices.MIN(data.quantity))>]
```

> **Note**
>
> Remember that `featuretools` names features with the function used to create them, followed by the DataFrame that was used in the computation, followed by the variable that was used in the computation. Thus, `MAX(data.price)` is the maximum price seen in the dataset for each customer. On the other hand, `MEAN(invoices.MAX(data.price))` is the mean value of all maximum prices observed in each invoice for a particular customer. That is, if a customer has six invoices, we first find the maximum price for each of the six invoices and then take the average of those values.

10. Let's now display the resulting DataFrame containing the original data and new features:

```
feature_matrix.head()
```

In the following output, we see *some* of the variables in the DataFrame returned by `dfs`:

customer_id	MAX(data.price)	MAX(data.quantity)	MEAN(data.price)	MEAN(data.quantity)	MIN(data.price)	MIN(data.quantity)	SUM(data.price)
13085.0	830.12	48.0	12.413587	9.076087	0.55	-48.0	1142.05
13078.0	12.75	300.0	3.961193	14.061988	0.19	-14.0	3386.82
15362.0	9.95	48.0	3.612000	9.200000	0.21	1.0	144.48
18102.0	3580.80	1008.0	10.831367	175.196629	0.27	-324.0	11567.90
18087.0	852.80	3906.0	11.971368	78.189474	0.36	-96.0	1137.28

SUM(data.quantity)	MAX(invoices.MEAN(data.price))	MAX(invoices.MEAN(data.quantity))	...	MIN(invoices.MEAN(data.price))	MIN(invoices.MEAN(data.quantity))
835.0	830.120000	20.750000	...	1.828571	-15.428571
12023.0	12.750000	61.333333	...	0.190000	-14.000000
368.0	3.628261	13.117647	...	3.590000	6.304348
187110.0	3580.800000	624.000000	...	0.480000	-324.000000
7428.0	852.800000	3906.000000	...	0.820000	-96.000000

Figure 9.12 – DataFrame with some of the features resulting from aggregations at the customer level

Due to space limitations, we can't display the entire output of *step 10*, so make sure you execute it on your computer or visit our accompanying GitHub repository for more details: `https://github.com/PacktPublishing/Python-Feature-Engineering-Cookbook-Third-Edition/blob/main/ch09-featuretools/Recipe6-Creating-features-with-aggregation-primitives.ipynb`.

To follow up, let's combine what we learned from the recipes using transform primitives with the aggregation functions from this recipe. First, we will create new features from existing datetime and text variables; then, we will aggregate those features along with the numerical variables, at the customer level.

11. Let's make lists with date and text primitives:

```
trans_primitives = ["month", "weekday", "num_words"]
```

12. Let's make a list with an aggregation primitive:

```
agg_primitives = ["mean"]
```

13. Let's now automatically create features by transforming and then aggregating variables:

```
feature_matrix, feature_defs = ft.dfs(
    entityset=es,
    target_dataframe_name=»customers»,
    agg_primitives=agg_primitives,
    trans_primitives=trans_primitives,
    max_depth=3,
)
```

The code from *step 13* triggers the creation of the features and their subsequent aggregation at the customer level.

14. Let's display the names of the new features:

```
feature_defs
```

In the following output, we see the names of the created variables:

```
[<Feature: MEAN(data.price)>,
 <Feature: MEAN(data.quantity)>,
 <Feature: MONTH(first_invoices_time)>,
 <Feature: WEEKDAY(first_invoices_time)>,
 <Feature: MEAN(invoices.MEAN(data.price))>,
 <Feature: MEAN(invoices.MEAN(data.quantity))>,
 <Feature: MEAN(data.NUM_WORDS(description))>,
 <Feature: MEAN(invoices.MEAN(data.NUM_
    WORDS(description)))>] WORDS(description)))>]
```

Note that in our recipes, we keep the creation of features to a minimum due to space limitations, but you can create as many features as you want and enrich your datasets dramatically with the functionality built into `featuretools`.

How it works...

In this recipe, we brought together the creation of features using transform primitives, which we discussed throughout the chapter, with the creation of features using aggregation primitives.

To create features with `featuretools` automatically, we first need to enter the data into an entity set and establish the relationships between the data. We discussed how to set up an entity set in the *Setting up an entity set and creating features automatically* recipe.

To aggregate existing features, we used the `dfs` class. We created a list with a string corresponding to the aggregation primitives and passed it to the `agg_primitives` parameter from `dfs`. To aggregate existing variables without creating new features, we passed an empty list to the `trans_primitives` parameter of `dfs`.

The `customers` DataFrame is the child of the `invoice` DataFrame, which is, in turn, the child of the original data. Thus, `dfs` created aggregations from the original data and the pre-aggregated data for each invoice. Thus, the `MEAN(data.price)` feature consists of the mean price for an item bought by a customer calculated from the entire data, whereas `MEAN(invoices.MEAN(data.price))` calculates the mean price per invoice first and then takes the mean of those values for a customer. Thus, if a customer has five invoices, `featuretools` first calculates the mean price paid for each of those invoices and then takes the mean of those values. As such, `MEAN(data.price)` and `MEAN(invoices.MEAN(data.price))` are not the same feature.

> **Note**
>
> An aggregate primitive aggregates information for a unique identifier. Aggregate primitives use mathematical operations such as the mean, standard deviation, maximum and minimum values, the sum, and the skew coefficient for numerical variables. For categorical variables, aggregate primitives use the mode and the count of unique items. For unique identifiers, aggregate primitives count the number of occurrences.

Next, we combined the creation of new features from date and text variables with aggregation. To do this, we passed a list of strings corresponding to the transform primitives to the `trans_primitives` parameter, and another list of strings corresponding to the aggregation primitives to the `agg_primitives` parameter of `dfs`.

One of the outputs of *step 13* is a list of the new features. From these, we can identify features created from the first invoice date for each customer, such as `MONTH(first_invoices_time)` and `WEEKDAY(first_invoices_time)`. We can also see features that were aggregated from features created from text, such as `MEAN(data.NUM_WORDS(description))` and `MEAN(invoices.MEAN(data.NUM_WORDS(description)))`. Finally, we can see the aggregations of existing numerical variables, such as `MEAN(data.price)` and `MEAN(invoices.MEAN(data.price))`.

> **Note**
>
> If you want to apply transform and aggregation primitives to specific variables, you can do so by specifying the primitive options as discussed here: `https://docs.featuretools.com/en/stable/guides/specifying_primitive_options.html`.

10

Creating Features from a Time Series with tsfresh

Throughout this book, we've discussed feature engineering methods and tools tailored for tabular and relational datasets. In this chapter, we will shift our focus to time-series data. A time series is a sequence of observations taken sequentially over time. Examples include energy generation and demand, temperature, air pollutant concentration, stock prices, and sales revenue. Each of these examples represents a variable and their values change over time.

The widespread availability of affordable sensors capable of measuring motion, movement, humidity, glucose, and other parameters has significantly increased the amount of temporally annotated data. These time series can be utilized in various classification tasks. For instance, by analyzing the electricity usage pattern of a household at a given time interval, we can infer whether a particular appliance was being used. Similarly, the signal of an ultrasound sensor can help determine the probability of a (gas) pipeline failure, and the characteristics of a sound wavelength can help predict whether a listener will like a song. Time-series data is also valuable for regression tasks. For example, signals from machinery sensors can be used to predict the remaining useful life of the device.

To use time series with traditional supervised machine learning models, such as linear and logistic regression, or decision-tree-based algorithms, we need to map each time series into a well-defined feature vector that captures its characteristics. Time-series patterns, including trends, seasonality, and periodicity, among other things, can be captured by a combination of simple and complex mathematical operations. Simple calculations include, for instance, taking the mean and the standard deviation of the time series. More complex methods include determining correlation or entropy, for example. In addition, we can apply non-linear time-series analysis functions to decompose the time-series signal, for example, Fourier or wavelet transformations, and use the parameters of these functions as features of the supervised models.

Creating features from time series can be very time-consuming; we need to apply various signal processing and time-series analysis algorithms to identify and extract meaningful features. The `tsfresh` Python package, which stands for **Time Series FeatuRe Extraction on the basis of Scalable Hypothesis** tests, streamlines this process. It integrates 63 time-series characterization methods to compute more than 750 features automatically. Additionally, `tsfresh` includes a feature selection algorithm that identifies the most predictive features for a given time series. By automating the application of complex time-series methods, `tsfresh` bridges the gap between signal-processing experts and machine learning practitioners, making it easier to extract valuable features from time-series data.

In this chapter, we will learn how to automatically create hundreds of features from time-series data by utilizing `tsfresh`. Following that, we will discuss how to fine-tune this feature creation process by selecting the most relevant features, extracting different features from different time series, and integrating the feature creation process into a scikit-learn pipeline to classify time-series data.

In this chapter, we will go through the following recipes:

- Extracting hundreds of features automatically from a time series

- Automatically creating and selecting predictive features from time-series data

- Extracting different features from different time series

- Creating a subset of features identified through feature selection

- Embedding feature creation into a scikit-learn pipeline

Technical requirements

In this chapter, we will use the open source `tsfresh` Python library. You can install `tsfresh` with `pip` by executing `pip install tsfresh`.

> **Note**
>
> If you have an old Microsoft operating system, you may need to update the Microsoft C++ build tools to proceed with the `tsfresh` package's installation. Follow the steps in this thread to do so: `https://stackoverflow.com/questions/64261546/how-to-solve-error-microsoft-visual-c-14-0-or-greater-is-required-when-inst`.

We will work with the **Occupancy Detection** dataset from the UCI Machine Learning Repository, available at `http://archive.ics.uci.edu/ml/datasets/Occupancy+Detection` and licensed under a Creative Commons Attribution 4.0 International (CC BY 4.0) license: `https://creativecommons.org/licenses/by/4.0/legalcode`. The corresponding citation for this data is as follows:

Candanedo, Luis. (2016). Occupancy Detection. UCI Machine Learning Repository. `https://doi.org/10.24432/C5X01N`.

I downloaded and modified the data as shown in this notebook: `https://github.com/PacktPublishing/Python-Feature-engineering-Cookbook-Third-Edition/blob/main/ch10-tsfresh/prepare-occupancy-dataset.ipynb`

For a copy of the modified dataset and a target variable, check out the files called `occupancy.csv` and `occupancy_target.csv`, available at the following link: `https://github.com/PacktPublishing/Python-Feature-engineering-Cookbook-Third-Edition/blob/main/ch10-tsfresh`

The Occupancy Detection dataset contains time-series data taken over 135 hours at one-minute intervals. The variables measure the temperature, humidity, CO_2 level, and light consumption in an office. Camera footage was used to determine whether someone was in the office. The target variable shows whether the office was occupied at any one hour. If the target takes the value 1, it means that the office was occupied during that hour; otherwise, it takes the value 0.

The dataset with the time series and that with the target variable have different numbers of rows. The time-series dataset contains 135 hours of records at one-minute intervals – that is, 8,100 rows. The target has only 135 rows, with a label indicating whether the office was occupied at each of the 135 hours.

> **Note**
>
> Check out the notebook in this book's GitHub repository for plots of the different time series to become familiar with the dataset: `https://github.com/PacktPublishing/Python-Feature-Engineering-Cookbook-Third-Edition/blob/main/ch10-tsfresh/prepare-occupancy-dataset.ipynb`

Extracting hundreds of features automatically from a time series

Time series are data points indexed in time order. Analyzing time-series sequences allows us to make various predictions. For example, sensor data can be used to predict pipeline failures, sound data can help identify music genres, health history or personal measurements such as glucose levels can indicate whether a person is sick, and, as we will show in this recipe, patterns of light usage, humidity, and CO_2 levels can determine whether an office is occupied.

To train regression and classification models using traditional machine learning algorithms, such as linear regression or random forests, we require a dataset of size $M \times N$, where M is the number of rows and N is the number of features or columns. However, with time-series data, what we have is a collection of M time series, and each time series has multiple rows indexed chronologically. To use time series in supervised learning models, each time series needs to be mapped into a well-defined feature vector, N, as shown in the following diagram:

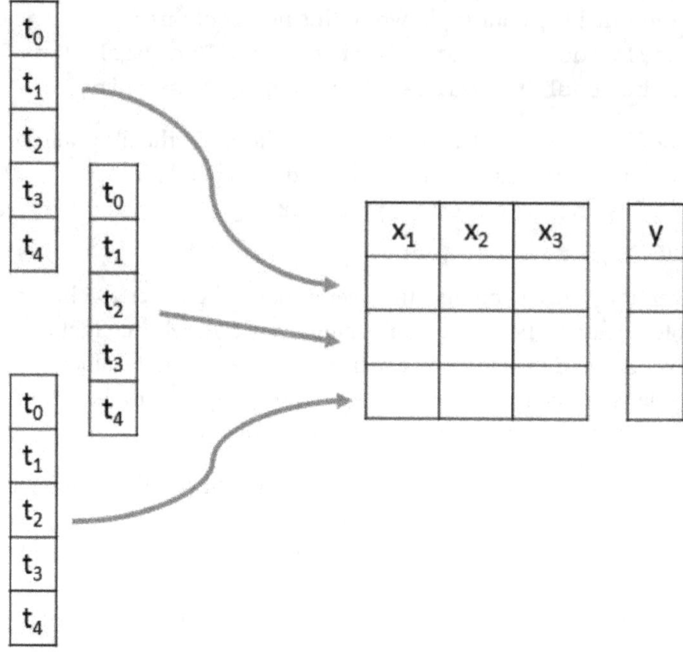

Figure 10.1 – Diagram showing the process of feature creation
from a time series for classification or regression

These feature vectors, which are represented as x_1, x_2, and x_3 in *Figure 10.1*, should capture the characteristics of the time series. For example, x_1 could be the mean value of the time series and x_2 its variance. We can create many features to characterize the time series concerning the distribution of data points, correlation properties, stationarity, or entropy, among others. Therefore, the feature vector, N, can be constructed by applying a series of **characterization methods** that take a time series as input and return one or more scalars as output. The mean, or the sum, takes the time-series sequence as input and returns a single scalar as output, with the mean value of the time series or the sum of its values. We can also fit a linear trend to the time-series sequence, which will return two scalars – one with the slope and one with the intercept.

`tsfresh` applies 63 characterization methods to a time series, each of which returns one or more scalars, therefore resulting in more than 750 features for any given time series. In this recipe, we will use `tsfresh` to transform time-series data into an M x N feature table, which we will then use to predict office occupancy.

Getting ready

In this recipe, we will use the Occupancy Detection dataset described in the *Technical requirements* section. This dataset contains measurements of temperature, humidity, CO_2 level, and light consumption in an office taken at one-minute intervals. There are 135 hours of measurements, and each hour is flagged with a unique identifier. There is also a dataset with a target variable that indicates in which of these 135 hours the office was occupied. Let's load the data and make some plots to understand its patterns:

1. Let's load `pandas` and `matplotlib`:

    ```
    import matplotlib.pyplot as plt
    import pandas as pd
    ```

2. Load the dataset and display the first five rows:

    ```
    X = pd.read_csv(
        "occupancy.csv", parse_dates=["date"])
    X.head()
    ```

    In the following figure, we can see the dataset containing a unique identifier, followed by the date and time of the measurements and values for five time series capturing temperature, humidity, lights, and CO_2 levels in the office:

id		date	temperature	humidity	light	co2	humidity_ratio
0	1	2015-02-04 18:00:00	23.075	27.175000	419.0	688.00	0.004745
1	1	2015-02-04 18:01:00	23.075	27.150000	419.0	690.25	0.004741
2	1	2015-02-04 18:02:00	23.100	27.100000	419.0	691.00	0.004739
3	1	2015-02-04 18:03:00	23.100	27.166667	419.0	683.50	0.004751
4	1	2015-02-04 18:04:00	23.050	27.150000	419.0	687.50	0.004734

Figure 10.2 – DataFrame with the time-series data

3. Let's create a function to plot the time series from *step 2* at a given hour (the `id` column is a unique identifier for each of the 135 hours of records):

    ```
    def plot_timeseries(n_id):
        fig, axes = plt.subplots(nrows=2, ncols=3,
        figsize=(20, 10))
        X[X[«id»] == n_id]["temperature"].plot(
            ax=axes[0, 0], title="temperature")
        X[X[«id»] == n_id]["humidity"].plot(
            ax=axes[0, 1], title="humidity")
        X[X[«id»] == n_id]["light"].plot(
            ax=axes[0, 2], title="light")
        X[X[«id»] == n_id]["co2"].plot(
    ```

```
            ax=axes[1, 0], title="co2")
        X[X[«id»] == n_id]["humidity_ratio"].plot(
            ax=axes[1,1], title="humidity_ratio")
        plt.show()
```

4. Let's plot the time series corresponding to an hour when the office was not occupied:

    ```
    plot_timeseries(2)
    ```

    In the following figure, we can see the time-series values during the second hour of records, when the office was empty:

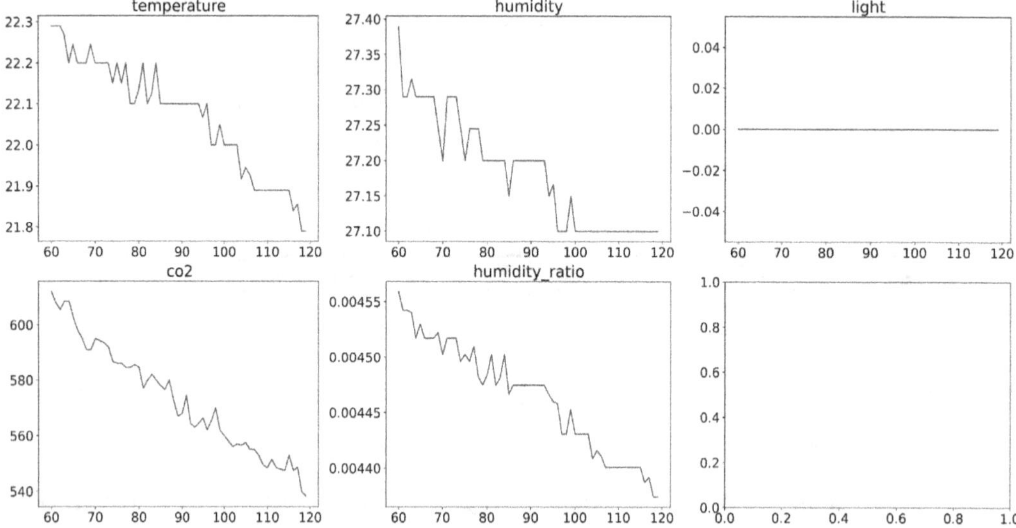

Figure 10.3 – Time-series values during the second hour of data collection when the office was empty

Note that the lights were off, and that is why we see the flat line at 0 in the plot of `light` consumption in the top-right corner.

5. Now, let's plot the time-series data corresponding to an hour when the office was occupied:

    ```
    plot_timeseries(15)
    ```

    In the following figure, we can see the time-series values during the fifteenth hour of records, when the office was occupied:

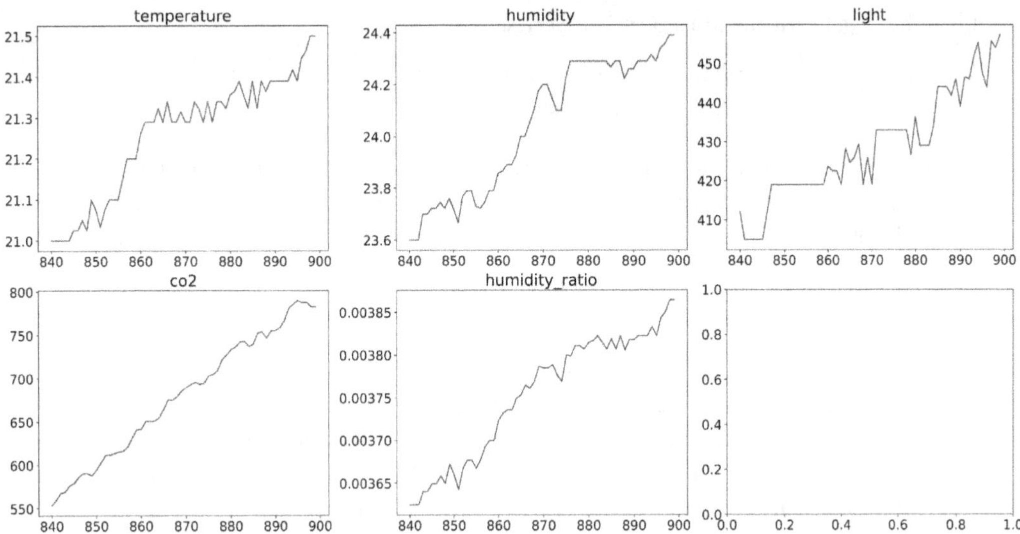

Figure 10.4 – Time-series values during the fifteenth hour of data collection, when the office was occupied

Notice that the lights were on this time (top-right panel).

In this recipe, we will extract features from each of these one-hour windows of time-series data, capturing various aspects of their characteristics. From each of these 60-minute time-series segments, we will automatically generate more than 750 features using `tsfresh`, ensuring a comprehensive representation of the data's properties.

How to do it...

We will begin by automatically creating hundreds of features from one time series, `lights`, and then use those features to predict whether the office was occupied at any given hour:

1. Let's import the required Python libraries and functions:

```python
import pandas as pd
from sklearn.linear_model import LogisticRegression
from sklearn.metrics import classification_report
from sklearn.model_selection import train_test_split
from tsfresh import extract_features
from tsfresh.utilities.dataframe_functions import (
    impute
)
```

2. Load the dataset described in the *Technical requirements* section:

```python
X = pd.read_csv("occupancy.csv", parse_dates=["date"])
```

3. Load the target variable into a `pandas` Series:

```
y = pd.read_csv("occupancy_target.csv",
    index_col="id")["occupancy"]
```

4. Let's create hundreds of features automatically for each hour of light records using `tsfresh`. To create features from the `light` variable, we pass the DataFrame containing this variable and the unique identifier for each time series to the `extract_features` function from `tsfresh`:

```
features = extract_features(
    X[[«id», «light»]], column_id="id")
```

If we execute `features.shape`, we'll obtain `(135, 789)` corresponding to the size of the resulting DataFrame, where each row represents an hour of records and each column one of the features created by `tsfresh`. There are 789 features that characterize light consumption at any given hour. Go ahead and execute `features.head()` to get a view of the resulting DataFrame. For space reasons, we can't display the entire DataFrame in the book. So, instead, we will explore some of the features.

5. Let's capture the names of five of the created features in an array:

```
feats = features.columns[10:15]
```

If we execute `feats`, we'll see the names of five features corresponding to the mean, length, standard deviation, coefficient of variation, and variance of the light consumption per hour:

```
Index(['light__mean', 'light__length',
    'light__standard_deviation',
    'light__variation_coefficient',
    'light__variance'], dtype='object')
```

6. Now, let's display the values of the features from *step 5* for the first five hours:

```
features[feats].head()
```

In the following DataFrame, we see the features extracted from the time series for the first five hours of light consumption:

	light__mean	light__length	light__standard_deviation	light__variation_coefficient	light__variance
1	48.875	60.0	134.485582	2.751623	18086.371875
2	0.000	60.0	0.000000	NaN	0.000000
3	0.000	60.0	0.000000	NaN	0.000000
4	0.000	60.0	0.000000	NaN	0.000000
5	0.000	60.0	0.000000	NaN	0.000000

Figure 10.5 – Features created for each hour of light consumption

Looking at the mean value of light consumption in *Figure 10.4*, we can see that the lights were on during the first hour, and then off in the following four hours. The length of the time series is 60 because we have 60 minutes of records per hour.

> **Note**
>
> `tsfresh` applies 63 feature creation methods to a time series. Based on the characteristics of the time series, such as its length or its variability, some of the methods will return missing values or infinite values. For example, in *Figure 10.4*, we see that the variation coefficient could not be calculated for those hours where the light consumption is constant. And the variance is also 0 in those cases. In fact, for our dataset, many of the resulting features contain only NaN values, or are constant, like the length, and are therefore not useful for training machine learning models.

7.   `tsfresh` includes an imputation function to impute features that contain NaN values. Let's go ahead and impute our features:

```
impute(features)
```

The `impute` function from `tsfresh` replaces NaN, `-Inf`, and `Inf` values with the variable's median, minimum, or maximum values, respectively.

Let's use these features to train a logistic regression model and predict whether the office was occupied.

8.   Let's begin by separating the dataset into training and test sets:

```
X_train, X_test, y_train, y_test = train_test_split(
    features,
    y,
    test_size=0.1,
    random_state=42,
)
```

9.   Now, let's set up and train a logistic regression model, and then evaluate its performance:

```
cls = LogisticRegression(random_state=10, C=0.01)
cls.fit(X_train, y_train)
print(classification_report(
    y_test, cls.predict(X_test)))
```

In the following output, we see the values of evaluation metrics that are commonly used for classification analysis, which suggests that the created features are useful for predicting office occupancy:

```
              precision    recall  f1-score   support

           0       1.00      1.00      1.00
          11
```

```
                     1            1.00           1.00           1.0
0                    3

       accu-
  racy                                                   1.00        14
      macro avg              1.00           1.00         1.00        14
  weighted avg              1.00           1.00          1.00        14
```

> **Note**
>
> To keep the recipe simple, I have not optimized the model hyperparameters or tuned the probability threshold – things that we normally do to ensure our models are accurate.

10. To finish off, let's extract features from every time series, that is, `light`, `temperature`, `humidity`, and `co2`, and this time, we will impute the features right after the extraction:

```python
features = extract_features(
    X,
    column_id="id",
    impute_function=impute,
    column_sort="date",
)
```

> **Note**
>
> In *step 10*, we indicated that we want to sort our time series based on the timestamp containing the time and date of the measurement, by passing the `date` variable to the `column_sort` parameter. This is useful when our time series are not equidistant or not ordered chronologically. If we leave this parameter set to None, `tsfresh` assumes that the time series are ordered and equidistant.

The output of *step 10* consists of a DataFrame with 135 rows, containing 3,945 features (execute `features.shape` to check that out) that characterize the five original time series – temperature, light, humidity and its ratio, and CO_2 in the office. These features were imputed in *step 10*, so you can go ahead and use this DataFrame to train another logistic regression model to predict office occupancy.

How it works...

In this recipe, we used `tsfresh` to automatically create hundreds of features from five time series, and then used those features to train a logistic regression model to predict whether the office was occupied.

> **Note**
>
> To create features with `tsfresh`, the time-series interval from which we want to extract features must be marked with a **unique identifier**. In our dataset, that was the `id` variable.

To create features from time series, we used the `extract_features` function from `tsfresh`. This function takes the DataFrame containing the time series and the unique identifier as input and returns a DataFrame containing the extracted features as output.

`extract_features` has three key parameters: `column_id`, `column_sort`, and `impute_function`. `column_id` receives the name of the column with the unique identifier for each sequence that'll be used to extract features. `column_sort` is used to reorder the time series before extracting features. When `column_sort` is left to None, `tsfresh` assumes that the data is ordered chronologically and that the timestamps are equidistant. In *step 10*, we passed the `date` variable as the sorting variable, which informs `tsfresh` how to sort the data before extracting the features.

> **Note**
>
> In our dataset, leaving `column_sort` set to None or passing the `date` variable made no difference, because our time series were already ordered chronologically and the timestamps were equidistant. If this is not the case in your time series, use this parameter to create features correctly.

Finally, `extract_features` also accepts the `impute` function through the `impute_function` parameter, to automatically remove infinite and NaN values from the created features. Will discuss additional parameters of `extract_features` in the coming recipes.

> **Note**
>
> For more details about the `extract_features` function, visit `https://tsfresh.readthedocs.io/en/latest/api/tsfresh.feature_extraction.html#module-tsfresh.feature_extraction.extraction`.

The `impute` function, which can be used independently, as we did in *step 7*, or within the `extract_features` function, as we did in *step 10*, replaced NAN, `-Inf`, and `Inf` values with the variable's median, minimum, or maximum values, respectively. If the feature contains only NaN values, they are replaced by zeroes. The imputation occurs in place – that is, in the same DataFrame that is being imputed.

The `extract_features` function returns a DataFrame containing as many rows as unique identifiers in the data. In our case, it returned a DataFrame with 135 rows. The columns of the resulting DataFrame correspond to the 789 values that were returned by 63 characterization methods applied to each of the 135 60-minute time series.

In *step 5*, we explored some of the resulting features, which captured the time series mean, variance, and coefficient of variation, as well as their length. Let's explore a few more of the resulting features.

Some of the created variables are self-explanatory. For example, the `'light__skewness'` and `'light__kurtosis'` variables contain the skewness and kurtosis coefficients, which characterize the data distribution. The `'light__has_duplicate_max'`, `'light__has_duplicate_min'`, and `'light__has_duplicate'` variables indicate whether the time series has duplicated values or duplicated minimum or maximum values within the time interval. The `'light__quantile__q_0.1'`, `'light__quantile__q_0.2'`, and `'light__quantile__q_0.3'` variables display the different quantile values of the time series. Finally, the `'light__autocorrelation__lag_0'`, `'light__autocorrelation__lag_1'`, and `'light__autocorrelation__lag_2'` variables show the autocorrelation of the time series with its past values, lagged by 0, 1, or 2 steps – information that is generally useful in forecasting.

Other characterization methods return features obtained from signal processing algorithms, such as the continuous wavelet transform for the Ricker wavelet, which returns the `'light__cwt_coefficients__coeff_0__w_2__widths_(2, 5, 10, 20)'`, `'light__cwt_coefficients__coeff_0__w_5__widths_(2, 5, 10, 20)'`, `'light__cwt_coefficients__coeff_0__w_10__widths_(2, 5, 10, 20)'`, and `'light__cwt_coefficients__coeff_0__w_20__widths_(2, 5, 10, 20)'` features, among others.

> **Note**
>
> We can't discuss each of these feature characterization methods or their outputs in detail in this book because there are too many. You can find more details about the transformations supported by `tsfresh` and their formulation at `https://tsfresh.readthedocs.io/en/latest/api/tsfresh.feature_extraction.html`.

Some of the features that are automatically created by `tsfresh` may not make sense or even be possible to calculate for some time series because they require a certain length or data variability, or the time series must meet certain distribution assumptions. Therefore, the suitability of the features will depend on the nature of the time series.

> **Note**
>
> You can decide which features to extract from your time series based on domain knowledge, or by creating all possible features and then applying feature selection algorithms or following up with data analysis. In fact, from our dataset, many of the resulting features were either constant or contained only missing data. Hence, we can reduce the feature space to informative features by taking those features out of the data.

See also

For more details about `tsfresh`, check out the article Christ M., Braun N., , Neuffer J., and Kempa-Liehr A., (2018). *Time Series FeatuRe Extraction on basis of Scalable Hypothesis tests (tsfresh – A Python package). Neurocomputing 307 (2018). Pages 72-77.* `https://dl.acm.org/doi/10.1016/j.neucom.2018.03.067`.

Automatically creating and selecting predictive features from time-series data

In the previous recipe, we automatically extracted several hundred features from time-series variables using `tsfresh`. If we have more than one time-series variable, we can easily end up with a dataset containing thousands of features. In addition, many of the resulting features had only missing data or were constant and were therefore not useful for training machine learning models.

When we create classification and regression models to solve real-life problems, we often want our models to take a small number of relevant features as input to produce interpretable machine learning outputs. Simpler models have many advantages. First, their output is easier to interpret. Second, simpler models are cheaper to store and faster to train. They also return their outputs faster.

`tsfresh` includes a highly parallelizable feature selection algorithm based on non-parametric statistical hypothesis tests, which can be executed at the back of the feature creation procedure to quickly remove irrelevant features. The feature selection procedure utilizes different tests for different features.

`tsfresh` uses the following tests to select features:

- Fisher's exact test of independence, if both the feature and the target are binary

- Kolmogorov-Smirnov test, if either the feature or the target is binary

- Kendall rank test, if neither the feature nor the target is binary

The advantage of these tests is that they are non-parametric, and thus make no assumptions on the underlying distribution of the variables being tested.

The result of these tests is a vector of p-values that measures the significance of the association between each feature and the target. These p-values are then evaluated based on the Benjamini-Yekutieli procedure to decide which features to keep.

> **Note**
>
> For more details about `tsfresh`'s feature selection procedure, check out the article Christ, Kempa-Liehr, and Feindt, *Distributed and parallel time series feature extraction for industrial big data applications.* Asian Machine Learning Conference (ACML) 2016, Workshop on Learning on Big Data (WLBD), Hamilton (New Zealand), arXiv, `https://arxiv.org/abs/1610.07717v1`.

In this recipe, we will automatically create hundreds of features from various time series, and then select the most relevant features by utilizing `tsfresh`.

How to do it...

We will begin by automatically creating and selecting features from one time series, `lights`, and then we will automate the procedure for multiple time series:

1. Let's import the required Python libraries and functions:

```python
import pandas as pd
from sklearn.linear_model import LogisticRegression
from sklearn.metrics import classification_report
from sklearn.model_selection import train_test_split
from tsfresh import (
    extract_features,
    extract_relevant_features,
    select_features,
)
from tsfresh.utilities.dataframe_functions import impute
```

2. Load the dataset and the target variable described in the *Technical requirements* section:

```python
X = pd.read_csv("occupancy.csv", parse_dates=["date"])
y = pd.read_csv("occupancy_target.csv",
    index_col="id")["occupancy"]
```

3. Let's create hundreds of features automatically for each hour of `light` use records and impute the resulting features:

```python
features = extract_features(
    X[["«id»", "«light»"]],
    column_id="id",
    impute_function=impute,
)
```

The output of the previous step is a DataFrame with 135 rows and 789 columns, corresponding to the features created from each hour of light consumption.

> **Note**
>
> For more details about *step 3*, or the Occupancy Detection dataset, check out the *Extracting hundreds of features automatically from a time series* recipe.

4. Now, let's select the features based on the non-parametric tests that we mentioned in the introduction of this recipe:

```
features = select_features(features, y)
```

If we execute `len(features)`, we'll see the value `135`, which means that from the 789 features created in *step 3*, only 135 are statistically significant. Go ahead and execute `features.head()` to display the first five rows of the resulting DataFrame.

5. For space reasons, we will only display the first five features:

```
feats = features.columns[0:5]
features[feats].head()
```

In the following DataFrame, we see the values of the first five features for the first five hours of light consumption:

	light__minimum	light__agg_linear_trend__attr_"intercept"__chunk_len_50__f_agg_"min"
1	0.0	0.0
2	0.0	0.0
3	0.0	0.0
4	0.0	0.0
5	0.0	0.0

light__quantile__q_0.1	light__quantile__q_0.3	light__quantile__q_0.4
0.0	0.0	0.0
0.0	0.0	0.0
0.0	0.0	0.0
0.0	0.0	0.0
0.0	0.0	0.0

Figure 10.6 – DataFrame with five of the selected features created from each hour of light consumption

Check the discussion in the *How it works...* section for a more detailed analysis of the DataFrame resulting from *step 4*.

6. Now, we will use the features from *step 4* to train a logistic regression model and predict whether the office was occupied. Let's begin by separating the dataset into training and test sets:

```
X_train, X_test, y_train, y_test = train_test_split(
    features,
    y,
    test_size=0.1,
    random_state=42,
)
```

7. Let's set up and train a logistic regression model and then evaluate its performance:

```python
cls = LogisticRegression(
    random_state=10, C=0.1, max_iter=1000)
cls.fit(X_train, y_train)
print(classification_report(
    y_test, cls.predict(X_test)))
```

In the following output, we see the values of commonly used evaluation metrics for classification analysis. These suggest that the selected features are useful for predicting office occupancy:

```
              precision    recall  f1-score   support

           0       1.00      0.91      0.95
11
           1       0.75      1.00      0.8
6          3

    accu-
racy                                    0.93        14
   macro avg       0.88      0.95      0.90        14
weighted avg       0.95      0.93      0.93        14
```

Go ahead and compare these results with those of *step 9* in the *Extracting hundreds of features automatically from a time series* recipe of this chapter. You will see that we obtained similar performance, with only a fraction of the features.

8. We can trigger the feature creation *and* feature selection procedures by using a single function, `extract_relevant_features`, and, like this, combine *steps 3* and *4*. We'll do that to create and select features automatically for the five time series in our dataset:

```python
features = extract_relevant_features(
    X,
    y,
    column_id="id",
    column_sort="date",
)
```

> **Note**
>
> The parameters of `extract_relevant_features` are very similar to those of `extract_features`. Note, however, that the former will automatically perform imputation to be able to proceed with the feature selection. We discussed the parameters of `extract_features` in the *Extracting hundreds of features automatically from time series* recipe.

The output of *step 8* consists of a DataFrame with 135 rows and 968 features, from the original 3,945 that are returned by default by `tsfresh` (you can check that out by executing `features.shape`). Go ahead and use this DataFrame to train another logistic regression model to predict office occupancy.

How it works...

In this recipe, we created hundreds of features from a time series and then selected the most relevant features based on non-parametric statistical tests. The feature creation and selection procedures were carried out automatically by `tsfresh`.

To create the features, we used `tsfresh`'s `extract_features` function, which we described in detail in the *Extracting hundreds of features automatically from a time series* recipe.

To select features, we used the `select_features` function, also from `tsfresh`. This function applies different statistical tests, depending on the nature of the feature and the target. Briefly, if the feature and target are binary, it tests their relationship with Fisher's exact test. If either the feature or the target is binary, and the other variable is continuous, it tests their relationship by using the Kolmogorov-Smirnov test. If neither the features nor the target is binary, it uses the Kendall rank test.

The result of these tests is a vector with one p-value per feature. Next, `tsfresh` applies the Benjamini-Yekutieli procedure, which aims to reduce the false discovery rate, to select which features to keep based on the p-values. This feature selection procedure has some advantages, the main one being that statistical tests are fast to compute, and therefore the selection algorithm is scalable and can be parallelized. Another advantage is that the tests are non-parametric and hence suitable for linear and non-linear models.

However, feature selection methods that evaluate each feature individually are unable to remove redundant features. In fact, many of the features automatically created by `tsfresh` will be highly correlated, like those capturing the different quantiles of light consumption. Hence, they will show similar p-values and be retained. But in practice, we only need one or a few of them to capture the information of the time series. I'd recommend following up the `tsfresh` selection procedure with alternative feature selection methods that are able to pick up feature interactions.

Finally, in *step 8*, we combined the feature creation step (*step 3*) with the feature selection step (*step 4*) by using the `extract_relevant_features` function. `extract_relevant_features` applies the `extract_features` function to create the features from each time series and imputes them. Next, it applies the `select_features` function to return a DataFrame containing one row per unique identifier, and the features that were selected for each time series. Note that different features can be selected for different time series.

See also

The selection algorithm from `tsfresh` offers a quick method to remove irrelevant features. However, it does not find the best feature subset for the classification or regression task. Other feature selection methods can be applied at the back of `tsfresh`'s algorithm to reduce the feature space further.

For more details on feature selection algorithms, check out the book *Feature Selection in Machine Learning with Python* by Soledad Galli on Leanpub: `https://leanpub.com/feature-selection-in-machine-learning/`.

Extracting different features from different time series

`tsfresh` extracts many features based on the time-series characteristics and distribution, such as their correlation properties, stationarity, and entropy. It also applies non-linear time-series analysis functions, which decompose the time-series signal through, for example, Fourier or wavelet transformations. Depending on the nature of the time series, some of these transformations make more sense than others. For example, wavelength decomposition methods can make sense for time series resulting from signals or sensors but are not always useful for time series representing sales or stock prices.

In this recipe, we will discuss how to optimize the feature extraction procedure to extract specific features from each time series, and then use these features to predict office occupancy.

How to do it...

`tsfresh` accesses the methods that will be used to create features through a dictionary that contains the method names as keys and, if they need a parameter, it has the parameter as a value. `tsfresh` includes some predefined dictionaries as well. We'll explore these predefined dictionaries first, which can be accessed through the `settings` module:

1. Let's import the required Python libraries and functions and the `settings` module:

    ```python
    import pandas as pd
    from sklearn.linear_model import LogisticRegression
    from sklearn.metrics import classification_report
    from sklearn.model_selection import train_test_split
    from tsfresh.feature_extraction import (
        extract_features
    )
    from tsfresh.feature_extraction import settings
    ```

2. Load the dataset and the target variable described in the *Technical requirements* section:

    ```python
    X = pd.read_csv("occupancy.csv", parse_dates=["date"])
    y = pd.read_csv("occupancy_target.csv",
        index_col="id")["occupancy"]
    ```

    `tsfresh` includes three main dictionaries that control the feature creation output: `settings.ComprehensiveFCParameters`, `settings.EfficientFCParameters`, and `settings.MinimalFCParameters`. Here, we'll explore the dictionary that returns the fewest features. You can repeat the steps to explore the additional dictionaries.

3. Display the feature creation methods that will be applied when using the dictionary that returns the fewest features:

```
minimal_feat = settings.MinimalFCParameters()
minimal_feat.items()
```

In the output of *step 3*, we see a dictionary with the feature extraction method names as keys, and the parameters used by those methods, if any, as values:

```
ItemsView({'sum_values': None, 'median': None, 'mean': None,
'length': None, 'standard_deviation': None, 'variance': None,
'root_mean_square': None, 'maximum': None, 'absolute_maximum':
None, 'minimum': None})
```

> **Note**
>
> Go ahead and explore the other two predefined dictionaries, `settings.ComprehensiveFCParameters` and `settings.EfficientFCParameters`, by adapting the code from *step 3*.

4. Now, let's use the dictionary from *step 3* to extract only those features from the `light` time series and then display the shape of the resulting DataFrame:

```
features = extract_features(
    X[["«id»", "«light»"]],
    column_id="id",
    default_fc_parameters=minimal_feat,
)
features.shape
```

The output of *step 4* is `(135, 10)`, which means that only 10 features were created for each of the 135 hours of light consumption data.

5. Let's display the resulting DataFrame:

```
features.head()
```

We see the values of the resulting features for the first five hours of light consumption in the following DataFrame:

	light__sum_values	light__median	light__mean	light__length	light__standard_deviation	light__variance
1	2932.5	0.0	48.875	60.0	134.485582	18086.371875
2	0.0	0.0	0.000	60.0	0.000000	0.000000
3	0.0	0.0	0.000	60.0	0.000000	0.000000
4	0.0	0.0	0.000	60.0	0.000000	0.000000
5	0.0	0.0	0.000	60.0	0.000000	0.000000

light__variance	light__root_mean_square	light__maximum	light__absolute_maximum	light__minimum
18086.371875	143.091361	419.0	419.0	0.0
0.000000	0.000000	0.0	0.0	0.0
0.000000	0.000000	0.0	0.0	0.0
0.000000	0.000000	0.0	0.0	0.0
0.000000	0.000000	0.0	0.0	0.0

Figure 10.7 – DataFrame with the features created for each hour of light consumption

Now, we will use these features to train a logistic regression model to predict whether the office was occupied.

6. Let's begin by separating the dataset into training and test sets:

```
X_train, X_test, y_train, y_test = train_test_split(
    features,
    y,
    test_size=0.1,
    random_state=42,
)
```

7. Now, let's set up and train a logistic regression model, and then evaluate its performance:

```
cls = LogisticRegression(random_state=10, C=0.01)
cls.fit(X_train, y_train)
print(classification_report(
    y_test, cls.predict(X_test)))
```

In the following output, we see the evaluation metrics that are commonly used for classification analysis. These suggest that the selected features are useful for predicting office occupancy:

```
              precision    recall  f1-score   support

           0       1.00      0.91      0.95
11
           1       0.75      1.00      0.8
    6            3
```

accuracy			0.93	14
macro avg	0.88	0.95	0.90	14
weighted avg	0.95	0.93	0.93	14

> **Note**
>
> Because light consumption is a very good indicator of office occupancy, with very simple features, we can obtain a predictive logistic regression model.

Now, let's learn how to specify the creation of different features for different time series.

8. Let's create a dictionary with the names of the methods that we want to use to create features from the `light` time series. We enter the method's names as keys, and if the methods take a parameter, we pass it as an additional dictionary to the corresponding key; otherwise, we pass `None` as the values:

```python
light_feat = {
    "sum_values": None,
    "median": None,
    "standard_deviation": None,
    "quantile": [{"q": 0.2}, {"q": 0.7}],
}
```

9. Now, let's create a dictionary with the features that we want to create from the co2 time series:

```python
co2_feat = {
    "root_mean_square": None,
    "number_peaks": [{"n": 1}, {"n": 2}],
}
```

10. Let's combine these dictionaries into a new dictionary:

```python
kind_to_fc_parameters = {
    "light": light_feat,
    "co2": co2_feat,
}
```

11. Finally, let's use the dictionary from *step 10* to create the features from both time series:

```python
features = extract_features(
    X[["id", "light", "co2"]],
    column_id="id",
    kind_to_fc_parameters=kind_to_fc_parameters,
)
```

The output of *step 11* consists of a DataFrame with 135 rows and 8 features. If we execute `features.columns`, we will see the names of the created features:

```
Index(['light__sum_values', 'light__median',
    'light__standard_deviation',
    'light__quantile__q_0.2',
    'light__quantile__q_0.7',
    'co2__root_mean_square',
    'co2__number_peaks__n_1',
    'co2__number_peaks__n_2'],
    dtype='object')
```

Note that in the output from *step 11*, different variables have been created from each of the `light` and `co2` time series.

How it works...

In this recipe, we extracted specific features from our time-series data. First, we created features based on a predefined dictionary that comes with `tsfresh`. Next, we created our own dictionary, specifying the creation of different features for different time series.

The `tsfresh` package comes with some predefined dictionaries that can be accessed through the `settings` module. The `MinimalFCParameters` dictionary is used to create 10 simple features based on basic statistical parameters of the time-series distribution, such as the mean, median, standard deviation, variance, sum of its values, count (or length), and minimum and maximum values. In *step 3*, we displayed the dictionary, with the method names as keys, and, as these methods do not require additional parameters, each key had None as the value.

`tsfresh` has two additional predefined dictionaries. `EfficientFCParameters` is used to apply methods that are fast to compute, whereas `ComprehensiveFCParameters` returns all possible features and is the one used by default by the `extract_features` function.

> **Note**
>
> For more details about the predefined dictionaries, check out `tsfresh`'s documentation: `https://tsfresh.readthedocs.io/en/latest/text/feature_extraction_settings.html`

By using these predefined dictionaries in the `default_fc_parameters` parameter of `tsfresh`'s `extract_features` function, we can create specific features from one or more time series, as we did in *step 4*. Note that `default_fc_parameters` instructs `extract_features` to create the same features from *all* the time series. What if we want to extract different features from different time series?

To create different features for different time series, we can use the `kind_to_fc_parameters` parameter of `tsfresh`'s `extract_features` function. This parameter takes a dictionary of dictionaries, specifying the methods to apply to each time series.

In *step 8*, we created a dictionary to specify the creation of specific features from the `light` time series. Note that the `"sum_values"` and `"mean"` methods take None as values, but the `quantile` method needs additional parameters corresponding to the quantiles that should be returned from the time series. In *step 9*, we created a dictionary to specify the creation of features from the `co2` time series. In *step 10*, we combined both dictionaries into one that takes the name of the time series as the key and the feature creation dictionaries as values. Then, we passed this dictionary to the `kind_to_fc_parameters` parameter of `tsfresh`'s `extract_features` function. This way of specifying features is suitable if we use domain knowledge to create the features, or if we only create a small number of features.

Do we need to type each method by hand into a dictionary if we want to create multiple features for various time series? Not really. In the following recipe, we will learn how to specify which features to create based on features selected by Lasso.

Creating a subset of features identified through feature selection

In the *Automatically creating and selecting predictive features from time-series data* recipe, we learned how to select relevant features using `tsfresh`. We also discussed the limitations of `tsfresh`'s selection procedures and suggested following up with alternative feature selection methods to identify predictive features while avoiding redundancy.

In this recipe, we will create and select features using `tsfresh`. Following that, we will reduce the feature space further by utilizing Lasso regularization. Then, we will learn how to create a dictionary from the selected feature names to trigger the creation of those features *only* from future time series.

How to do it...

Let's begin by importing the necessary libraries and getting the dataset ready:

1. Let's import the required libraries and functions:

```python
import pandas as pd
from sklearn.feature_selection import SelectFromModel
from sklearn.linear_model import LogisticRegression
from tsfresh import (
    extract_features,
    extract_relevant_features,
)
from tsfresh.feature_extraction import settings
```

2.   Load the Occupancy Detection dataset described in the *Technical requirements* section:

```
X = pd.read_csv("occupancy.csv", parse_dates=["date"])
y = pd.read_csv(
    "occupancy_target.csv",
    index_col="id")["occupancy"]
```

3.   Create and select features from our five time series and then display the shape of the resulting DataFrame:

```
features = extract_relevant_features(
    X,
    y,
    column_id="id",
    column_sort="date",
)
features.shape
```

The output of *step 3* is (135, 968), indicating that 968 features were returned from the five original time series, for each hour of records.

> **Note**
>
> We discussed the function from *step 3* in the *Automatically creating and selecting predictive features from time-series data* recipe.

Let's reduce the feature space further by selecting features with Lasso regularization.

4.   Set up logistic regression with Lasso regularization, which is the `"l1"` penalty. I also set some additional parameters arbitrarily:

```
cls = LogisticRegression(
    penalty="l1",
    solver=»liblinear",
    random_state=10,
    C=0.05,
    max_iter=1000,
)
```

5.   Let's set up a transformer to retain those features whose logistic regression coefficients are different from 0:

```
selector = SelectFromModel(cls)
```

6.   Train the logistic regression model and select the features:

```
selector.fit(features, y)
```

7. Now, capture the selected features in a variable:

```
features = selector.get_feature_names_out()
```

If we execute `features`, we'll see the names of the selected features:

```
array([
'light__sum_of_reoccurring_data_points',
'co2__fft_coefficient__attr_"abs"__coeff_0',
'co2__spkt_welch_density__coeff_2', 'co2__variance',
'temperature__c3__lag_1', 'temperature__abs_energy',
'temperature__c3__lag_2', 'temperature__c3__lag_3',
'co2__sum_of_reoccurring_data_points',
'light__spkt_welch_density__coeff_8',
'light__agg_linear_trend__attr_"intercept"__chunk_len_50__f_
agg_"var"',
        'light__agg_linear_trend__attr_"slope"__chunk_
len_50__f_agg_"var"',  'light__agg_linear_trend__
attr_"intercept"__chunk_len_10__f_agg_"var"'],
dtype=object)
```

8. To extract just the features from *step 6* from the time series, we need to capture the feature creation method name and corresponding parameters in a dictionary. We can do this automatically from the feature names with `tsfresh`:

```
kind_to_fc_parameters = settings.from_columns(
    selector.get_feature_names_out(),
)
```

If we execute `kind_to_fc_parameters`, we'll see the dictionary that was created from the names of the features from *step 6*:

```
{'light':
    {'sum_of_reoccurring_data_points': None,
    'spkt_welch_density': [{'coeff': 8}],
    'variance': None,
    'agg_linear_trend': [
        {'attr': 'slope','chunk_len': 50,
            'f_agg': 'var'},
        {'attr': 'intercept',
            'chunk_len': 10,'f_agg':'var'}
        ]
    },
    'co2':
    {'spkt_welch_density': [{'coeff': 2}],
    'variance': None,
    'sum_of_reoccurring_data_points': None
```

```
        },
        'temperature': {
            'c3': [{'lag': 1}, {'lag': 2}, {'lag':3}],
            'abs_energy': None}

    }
```

9. Now, we can use the dictionary from *step 8* together with the `extract_features` function
    to create only those features from our dataset:

```
features = extract_features(
    X,
    column_id="id",
    column_sort="date",
    kind_to_fc_parameters=kind_to_fc_parameters,
)
```

The new DataFrame, which can be displayed by executing `features.head()`, only contains the
12 features that were selected by Lasso. Go ahead and corroborate the result on your computer.

How it works...

In this recipe, we created 968 features from 5 time series. Next, we reduced the feature space to 12
features by using Lasso regularization. Finally, we captured the specifications of the selected features
in a dictionary so that, looking forward, we only created those features from our time series.

To automatically create and select features with `tsfresh`, we used the `extract_relevant_`
`features` function, which we described in detail in the *Automatically creating and selecting predictive
features from time-series data* recipe.

Lasso regularization has the intrinsic ability to reduce some of the coefficients of the logistic regression
model to 0. The contribution of the features whose coefficient is 0 to the prediction of office occupancy
is null and can therefore be removed. The `SelectFromModel()` class can identify and remove those
features. We set up an instance of `SelectFromModel()` with a logistic regression model that used
Lasso regularization to find the model coefficients. With `fit()`, `SelectFromModel()` trained
the logistic regression model using the 968 features created from our time series and identified those
whose coefficients were different from 0. Then, with the `get_feature_names_out()` method,
we captured the names of the selected features in a new variable.

To create only the 12 features selected by Lasso regularization, we created a dictionary from the variable
names by using the `from_columns()` function from `tsfresh`. This function returned a dictionary
with the variables from which features were selected as keys. The values were additional dictionaries,
containing the methods used to create features as keys, and the parameters used, if any, as values. To
create the new features, we used this dictionary together with the `extract_features` function.

> **Note**
>
> In *step 9*, we passed the entire dataset to the `extract_features` function. The resulting features only contained features extracted from three of the five time series. The additional two time series were ignored.

Embedding feature creation into a scikit-learn pipeline

Throughout this chapter, we've discussed how to automatically create and select features from time-series data by utilizing `tsfresh`. Then, we used these features to train a classification model to predict whether an office was occupied at any given hour.

`tsfresh` includes *wrapper* classes around its main functions, `extract_features` and `extract_relevant_features`, to make the creation and selection of features compatible with the scikit-learn pipeline.

In this recipe, we will set up a scikit-learn pipeline that extracts features from time series using `tsfresh` and then trains a logistic regression model with those features to predict office occupancy.

How to do it...

Let's begin by importing the necessary libraries and getting the dataset ready:

1. Let's import the required libraries and functions:

    ```python
    import pandas as pd
    from sklearn.pipeline import Pipeline
    from sklearn.linear_model import LogisticRegression
    from sklearn.model_selection import train_test_split
    from sklearn.metrics import classification_report
    from tsfresh.transformers import (
        RelevantFeatureAugmenter)
    ```

2. Load the Occupancy Detection dataset described in the *Technical requirements* section:

    ```python
    X = pd.read_csv("occupancy.csv", parse_dates=["date"])
    y = pd.read_csv(
        "occupancy_target.csv",
        index_col="id")["occupancy"]
    ```

3. Create an empty DataFrame that contains the index of the target variable:

    ```python
    tmp = pd.DataFrame(index=y.index)
    ```

4. Now, let's split the DataFrame from *step 3* and the target from *step 2* into training and test sets:

```
X_train, X_test, y_train, y_test = train_test_split(
    tmp, y, random_state=0)
```

> **Note**
>
> `X_train` and `X_test` will be used as containers to store the features created by `tsfresh`. They are needed for the functionality of `RelevantFeatureAugmenter()` that we will discuss in the coming steps.

5. Let's create a dictionary specifying the features to extract from each time series (I defined the following features arbitrarily):

```
kind_to_fc_parameters = {
    "light": {
        "c3": [{"lag": 3}, {"lag": 2}, {"lag": 1}],
        "abs_energy": None,
        "sum_values": None,
        "fft_coefficient": [
            {"attr": "real", "coeff": 0},
            {"attr": "abs", "coeff": 0}],
        "spkt_welch_density": [
            {"coeff": 2}, {"coeff":5}, {"coeff": 8}
        ],
        "agg_linear_trend": [
            {"attr": "intercept",
            "chunk_len": 50, "f_agg": "var"},
            {"attr": "slope",
            "chunk_len": 50, "f_agg":"var"},
        ],
        "change_quantiles": [
            {"f_agg": "var", "isabs": False,
            "qh": 1.0,"ql": 0.8},
            {"f_agg": "var", "isabs": True,
            "qh": 1.0,"ql": 0.8},
        ],
    },
    "co2": {
        "fft_coefficient": [
            {"attr": "real", "coeff": 0},
            {"attr": "abs", "coeff": 0}],
        "c3": [{"lag": 3}, {"lag": 2}, {"lag": 1}],
        "sum_values": None,
```

```
        «abs_energy": None,
        «sum_of_reoccurring_data_points": None,
        «sum_of_reoccurring_values": None,
        },
    "temperature": {"c3": [{"lag": 1},
        {«lag»: 2},{«lag»: 3}], «abs_energy": None},
    }
```

We discussed the parameters of this dictionary in the *Extracting different features from different time series* recipe.

6. Let's set up `RelevantFeatureAugmenter()`, which is a wrapper around the `extract_relevant_features` function, to create the features specified in *step 5*:

```
augmenter = RelevantFeatureAugmenter(
    column_id="id",
    column_sort="date",
    kind_to_fc_parameters=kind_to_fc_parameters,
)
```

> **Note**
>
> To create all possible features, use the `FeatureAugmenter()` class instead in *step 6*.

7. Let's combine the feature creation instance from *step 6* with a logistic regression model in a scikit-learn pipeline:

```
pipe = Pipeline(
    [
        ("augmenter", augmenter),
        («classifier», LogisticRegression(
    random_state=10, C=0.01)),
    ]
)
```

8. Now, let's tell `RelevantFeatureAugmenter()` which dataset it needs to use to create the features:

```
pipe.set_params(augmenter__timeseries_container=X)
```

9. Let's fit the pipeline, which will trigger the feature creation process, followed by the training of the logistic regression model:

```
pipe.fit(X_train, y_train)
```

10. Now, let's obtain predictions using the time series in the test set and evaluate the model's performance through a classification report:

```
print(classification_report(
    y_test, pipe.predict(X_test)))
```

We can see the output of *step 10* here:

```
                        precision      recall  f1-score      support

              0              1.00        0.96      0.98
       28
              1              0.86        1.00       0.9
       2              6

           accu-
       racy                                         0.97            34
          macro avg       0.93        0.98      0.95            34
       weighted avg       0.97        0.97      0.97            34
```

The values of the classification report suggest that the extracted features are suitable for predicting whether the office is occupied at any given hour.

How it works...

In this recipe, we combined creating features from a time series with `tsfresh` with training a machine learning algorithm from the scikit-learn library in a pipeline.

The `tsfresh` library includes two wrapper classes around its main functions to make the feature creation process compatible with the scikit-learn pipeline. In this recipe, we used the `RelevantFeatureAugmenter()` class, which wraps the `extract_relevant_features` function to create and then select features from a time series.

`RelevantFeatureAugmenter()` works as follows; with `fit()`, it creates and selects features by using `extract_relevant_features`. The names of the selected features are then stored internally in the transformer. With `transform()`, `RelevantFeatureAugmenter()` creates the selected features from the time series.

We overrode the default functionality of `RelevantFeatureAugmenter()` by passing a dictionary with the features we wanted to create to its `kind_to_fc_parameters` parameter. Therefore, with `transform()`, `RelevantFeatureAugmenter()` created the indicated features from the time series.

To create all features from the time series, `tsfresh` includes the `FeatureAugmenter()` class, which has the same functionality as `RelevantFeatureAugmenter()`, but without the feature selection step.

Both `RelevantFeatureAugmenter()` and `FeatureAugmenter()` need two DataFrames to work. The first DataFrame contains the time-series data and the unique identifiers (we loaded this DataFrame in *step 2*). The second DataFrame should be empty and contain the unique identifiers *in its index* (we created this DataFrame in *step 3*). The features are extracted from the first DataFrame with the time series (when applying `transform()`) and subsequently added to the second DataFrame, which is then used to train the logistic regression or obtain its predictions.

> **Note**
>
> The index of the empty DataFrame is used by `RelevantFeatureAugmenter()` and `FeatureAugmenter()` to identify the time series from which to extract the features. Hence, when applying `fit()` while passing `X_train`, features were extracted from time series whose `id` value was in the training set. After that, the model was evaluated by observing predictions made using the test set, which triggered the creation of features from time series whose `id` value was in `X_test`.

When we used `fit()` on the pipeline, we created features from our raw time series and trained a logistic regression model with the resulting features. With the `predict()` method, we created features from the test set and obtained the predictions of the logistic regression based on those features.

See also

For more details about the classes and procedures used in this recipe, visit the following links:

- The `tsfresh` documentation: `https://tsfresh.readthedocs.io/en/latest/api/tsfresh.transformers.html#tsfresh.transformers.relevant_feature_augmenter.RelevantFeatureAugmenter`

- A Jupyter notebook with a demo: `https://github.com/blue-yonder/tsfresh/blob/main/notebooks/02%20sklearn%20Pipeline.ipynb`

11

Extracting Features from Text Variables

Text can be one of the variables in our datasets. For example, in insurance, information describing the circumstances of an incident can come from free text fields in a form. If a company gathers customer reviews, this information will be collected as short pieces of text provided by the users. Text data does not show the **tabular** pattern of the datasets that we have worked with throughout this book. Instead, information in texts can vary in length and content, as well as writing style. We can extract a lot of information from text variables to use as predictive features in machine learning models. The techniques we will cover in this chapter belong to the realm of **Natural Language Processing (NLP)**. NLP is a subfield of linguistics and computer science. It is concerned with the interactions between computer and human language, or, in other words, how to program computers to understand human language. NLP includes a multitude of techniques to understand the syntax, semantics, and discourse of text. Therefore, to do this field justice would require an entire book.

In this chapter, we will discuss the methods that will allow us to quickly extract features from short pieces of text to complement our predictive models. Specifically, we will discuss how to capture a piece of text's complexity by looking at some statistical parameters of the text, such as the word length and count, the number of words and unique words used, the number of sentences, and so on. We will use the `pandas` and `scikit-learn` libraries, and we will make a shallow dive into a very useful Python NLP toolkit called the **Natural Language Toolkit (NLTK)**.

This chapter includes the following recipes:

- Counting characters, words, and vocabulary
- Estimating text complexity by counting sentences
- Creating features with bag-of-words and n-grams
- Implementing term frequency-inverse document frequency
- Cleaning and stemming text variables

Technical requirements

In this chapter, we will use the `pandas`, `matplotlib`, and `scikit-learn` Python libraries. We will also use NLTK, a comprehensive Python library for NLP and text analysis. You can find the instructions to install NLTK at `http://www.nltk.org/install.html`.

If you are using the Python Anaconda distribution, follow the instructions to install NLTK at `https://anaconda.org/anaconda/nltk`.

After you have installed NLTK, open up a Python console and execute the following:

```
import nltk
nltk.download('punkt')
nltk.download('stopwords')
```

These commands will download the necessary data for you to be able to run the recipes in this chapter successfully.

> **Note**
>
> If you haven't downloaded these or the other data sources necessary for NLTK functionality, NLTK will raise an error. Read the error message carefully because it will direct you to download the data required to run the command that you are trying to execute.

Counting characters, words, and vocabulary

One of the salient characteristics of text is its complexity. Long descriptions are more likely to contain more information than short descriptions. Texts rich in different, unique words are more likely to be richer in detail than texts that repeat the same words over and over. In the same way, when we speak, we use many short words such as articles and prepositions to build the sentence structure, yet the main concept is often derived from the nouns and adjectives we use, which tend to be longer words. So, as you can see, even without reading the text, we can start inferring how much information the text provides by determining the number of words, the number of unique words (non-repeated occurrences of a word), the lexical diversity, and the length of those words. In this recipe, we will learn how to extract these features from a text variable using `pandas`.

Getting ready

We are going to use the **20 Newsgroup** dataset that comes with `scikit-learn`, which comprises around 18,000 news posts on 20 different topics. More details about this dataset can be found on the following sites:

- The scikit-learn dataset website: `https://scikit-learn.org/stable/datasets/real_world.html#newsgroups-dataset`
- The home page for the 20 Newsgroup dataset: `http://qwone.com/~jason/20Newsgroups/`

Before jumping into the recipe, let's discuss the features that we are going to derive from these text pieces. We mentioned that longer descriptions, more words in the article, a greater variety of unique words, and longer words tend to correlate with the amount of information that the article provides. Hence, we can capture text complexity by extracting the following information about the text:

- The total number of characters

- The total number of words

- The total number of unique words

- Lexical diversity (total number of words divided by number of unique words)

- Word average length (number of characters divided by number of words)

In this recipe, we will extract these numerical features using `pandas`, which has extensive string processing functionalities that can be accessed via the `str` vectorized string functions for series.

How to do it...

Let's begin by loading `pandas` and getting the dataset ready:

1. Load `pandas` and the dataset from `scikit-learn`:

```python
import pandas as pd
from sklearn.datasets import fetch_20newsgroups
```

2. Let's load the train set part of the 20 Newsgroup dataset into a `pandas` DataFrame:

```python
data = fetch_20newsgroups(subset='train')
df = pd.DataFrame(data.data, columns=['text'])
```

> **Tip**
>
> You can print an example of a text from the DataFrame by executing `print(df['text'][1])`. Change the number between `[` and `]` to display different texts. Note how every text description is a single string composed of letters, numbers, punctuation, and spaces. You can check the datatype by executing `type(df["text"][1])`.

Now that we have the text variable in a `pandas` DataFrame, we are ready to extract the features.

3. Let's capture the number of characters in each text piece in a new column:

```python
df['num_char'] = df['text'].str.len()
```

> **Tip**
>
> You can remove trailing white spaces in a string, including those from new lines, before counting the number of characters by adding the `strip()` method before the `len()` method, as shown here: `df['num_char'] = df['text'].str.strip().str.len()`.

4. Let's capture the number of words in each text in a new column:

    ```python
    df['num_words'] = df['text'].str.split().str.len()
    ```

    To count words, we use the `pandas` library's `split()` method, which splits a text at white spaces. Check out the output of `split()` by executing, for instance, `df["text"].loc[1].split()` to separate the words of the second text of the DataFrame.

5. Let's capture the number of *unique* words in each text in a new column:

    ```python
    df['num_vocab']df[
        'text'].str.lower().str.split().apply(
            set).str.len()
    ```

> **Note**
>
> Python interprets the same word as two different words if one has a capital letter. To avoid this behavior, we can apply the `lower()` method before the `split()` method.

6. Let's create a feature that captures the lexical diversity – that is, the total number of words (*step 4*) compared to the number of unique words (*step 5*):

    ```python
    df['lexical_div'] = df['num_words'] / df['num_vocab']
    ```

7. Let's calculate the average word length by dividing the number of characters (*step 3*) by the number of words (*step 4*):

    ```python
    df['ave_word_length'] = df[
        'num_char'] / df['num_words']
    ```

    If we execute `df.head()`, we will see the first five rows of data with the text and the newly created features:

	text	num_char	num_words	num_vocab	lexical_div	ave_word_length
0	From: lerxst@wam.umd.edu (where's my thing)\nS...	716	123	93	1.322581	5.821138
1	From: guykuo@carson.u.washington.edu (Guy Kuo)...	857	123	99	1.242424	6.967480
2	From: twillis@ec.ecn.purdue.edu (Thomas E Will...	1980	339	219	1.547945	5.840708
3	From: jgreen@amber (Joe Green)\nSubject: Re: W...	814	113	96	1.177083	7.203540
4	From: jcm@head-cfa.harvard.edu (Jonathan McDow...	1117	171	139	1.230216	6.532164

Figure 11.1 – A DataFrame with the text variable and features
that summarize some of the text's characteristics

With that, we have extracted five different features that capture the text complexity, which we can use as inputs for our machine learning algorithms.

> **Note**
>
> In this recipe, we created new features from the raw data straight away without doing any data cleaning, removing punctuation, or even stemming words. Note that these are steps that are performed ahead of most standard NLP procedures. To learn more about this, visit the *Cleaning and stemming text variables* recipe at the end of this chapter.

How it works...

In this recipe, we created five new features that capture text complexity by utilizing pandas' `str` to access the built-in `pandas` functionality to work with strings. We worked with the text column of the `train` subset of the 20 Newsgroup dataset that comes with `scikit-learn`. Each row in this dataset is composed of a string with text.

We used pandas' `str`, followed by `len()`, to count the number of characters in each string – that is, the total number of letters, numbers, symbols, and spaces. We also combined `str.len()` with `str.strip()` to remove trailing white spaces at the beginning and end of the string and in new lines, before counting the number of characters.

To count the number of words, we used pandas' `str`, followed by `split()`, to divide the string into a list of words. The `split()` method creates a list of words by breaking the string at the white spaces between words. Next, we counted those words with `str.len()`, obtaining the number of words per string.

> **Note**
>
> We can change the behavior of `str.split()` by passing a string or character that we would like to use to split the string. For example, `df['text'].str.split(';')` divides a string at each occurrence of `;`.

To determine the number of unique words, we used pandas' `str.split()` function to divide the string into a list of words. Next, we applied the built-in Python `set()` method within pandas' `apply()` to return a set of words. Remember that a set contains *unique occurrences* of the elements in a list – that is, unique words. Next, we counted those words with pandas' `str.len()` function to return the **vocabulary**, or in other words, the number of unique words in the string. Python interprets words that are written in uppercase differently from those in lowercase; therefore, we introduced pandas' `lower()` function to set all the characters to lowercase before splitting the string and counting the number of unique words.

To create the lexical diversity and average word length features, we simply performed a vectorized division of two `pandas` series. That's it; we created five new features with information about the complexity of the text.

There's more...

We can check out the distribution of the features extracted from text in each of the 20 different news topics present in the dataset by using visualizations.

To make histogram plots of the newly created features, after you run all of the steps in the *How it works...* section of this recipe, follow these steps:

1. Import `matplotlib`:

    ```
    import matplotlib.pyplot as plt
    ```

2. Add the target with the news topics to the 20 Newsgroup DataFrame:

    ```
    df['target'] = data.target
    ```

3. Create a function that displays a histogram of a feature of your choice for each of the news topics:

    ```
    def plot_features(df, text_var):
        nb_rows = 5
        nb_cols = 4
        fig, axs = plt.subplots(
            nb_rows, nb_cols,figsize=(12, 12))
        plt.subplots_adjust(wspace=None, hspace=0.4)
        n = 0
        for i in range(0, nb_rows):
            for j in range(0, nb_cols):
                axs[i, j].hist(
                    df[df.target==n][text_var], bins=30)
                axs[i, j].set_title(
                    text_var + ' | ' + str(n))
                n += 1
        plt.show()
    ```

4. Run the function for the number of words feature:

    ```
    plot_features(df, 'num_words')
    ```

The previous command returns the following plot, where you can see the distribution of the number of words in each of the 20 news topics, numbered from 0 to 19 in the plot title:

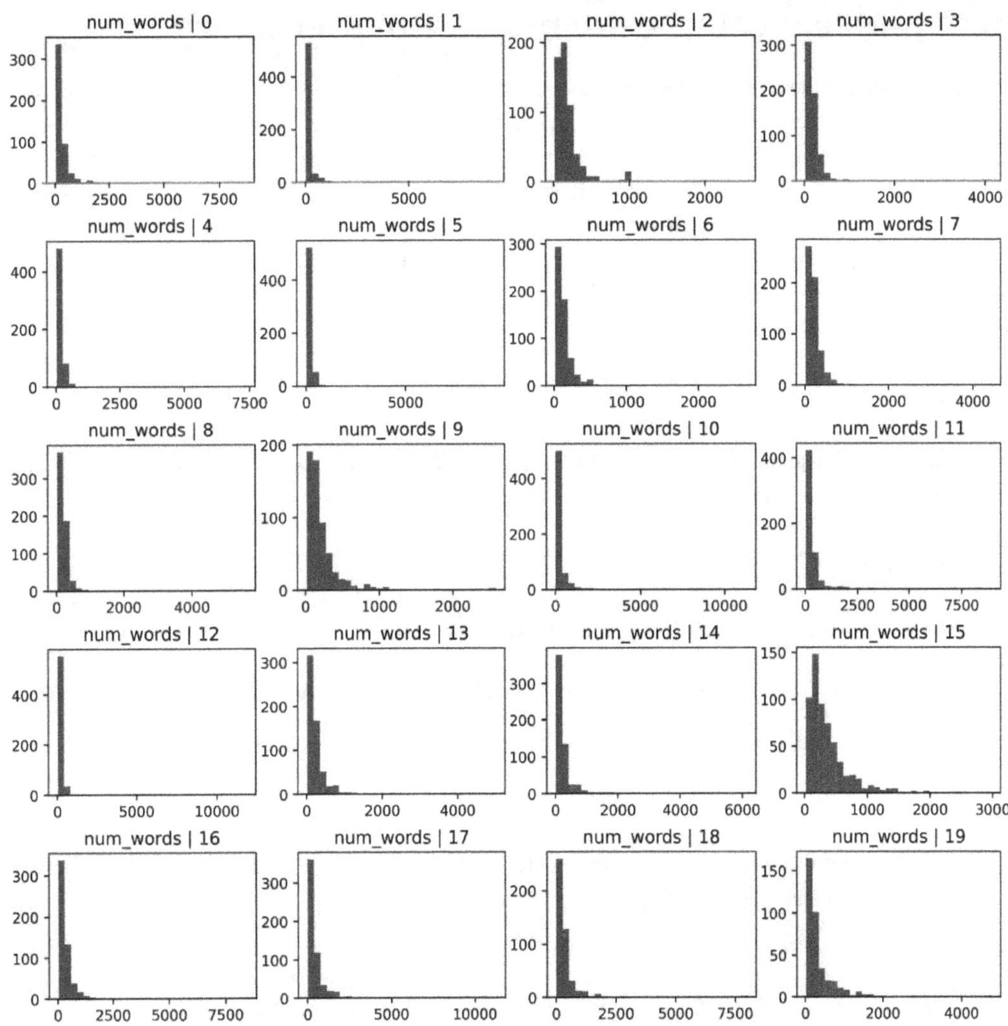

Figure 11.2 – Histograms showing the distribution of the number of
words per text, segregated by topic discussed in each text

The number of words shows a different distribution across the different news topics. Therefore, this feature is likely useful in a classification algorithm to predict the topic of the text.

See also

To learn more about pandas' built-in string processing functionality visit `https://pandas.pydata.org/pandas-docs/stable/user_guide/text.html#method-summary`.

Estimating text complexity by counting sentences

One aspect of a piece of text that we can capture in features is its complexity. Usually, longer descriptions that contain multiple sentences spread over several paragraphs tend to provide more information than descriptions with very few sentences. Therefore, capturing the number of sentences may provide some insight into the amount of information provided by the text. This process is called **sentence tokenization**. Tokenization is the process of splitting a string into a list of pieces or tokens. In the *Counting characters, words, and vocabulary* recipe, we did word tokenization – that is, we divided the string into words. In this recipe, we will divide the string into sentences, and then we will count them. We will use the NLTK Python library, which provides this functionality.

Getting ready

In this recipe, we will use the NLTK Python library. For guidelines on how to install NLTK, check out the *Technical requirements* section of this chapter.

How to do it...

Let's begin by importing the required libraries and dataset:

1. Let's load pandas, the sentence tokenizer from NLTK, and the dataset from scikit-learn:

    ```
    import pandas as pd
    from nltk.tokenize import sent_tokenize
    from sklearn.datasets import fetch_20newsgroups
    ```

2. To understand the functionality of the sentence tokenizer from NLTK, let's create a variable that contains a string with multiple sentences:

    ```
    text = """
    The alarm rang at 7 in the morning as it usually did on
    Tuesdays. She rolled over, stretched her arm, and stumbled
    to the button till she finally managed to switch it off.
    Reluctantly, she got up and went for a shower. The water was
    cold as the day before the engineers did not manage to get the
    boiler working. Good thing it was still summer.
    Upstairs, her cat waited eagerly for his morning snack. Miaow!
    He voiced with excitement as he saw her climb the stairs.
    """
    ```

3. Now, let's separate the string from *step 2* into sentences using NLTK library's sentence tokenizer:

    ```
    sent_tokenize(text)
    ```

> **Tip**
>
> If you encounter an error in *step 3*, read the error message carefully and download the data source required by NLTK, as described in the error message. For more details, check out the *Technical requirements* section.

The sentence tokenizer returns the list of sentences shown in the following output:

```
['\nThe alarm rang at 7 in the morning as it usually did on
Tuesdays.',
 'She rolled over,\nstretched her arm, and stumbled to the
button till she finally managed to switch it off.',
 'Reluctantly, she got up and went for a shower.',
 'The water was cold as the day before the engineers\ndid not
manage to get the boiler working.',
 'Good thing it was still summer.',
 'Upstairs, her cat waited eagerly for his morning snack.',
 'Miaow!',
 'He voiced with excitement\nas he saw her climb the stairs.']
```

> **Note**
>
> The escape character followed by the letter, \n, indicates a new line.

4. Let's count the number of sentences in the `text` variable:

    ```
    len(sent_tokenize(text))
    ```

    The previous command returns 8, which is the number of sentences in our `text` variable. Now, let's determine the number of sentences in an entire DataFrame.

5. Let's load the `train` subset of the 20 Newsgroup dataset into a `pandas` DataFrame:

    ```
    data = fetch_20newsgroups(subset='train')
    df = pd.DataFrame(data.data, columns=['text'])
    ```

6. To speed up the following steps, we will only work with the first `10` rows of the DataFrame:

    ```
    df = df.loc[1:10]
    ```

7. Let's also remove the first part of the text, which contains information about the email sender, subject, and other details that we are not interested in. Most of this information comes before the word `Lines` followed by `:`, so let's split the string at `Lines:` and capture the second part of the string:

    ```
    df['text'] = df['text'].str.split('Lines:').apply(
        lambda x: x[1])
    ```

8. Finally, let's create a variable containing the number of sentences per `text`:

```
df['num_sent'] = df['text'].apply(
    sent_tokenize).apply(len)
```

With the `df` command, you can display the entire DataFrame with the `text` variable and the new feature containing the number of sentences per text:

	text	num_sent
1	11\nNNTP-Posting-Host: carson.u.washington.ed...	6
2	36\n\nwell folks, my mac plus finally gave up...	9
3	14\nDistribution: world\nNNTP-Posting-Host: a...	7
4	23\n\nFrom article <C5owCB.n3p@world.std.com>...	10
5	58\n\nIn article <1r1eu1$4t@transfer.stratus....	21
6	12\n\nThere were a few people who responded t...	8
7	44\nDistribution: world\nNNTP-Posting-Host: d...	15
8	10\n\nI have win 3.0 and downloaded several i...	3
9	29\n\njap10@po.CWRU.Edu (Joseph A. Pellettier...	12
10	13\n\nI have a line on a Ducati 900GTS 1978 m...	11

Figure 11.3 – A DataFrame with the text variable and the number of sentences per text

Now, we can use this new feature as input to machine learning algorithms.

How it works...

In this recipe, we separated a string with text into sentences using `sent_tokenizer` from the NLTK library. `sent_tokenizer` has been pre-trained to recognize capitalization and different types of punctuation that signal the beginning and the end of a sentence.

First, we applied `sent_tokenizer` to a manually created string to become familiar with its functionality. The tokenizer divided the text into a list of eight sentences. We combined the tokenizer with the built-in Python `len()` method to count the number of sentences in the string.

Next, we loaded a dataset with text and, to speed up the computation, we only retained the first 10 rows of the DataFrame using pandas' `loc[]` function. Next, we removed the first part of the text, which contained information about the email sender and subject. To do this, we split the string at `Lines:` using pandas' `str.split("Lines:")` function, which returned a list with two elements: the strings before and after `Lines:`. Utilizing a lambda function within `apply()`, we retained the second part of the text – that is, the second string in the list returned by `split()`.

Finally, we applied `sent_tokenizer` to each row in the DataFrame with the pandas `apply()` method to separate the strings into sentences, and then applied the built-in Python `len()` method to the list of sentences to return the number of sentences per string. This way, we created a new feature that contained the number of sentences per text.

There's more...

`NLTK` has functionalities for word tokenization among other useful features, which we can use instead of `pandas` to count and return the number of words. You can find out more about `NLTK`'s functionality here:

- *Python 3 Text Processing with NLTK 3 Cookbook*, by Jacob Perkins, Packt Publishing

- The `NLTK` documentation at `http://www.nltk.org/`.

Creating features with bag-of-words and n-grams

A **Bag-of-Words (BoW)** is a simplified representation of a piece of text that captures the words that are present in the text and the number of times each word appears in the text. So, for the text string *Dogs like cats, but cats do not like dogs*, the derived BoW is as follows:

dogs	like	cats	but	do	not
2	2	2	1	1	1

Figure 11.4 – The BoW derived from the sentence Dogs like cats, but cats do not like dogs

Here, each word becomes a variable, and the value of the variable represents the number of times the word appears in the string. As you can see, the BoW captures multiplicity but does not retain word order or grammar. That is why it is a simple, yet useful way of extracting features and capturing some information about the texts we are working with.

To capture some syntax, BoW can be used together with **n-grams**. An n-gram is a contiguous sequence of *n* items in a given text. Continuing with the sentence *Dogs like cats, but cats do not like dogs*, the derived 2-grams are as follows:

- Dogs like

- like cats

- cats but

- but do

- do not

- like dogs

We can create, together with a BoW, a bag of n-grams, where the additional variables are given by the 2-grams and the values for each 2-gram are the number of times they appear in each string; for this example, the value is 1. So, our final BoW with 2-grams would look like this:

dogs	like	cats	but	do	not	dogs like	like cats	cats but	but do	do not	like dogs
2	2	2	1	1	1	1	1	1	1	1	1

Figure 11.5 – The BoW with 2-grams

In this recipe, we will learn how to create BoWs with or without n-grams using `scikit-learn`.

Getting ready

Before jumping into this recipe, let's get familiar with some of the parameters of a BoW that we can adjust to make the BoW comprehensive. When creating a BoW over several pieces of text, a new feature is created for each unique word that appears at least once in *any* of the text pieces we are analyzing. If the word appears only in one piece of text, it will show a value of 1 for that particular text and 0 for all of the others. Therefore, BoWs tend to be sparse matrices, where most of the values are zeros.

The number of columns – that is, the number of words – in a BoW can be quite large if we work with huge text corpora, and even larger if we also include n-grams. To limit the number of columns and the sparsity of the returned matrix, we can retain words that appear across multiple texts; or, in better words, we can retain words that appear in, at least, a certain percentage of texts.

To reduce the number of columns and sparsity of the BoW, we should also work with words in the same case – for example, lowercase – as Python identifies words in a different case as different words. We can also reduce the number of columns and sparsity by removing **stop words**. Stop words are very frequently used words that make sentences flow, but that do not, per se, carry any useful information. Examples of stop words are pronouns such as I, you, and he, as well as prepositions and articles.

In this recipe, we will learn how to set words in lowercase, remove stop words, retain words with a minimum acceptable frequency, and capture n-grams all together with a single transformer from `scikit-learn`: `CountVectorizer()`.

How to do it...

Let's begin by loading the necessary libraries and getting the dataset ready:

1. Load pandas, `CountVectorizer`, and the dataset from `scikit-learn`:

    ```python
    import pandas as pd
    from sklearn.datasets import fetch_20newsgroups
    from sklearn.feature_extraction.text import (
    ```

```
        CountVectorizer
    )
```

2. Let's load the train set part of the 20 Newsgroup dataset into a pandas DataFrame:

```
data = fetch_20newsgroups(subset='train')
df = pd.DataFrame(data.data, columns=['text'])
```

3. To make interpreting the results easier, let's remove punctuation and numbers from the text variable:

```
df['text'] = df['text'].str.replace(
    '[^\w\s]','', regex=True).str.replace(
    '\d+','', regex=True)
```

> **Note**
>
> To learn more about regex with Python, follow this link: `https://docs.python.org/3/howto/regex.html`

4. Now, let's set up `CountVectorizer()` so that, before creating the BoW, it puts the text in lowercase, removes stop words, and retains words that appear in, at least, 5% of the text pieces:

```
vectorizer = CountVectorizer(
    lowercase=True,
    stop_words='english',
    ngram_range=(1, 1),
    min_df=0.05)
```

> **Note**
>
> To introduce n-grams as part of the returned columns, we can change the value of `ngrams_range` to, for example, `(1,2)`. The tuple provides the lower and upper boundaries of the range of n-values for different n-grams. In the case of `(1,2)`, `CountVectorizer()` will return single words and arrays of two consecutive words.

5. Let's fit `CountVectorizer()` so that it learns which words should be used in the BoW:

```
vectorizer.fit(df['text'])
```

6. Now, let's create the BoW:

```
X = vectorizer.transform(df['text'])
```

7. Finally, let's capture the BoW in a DataFrame with the corresponding feature names:

```python
bagofwords = pd.DataFrame(
    X.toarray(),
    columns = vectorizer.get_feature_names_out()
)
```

With that, we have created a `pandas` DataFrame that contains words as columns and the number of times they appeared in each text as values. You can inspect the result by executing `bagofwords.head()`:

	able	access	actually	ago	apr	article	articleid	ask	available	away	...	works	world	writes	wrong	wrote	xnewsreader	year	years	yes	youre
0	0	0	0	0	0	0	0	0	0	0	...	0	0	0	0	0	0	0	1	0	0
1	0	0	0	0	0	0	1	0	0	0	...	0	0	0	0	0	0	0	0	0	0
2	0	1	1	0	0	0	0	0	0	0	...	0	0	0	0	0	0	0	0	0	0
3	0	0	0	0	0	1	0	0	0	0	...	0	1	1	0	1	1	0	0	0	0
4	0	0	0	0	0	2	0	0	0	0	...	0	0	1	0	0	0	0	0	1	0

5 rows × 191 columns

Figure 11.6 – A DataFrame with the BoW resulting from the 20 Newsgroup dataset

We can use this BoW as input for a machine learning model.

How it works...

scikit-learn's `CountVectorizer()` converts a collection of text documents into a matrix of token counts. These tokens can be individual words or arrays of two or more consecutive words – that is, n-grams. In this recipe, we created a BoW from a text variable in a DataFrame.

We loaded the 20 Newsgroup text dataset from `scikit-learn` and removed punctuation and numbers from the text rows using pandas' `replace()` function, which can be accessed through pandas' `str` module, to replace digits, `'\d+'`, or symbols, `'[^\w\s]'`, with empty strings, `''`. Then, we used `CountVectorizer()` to create the BoW. We set the `lowercase` parameter to `True` to put the words in lowercase before extracting the BoW. We set the `stop_words` argument to `english` to ignore stop words – that is, to avoid stop words in the BoW. We set `ngram_range` to the `(1, 1)` tuple to return only single words as columns. Finally, we set `min_df` to `0.05` to return words that appeared in at least 5% of the texts, or, in other words, in 5% of the rows in the DataFrame.

After setting up the transformer, we used the `fit()` method to allow the transformer to find the words that fulfill the preceding criteria. Finally, using the `transform()` method, the transformer returned an object containing the BoW with its feature names, which we captured in a `pandas` DataFrame.

See also

For more details about `CountVectorizer()`, visit the `scikit-learn` library's documentation at `https://scikit-learn.org/stable/modules/generated/sklearn.feature_extraction.text.CountVectorizer.html`.

Implementing term frequency-inverse document frequency

Term Frequency-Inverse Document Frequency (TF-IDF) is a numerical statistic that captures how relevant a word is in a document considering the entire collection of documents. What does this mean? Some words will appear a lot within a text document as well as across documents, such as the English words *the*, *a*, and *is*, for example. These words generally convey little information about the actual content of the document and don't make the text stand out from the crowd. TF-IDF provides a way to *weigh* the importance of a word by considering how many times it appears in a document with regards to how often it appears across documents. Hence, commonly occurring words such as *the*, *a*, or *is* will have a low weight, and words that are more specific to a topic, such as *leopard*, will have a higher weight.

TF-IDF is the product of two statistics: **Term Frequency (tf)** and **Inverse Document Frequency (idf)**, represented as follows: **tf-idf = td × idf**. tf is, in its simplest form, the count of the word in an individual text. So, for term t, the tf is calculated as $tf(t) = count(t)$ and is determined on a text-by-text basis. The idf is a measure of how common the word is across *all* documents and is usually calculated on a logarithmic scale. A common implementation is given by the following:

$$idf(t) = \log\left(\frac{n}{1 + df(t)}\right)$$

Here, n is the total number of documents, and $df(t)$ is the number of documents in which the term t appears. The bigger the value of $df(t)$, the lower the weighting for the term. The importance of a word will be high if it appears a lot of times in a text (high tf) or few times across texts (high idf).

> **Note**
>
> TF-IDF can be used together with n-grams. Similarly, to weigh an n-gram, we compound the n-gram frequency in a certain document with the frequency of the n-gram across documents.

In this recipe, we will learn how to extract features using TF-IDF with or without n-grams using `scikit-learn`.

Getting ready

`scikit-learn` uses a slightly different way to calculate the IDF statistic:

$$idf(t) = \log\left(\frac{1 + n}{1 + df(t)}\right) + 1$$

This formulation ensures that a word that appears in all texts receives the lowest weight of 1. In addition, after calculating the TF-IDF for every word, `scikit-learn` normalizes the feature vector (that with all the words) to its Euclidean norm. For more details on the exact formula, visit the `scikit-learn` documentation at `https://scikit-learn.org/stable/modules/feature_extraction.html#tfidf-term-weighting`.

TF-IDF shares the characteristics of BoW when creating the term matrix – that is, high feature space and sparsity. To reduce the number of features and sparsity, we can remove stop words, set the characters to lowercase, and retain words that appear in a minimum percentage of observations. If you are unfamiliar with these terms, visit the *Creating features with bag-of-words and n-grams* recipe in this chapter for a recap.

In this recipe, we will learn how to set words into lowercase, remove stop words, retain words with a minimum acceptable frequency, capture n-grams, and then return the TF-IDF statistic of words, all using a single transformer from scikit-learn: `TfidfVectorizer()`.

How to do it...

Let's begin by loading the necessary libraries and getting the dataset ready:

1. Load `pandas`, `TfidfVectorizer()`, and the dataset from `scikit-learn`:

```python
import pandas as pd
from sklearn.datasets import fetch_20newsgroups
from sklearn.feature_extraction.text import (
    TfidfVectorizer
)
```

2. Let's load the train set part of the 20 Newsgroup dataset into a pandas DataFrame:

```python
data = fetch_20newsgroups(subset='train')
df = pd.DataFrame(data.data, columns=['text'])
```

3. To make interpreting the results easier, let's remove punctuation and numbers from the text variable:

```python
df['text'] = df['text'].str.replace(
    '[^\w\s]', '', regex=True).str.replace(
    '\d+', '', regex=True)
```

4. Now, let's set up `TfidfVectorizer()` from `scikit-learn` so that, before creating the TF-IDF metrics, it puts all text in lowercase, removes stop words, and retains words that appear in at least 5% of the text pieces:

```python
vectorizer = TfidfVectorizer(
    lowercase=True,
    stop_words='english',
    ngram_range=(1, 1),
    min_df=0.05)
```

> **Note**
>
> To introduce n-grams as part of the returned columns, we can change the value of `ngrams_range` to, for example, `(1,2)`. The tuple provides the lower and upper boundaries of the range of n-values for different n-grams. In the case of `(1,2)`, `TfidfVectorizer()` will return single words and arrays of two consecutive words as columns.

5. Let's fit `TfidfVectorizer()` so that it learns which words should be introduced as columns of the TF-IDF matrix and determines the words' `idf`:

```
vectorizer.fit(df['text'])
```

6. Now, let's create the TF-IDF matrix:

```
X = vectorizer.transform(df['text'])
```

7. Finally, let's capture the TF-IDF matrix in a DataFrame with the corresponding feature names:

```
tfidf = pd.DataFrame(
    X.toarray(),
    columns = vectorizer.get_feature_names_out()
)
```

With that, we have created a `pandas` DataFrame that contains words as columns and the TF-IDF as values. You can inspect the result by executing `tfidf.head()`:

	able	access	actually	ago	apr	article	articleid	ask	available	away	...
0	0.0	0.000000	0.000000	0.0	0.0	0.000000	0.000000	0.0	0.0	0.0	...
1	0.0	0.000000	0.000000	0.0	0.0	0.000000	0.356469	0.0	0.0	0.0	...
2	0.0	0.135765	0.123914	0.0	0.0	0.000000	0.000000	0.0	0.0	0.0	...
3	0.0	0.000000	0.000000	0.0	0.0	0.110035	0.000000	0.0	0.0	0.0	...
4	0.0	0.000000	0.000000	0.0	0.0	0.262692	0.000000	0.0	0.0	0.0	...

works	world	writes	wrong	wrote	xnewsreader	year	years	yes	youre
0.0	0.000000	0.000000	0.0	0.000000	0.000000	0.0	0.27302	0.000000	0.0
0.0	0.000000	0.000000	0.0	0.000000	0.000000	0.0	0.00000	0.000000	0.0
0.0	0.000000	0.000000	0.0	0.000000	0.000000	0.0	0.00000	0.000000	0.0
0.0	0.169635	0.100554	0.0	0.218197	0.233578	0.0	0.00000	0.000000	0.0
0.0	0.000000	0.120029	0.0	0.000000	0.000000	0.0	0.00000	0.264836	0.0

Figure 11.7 – A DataFrame with features resulting from TF-IDF

Now, we can use this term frequency DataFrame to train machine learning models.

How it works...

In this recipe, we extracted the TF-IDF values of words present in at least 5% of the documents by utilizing `TfidfVectorizer()` from scikit-learn.

We loaded the 20 Newsgroup text dataset from `scikit-learn` and then removed punctuation and numbers from the text rows using pandas' `replace()`, which can be accessed through pandas' `str`, to replace digits, `'\d+'`, or symbols, `'[^\w\s]'`, with empty strings, `''`. Then, we used `TfidfVectorizer()` to create TF-IDF statistics for words. We set the `lowercase` parameter to `True` to put words into lowercase before making the calculations. We set the `stop_words` argument to `english` to avoid stop words in the returned matrix. We set `ngram_range` to the `(1,1)` tuple to return single words as features. Finally, we set the `min_df` argument to `0.05` to return words that appear at least in 5% of the texts or, in other words, in 5% of the rows.

After setting up the transformer, we applied the `fit()` method to let the transformer find the words to retain in the final term matrix. With the `transform()` method, the transformer returned an object with the words and their TF-IDF values, which we then captured in a pandas DataFrame with the appropriate feature names. We can now use these features in machine learning algorithms.

See also

For more details on `TfidfVectorizer()`, visit scikit-learn's documentation: `https://scikit-learn.org/stable/modules/generated/sklearn.feature_extraction.text.TfidfVectorizer.html`

Cleaning and stemming text variables

Some variables in our dataset come from free text fields, which are manually completed by users. People have different writing styles, and we use a variety of punctuation marks, capitalization patterns, and verb conjugations to convey the content, as well as the emotions surrounding it. We can extract (some) information from text without taking the trouble to read it by creating statistical parameters that summarize the text's complexity, keywords, and relevance of words in a document. We discussed these methods in the previous recipes of this chapter. However, to derive these statistics and aggregated features, we should clean the text variables first.

Text cleaning or preprocessing involves punctuation removal, stop word elimination, character case setting, and word stemming. Punctuation removal consists of deleting characters that are not letters, numbers, or spaces; in some cases, we also remove numbers. The elimination of stop words refers to removing common words that are used in our language to allow for the sentence structure and flow, but that individually convey little or no information. Examples of stop words include articles such as *the* and *a* for the English language, as well as pronouns such as *I, you* and *they*, and commonly used verbs in their various conjugations, such as the verbs *to be* and *to have*, as well as the auxiliary verbs *would* and *do*.

To allow computers to identify words correctly, it is also necessary to set all the words in the same case, since the words *Toy* and *toy* would be identified as being different by a computer due to the uppercase *T* in the first one.

Finally, to focus on the *message* of the text, we don't want computers to consider words differently if they show different conjugations. Hence, we would use word stemming as part of the preprocessing pipeline. Word stemming refers to reducing each word to its root or base so that the words *playing*, *plays*, and *played* become *play*, which, in essence, conveys the same or very similar meaning.

In this recipe, we will learn how to remove punctuation and stop words, set words in lowercase, and perform word stemming with pandas and NLTK.

Getting ready

We are going to use the NLTK stem package to perform word stemming, which incorporates different algorithms to stem words from English and other languages. Each method differs in the algorithm it uses to find the *root* of the word; therefore, they may output slightly different results. I recommend reading more about it, trying different methods, and choosing the one that serves the project you are working on.

More information about NLTK stemmers can be found at `https://www.nltk.org/api/nltk.stem.html`.

How to do it...

Let's begin by loading the necessary libraries and getting the dataset ready:

1. Load `pandas`, `stopwords`, and `SnowballStemmer` from NLTK and the dataset from `scikit-learn`:

```python
import pandas as pd
from nltk.corpus import stopwords
from nltk.stem.snowball import SnowballStemmer
from sklearn.datasets import fetch_20newsgroups
```

2. Let's load the train set part of the 20 Newsgroup dataset into a pandas DataFrame:

```python
data = fetch_20newsgroups(subset='train')
df = pd.DataFrame(data.data, columns=['text'])
```

Now, let's begin with the text cleaning.

> **Note**
>
> After executing each of the commands in this recipe, print some example texts by executing, for example, `print(df['text'][10])` so that you can visualize the changes introduced to the text. Go ahead and do it now, and then repeat the command after each step.

3. Let's begin by removing the punctuation:

```
df["text"] = df['text'].str.replace('[^\w\s]','')
```

> **Tip**
>
> You can also remove the punctuation using the built-in `string` module from Python. First, import the module by executing `import string` and then execute `df['text'] = df['text'].str.replace('[{}]'.format(string.punctuation), '')`.

4. We can also remove characters that are numbers, leaving only letters, as follows:

```
df['text'] = df['text'].str.replace(
    '\d+', '', regex=True)
```

5. Now, let's set all words into lowercase:

```
df['text'] = df['text'].str.lower()
```

Now, let's start the process of removing stop words.

> **Note**
>
> *Step 6* may fail if you did not download the NLTK library's `stopwords`. Visit the *Technical requirements* section in this chapter for more details.

6. Let's create a function that splits a string into a list of words, removes the stop words, and finally concatenates the remaining words back into a string:

```
def remove_stopwords(text):
    stop = set(stopwords.words('english'))
    text = [word
    for word in text.split() if word not in stop]
    text = ' '.join(x for x in text)
    return text
```

> **Note**
>
> To be able to process the data with the `scikit-learn` library's `CountVectorizer()` or `TfidfVectorizer()`, we need the text to be in string format. Therefore, after removing the stop words, we need to return the words as a single string. We have transformed the NLTK library's stop words list into a set because sets are faster to scan than lists. This improves the computation time.

7. Now, let's use the function from *step 6* to remove stop words from the `text` variable:

```
df['text'] = df['text'].apply(remove_stopwords)
```

If you want to know which words are stop words, execute `stopwords.words('english')`.

Finally, let's stem the words in our data. We will use `SnowballStemmer` from NLTK to do so.

8. Let's create an instance of `SnowballStemer` for the English language:

```
stemmer = SnowballStemmer("english")
```

> **Tip**
>
> Try the stemmer in a single word to see how it works; for example, run `stemmer.stem('running')`. You should see `run` as the result of that command. Try different words!

9. Let's create a function that splits a string into a list of words, applies `stemmer` to each word, and finally concatenates the stemmed word list back into a string:

```
def stemm_words(text):
    text = [
        stemmer.stem(word) for word in text.split()
    ]
    text = ' '.join(x for x in text)
    return text
```

10. Let's use the function from *step 9* to stem the words in our data:

```
df['text'] = df['text'].apply(stemm_words)
```

Now, our text is ready to create features based on character and word counts, as well as create BoWs or TF-IDF matrices, as described in the previous recipes of this chapter.

If we execute `print(df['text'][10])`, we will see a text example after cleaning:

```
irwincmptrclonestarorg irwin arnstein subject recommend duc
summari what worth distribut usa expir sat may gmt organ
computrac inc richardson tx keyword ducati gts much line line
ducati gts model k clock run well paint bronzebrownorang fade
leak bit oil pop st hard accel shop fix tran oil leak sold bike
```

```
owner want think like k opinion pleas email thank would nice
stabl mate beemer ill get jap bike call axi motor tuba irwin
honk therefor computracrichardsontx irwincmptrclonestarorg dod r
```

> **Note**
>
> If you are counting sentences, you need to do that before removing punctuation, as punctuation and capitalization are needed to define the boundaries of each sentence.

How it works...

In this recipe, we removed punctuation, numbers, and stop words from a text variable, set the words in lowercase, and finally, stemmed the words to their root. We removed punctuation and numbers from the text variable using pandas' `replace()`, which can be accessed through pandas' `str`, to replace digits, `'\d+'`, or symbols, `'[^\w\s]'`, with empty strings, `''`. Alternatively, we can use the `punctuation` module from the built-in `string` package.

> **Tip**
>
> Run `string.punctuation` in your Python console after importing `string` to check out the symbols that will be replaced with empty strings.

Next, utilizing pandas' string processing functionality through `str`, we set all of the words to lowercase with the `lower()` method. To remove stop words from the text, we used the `stopwords` module from NLTK, which contains a list of words that are considered frequent – that is, the stop words. We created a function that takes a string and splits it into a list of words using pandas' `str.split()`, and then, with list comprehension, we looped over the words in the list and retained the non-stop words. Finally, with the `join()` method, we concatenated the retained words back into a string. We used the built-in Python `set()` method over the NLTK stop words list to improve computation efficiency since it is faster to iterate over sets than over lists. Finally, with pandas' `apply()`, we applied the function to each row of our text data.

> **Tip**
>
> Run `stopwords.words('english')` in your Python console after importing `stopwords` from NLTK to visualize the list with the stop words that will be removed.

Finally, we stemmed the words using `SnowballStemmer` from NLTK. `SnowballStemmer` works one word at a time. Therefore, we created a function that takes a string and splits it into a list of words using pandas' `str.split()`. In a list comprehension, we applied `SnowballStemmer` word per word and then concatenated the list of stemmed words back into a string using the `join()` method. With pandas' `apply()`, we applied the function to stem words to each row of the DataFrame.

The cleaning steps we performed in this recipe resulted in strings containing the original text, without punctuation or numbers, in lowercase, without common words, and with the root of the word instead of its conjugated form. The data, as it is returned, can be used to derive features, as described in the *Counting characters, words, and vocabulary* recipe, or to create BoWs and TI-IDF matrices, as described in the *Creating features with bag-of-words and n-grams* and *Implementing term frequency-inverse document frequency* recipes.

Cleaning the texts as we have shown in this recipe can incur data loss, depending on the characteristics of the text, and if we seek to interpret the models after creating BoW or TF-IDF matrices, understanding the importance of stemmed words may not be so straightforward.

Index

N

S

Scikit-learn
  reference link 27
scikit-learn pipeline
  feature creation, embedding into 333-337
sentence tokenization 346
sine transformation 286
spline features
  creating 259-267
square root transformation
  used, for transforming variables 96-98
standardization 204
stop words 350

T

tabular pattern 339
target mean encoding 69
  implementing 69-73
Term Frequency-Inverse Document Frequency (TF-IDF)
  implementing 353-356
  reference link 356
Term Frequency (tf) 353
text complexity
  estimating, by counting sentences 346-349
text features
  extracting 295-299
text variables
  cleaning 356-361
  stemming 356-361
time
  features, extracting from 184-187
time/date components
  reference link 188
timedelta
  reference link 193

time, in different time zones
  working with 193-196
time series
  different features, extracting from different 324-329
  features, extracting automatically from 309-319
  subset, creating of features identified through feature selection 329-332
time-series data
  predictive features, creating and selecting automatically 319-323
to_datetime(), pandas
  reference link 197
transform primitive 280, 281
tsfresh
  reference link 318, 337
  used, for selecting relevant features 329-332
tz_convert(), pandas
  reference link 197

U

unique identifier 317

V

variables
  discretizing, into arbitrary intervals 130-134
  transforming, with logarithm function 84-90
  transforming, with reciprocal function 91-95
  transforming, with square root transformation 95-98
variance stabilizing transformations 83
vector unit length
  scaling to 224-227
vocabulary
  counting 340-345

W

X

Y

Z

packtpub.com

Subscribe to our online digital library for full access to over 7,000 books and videos, as well as industry leading tools to help you plan your personal development and advance your career. For more information, please visit our website.

Why subscribe?

- Spend less time learning and more time coding with practical eBooks and Videos from over 4,000 industry professionals

- Improve your learning with Skill Plans built especially for you

- Get a free eBook or video every month

- Fully searchable for easy access to vital information

- Copy and paste, print, and bookmark content

Did you know that Packt offers eBook versions of every book published, with PDF and ePub files available? You can upgrade to the eBook version at packtpub.com and as a print book customer, you are entitled to a discount on the eBook copy. Get in touch with us at customercare@packtpub.com for more details.

At www.packtpub.com, you can also read a collection of free technical articles, sign up for a range of free newsletters, and receive exclusive discounts and offers on Packt books and eBooks.

Other Books You May Enjoy

If you enjoyed this book, you may be interested in these other books by Packt:

Causal Inference and Discovery in Python

Aleksander Molak

ISBN: 978-1-80461-298-9

- Master the fundamental concepts of causal inference
- Decipher the mysteries of structural causal models
- Unleash the power of the 4-step causal inference process in Python
- Explore advanced uplift modeling techniques
- Unlock the secrets of modern causal discovery using Python
- Use causal inference for social impact and community benefit

Mastering Transformers

Savaş Yıldırım, Meysam Asgari- Chenaghlu

ISBN: 978-1-83763-378-4

- Focus on solving simple-to-complex NLP problems with Python
- Discover how to solve classification/regression problems with traditional NLP approaches
- Train a language model and explore how to fine-tune models to the downstream tasks
- Understand how to use transformers for generative AI and computer vision tasks
- Build transformer-based NLP apps with the Python transformers library
- Focus on language generation such as machine translation and conversational AI in any language
- Speed up transformer model inference to reduce latency

Packt is searching for authors like you

If you're interested in becoming an author for Packt, please visit `authors.packtpub.com` and apply today. We have worked with thousands of developers and tech professionals, just like you, to help them share their insight with the global tech community. You can make a general application, apply for a specific hot topic that we are recruiting an author for, or submit your own idea.

Share Your Thoughts

Now you've finished *Python Feature Engineering Cookbook*, we'd love to hear your thoughts! Scan the QR code below to go straight to the Amazon review page for this book and share your feedback or leave a review on the site that you purchased it from.

`https://packt.link/r/1835883591`

Your review is important to us and the tech community and will help us make sure we're delivering excellent quality content.

Download a free PDF copy of this book

Thanks for purchasing this book!

Do you like to read on the go but are unable to carry your print books everywhere?

Is your eBook purchase not compatible with the device of your choice?

Don't worry, now with every Packt book you get a DRM-free PDF version of that book at no cost.

Read anywhere, any place, on any device. Search, copy, and paste code from your favorite technical books directly into your application.

The perks don't stop there, you can get exclusive access to discounts, newsletters, and great free content in your inbox daily

Follow these simple steps to get the benefits:

1. Scan the QR code or visit the link below

```
https://packt.link/free-ebook/978-1-83588-358-7
```

2. Submit your proof of purchase

3. That's it! We'll send your free PDF and other benefits to your email directly